D0107492

Europe After Democracy

by
Arthur H. Brown

Bridge Publishing, Inc.
South Plainfield, NJ

Europe After Democracy

Copyright © 1993 by Arthur H. Brown
Library of Congress
  Catalog Card Number 93-070309
ISBN 0-88270-663-2

Published by:
Bridge Publishing Inc.
2500 Hamilton Blvd.
South Plainfield, NJ 07080

DEDICATION

TO MY FAMILY

Lawson, Garth, Peggy, Amanda, and Adlai. And to my wife, Ruth, who has stood with me in 32 years of pastoral work and evangelistic crusades. Her talents in singing and keyboards has greatly enhanced our ministry.

TABLE OF CONTENTS

INTRODUCTION

The Book of Revelation is the most contemporary book in all of the Bible and the least read, studied, and expounded . I have heard Bible scholars mock its authenticity, relegating it to nothing more than a little literature which does a lot of "horsing around." Many argue that because of the extreme differences in scholarly interpretations, it is best to ignore this book altogether. The time has come to confront this skepticism. When it comes to the Word of God, there is no room for multiple theories and interpretations. If there were only two different opinions about Scripture, at least one of them would be wrong.

You are embarking upon a joyful, fresh journey into understanding the Book of Revelation. This book is wonderfully organized and precise in its presentation of prophecy, and, when our Lord gave it to John, He intended for us to understand it.

I have felt constrained to write this book for some time. God has given me a curious fascination for the mystique in which the Book of Revelation is robed and the truth inherent in its picturesque symbols. This book is filled with the breath of tragedy and joy, defeat and victory, sorrow and rejoicing. Wonder fills the heart as one begins to comprehend the meaning of its symbols, signs, metaphors and figures of speech.

It is a most dreadful book for those who fall under its judgments. This same book, however, is delightful to those who live and walk in its light and thus qualify to partake of the blessings it promises.

1

Yet, when this book's terrible message to those who will fall under its judgments begins to claw its way into the believer's heart, a new commitment to sound the truth rises within the believing individual. A desire to act upon the responsibilities of this commitment begins to propel one forward. I now give myself to this task.

MY GUIDING PRINCIPLE

Listen to thine heart,
for the Holy Spirit talks to it.
It is He who knows
all that can be known about
sin and righteousness
and of "the judgments to come."

HOW IS THIS BOOK CONTEMPORARY?

Socially

No one but Jesus Christ could have predicted the social dilemma of our day. Law enforcement agencies are spending billions of dollars trying to reestablish some semblance of decency in our society. Immorality, dishonesty, murder, robbery, substance abuse, homosexuality, abortion and scores of other vices have plunged our world into utter despair.

Spiritually

No one but Jesus Christ could have predicted the evil spiritual subversion into which our world has plunged. The worship of Satan has summoned the most base elements of man's nature, making man a true slave of sin and Satan. Cain, Ahab, Pharaoh, Herod, Pilate, Caiaphas, Nebuchadnezzar and Antiochus Epiphanes have many "brothers." Jezabel and Herodias have many "sisters."

The Book of Revelation presents a sad commentary of man's spiritual condition in the last days. False prophets, false christs and atheist and occult leaders abound. A multitude of them are being given

2

prime time visibility through the media, thereby subverting disciples and adding many to their cause.

Many of the tribulation's judgments will come directly from Hell. All of the forces available to Satan will be permitted by God to "have their way" during these last three and a half years of history.

Economically

The matter of economics weighs heavy on the minds of our debt-ridden society. Financiers are looking for the way out. The Book of Revelation tells us how this will be done.

Politically

The world is in political ferment. The common people are weary of headlines revealing corruption and embezzlement. Using a political position as an opportunity for personal financial advantage has sent Marcos, Noriega, Ceausescu and many others to imprisonment, obscurity, or death.

The cry for democracy is being heard in Russia, East Germany, Romania, Poland, Bulgaria, Hungary, Czechoslovakia, Estonia, Latvia, Lithuania, Georgia, Armenia, Albania, South Africa, and many of the Latin American countries.

The Book of Revelation has a surprise for us. Democracy is a wonderful form of government, but, regardless of the fact that it seems to be spreading, something will go wrong in the scheme of things. Europe, along with many other democratic countries, will ultimately end up with the most diabolical dictatorship the world has ever known.

Militarily

The world's super powers are on constant alert as they monitor what is being sold, to whom it is being sold, and how it could become a military threat. There are basically two unwritten and unverbalized military philosophies abroad today. One is to trust America and her allies to police the world at their expense, without fear of any ulterior monetary motives or territorial usurpation. The other is to hate America and her God and to dispose of them as soon as possible.

America cannot continue policing the world forever. Inevitably she will say, "We are tired of sacrificing our young men and women for the sake of freedom in a country on the other side of the world. If you want our liberty, fight for it like we did. If you envy our democracy, enshrine it in your nation like we did. If you want our standard of living, be creative and struggle to achieve it like we did. If you want the blessings of the Americans, then serve the God of the Americans from whom all blessings flow."

The New World Order

The Bible graphically describes a world order in which a large segment of the world's religion, commerce, politics and military forces will be marshalled under the command of a single leader called the beast. This beast will come out of a small people (Dan. 8:23) who were badly wounded (Rev. 13:3-4). This new world order will ultimately become the worst world disorder ever imagined. It is incredible and nothing short of supernatural that the Book of Revelation should record future history in such graphic detail.

The Ultimate Battle

The story of Satan's struggle for the mastery of the soul of man started at the very dawn of creation. Essentially, the battle lines of Armageddon and of good and evil were already drawn even then. The conflict of the ages started in a garden (Gen. 3:1-6) and will end in a garden (Rev. 22:1-2). The central players in the drama are the Jews, God's holy people. God began with them in Babylon by calling Abraham from that region. He will conduct His final judgments in that same region, now known as Iraq, with the destruction of the soon-to-be-built new city of Babylon.

The New World Religion

The Book of Revelation depicts a world church composed of anti-God religions (Rev. 17:3). The word blasphemy, used in describing the religious beast, reveals that the leaders of this world church will

4

bask in the sacrilege of worshiping themselves, thereby usurping the honor due God.

Israel: The Focal Point

Saddam Hussein will not go down without trying to drag Israel down with him. World consciousness regarding the occupied territories and the Palestinian problem has been rekindled as a result of the Gulf War. Israel's unwillingness to surrender land now occupied continues to create a rift between her and her allies. A peace will be worked out, but it will die in its infancy (I Thess. 5:3; Rev. 6:4).

Beginning with chapter six and ending with chapter nineteen, the Book of Revelation exposes the trials of Israel's great tribulation or Jacob's trouble (Jer. 30:7). This entire passage speaks of a spiritual, political, and military struggle over Israel. The entire world will eventually be drawn into the conflict. The Jews, God's chosen people, will be defended by their Messiah, Jesus, who will appear at Jerusalem upon a white horse. He will have a sharp sword in His mouth to face the armies of the world (Rev. 19:11-16).

The Church will have been raptured to safety before this time of trouble begins. Israel, because of its rejection of Christ and its handing Him over to the Romans to be crucified, will have been smitten with spiritual blindness. It will take the sorrows of the Great Tribulation to awaken the nation of Israel and to bring its people to repentance. Paul declared, "And so all Israel shall be saved" (Rom. 11:26). It will be Israel's acceptance of Jesus Christ (the Son of God) as its true Messiah and its rejection of the antichrist (the son of perdition) that will unleash the powers of heaven and hell against each other.

Satan: The Underlying Universal Malignancy to Peace

In the beginning, Lucifer lost his position with God because of pride. Adam was created to be the custodian of this world and everything went well until Lucifer (Satan), through a serpent, succeeded in tempting Adam and Eve to sin by disobeying God. This necessitated the sending of Jesus Christ, the second Adam, into the world, through Israel, to redeem the world back to God. Jesus' ultimate goal will be to dethrone Satan, the prince of this world, in the final conflict of good against evil in the battle of Armageddon.

Satan attempted, through cold war tactics, to cause our Savior to sin. He said, "I will give you the kingdoms of this world if you will fall down and worship me" (Matt. 4:8-9). Satan also used a thief, while Jesus hung dying upon the cross, to suggest a short cut to the kingdom with these words, "If you are Christ, save yourself and us" (Luke 23:39-43). Satan used Roman soldiers to proclaim a story fabricated by the crucifiers to discount the truth of the resurrection, "While we slept, his disciples came in the night and stole the body of Jesus" (Matt. 28:11-15).

But Satan lost the cold war; he failed in each of these three attacks. Millions have, and still are, believing the witnesses who saw Jesus Christ alive. They are experiencing His living presence in their lives.

Next, the Kingdom of Peace

Jesus taught us to pray, "Thy kingdom come." This prayer is about to be answered as the powers of heaven square off against the powers of hell in the great tribulation. The powers of heaven will win and "the kingdoms of the world will become the kingdoms of his Christ" (Rev. 11:15), for He is indeed the "KING OF KINGS, AND THE LORD OF LORDS" (Rev. 19:16).

Why is Satan so infuriated against Jesus, the Jews, and Jerusalem? He is so infuriated because Jesus is God's choice for Messiah. Because the Jews are God's people who, with the Church, will rule the world. And, finally, he is so infuriated because Jerusalem is God's choice to be the Messiah's capital. Satan's jealousy will lead to his humiliating defeat, clearing the way for Christ's ascension to the millennial throne.

Isaiah said, "Of the increase of his government and peace there shall be no end..." (Isa. 9:7). The angelic messengers on the night of Christ's birth proclaimed, "Glory to God in the highest, and on earth peace, good will toward men" (Luke 2:14). The Book of Revelation brings to fruition these messianic prophecies.

The Temple Desecration Tips the Cup

A soon-to-emerge leader of the European Economic Community, called the beast, will sign a seven-year peace treaty involving Israel

6

and other countries (Dan. 9:27). In the middle of the seven years, this leader will break the treaty. An image representing the beast will be erected in the soon-to-be-built temple in Jerusalem. All subjects of the new world order will be commanded to worship this image, including the Jews, but the Jews will refuse. This will be the flash point of the tribulation explosion.

The Jews' rejection of the antichrist results in their acceptance of Jesus Christ. The ungodly who will accept the mark of the beast will fiercely persecute Israel. The drama in the Book of Revelation will become an intense struggle, with seven righteous forces rising to protect Israel from the wrath of the antichrist by warring against the six evil forces bent on Israel's annihilation, as illustrated in the drawing.

Israel may be small, but the Almighty God is on her side! What Moses saw in the bush that burned, yet was not consumed (Exod. 3:2-5), is nothing less than a message to us that God will never allow Israel to be destroyed.

The Fig Tree

"And in the morning, as they passed by, they saw the fig tree dried up from the roots. And Peter calling to remembrance saith unto him, Master, behold, the fig tree which thou cursedst is withered away. And Jesus answering saith unto them, Have faith in God" (Mark 11:20-22).

The fig tree represents the Jewish nation. A tree dried from the roots up has absolutely no chance for survival. Neither did the Jews, but Jesus said to "have faith in God." When John penned the Book of Revelation, the Jewish nation had already been completely decimated by the Romans under Titus Vespasian in 70 A.D. Even to this day, the temple lies in ruin and no one seems absolutely sure of its original location, for there was not left "one stone upon another" that was not thrown over. However, the Lord said to them, "Now learn a parable of the fig tree; When his branch is yet tender, and putteth forth leaves, ye know that summer is nigh" (Matt. 24:32).

The reestablishment of the Jewish nation is a twentieth-century miracle. To recreate a paradise out of a rocky wasteland takes more than the ingenuity of man. For Israel to rise from a national junk heap in history to such a place of prominence and power, so that she is now considered to be among the super powers of the world, is an ingenuity of omnipotence. Such a rise is also fraught with great dan-

THE STRUGGLE OVER ISRAEL

HER PERSECUTORS
   Satan (Rev. 12:12-13; 17)
   Antichrist (Rev. 13:7)
   False Prophet (Rev. 13:11-16)
   The Flood (Rev. 12:15)
   Three Unclean Spirits (Rev. 16:13-16)
   All Nations (Zech. 14:2)

HER PROTECTORS
   God (Ps. 121:4)
   Jesus (Rev. 19:11-16)
   The Spirit (Zech. 12:10)
   The 144,000 (Rev. 14:14)
   Moses and Elijah (Rev. 11:3-6)
   Michael the Archangel
          (Rev. 12:7; Dan. 12:1)
   The Earth (Rev. 12:16)

Sea of Galilee

Jordan River

THE
MEDITERRANEAN
SEA

The
Dead Sea

ger. The military forces of the world are keeping a watchful eye upon Israel and the rationale espoused by many is, "Dispose of her as soon as possible. If we wait too long, it will be too late!"

The prophet Ezekiel tells the sad story of Russia's future attempt to invade and destroy Israel. Russia will be defeated by Israel (Ezek. 38 and 39). Do not presuppose that the breakup of the Soviet Union has insured her military demise or that we have heard the last of her as a military threat. Nothing has changed as far as Russia's irreversible destiny to attempt the annihilation of Israel. It is all in the Bible. Is there any other book in the world that could possibly have predicted contemporary history as the Bible has?

Gulf War Revives Messianic Hope

Since God's miraculous protection over Israel from the SCUD missiles launched by Iraq, the people of Israel are secretly admitting that an omnipotent hand must have guided those missiles away from heavily populated areas. This awareness requires a subsequent conclusion that something of great import is in store for them.

Even while missiles were falling, Jewish leaders met behind closed doors. Many of the religious Jews concluded that the true meaning of the Gulf War foreshadows only good things for Israel. They see signs in this conflict that the Messiah is coming soon. Jews are preparing themselves once more to fulfill their designated roles as the conscience and the sufferers of the world. This experience of war has put the name of God upon the lips of everyone in Israel. These are but the initial spiritual breezes that will intensify into a mighty wind of the Spirit of God which will bring Israel to repentance, resulting in the salvation of the world!

CHAPTER ONE

Europe After Democracy deals with conditions in Europe and those parts of the world under the domination of the beast just prior to and during the great tribulation. This period of time is delineated in the Book of Revelation from chapters six through nineteen. In order to understand what transpires during these fourteen chapters, we must first understand what transpires during the first five chapters. The last three chapters of the Book of Revelation deal with the world after Armageddon. This will be dealt with in a sequel to this book entitled *Life After Armageddon*.

Because the author of the Book of Revelation is Jesus Christ, the perfect number seven is consistently a natural division of its passages. In this book, I am following the seven master topical divisions of the Book of Revelation. Each one of these divisions is divided into seven subjects, each containing seven pronouncements of exposition.

FORTY-NINE PRONOUNCEMENTS
CONCERNING JESUS AND HIS DIRECTIVES
(Revelation 1)

I. THE PURPOSE OF THE BOOK OF REVELATION
(Revelation 1:1-3)

The revelation of Jesus Christ, which God gave unto him, to show unto his servants things which must shortly come to pass; and he sent and signified it by his angel unto his servant John: Who bare record of the word of God, and of the testimony of Jesus Christ, and of all things that he saw. Blessed is he that readeth, and they that hear the words of this prophecy, and keep those things which are written therein: for the time is at hand.

1. Revelation: "The revelation of Jesus Christ, which God gave unto Him..." (Rev. 1:1).

The magnitude of the happenings in the Book of Revelation clearly reveals that the one executing these events is no mere human. An omnipotent power moves these events steadily forward to bring to fruition every word that has been promised and prophesied until Messiah has made His enemies His "footstool" (Ps. 110:1).

This revealing of future events has nothing to do with the occult or various occult paraphernalia, such as the crystal ball. The Book of Revelation is a prophetical treatise that precisely describes the future from here to Armageddon and beyond. Its fountainhead is Jesus Christ, the source of all knowledge, wisdom, understanding, and truth.

Jesus Christ is revealed as the one which is, which was, and which is to come: the Alpha and Omega; He that liveth and was dead, and is alive for evermore; He that walketh in the midst of the seven golden candlesticks; He which hath the sharp sword with two edges; the Son of man...(whose) eyes were as a flame of fire and his feet like unto fine brass; He that hath the seven spirits of God and the seven stars; the Lion of the tribe of Judah; the root of David; the Lord God omnipotent; the Lamb; the Word of God; KING OF KINGS AND LORD OF LORDS.

There are over 200 names attributed to Jesus Christ in the Bible, each one attesting to the scope of His invincible power, His wisdom and the infallible justice of His judgments. It is Jesus alone who can redeem the universe. Unless we grasp and embrace the absolute truth of His supreme authority and power, there is no use in us attempting to understand the Book of Revelation.

2. Information: "...To show unto his servants things which must shortly come to pass..." (Rev. 1:1).

12

Before setting world events of great consequence into motion, God has always informed His prophets about His intentions to do so. Jude 14 and 15 declares that "...Enoch also, the seventh from Adam, prophesied of these, saying, Behold, the Lord cometh with ten thousands of his saints, to execute judgement upon all...."

John received this same revelation, "Behold, he cometh with clouds..." (Rev. 1:7). It is God's deepest concern that His message not be misunderstood and become nothing more than mystical writings with figurative overtones. The message John was to deliver to the churches was that Jesus was personally coming back!

Twice John was emphatically told by Jesus that He had sent an angel all the way from heaven with this message—in the very first verse of this book, as well as in the last chapter, verse sixteen. John was also warned not to change the meaning of this truth by adding anything or taking away anything (Rev. 22:18, 19).

The expression, "shortly come to pass," in Revelation 1:1 must be viewed in relative terms. When God speaks about time, we need to heed the words of Peter who wrote, "But, beloved, be not ignorant of this one thing, that one day is with the Lord as a thousand years, and a thousand years as one day" (2 Pet. 3:8).

I am in agreement with those scholars who understand the divine pattern that can be taken from the days of creation in which God worked for six days and rested on the seventh. I understand this to mean that God has allotted mankind six thousand years of history. The seventh day, or the seventh millennium, corresponds to the Lord's sabbath of rest when Christ shall reign over a world of peace for one thousand years. The conclusion regarding the phrase "shortly come to pass," when considered relatively as pertaining to God's time, would encompass a mere two days (2,000 years).

3. Communication: "...He sent and signified it..." (Rev. 1:1).

The word "signified" forewarns that the contents of the Book of Revelation are delivered via grammatical vehicles referred to as signs, wonders, seals, trumpets, vials and other symbols. Jesus often utilized parables during His earthly ministry. It should not be surprising to note that the same style would prevail here.

When the word "signified" is divided to read SIGN-ified, we see the prefix as "sign" which clarifies the procedure. This makes the word "signified" a relative to the family of words which convey a common idea, words like sign, symbol, signal, etc. These same words convey the idea that a figure requiring interpretation is employed. Jesus knew that the Jews were a sign-seeking generation; faith does not come easy to a Jew. The main burden of the Book of Revelation deals with Israel's salvation through tribulation, and God speaks to them in a language they are accustomed to, with the hope that they will understand and be saved.

I am fully convinced that Jesus Christ did not give us this book to confuse us. It was written with the intent that we should understand the marvelous mysteries hidden within these signs and symbols.

4. Preservation: "...Sent and signified it by his angel unto his servant John" (Rev. 1:1).

Who is this angel? Without this angel's hand to guide, an exegesis of the Book of Revelation can be quite frustrating. I believe the evidence clearly states that the angel is Daniel.

At the end of his vision and encounter with the angel, John was completely overwhelmed by what he saw. He wanted to fall down and worship the angel who delivered the prophecy of signs and symbols (Rev. 19:10; 22:8-9). But the angel forbade him, saying:

> ...See thou do it not: for I am thy fellowservant, and of thy
> brethren the prophets, and of them which keep the sayings
> of this book: worship God (Rev. 22:9).

A fellow servant is one who works toward and represents the same cause. Angels have been described elsewhere in the Scriptures as "ministering spirits" (Heb. 1:14), but not fellow servants. This angel identifies so intimately with John that one must conclude that he is one like John, a Hebrew brother. It is my firm belief that the angel who appeared to John was actually the prophet Daniel.

Most eschatological scholars acknowledge that the Books of Daniel and Revelation need to be studied as companion volumes, but no one (to my knowledge) has discovered this interpretive link between the two. Herein lies the secret of properly understanding the first seal of Revelation in chapter six. To misunderstand this first seal creates

14

great difficulty for any student of prophecy who then tries to make sense of all the seals which follow.

Having said this, let me proceed to draw some interesting parallels between the two prophets:

- A Common Relationship: Both prophets are highly praised as to their relationship to God. Daniel is spoken of as a man "greatly beloved" (Dan. 9:23; 10:11, 19); John was the "disciple whom Jesus loved" (John. 13:23).

- A Common Vision: Both men had an unusual vision of Jesus (Dan. 10:4-6; Rev. 1:11-20).

- A Common Encounter: Both were overcome by near death experiences after having seen the vision (Dan. 10:8-9; Rev. 1:17).

- A Common Renewal: Both were restored by the touch of Jesus (Dan. 10:10; Rev. 1:17)

- A Common Document: Both were entrusted with the stewardship of a divinely authored book. Daniel was told to "shut up the words, and seal the book, even to the time of the end" (Dan. 12:4). John was told to "seal not the sayings of the prophecy of this book, for the time (the end) is at hand" (Rev. 22:10).

- A Common Commission: Both prophets died being told their tasks were unfinished. Daniel was told to rest and "stand in his lot at the end of the days" (Dan. 12:13). John's commission was to prophecy again regarding the seven messages the thunders uttered, which he was commanded to "seal up" in verse four (Rev. 10:11).

- A Common Time Frame: Both prophets were enlightened about a short (three and a half years), but critical, space of time in the distant future (Dan. 9:27; 12:6-7; Rev. 11:2-3; 12:6, 14; 13:5; 6:11; 10:6-7).

Also, there is a common scriptural descriptive comparison regarding their sealed book:

Daniel's Account:

> But thou, O Daniel, shut up the words, and seal the book, even to the time of the end... (Dan. 12:4),

> And I heard, but I understood not: then said I, O my Lord, what shall be the end of these things? And he said, Go thy way, Daniel: for the words are closed up and sealed till the time of the end (Dan. 12:8-9).

The "wonders" contained in Daniel's sealed book were not relevant for his day. Consequently, he was told to seal the book until such a time when they would be relevant. Since Daniel was the only one having information about this sealed book, it goes without saying that he was responsible for its custody "until the time of the end." Only by delivering the book to John would Daniel discharge himself of his final obligation referred to as "standing in his lot." This is even more aptly expressed by Menge, *Du wirst zu deinem Anteil aufstehen am Ende der Tage*, meaning, "You will rise for your duty at the end of days" (Dan. 12:13).

John's Account:

> And I saw in the right hand of him that sat on the throne a book written within and on the backside, sealed with seven seals. And I saw a strong angel proclaiming with a loud voice, Who is worthy to open the book, and to loose the seals thereof? (Rev. 5:1-2)

> And I beheld, and, lo, in the midst of the throne...stood a Lamb as it had been slain...he came and took the book out of the right hand of him that sat upon the throne (Rev. 5:6-7).

> And I saw when the Lamb opened one of the seals, and I heard, as it were the noise of thunder... (Rev. 6:1).

The time had come for God to reveal the contents of Daniel's sealed book.

THE WONDERS IN THE SEALED BOOK

Daniel's Account:

> And at that time shall Michael stand up, the great prince which standeth for the children of thy people: and there shall be a time of trouble, such as never was...and at that time thy people shall be delivered, every one that shall be found written in the book...and when he shall have accomplished to scatter the power of the holy people, all these things shall be finished (Dan. 12:1, 7).

Daniel's information was limited. He knew Michael would be involved in defending Israel, but had no further details about the conflict. Daniel knew that a time of great trouble was coming which would last for three and a half years, but he was not told of the white, red, black, or pale horse. He knew nothing about the seals, trumpets, or vials. Daniel was told that all those whose names were in the book of life at the beginning of the tribulation would escape it. What he saw was through a glass, darkly.

John's Account:

> ...Come up hither, and I will show thee things which must be hereafter...And they sung a new song, saying, Thou art worthy to take the book, and to open the seals thereof: for thou wast slain, and has redeemed us to God by thy blood out of every kindred, and tongue, and people and nation (Rev. 4:1; 5:9).

> And I saw when the Lamb opened one of the seals...a white horse...another horse that was red...a black horse...a pale horse...I saw under the altar the souls of them that were slain for the word of God...the sun became black as sackcloth of hair, and the moon became as blood (Rev. 6:1-2, 4-5, 8-9, 12).

> And I saw the seven angels which stood before God; and to them were given seven trumpets....And I saw another

17

sign in heaven...seven angels having the seven last plagues... (Rev. 8:2; 15:1).

And there was war in heaven: Michael and his angels fought against the dragon; and the dragon fought and his angels (Rev. 12:7).

We observe that John's knowledge of the book's contents is more detailed than Daniel's who was told to seal its contents until the end. John, on the other hand, saw the book being opened with symbols issuing from it. The time of the end had come when these things must be divulged.

THE MAN UPON THE WATER

Daniel's Account:

And I heard the man clothed in linen, which was upon the waters of the river, when he held up his right hand and his left hand unto heaven, and sware by him that liveth for ever that it shall be for a time, times, and an half... (Dan. 12:7).

This angel appears at the beginning of the three and a half year period of time. All that Daniel was told about this era is that it "shall be a time of trouble, such as never was since there was a nation."

John's Account:

And the angel which I saw stand upon the sea and upon the earth lifted up his hand to heaven, and sware by him that liveth for ever and ever...that there should be time no longer...And the voice which I heard from heaven spake unto me again, and said, Go and take the little book which is open in the hand of the angel which standeth upon the sea and upon the earth (Rev. 10:5-6, 8).

The angel who swore to John that "there should be time no longer" appeared after the three and a half years had transpired. All of the seals had been opened as exemplified by the book being "open" in the angel's hand.

18

Correlation

Daniel saw a book which he was commanded to seal "till the time of the end." This must mean the contents of the book are imperative as touching the unfolding of those events yet to take place in "the time of the end." John, on the other hand, actually saw the symbols and pictures which illustrated the world scenario at "the time of the end." Is it not possible that Daniel's sealed book and the sealed book of Revelation 5 are the same book?

Many have assumed the Book of Daniel is the sealed book. In reality, the Book of Daniel has never been sealed. It is widely available and readable even today. The only other book spoken of by Daniel is the book of life. This book is indeed closed and will not be opened until the great white throne judgement comes to pass (Rev. 20:11,12).

I am certain that Daniel delivers the book containing the itinerary of events to John. The contents of this book are unveiled in the revelations of John through seals, trumpets and vials. Daniel simply spoke of these events as wonders which he understood not (Dan. 12:6,8). These wonders are summarized in skeleton form for Daniel, but they are fleshed out in detail in the awesome revelations given to John.

The Significant Interpretive Linkage

When once you establish that Daniel's book and John's book are the same, many interpretive problems are solved:

- The four apocalyptic horsemen need no longer gallop all over history seeking to corral themselves in some historical event that seems to symbolize them. If Daniel's book is John's book, then Daniel's wonders, which include the horsemen, are restricted to the three and a half years precisely called "the time of the end."

- The first seal, which depicts the white horse and is the supreme seal, is also no longer a mystery. Immediately after Daniel is told that the book is sealed till "the time of the end," the man on the water says, "Many shall be purified and made white, and tried..."

19

(Dan. 12:10). This is Daniel's clue as to what he is to expect to see first when the book is finally opened in the "time of the end."

The purifying and making white is the prophesied spiritual revival of Israel and their acceptance of Jesus Christ, symbolized by the white horse. This comes about because of the antichrist breaking his promise to allow religious freedom for the Jews and the desecration of the temple by erecting an image called "the abomination that maketh desolate" (Dan. 12:11).

It takes little imagination to see that such a spiritual revival will infuriate the antichrist and bring the murderous red horse into action. The destruction brought by the rider of the red horse automatically compels the black famine and pale pestilence horses to follow him. This irrevocable chain of destruction is set in motion with each seal becoming the consequence of the preceding one. An interpretation of the Book of Revelation from here on becomes possible for most laymen.

- The age-old error of trying to fit the Church into the tribulation is also eliminated. The Church, called "thy people," shall be delivered before the tribulation begins, because their names are found written in the book (Dan. 12:1; Rev. 20:12). Israel, whose temple is desecrated, is the "holy people" whose scattering signals the end of the tribulation (Dan. 12:7, 11).

5. Validation: "(John) Who bare record of the Word of God, and of the testimony of Jesus Christ, and of all the things that he saw" (Rev. 1:2).

What a preface from the one who has been chosen to pen this profound book of the Bible. John's qualifications were not based on his education or by any other modern-day criterion. He was chosen because of his genuine faith in Jesus Christ, the Son of God. John was so overwhelmed with the birth, life, miracles, death, and resurrection of Jesus that he said he was

...the disciple, which testifieth of these things, and wrote these things: and we know that his testimony is true. And there are also many other things which Jesus did, the which, if they should be written every one, I suppose that even the

20

world itself could not contain the books that should be written (John 21:24-25).

John's qualifications were validated by the angelic messenger's delivering of the revelation that was to be recorded for all who would come thereafter.

- "Who bare record of the word (Jesus) of God..." (Rev. 1:2). The expression "bare record" means John wrote the record. He also wrote the Gospel of John, which has become to many the favorite book of the Bible. He records the birth of Christ not as a baby in a manger at Bethlehem, rather as the co-creator who was "in the beginning with God" (John. 1:2). Not only was Jesus Christ *with* God, He *was* God (John. 1:1).
John's concept of Jesus is one we need to grasp as we approach the awesome works of Christ as they are depicted in the Book of Revelation. Unless we are convinced that Jesus is God, the Book of Revelation will seem like a fairy tale or a wild novel written by someone with a vivid imagination.

- "Who bare record...of the testimony of Jesus Christ..." (Rev. 1:2). John recorded everything he heard Jesus say about himself. An entire volume would be required to research this subject. Let me suggest John 8:14-58 as an introduction to such a pursuit.
John was a very observant disciple. Note the various titles he attributes to Jesus in the Gospel of John after hearing his Master speak of himself: The Son of God (ch. 1), the Son of man (ch. 2), the great teacher (ch. 3), a soul winner (ch. 4), the great physician (ch. 5), the bread of life (ch. 6), the water of life (ch. 7), the merciful one (ch. 8), the light of the world (ch. 9), the good shepherd (ch. 10), the resurrection and the life (ch. 11), the King (ch. 12), the servant (ch. 13), the Comforter (ch. 14), the true vine (ch. 15), the imparter of the Spirit (ch. 16), the intercessor (ch. 17), our prayer model (ch. 18), the sin bearer (ch. 19), victor over death (ch. 20), forgiver and Savior (ch. 21).

- "Who bare record...of all the things that he saw" (Rev. 1:2). John was divinely endowed with a spiritual cognizance that far exceeded the capabilities of his natural eyes. He possessed a soul sight, a

21

kind of heart-discerning scrutiny that looked beyond the form of man as evidenced by the many names and titles he ascribes to the Lord.

6. Stipulation: "Blessed is he that readeth, and they that hear the words of this prophecy, and keep those things which are written therein..." (Rev 1:3).

This is the only book in the Bible where a blessing is specifically promised for the reading, the hearing, and the keeping of the writing. This threefold diligence will be rewarded with a "part in the first resurrection (Rev. 20:6), being invited to "the marriage supper of the Lamb" (Rev. 19:9) and being one who has right "to the tree of life and may enter in through the gates to the city" (Rev. 22:14).

7. Expectation: "...for the time is at hand" (Rev. 1:3).

This seventh pronouncement annunciates the primary purpose for the writing of the Book of Revelation. Herein lies the rich heritage and legacy of the child of God, the "blessed hope" of every born-again Christian. Jesus is coming and the time is at hand. Man grows calloused and careless with the passing of time; however, God's time-piece ticks unrelentlessly onward, marking the record of our lives. Every time the reader ponders the pages of this book, he has advanced even nearer to the day when these things shall unfold.

II. THE PROLOGUE TO THE BOOK OF REVELATION
(Revelation 1:4-6)

John to the seven churches which are in Asia: Grace be unto you, and peace, from him which is, and which was, and which is to come; and from the seven Spirits which are before his throne; and from Jesus Christ, who is the faithful witness, and the first begotten of the dead, and the prince of the kings of the earth. Unto him that loved us, and washed us from our sins in his own blood, and hath made us kings and priests unto God and his Father; to him be glory and dominion for ever and ever. Amen.

1. Informant: "John..." (Rev. 1:4).

The informant, John, is that apostle who was the brother of James and a son of Zebedee. He is the disciple who was so loved by Jesus. Unlike modern-day correspondence, a writer living in the time the New Testament was written always identified himself at the beginning of his letter.

2. Recipients: "...To the seven churches which are in Asia..." (Rev. 1:4).

The geographic region here called Asia (where the seven churches were located) is modern Turkey. The Christian faith is scarcely known in Turkey today; ninety-eight percent of its people embrace the Moslem faith. The first churches to see a copy of the Book of Revelation were Ephesus, Smyrna, Pergamos, Thyatira, Sardis, Philadelphia and Laodicea.

3. Endowment:

> ...Grace be unto you, and peace, from him which is, and which was, and which is to come; and from the seven Spirits which are before his throne; and from Jesus Christ, who is the faithful witness, and the first begotten of the dead, and the prince of the kings of the earth (Rev 1:4-5).

This grace greeting is not written exclusively to the seven churches. Seated now at the right hand of power, sixty years after they nailed Him to a cross, Jesus greets the reader with the words "grace" and "peace"! This message of grace was to be preached to those who spit in His face and who scourged, mocked, and crucified Him. It was written for those who cursed Him. *"I hold nothing against you," is what I seem to hear Him say. "I extend the best to you, even the life I procured through my death. You cannot offend me by crucifixion and death, because my love is greater than these. You have not insulted me, because I know you did not know who I was. I am not angry with you. Please come near, I want to comfort, forgive and cleanse you. My grace and unmerited favor is my heaven-sent greeting to you."*

Along with His grace, Jesus offers His peace to the Church and the world. The touchstone word of our generation is peace. Men are flying around the world, sitting for long periods of time at round tables, spending many dollars, and engaging the best minds — all in search of peace. When they finally "say peace," the Bible reminds us, "...then sudden destruction cometh upon them, as travail upon a woman with child; and they shall not escape" (1 Thess. 5:3).

The kind of peace proclaimed at peace tables is signed, sealed, verified, and authorized only to be broken. It is not the kind of peace Jesus imparts. Lasting peace will never come about through legislation or diplomacy. The world will be at peace only when every soul in the world is personally at peace with God!

Peace has been defined in many ways. Some say, "Peace is the absence of war." Another has said, "Peace comes out of the end of a gun barrel." Others affirm that a strategic defense system (SDI) will assure peace. Some hold that the morbid Mutual Assured Destruction theory (MAD) would guarantee peace. The defunct League of Nations failed in its quest for peace. The North Atlantic Treaty Organization (NATO), with its Security Council, is engaged in the unending search for peace. Summit talks, ambassadors, Olympic games, exchange students, and a sharing of technology in science and medicine...all are intended to nurture and encourage the peace process. However, the waters of peace are getting deeper and more poisonous with every passing generation.

In addition to international peace pursuits, as individuals we are all trying to find inner peace. The world is tired of man's "religion," which has been proven to be nothing more than a notion in the head. Eastern mysticism and occultism have been seeded profusely in the West; however, their efforts will never succeed in bringing true inner peace. The wound of sin is deeply, malignantly infected and man's religions cannot cleanse and heal it. That can be accomplished only through the blood of Christ.

Fame, fun, immorality, drugs, alcohol, money, and music have, for the most part, failed man in his quest for inner peace. People are more phobic and frustrated than ever before. Psychiatrists, counselling services, and corporations manufacturing mood-altering drugs are doing big business today. Jesus offers an open clinic, a free prescription and the only sure cure for the hurts of mankind today — His peace. His last promise to His disciples was, "Peace I leave with you, my peace I give unto you: not as the world giveth, give I unto you. Let not your heart be troubled, neither let it be afraid" (John 14: 27). And now, sixty years after He made that promise, Jesus appears to John on a lonely, rocky island and assures him that this provision still stands.

There is a post-Desert Storm peace being contrived by the United Nations. It is garbed in a hopeful atmosphere called the New World Order. This new agreement will be primarily centered around the Jews and the Arabs; but, alas, it will be ultra temporary in its tenure. It will be only a matter of time until the world will awaken to what Ezekiel describes as "Gog Storm" (Ezek. 38:9). The Allied forces will have to fight again, with Israel joining them in a battle which might be called "Mountain Storm" (Ezek. 39:4). This is the battle which will unmask the friendly face of *glasnost* and *perestroika* . Russia and her "bands" (The Commonwealth of Independent States) will invade Israel and be soundly defeated by Israel and her allies in a victory which might be called "Fire Storm" (Ezek. 38:22; 39:6, 9-10).

Following the destruction of five-sixths of the armies of the Septentrional confederacy (northern, see Ezek. 39:2), a charlatan will come on the scene who will smile his way into the hearts of the United Nations and the European Economic Community . He will present the "ultimate" proposal to peace, and the world will be convinced that war is now obsolete. This peace treaty will be the most deviant enigma the world has ever experienced. It will be Satan's most murderous masterpiece, having the destruction of Israel as its goal. The consequences will be Armageddon.

The finest proposal for peace is inherent only in the Trinity, guaranteed and bonded by absolute divine truth. It is bona fide by God the Father, verified by Jesus Christ the faithful witness, and ratified by the Holy Spirit through His seven-fold administration of "wisdom, understanding, counsel, might, knowledge, fear of the Lord, and judgment (Isa. 11:2-3). I have known, relaxed in, and enjoyed this peace for over forty years. I recommend this precious peace of God "which passes all understanding" to a world filled with fear!

4. Endearment: "...Unto him that loved us..." (Rev. 1:5).

The peace Jesus gives does not come out of the end of a gun barrel. He does not beat us into submission and force us to sit down at a peace table. His "weapon" is the most powerful force in the universe — His immeasurable love.

5. Improvement: "...Washed us from our sins in his own blood" (Rev. 1:5).

The killing and offering of blood sacrifices for sin by Israel's temple priests could not cease, because sin never ceased. The sacrifice of Christ upon the cross is an everlasting sacrifice, because He lives. Hebrews 10:12-14 points out how shedding His own blood qualifies Christ to be the priest who now "perfects and sanctifies" those "who come boldly to the throne of grace."

Notice the order in which this is done: He loved us before He washed us, when we were still unlovely, filthy with sin, and disobedient in pride. "But God commended his love toward us, in that, while we were yet sinners, Christ died for us" (Rom. 5:8).

6. Benevolent: "And hath made us kings and priests unto God and his Father..." (Rev. 1:6).

Are not these tender and kind words of grace and peace beyond anything that those who offended Him are worthy to accept? Is this not more than a world deserves whose service to Him was crucifixion? But God does not dispense His love within the borders of what man deserves or has earned. His love knows no limits and His grace is not measured; both are freely bestowed. The grace, peace, and love expressed in the act of His "washing us from our sins in his own blood" are but the first fruits of a glorious harvest of blessings that will yet follow.

Unbelievable joy must have spilled over in the soul of the apostle on the Isle of Patmos when he realized what he was hearing from the mouth of the resurrected Christ. But then he saw still more. The Book of Revelation never stops with satisfactions or contentments of today's blessings in Christ. This is a revelation of Jesus Christ that views salvation in its fulfilled dimension and glory.

How can we declare the marvelous consideration of the Trinity towards the children of men? The benefits bestowed upon sinful man exceed the receptive capabilities of our spiritual sensibilities to understand why "He hath made us kings and priests unto God and His Father."

I speak two languages. Both of them leave me frustrated as I grasp for a paragraph that would express what I see in the above statement. I see fishermen and finishing carpenters, murderers and musicians, adulterers and artists, thieves and technicians, farmers and fortune tellers, doctors and dentists, servants and secretaries, slaves and soldiers. I see anybody and everybody who has appropriated the benefits of His grace, peace, and love (by the washing of His blood) included in this wonderful promise: "He hath made us kings and priests unto God." This is a promise embodying a regal partnership with the King of kings himself (Luke 22:29-30).

Have you agonized for hours in intercessory prayer? Have you lived below your means that you could give sacrificially? Have you approached every opportunity with the goal of drawing yet another into His kingdom? Have you invited the street person into your home? Have you shared Christ with the prisoner? Have you served joyfully in the kingdom without murmuring? If you have done these things, do them more! Lose your life—lay it down, offering it as a daily sacrifice unto God.

> And the King shall answer and say unto them, Verily I say unto you, Inasmuch as ye have done it unto one of the least of these my brethren, ye have done it unto me (Matt. 25:40).

We may be servants in His kingdom on earth today, but we shall be kings in His kingdom tomorrow. There is no believer, however humble or or ill-gifted, who, serving in some lowly outpost in the kingdom, may not rejoice in this prospect.

7. Excellence: "...To him be glory and dominion forever and ever. Amen" (Rev. 1:6).

What we are about to consider renders human speech poverty-stricken and naked. There is no language in terrestrial terms, no music, no instrument, no sound, no color, no aroma, no taste, no sensation that can adequately portray the sublime white light of the throne of His excellence. We simply have never seen the glory which John saw.

As she lay dying, my mother-in-law said to her daughters, "Last night I saw my mother and the room I have in heaven." She tried to explain how she saw the image of her aged mother in the face of the clock on the table. We understood that to mean that it was "just a matter of time" until the angels would carry her home.

Her daughters asked, "What did your room look like?"

My mother-in-law laughed softly as she said, *Das kann ich euch nicht sagen* (meaning: That I am unable to tell you).

At that moment, these words of John seemed to ring in my ears, "I was caught away into the third heaven and saw things there which I cannot describe" (author's paraphrase).

Confronted by the glory of God, Isaiah said, "Woe is me" (Isa. 6:5). Daniel said, "There remained no strength in me, for my comeliness was turned in me into corruption, and I retained no strength" (Dan. 10:8). Peter cried, "Depart from me, for I am a sinful man, O Lord" (Luke 5:8). John said, "When I saw him, I fell at his feet as dead" (Rev. 1:17).

Man will not be capable of truly praising Him who is in heaven until "that which is corruptible shall have put on incorruption" (1 Cor. 15:54). An earthly choir trying to sing God's glory in His actual presence would faint dead away as did John on Patmos. Musical instruments of earth, trying to produce celestial tones acceptable at His throne, would probably explode. Sound systems would probably destroy their own speaker columns. The presence of God can be survived only by those "who have been changed, in a moment, in the twinkling of an eye" (1 Cor. 15:52 — author's paraphrase).

III. PERSUASIVE PROMPTINGS (Revelation 1:7-8)

Behold, he cometh with clouds; and every eye shall see him, and they also which pierced him: and all kindreds of the earth shall wail because of him. Even so, Amen. I am Alpha and Omega, the beginning and the ending, saith the Lord, which is, and which was, and which is to come, the Almighty.

1. Wake Up: "Behold..." (Rev. 1:7).

The word "behold" is designed to arrest our attention. John uses the word here to jab us wide awake, for he knew very well that the greater part of our world's population would be spiritually asleep or unaware of Christ's return. Jesus cautioned His disciples, "Watch therefore: for ye know not what hour your Lord doth come" (Matt. 24:42). Paul sounded the warning, "It is high time to awake out of sleep: for now is our salvation nearer than when we believed" (Rom. 13:11).

There are myriads of signs pointing to Christ's soon return. Earthquakes, floods, violence, drug abuse (sorcery), broken marriages, starvation, disease, witchcraft, false prophets, devil worship, a falling away from the truth, and a resorting to fables. All of these are eschatological flags waving in the breezes of prophecy as a message loud and clear: Wake up, shape up, Jesus is coming soon!

2. Look Up: "...He cometh with clouds..." (Rev. 1:7).

The Bible makes this pronouncement many times. One of the shortest books in the Bible tells about it (Jude 14) and the longest book declares it (Ps. 96:13). The prophets have told us. We have been singing, preaching, teaching, hoping, and praying for it for centuries. Jesus promised that He was going to "prepare a place" and then He said, "I will come again, and receive you unto myself; that where I am ye may be also" (John. 14:2-3). I believe it.

Unfortunately, many of His servants no longer anticipate His return. Some laugh and mock those who still lay it to heart. A religion without a Christ returning to this world is not the religion of this revelation. We must embrace His words, "Behold I come quickly" (Rev. 3:11).

Let us never forget or reject the doctrine proclaimed by the two men on the day of Christ's ascension, "This same Jesus, which is taken up from you into heaven, shall so come in like manner as ye have seen him go into heaven" (Acts 1:11). How I love those two men. I think they must be Moses and Elijah. It was these two who talked with Him on the mount of transfiguration and who will appear again during the tribulation, performing miracles to convince Israel that Jesus is their Messiah (Rev. 11:3-12).

"He cometh, with clouds." What clouds does John speak of here? Paul answers this in Ephesians 4:8 where he writes, "...When he ascended up on high, he led captivity captive...." The "captivity" freed at His ascension are the souls of Old Testament saints to whom He preached deliverance and announced their release from the bondage of death (1 Pet. 3:19). These delivered saints are themselves the cloud which the disciples saw as Jesus was ascending into heaven. Paul, speaking about the fathers of the faith, alludes to them as this same cloud when he says, "Seeing we are compassed about with so great a cloud of witnesses, let us run with patience the race..." (Heb. 11:1).

When Jesus returns to earth, He will return with clouds (plural). I understand this to mean that the saints He took captive at His ascension will be joined by the Church which will have been raptured before the tribulation. This truth is fortified by the words, "...The Lord cometh with ten thousands of his saints..." (Jude 14).

3. Lift Up: "...And every eye shall see him..." (Rev. 1:7).

The rapture of the Church is not being alluded to here. This is the revelation of Jesus to the Jews (1 Pet. 1:13). Jesus also said, "And when these things begin to come to pass, then look up, and lift up your heads; for your redemption draweth nigh" (Luke 21:28).

4. Shake Up: "...And they also which pierced him..." (Rev. 1:7).

You cannot kill God by crucifixion. The crucifiers were sure He was dead because blood and water ran from His side. They saw Him bow His head and give up the ghost. They heard Him say to His Father, "...Into thy hands I commend my spirit" (Luke 23:46). But somehow they did not see that over those eyelids closed in death hovered the dawn of a resurrection. What a paralyzing fear will grip their conscience when He presents the scars in His hands as evidence against them.

5. Break Up: "...And all kindreds of the earth shall wail because of him. Even so, Amen" (Rev. 1:7).

It would appear that both the Romans and the Jews are indicted for the crucifixion of Jesus. The Jews condemned Him to death and the Romans crucified and pierced Him. The prophet Zechariah beholds the same terrible scene when he writes these words of God, "...And they shall look upon me whom they have pierced..." (Zech. 12:10).

"All kindreds of the earth" is in keeping with the judgment of dispersion for the Jews into the four corners of the earth. The rapture of Israel, as described in Matthew 24:30-31, confirms this:

> And then shall appear the sign of the Son of man in heaven: and then shall all the tribes of the earth mourn, and they shall see the Son of man coming in the clouds of heaven with power and great glory. And he shall send his angels with a great sound of a trumpet, and they shall gather together his elect from the four winds of heaven, from one end of heaven to the other.

6. Shut Up: "I am Alpha and Omega, the beginning and the ending, saith the Lord..." (Rev. 1:8).

Alpha and Omega are the first and last letters of the Greek Alphabet. The message I hear is that He alone, not His crucifiers or anyone who has ever opposed Him, will have the first or the last word. His judgments are so absolute that Paul cried out, "... every mouth shall be stopped, and all the world shall become guilty before God" (Rom. 3:19, author's paraphrase).

Christ is not only the first and last letter of the alphabet; He is the absolute Word which was in the beginning with God (John. 1:1), and He will still be that absolute Word at the end with God (Rev. 19:13).

7. High Up: "...The Almighty, which is, and which was, and which is to come" (Rev. 1:8, word order reversed by author).

No violence is being done in rearranging the text. By naming "the Almighty" first, the implication of Christ's divinity becomes even more conspicuous. Jesus was very deliberate when He asserted, "I and my Father are one" (John. 10:30). Upon making this claim, the Jews immediately took up stones to destroy Him. This did not keep Him from insisting upon speaking the truth again, four chapters later, where He says, "He that hath seen me hath seen the Father" (John. 14:9).

What John experienced on the Isle of Patmos that day thoroughly convinced him that Jesus indeed was God. The world would be a much better place if all men would embrace this truth.

IV. PERSECUTED, BUT PRESERVED
(Revelation 1:9)

I John, who also am your brother, and companion in tribulation, and in the kingdom and patience of Jesus Christ, was
in the isle that is called Patmos, for the word of God and
for the testimony of Jesus Christ.

1. The Person: "I John..." (Rev. 1:9).

"Just call me John Zebedee." I can almost hear him saying, with
a sting of irony, "Leave off the ego-inflating accolades on my achievements, travels, epistles authored, honors earned, and how congested
my schedule is with invitations. Just call me John."

He was no doubt a most prestigious saint and the only surviving
apostle at this time. He no doubt had an audience with every age
group. Who would not want to talk with a man known as Jesus'
closest companion — one who had personally witnessed the life,
death, resurrection, and ascension of Jesus Christ? And now John is
being doubly honored with prophetic secrets that Jesus is about to
divulge.

Much had already been written about Jesus. Yet John said, "There
are many things, if all of them were recorded, the world could not
contain all the books of those things Jesus said and did" (John 21:25,
author's paraphrase). When I get toHeaven, I want John to tell me
all about those things Jesus did and said that have never been recorded.

John was also the pastor of the church at Ephesus where Mary,
the mother of Jesus, was a member. Ephesus was the city where a
two-hour demonstration took place because the god-makers were
threatened by Paul (Acts 19:28-34). In spite of this idolatrous strong-
hold, when John was banished to Patmos in about 95 A.D. (some forty
years after Paul's visit), the temple of Diana was all but forsaken.
Christianity had become the popular religion. This is a testimony to
the effectiveness of John's ministry.

2. The Parentage: "... Who also am your brother..." (Rev. 1:9)

The spirit of the early Church lives on. We are a family, the children of one heavenly Father. We are equal heirs of the promise.

32

There is no one who is to lord over another. Jesus said, "And whosoever of you will be the chiefest, shall be servant of all" (Mark 10:44).

3. The Partnership: "...Companion in tribulation..." (Rev. 1:9).

At the time of this writing, the early Church was experiencing much persecution under the cruel Roman Emperor Domitian. Tradition tells us that John was thrown into a boiling caldron of oil, but was unharmed. He was then banished to a lonely, desolate island called Patmos some seventy miles southwest of Ephesus in the Aegean Sea.

There are many things the children of God have in common, and persecution has always been the hallmark of genuine Christian experience. The world has always clubbed its Abels, mocked its Noahs, denned its Daniels, jailed its Josephs, beheaded its Pauls, banished its apostles, and crucified its Christ. The Lord warned us that we should not be surprised at this; the world hated Him and it will hate us, too. Then He said, "In the world ye shall have tribulation, but be of good cheer; I have overcome the world" (John 16:33). Many have graciously accepted this suffering. How little our Western world has tasted of this bitter cup.

4. The Parameter: "...The kingdom..." (Rev. 1:9).

The kingdom is the thorn in Satan's side. He revealed his malicious ambitions when he said to Jesus, "All these things (kingdoms) I will give thee, if thou wilt fall down and worship me" (Matt. 4:9). Either Satan has never realized it, or else he has forgotten that Jesus was endowed with the seven spirits of God (Isa. 11:1-4). It is completely impossible for Satan to ever intellectually out-maneuver our Lord.

What is this kingdom of God? Unfortunately, the subject of the kingdom of God has become something of a theological freeway interchange. Indeed, this kingdom begins in the life of one whose heart is fully given to the Lordship of Christ. The Book of Revelation assumes this, but we must look further down the highway which consummates in something corporate as well as personal. Jesus taught us to pray, "Thy kingdom come on earth," implying more than just a heart commitment to this kingdom.

...The kingdoms of this world are become the kingdoms of our Lord, and of his Christ, and he shall reign for ever and ever (Rev. 11:15).

What would the apostle John say to us today about the kingdom? He would tell us to get busy, there is much work to be done. John the Baptist was the kingdom's spiritual road contractor; he land-filled, graded, and built bridges and overpasses. He was in full obedience to his mission, "Prepare ye the way of the Lord, make his paths straight" (Matt. 3:3). John's message was straight and forthright: "Repent, for the kingdom of God is at hand."

The scriptural references to the kingdom are profuse. The teaching of our Lord was punctuated with terse remarks, parables, and sermons about the kingdom. The worldly Samaritan woman at the well said, "I know that Messiah cometh, which is called Christ: when he is come, he will tell us all things" (John 4:25). Who is the Messiah? He is the one who will restore again the kingdom to Israel. He alone will bring peace to this earth and goodwill to men. The government of the world will be upon His shoulders. The kingdoms of this world are to become His kingdom and He is to reign for a thousand years. If He is to be the "King of kings and Lord of lords," then where and when is this to be?

The following Scriptures are just a few dealing with the messianic plan of God for Jesus: Genesis 49:10; Psalm 2; 110:1-2; Isaiah 9:6; 40:3; 42:1-7; Ezekiel 37:21-22; Daniel 2:44-45; 7:13-14; Micah 5:1-4, and Zechariah 9:9. The four Gospels, the Book of Acts, and the Book of Revelation are filled with such references as well. Jesus is far more than a penniless Jew who died upon a Roman cross to atone for the sins of the world. That was but the first step in an obedience that would lead to great honor.

5. The Practice: "...Patience of Jesus Christ..." (Rev. 1:9).

Patience is an attribute which verifies Christian maturity, and tribulation is the thorny branch which bears the flowers of patience (Rom. 5:3). "In your patience possess ye your souls" (Luke 21:19). Luke said, "...We must through much tribulation enter into the kingdom of God" (Acts 14:22). Tribulation is the parent of patience. Patience is that grace which enables us to bear afflictions with steadfast calmness of mind and a ready submission to the will of God. Patience is the grace to be calm when all around the tempest rages.

The Scriptures exhort us that waiting for the coming of Christ will require patience (2 Thess. 3:5). The theme of many of the parables of Christ that deal with His return are all about patience.

Patmos must be one of the loneliest and most desolate places in all the world. It must have required great patience as John literally crawled about on a rock pile while God gave him this revelation. There were no trees for shade, parks for beauty, or lakes for serenity on this island. Yet, it is in precisely such a setting of stark solitude that God often reveals the most intimate secrets of His heart to patient men and women. "Be still and know that I am God..." (Ps. 46:10).

Bible scholars know that God speaks to men in the most unlikely places and times. He spoke to Elijah in a cave, to Moses on a mountain, to Paul in the desert of Arabia, to John the Baptist in the wilderness, to Joseph in prison, and to Daniel in a lion's den. Most of Paul's letters were written from a prison. Martin Luther translated the Bible into the German language under duress and imprisonment. It should come as no surprise that the Lord chose Patmos, the loneliest place on earth, to give John the revelation of Himself.

6. The Problem: "...The word of God..." (Rev. 1:9).

Whenever a man utters the phrase, "Hear the word of the Lord," it creates a problem. It may be true that the basic reason behind every Christian martyrdom is the love for the Lord and defense of the Word of God. Daniel, Joseph, Elijah, John the Baptist, Paul, and scores of others encountered great difficulty because of such conviction.

Stephen, while on trial, spoke these words, "Which of the prophets have not your fathers persecuted? And they have slain them which showed before of the coming of the Just One... When they heard these things, they were cut to the heart, and they gnashed on him with their teeth" (Acts 7:52, 54). Men become as snarling animals when their lives are exposed by the Word of God. John had been banished to this rock island called Patmos because of his proclamation of the Word.

35

7. The Provocation: "...The testimony of Jesus Christ" (Rev. 1:9).

The testimony of Jesus refers to all of the claims He made regarding Himself and the miracles He performed (which vindicated His claims). He claimed to be the Son of God. This claim was vindicated on both the mount of transfiguration and at His baptism when the voice of God was heard to say from heaven, "This is my beloved Son" (Matt. 3:17; 17:5). Jesus claimed that He and the Father were one (John 10:30). He vindicated this claim by revealing that the Father had vested all power and authority in Him (John 5:20-23). Others called Him a great teacher, a prophet, the son of David, and the King of the Jews, which provoked men and invoked the jealousy of the Jewish leaders.

One of the greatest irritants to the non-believers was the mention of the blood of Christ. If the blood of Christ saved, then the sacrificing of animals and the shedding of their blood by Jewish priests would become obsolete. To accept this would have meant the dismantling of the entire Jewish religion which the scribes and pharisees would not allow. Before they would see this happen, they would take Him out of the way.

Another great provocation, actually leading to His crucifixion, was the testimony that Jesus was the Jewish Messiah and King. The vindication of this truth has not yet been realized, but it is not far away. The supreme testimony, which ratifies all the works and claims of Jesus, was vindicated in His resurrection. The priests bribed the guards of Jesus's tomb to give this testimony: "Say ye, his disciples came by night, and stole him away while we slept" (Matt. 28:13). The stifling of the message of His resurrection resulted in spiritual blindness to the Jews until this day.

The fact of the resurrection is a showdown of all the religions of the world. I could never feel spiritually secure in a religion that can only take me to an elaborate monument commemorating its dead leader. A religion's power and life can only be as potent and alive as its leader. A dead leader infers and implies a dead religion. Only the Christian religion can take you to a crude cave in a garden at Jerusalem where we celebrate the message of an epitaph which reads, "He is not here: for he is risen, as he said..." (Matt. 28:6).

The resurrection of Jesus Christ guarantees His return to earth and His coronation as the King of all the world. How Satan wishes that the lie and the fraud the Jewish leaders tried to perpetrate were true.

V. PREPARATION FOR THE VISION
(Revelation 1:10-12)

I was in the Spirit on the Lord's day, and heard behind me
a great voice, as of a trumpet, saying, I am Alpha and Omega, the first and the last: and, What thou seest, write in a
book, and send it unto the seven churches which are in Asia;
unto Ephesus, and unto Smyrna, and unto Pergamos, and
unto Thyatira, and unto Sardis, and unto Philadelphia, and
unto Laodicea. And I turned to see the voice that spake with
me. And being turned, I saw seven golden candlesticks.

1. For Worship: "I was in the Spirit..." (Rev. 1:10).

The barren wasteland of the Isle of Patmos certainly contributed
to objects of inspiration for John's worship. Modern man often finds
it difficult to reach God unless there are stained glass windows, a
choir, candles, and padded pews to provide comfort and inspiration.
John needed no such amenities, for he was "in the Spirit on the Lord's
day." He intended to worship, but what happened to him in that
rocky rubble changed his life and influenced the Church of Jesus
Christ forever.

A Greek transliteration of "I was in the Spirit" would read, "I came
to be in Spirit." This seems somehow to say that some activity of
the Holy Spirit happened to him. A process was at work as though
some kind of metamorphosis had taken place. Menge, in his German translation says, *Da geriet ich durch den Geist in Verzuekung*, meaning: "There fell I through the Spirit into trance." The German word
geriet cannot be expressed with another English word; it requires a
sentence like, "I fell unknowingly into..."

God required John's undivided attention, so even the desolation
of Patmos needed to be eliminated. John was about to encounter spiritual realities which flesh and blood could not survive, thus a temporary spiritual state needed to be engaged to accommodate such
supernatural confrontations. When God gives a heavenly vision to
a human, He generally does it while the person is in a trance. Balaam, while in a trance, blessed Jacob (Num. 24:4, 16). Daniel saw a
vision of Jesus while in a "deep sleep" (Dan. 10:9). Peter received
his vision of all manner of creatures while in a trance (Acts 10:10).

Paul fell into a trance while praying in the temple at Jerusalem (Acts 22:17).

God places Man's human quotient on hold, transforming him "into the Spirit" to receive His heavenly visions. There must be an awesome silence surrounding a man or woman under God's omnipotent anesthesia.

2. For A Special Day: "... The Lord's day..." (Rev. 1:10).

If our Lord has a special day, it surely must be Sunday. Sunday was the day of Jesus' coronation (albeit misunderstood) when He rode into the city of Jerusalem on a donkey. Sunday is also the day that Jesus rose triumphantly from the grave and conquered death. The early Church always observed the Eucharist on Sunday. The day of Pentecost came on a Sunday. Christians observe the Lord's Supper on Sunday. I cannot help but wonder if Jesus Christ will return on His special day, as well.

3. To Listen: "...Heard behind me a great voice, as of a trumpet" (Rev. 1:10).

Jesus is God and no mortal could survive a face-to-face confrontation with God. When John turned towards the voice, he saw only seven golden candlesticks. Then the vision expands and he sees not God, but one "like unto the Son of man." John recognized the person of Jesus. This is the only way God could reveal Himself to mortal man, incarnate in the body of Jesus as "one like the Son of man." And even in this form, John fell as though he were a dead man at His feet.

The voice of a trumpet is God's way of getting our attention. The voice of God was heard from Mount Sinai as the sound of a trumpet. The people of Israel were summoned for worship in the temple by the sound of a trumpet. First Thessalonians 4:16 reveals that:

> ...The Lord himself shall descend from heaven with a shout, with the voice of the archangel, and with the trump of God: and the dead in Christ shall rise first.

God will gather Israel for the last time with the sound of a trumpet:

> And he shall send his angels with a great sound of a trumpet, and they shall gather together his elect from the four winds, from one end of heaven to the other" (Matt. 24:31).

When John returned to Ephesus with this document in his hand, I wonder if he asked his congregation whether on a certain Sunday they heard that trumpet from seventy miles away. What an omnipotent signal it must have produced. It was enough to awaken Lazarus from sleep after being dead for four days. And it is quite capable of awaking all of the dead in Christ from every cemetery of the world and every cremation crypt — even those who perished in the sea.

4. For A Great Message: "...I am Alpha and Omega, the first and the Last..." (Rev. 1:11).

Four times in the Book of Revelation Jesus declares Himself to be either the Alpha and Omega, the first and the last, or the beginning and the end. Many of today's best minds have not yet acknowledged this reality. The first chapter of Genesis tells how God created the heavens and the earth and all that is in them. The words "And God said..." are repeated nine times in this first chapter as a preface to each phase of creation. Peter also affirms this with the words, "...By the word of God the heavens were of old..." (2 Pet. 3:5).

How incredible it is that man believes he can explain the origin of all things without so much as even the mention of God. What an insult to the Almighty that those who have been created in His own image are unwilling to acknowledge Him as the creator of anything. God is here telling us, "I was and I am the first."

No speck of protoplasm was responsible for procreating anything that is alive in the universe. The theory of evolution must be the biggest joke in Heaven and no doubt has caused the angels either to laugh or cry many times. The Alpha and Omega and evolution are on a collision course. They remind me of a mighty locomotive speeding down the tracks at three hundred miles an hour while a little signal-fixer is on the same track coming from the opposite direction. The small upstart proceeds confidently on, blowing its horn to warn the huge train to get off the tracks because there is not enough room for both of them. When the inevitable happens, the experts gather around to shake their heads and assess the remains of the accident. Meanwhile, back in the depot the next morning, the report reads, "*It appears we might have struck a monkey yesterday as there seems to be fragments of banana peels on our front bumper.*"

Of course, this sounds silly and facetious. But in reality, how do these man-made theories sit with the Almighty? The mockery of the theory of evolution will be deadly silent when its perpetrators stand in judgment for the spiritual wreck many have suffered because of this teaching. There is a collision coming!

5. For A Great Revelation: "...What thou seest..." (Rev. 1:11).

What John turned to see was not the same as that which he had heard from behind him. The voice behind him was the voice of Jesus, the Almighty God. But when John turned, he saw seven golden candlesticks. Looking more closely, he saw "one like the Son of man." If Jesus had not transformed Himself at that point into that which He became through the virgin birth, namely "the Son of man," John would not have lived.

What kind of love caused the Son of God to become the Son of man, so that sons of men might be able to become sons of God? In order for Christ to save humanity, He left the praises of angels to come to earth to receive the persecution of Man. He went from coronation to crucifixion, from exaltation to degradation, and from the hails of Heaven to the nails of the cross. He laid down His righteous name to suffer blasphemy. But, in spite of it all, He returned to further reveal Himself and His love to His friend, John, to be recorded for all who would receive what He offered.

6. For A Great Responsibility: "...What thou seest, write in a book, and send it unto the seven churches which are in Asia..." (Rev. 1:11).

God knows how to bring disgrace upon His enemies. The haughty Goliath was humiliated by a single stone from little David's sling shot. The hateful Haman hung from the gallows he had built for Morde-

40

cai. When the Pharaohs of Egypt persisted in drowning the first-born sons of the Hebrews in the river Nile, God responded by killing all the first-born of man and beast.

John was exiled, by God's enemies, to Patmos for the "word of God and the testimony of Jesus "which he proclaimed in a single church at Ephesus. John returned from Patmos with a "more sure word of prophecy," which possessed a seven-fold potential after it was distributed to the seven Asian congregations.

7. For A Great Representation:

> And I turned to see the voice that spake with me. And being turned, I saw seven golden candlesticks; and in the midst of the seven candlesticks one like unto the Son of man, clothed with a garment down to the foot, and girt about the paps (breast) with a golden girdle (Rev. 1:12-13).

Three representations within this pronouncement require serious attention. The candlesticks represent the seven chruches (Rev. 1:20), which will be studied in depth in chapters two and three. The fact that Christ is here standing among the seven chruches indicates that His chief interest in this world is His Church, which after all is His bride. In Ephesians 5, Paul draws an analogy between Christ and His Church as being likened to a husband and his wife. Paul tells us that Christ is willing to identify himself as the "head" of the Church, reminding us that Christ "loved the church and gave himself for it."

The fact that the Church is symbolized as "golden candlesticks" is also significant. Gold is the most precious metal known to man. Christ's estimate of the Church is embodied within this symbol.

The fact that the Church is symbolized by candlesticks conveys its responsibility. A candlestick is a light-bearer. Christ is surely reminding the Church that she is to be a light in this dark world. Christ is Himself the Light of the World, and if His Church fails in holding forth this light, His death upon the cross will have been in vain.

Second, Christ is seen standing "in the midst" of the candlesticks. This is a reminder to John that Jesus has not forgotten His ascension promise, "Lo I am with you always, even unto the end of the world" (Matt. 28:20). This is also a reaffirmation of His presence in our worship, for He said, "Where two or three are gathered together in my name, there am I in the midst of them" (Matt. 18:20). It is further a warning that if He is indeed in the midst of the Church, He is aware of her activity and will be a "rewarder of them that diligently seek him" (Heb. 11:6).

Finally, it is "the Son of man" who is standing here. I cannot help but feel that He was standing there long before John caught sight of Him. It is my belief that He is always walking among the churches, never resting or at ease. How can He be when the Devil, our adversary, never ceases to see who he may take out of the Church? Peter expresses this awful truth in these words, "Be sober, be vigilant; because your adversary the devil, as a roaring lion, walketh about, seeking whom he may devour" (1 Pet. 5:8).

Do not get the impression that the "Son of man" is someone less than the Son of God, the Alpha and Omega, or the Almighty. His intimate association and identification with Mankind as "the Son of man" alters nothing of His awesome person. Never forget that John fell as dead before the "Son of man."

In the prominent twenty-fourth chapter of Matthew, which has distinguished itself as being Jesus' greatest discourse of His coming, our Lord is referred to as "the Son of man" at least six times. There are scores of references in the Bible that call Jesus "the Son of man" in connection with His second coming.

VI. PORTRAIT OF THE POTENTATE - HIS SEVEN-FOLD GLORY (Revelation 1:14-16).

His head and his hairs were white like wool, as white as snow; and his eyes were as a flame of fire; and his feet like unto fine brass, as if they burned in a furnace; and his voice as the sound of many waters. And he had in his right hand seven stars: and out of his mouth went a sharp two-edged sword: and his countenance was as the sun shineth in his strength.

I am very aware here that I have just entered into the holy of holies of this first chapter. The personage we are trying to understand in the symbols here portrayed is the one John fell before as a dead man. I tremble as a human in trying to understand and explain deity, which has never yet and never will be satisfactorily done. Per-

42

haps this assignment should be attempted only in the seclusion of a wilderness, a desert, a forest, or on a mountain top. The world's distractions hinder the expression of the mysteries here embodied.

Technology offers sophisticated electronic equipment to help us transfer the thoughts of our mind to paper, but these conveniences have no heart, soul, or conscience. We are left entirely alone to cry out, *"Speak Lord, thy servant heareth."*

1. His Head And His Hairs Were White: (Rev. 1:14).

As John laid eyes upon this personage, he was captivated first by the whiteness of His head and His hair. John found it necessary to emphasize this by saying it in two ways: "white like wool" and "white as snow." The Son of man is here depicted as a judge. It is necessary to make this statement at the outset, so that our minds may be constantly thinking in these terms which will help us to understand the vision. This statement will vindicate itself as we proceed.

A white wig is an accoutrement of a judge which speaks of justice, honor, honesty, trustworthiness, and integrity. Scripturally, white represents righteousness (Rev. 19:8) and cleansing and forgiveness (Isa. 1:18). The process of purification is referred to as being "made white" (Dan. 12:10). The saints are referred to as the "children of light" (Eph. 5:8), having been washed in the blood of the Lamb to become white (Rev. 7:14). In Revelation 20:11, John sees the judgment seat as "a great white throne."

Black is in opposition to white. The works of Satan are referred to as the powers of darkness (Eph. 6:12). The evil deeds of men are called darkness (John 3:19). Evil-doers hate light (John 3:20), and Hell is a terrible place of darkness (Matt. 8:12; 22:13; 25:30).

Jesus is here depicted (Rev. 1:14) as a judge because God wants us to understand that the principle position and function of Jesus will be judicial throughout the last three and a half years of this world's systems.

2. His Eyes Were As A Flame Of Fire: (Rev. 1:14).

We have high expectations of judges. They are ideally chosen for their compulsion to execute justice tempered with compassion and mercy. They are to possess an innate ability to recognize truth or fraud, and they must be firm and courageous enough to pronounce the verdict. The judge of the Revelation is the supreme judge, making all others pale by inferiority.

If eyes speak of intelligence, what kind of eyes are described as being flames of fire? Such eyes possess an omnipotent ability to penetrate the remotest recesses of the human heart with an omniscient comprehension of the past, present, and future. These eyes are their own advocate, jury, evidence, verdict, and sentence.

Somehow, I feel that not a word will need to be spoken at the Great White Throne Judgment. Jesus will just look at the unrepentant with those eyes of fire, immediately making him aware of his guilt and the verdict. Peter knew when the Lord "looked at him" that his cowardly denial was known and he went out and "wept bitterly" (Luke 22: 56-62).

The Great White Throne Judgment will be a terrible scene. I believe every crime perpetrated against God and man will be relived right before the eyes of the offenders. Those who killed babies by abortion will see a sordid scene flash before their eyes as aborted infants point fingers at them. Those who murdered and raped will stand face-to-face with their victims before a just and Almighty God. Every conceivable unsolved crime will be revealed. When the fiery eyes of the judge of the Book of Revelation begin staring into the eyes of sinners, every seemingly justifiable defense and alibi will suddenly become the sinner's own verdict of guilt. No one will stand up in defiance, as they once did on earth, to justify their deeds.

3. His Feet Like Unto Fine Brass: (Rev. 1:15).

The feet of Jesus, the Supreme Judge, will appear as if they burned in a furnace. His eyes and His feet are symbolized by fire, which is a symbol of judgment. When the eyes witness an injustice, the feet hasten to take appropriate judicial action.

There are two characteristics of Christ's feet which are significant. First, they are of brass. In the Old Testament, the altar upon which sin was judged by the sacrificing of blood was made of brass. The serpent which Moses lifted up in the wilderness, the one that saved the people from death when they gazed upon it in faith, was also made of brass. Brass is a type of judgment against sin. Second, the

44

brass representing Christ's feet is a fine molten brass. This means that a perpetual refining process is always at work, making it impossible for impurities or dross to become a part of them. King David had high respect for the judgments of God when he said, "...The judgments of the Lord are true and righteous altogether" (Ps. 19:9).

Several times, the Bible employs the figure of speech, "Sit thou on my right hand till I make thine enemies thy footstool." A footstool is used to rest feet. The above figure of speech substantiates the truth of the judicial authority of Christ's feet by representing Him as resting them upon His enemies. When our Lord reclines and uses His enemies as a footstool, the terror of any enemy shall forever "be put to rest."

4. His Voice As The Sound Of Many Waters: (Rev. 1:15).

On the occasion of my oldest son's wedding, I experienced the privilege of seeing the Oregon coast for the first time. I cannot explain how I felt when we got out of the car and the power of that magnificent ocean burst upon me. The sun was setting, and a blinding band of white light reflecting from the heaving waters almost took my breath away. Our eyes followed the ships, as one after another they disappeared over the horizon. I marveled at the power of the ocean, at how it could carry those large ocean liners with their tonnage to another hemisphere, and at how it came crashing in upon the rocky shoreline, its waters exploding like a white volcano high into the air.

The sound that John heard was not that of one powerful water as expressed by an ocean. He heard the sound of "many waters" here which must surely include the voices of all the prophets and messengers of God who told of the coming of the "Just One." These messages now all converged on the Isle of Patmos, being fulfilled in this one voice of the Supreme Judge, the Word. This same voice prayed on another occasion and caused the people to exclaim that it had thundered (John 12:29).

In the Gospel of John, it is recorded that Jesus said, "He that believeth on me, as the scripture saith, out of his inner most being shall flow rivers of living water" (John 7:38). Then John says in the Book of Revelation that Christ's voice was as the sound of many waters. The message regarding the Word of God, Jesus Himself, is the verbal stream that the Church must keep flowing freely until He returns. The true messenger of God begins with the Word and ends with the Word!

5. He Had In His Right Hand Seven Stars: (Rev. 1:16)

The mystery of the seven stars is explained in verse 20, "...The seven stars are the angels of the seven churches...." Popular opinion regarding angels would insist that their habitation is Heaven. While this may be true, our Lord here reserves the right to call the ministers of the seven chruches angels as well. While these written messages were to be "sent" to the seven churches (Rev. 1:11), John was, nevertheless, instructed to direct them to the "angel" of each church. If the angels referred to here had their abode in Heaven, what address would John use for delivery instructions? We can only conclude that these angels are the ministers of the seven churches, and it is their responsibility to read the letters in a public worship service.

6. Out Of His Mouth Went A Sharp Two-edged Sword: (Rev. 1:16)

The two-edged sword proceeding from the Savior's mouth and the voice as the sound of many waters call attention to the intensity and immensity of His Word. The two-edged sword proceeding from His mouth speaks of the merciless executions of His Word which are here being initiated. This sword is mentioned several more times.

We read in Hebrews 4:12 that "the word of God is quick, and powerful, and sharper than any towedged sword." We read in Ephesians 6:17 that "the sword of the Spirit...is the word of God." The Word of God is infinitely powerful when wielded by the Holy Spirit. When we are dealing with the sword in the Book of Revelation, for the most part, God is not talking to people. Here the sword speaks of a dispensation of judgement. The judge of Revelation does more than pronounce verdicts, He carries out His own executions. The sword in the Savior's mouth represents the power of His Word with the sheath of mercy removed.

When the Savior uses this sword in chapter 19, it will not be in the manner known to us today. His Word today is used for doctrine, reproof, correction, and instruction in righteousness (2 Tim. 3:16). The Scriptures referring to the sword in chapter 19 have to do with judgment. In Revelation 2:16, the word "fight" is used. In Revelation 19:15, the word "smite" is used.

What will it be like when God finally refuses to talk or listen to Man? Of King Saul, it is said that "when Saul inquired of the Lord, the Lord answered him not" (1 Sam. 28:6). Saul must have believed it would be better to be dead than to have God against him, for he committed suicide the next day.

What will it be like when Jesus the Judge strips the sheath of mercy from His sword? It would be better for us to have earthquakes, tornados, floods, and fire worldwide than to have Christ fight against us with his sharp two-edged sword.

When our Lord goes to battle, His sword does not get bloodied. He destroys men by the power of His Word. I believe all of the first-born in Egypt were found dead with not a mark on them. I believe Ananias and Sapphira had not a mark on them. He breathed over His disciples and they received the gift of the Holy Ghost. He spoke the word of judgment over Sodom and Gomorrah and they disappeared. He and the saints will fight against the enemies of Israel in the final battle of the tribulation and there will not be a drop of blood on their garments. He will just speak the Word and "it is done" (Rev. 16:17).

7. His Countenance Was As The Sun Shineth In His Strength: (Rev. 1:16).

Have you ever tried looking into the sun? What kind of shock must have paralyzed John when that which cannot be viewed 93,000,000 miles away suddenly stood before him in the form of a man? This scene so electrified and overwhelmed the apostle that it rendered him defenseless and prostrate on the ground as a dead man. Daniel, who feared neither king nor lion, saw this same vision centuries earlier by the great river Hiddekel and said, "I retained no strength, and my comliness was turned in me into corruption."

Reflect for a moment upon this personage with ultra-white hair, lightning-like eyes of fire, a countenance like the full-strength power of the sun, a voice like many waters, one hand holding seven brilliant stars, the other hand holding a sharp two-edged sword and glistening feet of molten brass. The one who suddenly appeared before John was a being whose forbidding form would send any human into a state of unconsciousness. No human could have remained unaffected in such a presence. Had John not been in the spirit (in a trance), his life would surely have been snuffed out. John, Christ's closest friend on earth, fell at His feet as a dead man at the sight of Him. Only Jesus' touch and voice, saying, "Fear not," obtained John's survival.

The transfiguration of Jesus was the maximum divine exposure allowed for His inner circle. That was as close as men dared to approach omnipotence. Saul of Tarsus got so close that, except for divine intervention, he probably would have remained blind to his dying day. Matthew 24:27 declares that the impact upon the world of the coming of Jesus Christ will be like a lightning flash out of the East and covering the globe to the West. All of this world's arc welders striking an arc in unison could not so illuminate the planet.

The New Jerusalem, resplendent with supernatural light, requires no sun or moon, for the glory of God and the Lamb are the light of it. So penetrating are its rays that "the nations which are saved shall walk in its light" (Rev. 21:24). This is the light which illuminated Patmos that day.

As we approach the Book of Revelation, we must have a proper concept of the author of our faith and executioner of these judgments. If you do not, you will scarcely have enough faith to believe what you will discover as He finishes your faith!

VII. PROCLAMATION OF AUTHORIZATION
(Revelation 1:17-18).

And when I saw him, I fell at his feet as dead. And he laid his right hand upon me, saying unto me, Fear not; I am the first and the last: I am he that liveth, and was dead; and behold, I am alive forevermore, Amen; and have the keys of hell and of death.

In this, the final section of Forty-Nine Pronouncements Concerning Jesus and His Directives, He makes seven declarations regarding His authority. These declarations begin with the personal pronoun "I."

1. I Am The First: (Rev. 1:17).

The Holy Spirit did a good work in the heart of John when He inspired him to write, "In the beginning was the Word (Jesus), and the Word (Jesus) was with God, and the Word (Jesus) was God" (John 1:1). I am quite sure that John understood what that meant. Our Lord knew if He addressed Himself to John as "the first" on the Isle of Patmos, John would immediately equate this first as being the same as the Word which was with God in the beginning.

If He is the "first," then He was present in the world first. Whoever was here first created everything that exists. Whoever created everything owns everything. Whoever owns everything governs everything and has kept it running since the beginning. Whoever has kept everything running has a plan for that which He has created. We must, therefore, conclude that He is also responsible for His creation and has the authority to continue doing whatever He feels needs to be done. He is the one and only true God!

2. I...Am The Last: (Rev. 1:17).

If He was here first and created everything and owns everything, then He also has power over everything. If He has that kind of power, then no one can withstand Him. If no one can withstand Him, He will never be defeated. If He can never be defeated, then He will always be. If He will always be, then, obviously, He is the last. Our God comes from an eternity past and is going into an eternity future. He has plans for Mankind which are still unwritten and sealed in the seven thunders (Rev. 10:4).

God is the first and the last in many ways. The pronouncement that "I am the first and the last" is made in the first and the last chapters of the Book of Revelation. What He did in creation the first time is recorded in the first two chapters of the Bible: "In the beginning God created the heaven and the earth" (Gen. 1:1). "And the Lord God planted a garden eastward in Eden..." (Gen. 2:8). He will repeat His acts of creation again in the last two chapters of the Bible: "And I saw a new heaven and a new earth..." (Rev. 21:1). "And he shewed me a pure river of water of life, clear as crystal...and on either side of the river, was there the tree of life..." (Rev. 22:1-2). God's designs for Mankind are the same, whether they be of the first order or of the order still to come.

The fellowship that God had with Man in the beginning will again be restored at the end. "...God himself shall be with them, and be their God" (Rev. 21:3). IT ALL STARTED IN A GARDEN IN THE BEGINNING WITH GOD, AND IT WILL ALL END IN A GARDEN AT THE ENDING WITH GOD!

How great and wonderful is our Lord. He started His earthly ministry in the wilderness with the Devil dogging His every step. He ended it on the cross with the Devil still harassing Him. The greatest revelation of His plans for Mankind were given to John on a rock island called Patmos. He will bring it all to fruition on Mount Zion. From the hill called Calvary and that rock pile on Patmos flow blessings and promises which will end in the Holy City, where the eternal river never stops flowing.

3. I Am He That Liveth: (Rev. 1:18).

Life is the true test of deity, for a dead god cannot be regarded to be a god at all. Menge, in his German translation, says, *Ich bin's, der lebende.* A direct transliteration would be "Iam it; the living." The Greek simply says, "I am the Living One."

Crucifixion and concealment in a rock tomb did not render Him dead. Only the flesh He received from His mother Mary, that body in which our God tabernacled here on earth, had been put to death. The God who is a spirit, who must be worshipped in "spirit and in truth," had spiritual work to do in Hell. While His body lay sleeping in death for three days, His Spirit was functioning in the same manner as in the pre-eternity before Bethlehem. First Peter 3:18-19 declares, "For Christ also hath once suffered for sins, the just for the unjust, that he might bring us to God, being put to death in the flesh, but quickened by the Spirit: By which also he went and preached unto the spirits in prison."

This pronouncement speaks to a self-existent life that needs no one to prolong or sustain it. Jesus existed long before Bethlehem. The prophet Micah affirms this, "But thou, Bethlehem Ephratah, though thou be little among the thousands of Judah, yet out of thee shall he come forth unto me that is to be ruler in Israel; whose goings forth have been from of old, from everlasting" (Mic. 5:2). Other Scriptures that attest to this truth are John 1:1, 8:58, 17:5; Hebrews 7:3; and Hebrews 13:8.

A god who came into existence in the process of time (somewhere after the beginning) would be of no use to those who lived before he came. If a god cannot help everyone, then he is not God at all. Only the God who has always been is the true and living God. I can be satisfied with nothing less!

4. I Am He That...Was Dead: (Rev. 1:18).

Jesus possessed both a human and a divine nature. The essence of His humanity was crucifiable. However, the quintessence of His divinity could never be marred by crucifixion. That substance and presence of the person of Jesus which entered through closed doors and windows, appearing at different places of the country on the day of His resurrection, cannot be killed.

Sin created a terrible dilemma for God. In order to reinstate life that was lost by a human because of sin, it became necessary to punish a sinless human with death. Because there was no human to be found without sin, it was necessary for the sinless Son of God to become human and die this death. The original Greek says, "I became dead." This implies a willingness on His part to participate in Man's redemption. In order that death might be destroyed and eternal life again enjoyed, Jesus became willing to "become flesh" (John 1:14), and "became dead," that we might become alive.

There was no other way that humans could have crucified Jesus Christ. Imagine any human trying to crucify the person John saw on the Isle of Patmos. The thought of it is ludicrous. In order that Man was ever able to lay hands on Jesus, it was necessary for Him to take on a human form. Paul expressed it perfectly, saying, "And being found in fashion as a man, he humbled himself, and 'became' obedient unto death..." (Phil. 2:8).

This makes the love and mercy of God, as expressed in the incarnation, even more incredible. God was born into the body of a man — so He could be crucified by Man — in order to save Man.

5. I Am Alive Forevermore: (Rev. 1:18).

Physical death was only able to contain Him as long as He chose. Jesus Himself declared, "Destroy this temple, and in three days I will raise it up" (Matt. 12:40; John 2:19). The assertion "I am alive forevermore" is an assurance that crucifixion could not weaken the quality of His eternity. His life was immune to death.

When the thunder and lightning and the weeping and wailing of tribulation terror echo through this sinful world, it will be the one John saw on the isle called Patmos who stands at this creation's exit. Jesus Christ will call out to whoever and whatever is left at that time, "I live forevermore!"

6. I...Have The Keys Of Hell: (Rev. 1:18).

If I had been the Devil, I would have hoisted the white flag upon first sight of Jesus walking around in my prison of eternal death. For three days while Jesus' body rested in the sepulcher, His eternal Spirit could not rest. The message that a satisfactory eternal settlement had been reached needed to be delivered to those whom Satan held captive.

His message probably was delivered like this: *"Your service of sacrificing little lambs for the forgiveness of every transgression has now been ratified and certified by the blood of the Lamb of God. My Father will wrench the key from the hands of the prince of this world and give it to me. I will unlock this prison house, and all who exercised faith that the blood of every little lamb sacrificed would one day be validated, when it was substituted and certified by the blood of the Lamb of God, may come out with me."*

"It will be on a Thursday about two score days from now when you, my blood-washed ones, will take to the skies and become a white cloud to be re-united with Him from whom you hid in the garden as He called, 'Adam where art thou?' Hand in your rain cheques of salvation. You may cash them today in the currency of eternal life which I purchased for you yesterday on a Roman cross outside of Jerusalem."

7. I...Have The Keys Of...Death: (Rev. 1:18).

The word "death" was very much on the mind of Jesus. The purpose for which Jesus Christ came into the world was "that he might destroy the works of the devil" (1 John 3:8). The purpose of the works of the Devil is death.

Revelation 20:14 tells us that "death and hell (will be) cast into the lake of fire..." at the Great White Throne Judgment. Death and Hell are the wages of Satan — his ultimate goal for humanity. But Jesus said here, "Dying must stop." Our Lord will not rest until the Devil, the false prophet, the beast, Death, and Hell are all cast into their own hell. Only then can the divine gift, the breath of God which made us living souls, be fully restored. Our Lord made certain to inform John that there would be no more death in the New Jerusalem (Rev. 21:4).

Hundreds of times I have stood by a grave with my hand on the casket saying, "Earth to earth, ashes and dust to dust," as the tears flowed from the eyes of loved ones. Most always there was a conscious assurance that we were standing on holy ground and that one day every cemetery would become a resurrection field.

God will restore to us our "dead in Christ," no matter where they lie. He is the only one who is the champion of life and the overcomer of death. If in the beginning He created us out of the dust of the earth, is it unreasonable to believe that He can renew us out of the dust? How the corridors of Heaven will echo with shouts of recognition, and, if tears of separation were bitter while parting here on earth, how sweet they shall be in the long embrace of those we miss so much today.

I do not know if I shall march in the parade of the resurrected ones or if He shall spare me the terror of dying, by way of the rapture. But I do think that when the long procession reaches the gates of Heaven, the angels will set the celestial fireworks of Heaven ablaze in the skies. There will be choirs and bands and palms and shouting which will be hushed only as we join together with all the redeemed in a "new song." Then and only then will the truth of the pronouncement, "I have the keys of hell and of death, " be fully understood. Then we will thrill to the words, "I am the resurrection and the life" (John 11:25). Then we will fully appreciate the miracle of the new birth, when the seeds of eternal life planted in our hearts burst into full bloom.

There are two words, "FEAR NOT," which preface and are a part of Christ's seven-fold proclamation of authority. Our Lord assures us that because He is the first, the last, was dead and now lives, has the keys to Death and Hell, and that He is alive forevermore, we should not be afraid. He saw the tribulation horses, seals, trumpets, and vials already approaching on that day on the Isle of Patmos.

Jesus warned that in the last days, men's hearts would fail them because of the fear of the future. We need to hear Him repeat the words, "FEAR NOT," to us today.

John had heard these words before when the disciples were in the midst of a storm at sea. They were sure their little craft was sinking when they saw what they conjectured to be a ghost walking on the water. Then they heard the voice of Jesus speaking out of the storm to say, "Fear not, it is I."

Jesus stands in the midst of His Church watching the prophetical horizons for the first signs of a far greater storm. Little whirlwinds of wrath are already making their presence felt. But today, as then, he raises His hand against the storm of the great tribulation and says to His people, "Fear not, it is I." It is my belief that the Church will be taken away before the storm strikes. I rest in His promise, "Lo, I am with you always, even to the end of the world" (Matt. 28:20).

CHAPTER TWO

When John received the revelation, there were actually seven churches in Asia (today known as Turkey). They existed in the cities named as Ephesus, Smyrna, Pergamos, Sardis, Thyatira, Philadelphia and Laodicea. These were congregations which were organized after Pentecost by Christians, many of whom were driven from Palestine because of persecution. Each of these churches had its problems and its points of praise as delineated by our Lord in these letters.

To our knowledge, none of these churches exist today, for Turkey is currently ninety-eight percent Moslem. However, these letters continue to have their lasting impact upon the Christian Church. Much blessing and correction has been derived over the centuries by congregations and individuals with similar needs as those typified by these churches.

The Savior was very deliberate in His selection of these seven churches. He saw the Church from Pentecost to His return as experiencing seven spiritual stages. Each church chosen typified a certain era, beginning with the Ephesus period which forsook its initial vibrant love and closing out the history of the Church with the Laodicean period, typified by the apostate, rich/poor, blind church of the last days.

The story of the seven churches represents an account of the spiritual ups and downs of the early Church, moving through the seven stages into future Church history. This finally culminates in a one-world church system as symbolized by the mother of harlots and her daughters (Rev. 17:5). We now give our attention to that which was prophecy when John received it, but is, for the most part, history for us today.

FORTY-NINE PRONOUNCEMENTS
ABOUT THE CHURCH

I. EPHESUS, THE CARELESS CHURCH (Revelation 2:1-7)

1. Place and People: "Unto the angel of the church of Ephesus write..." (Rev. 2:1).

The name Ephesus means "desirable." Ephesus was the capital city of the Roman Province of Asia situated seventy miles northeast of the Isle of Patmos in the Aegean Sea. It was known as "the first of cities," which means it ranked first among the names of great cities. It had a large seaport and was engaged in vigorous trade through imports and exports. Ephesus was also famous for its great artists and their notable works. Magicians, coppersmiths and craftsmen of every sort devoted to idol making abounded.

The religion was predominantly Diana worship, the star goddess who was said to have fallen from Jupiter. Her temple, situated in Ephesus, was one of the seven wonders of the world and a famous tourist attraction. It was a magnificent structure undergirded with one hundred and twenty great pillars which were sixty feet high and six feet in diameter. Some of these pillars were gifts of kings.

The Apostle Paul founded the church at Ephesus. He spent two years in Ephesus and the power of God rested upon him as he healed the sick and cast out demons, even with handkerchiefs and aprons which he had touched. Satan was dealt a serious blow when exorcists and magicians brought their books, worth 50,000 pieces of silver, and burned them before all men. So great was Paul's success in the gospel "that all which dwelt in Asia heard the word of the Lord Jesus, both Jews and Greeks" (Acts 19:10). Fearful for their livelihood, the silversmiths engaged in the making of gods organized a great revolt. Acts 19 records a sensational rampage that lasted for two hours as these Ephesians marched and demonstrated in the streets shouting, "Great is the goddess Diana."

Forty years after Paul's first visit to Ephesus, Christianity had so flourished that the heathen temples were all but forsaken. In addition to John, who ministered at the church of Ephesus, other notable people like Mary (the mother of Jesus), Priscilla, Aquilla, Timothy and Apollos were members of this church. The time period represented by the Ephesian church would probably be from about 63 A.D. (when Paul wrote his letter to the Ephesians) to about 170 A.D. (when the Roman persecutions began).

2. Personification: "...These things saith he that holdeth the seven stars in his right hand, who walketh in the midst of the seven golden candlesticks" (Rev. 2:1).

A definite pattern emerges as one studies these letters. Christ represents Himself to each of the seven churches by one of His distinctive physical attributes as the "Son of man" described in chapter one. Each attribute has a special message and connotation. We can only conclude that He has deliberately chosen a certain attribute because it specifically addresses the need of that church. In this instance, He zeros in on the seven stars in His right hand. As we have already discovered, the stars are ministers. I believe the problem in the church at Ephesus rested somewhere in the ranks of its leadership.

3. Praise:

> I know thy works, and thy labour, and thy patience, and how thou canst not bear them which are evil: and thou hast tried them which say they are apostles, and are not, and hast found them liars: and hast borne, and hast patience, and for my name's sake hast not fainted (Rev. 2:2, 3).

> But this thou hast, that thou hatest the deeds of the Nicolaitans, which I also hate (Rev. 2:6).

Graciously, the Lord approaches the problem which is at the very heart and core of this church. Before confronting the issue, He compliments them for the good He observes in their fellowship with a sevenfold praise statement. He assures them that He is aware of their works, labor, patience, uncompromising standards, endurance, stability, and intolerance of sin.

One would scarcely expect a sad ending to this letter in view of the good things our Lord here enumerates. The Ephesian church had so many good qualities that one could rationalize the Lord might have overlooked a single fault.

4. The Problem: "Nevertheless, I have somewhat against thee, because thou hast left thy first love" (Rev. 2:4).

It seems incomprehensible that, in the sixty years transpiring from Pentecost to Patmos, the Ephesian church (the early New Testament Church of the Acts of the Apostles) could have forsaken the very virtue by which they were known. They had sold their possessions and shared among themselves, so much so that the world took note of the love which was practiced between them.

John wrote a Gospel and three Epistles here which contain the greatest statements in all of the Bible regarding love. John himself had the reputation as being known as "the disciple of love." Whatever could have gone wrong? Could it be that the very seed of love, which produced the blossoms of Christian virtues that the Savior enumerated when He said, "I know thy works," had withered and died?

Jesus said, "I have somewhat against thee." This "somewhat" may only be one thing, but it is the quintessence of discipleship. God is not too impressed with a long list of spiritual goods if the motive for their existence is anything other than love.

A good friend of mine, a man whose wife lay dying, seemed not to be sad over her terminal condition. I asked him one day how she was doing and he said, *I really don't know, I haven't been to see her yet.* In a broken voice, he continued, *Love died at our house a long time ago. When love is gone, everything else worth having might as well be gone too.* He wept for a long time before being able to speak further. He told me how he tried in vain to fabricate love for her by buying her things. He said, *I've even brought her flowers, but there was no heart or joy to any of it because I had no love for her.*

When I recall the unhappy life of my friend, I think of the Ephesian church. What went wrong? Is the problem really to be found among the stars which the Savior held in His right hand? What so leavened the lump until the Bread of Life needed to say, "I have somewhat against thee"?

The early church of Ephesus appointed seven deacons to be leaders. Their names are Stephen, Philip, Prochorus, Nicanor, Timon, Parmenas and Nicolas. Nicolas was a Greek proselyte from Antioch. Many scholars point their finger at him as being the leader and founder of the "NICOLA"itans. Jesus identified them by saying, "He hated their deeds" (their doctrine) ,in Revelations 2:6 and 15. The last reference to their doctrine is alluded to again as the "depths of Satan" (Rev. 2:24), where Jezabel is indicted (from verse 20). Anything associated with Jezabel is not good. All three of these references appear to refer to the same problem.

What seems to have happened is that Nicolas was not completely weaned from his heathenish religion which practiced love, but not the kind of love Jesus was talking about. The churches of Pergamos and Thyatira, where this doctrine was prevalent, were plagued with immorality and licentiousness. The doctrine of the Nicolaitans also espoused sacrificing like they had in Judaism, but their ceremonies deteriorated into licentiousness where the meat sacrificed to idols was eaten and sexual orgies followed.

I cannot imagine that the entire Ephesian church was guilty of this sin. However, one leader with a bad influence can rob an entire assembly of God's blessings. It was only a little "somewhat," but it soured the entire fellowship. Anything that comes between Christ and His Church is spiritual fornication. There can be no other lovers in Christianity.

In studying the Ephesian church, a Bible scholar has extra advantages. For the most part, the other churches are given little attention outside of the Book of Revelation. Much can be learned about this church from Paul who warned that ravenous wolves would not spare the flock of God (Acts. 20:28-31). Paul also wrote a complete letter addressed to the Ephesians. Finally, since Timothy was a member of that church, the letters addressed to him would reflect conditions which existed in Ephesus.

Note that these thrice-baptized Ephesians (Acts 19:1-6) did a very deliberate thing. They did not lose, they were not robbed, nor were they threatened — they simply left and ignored their first love.

5. Prescription: "Remember therefore from whence thou art fallen, and repent, and do the first works..." (Rev. 2:5).

Remembering is a wonderful therapy for restoring lost love. Looking at courtship pictures, reading old love letters, talking about things you used to do together, going to the place you first met or the spot you were engaged, always does wonders for a marriage.

Remembering the overwhelming joy which inundated our souls in our initial experience of conversion or sanctification, and the intense love we had for the Scriptures and worship services and the singing of hymns, will do a lot to restore a lethargic spiritual existence. Paul Smith, in his book *Church Aflame,* names the following as sure signs of a wholesome first love: a desire to be near, an intense enthusiasm, a desire to serve.(1)

Remember, repent, do the first works is the spiritual therapy here prescribed. First works are like those a young husband is willing to do for his tender bride. Nothing is an inconvenience and no request prompts even a hint of a negative response. But when the first love is gone, serving becomes a dead ritual, a compulsory obligation. God does not care about our works unless they are of the kind which characterizes the first works which radiate and emanate from first love.

6. Penalty: "...I will come unto thee quickly, and remove thy candlestick out of his place except thou repent" (Rev. 2:5).

Repentance restores favor with God. Repentance spared Nineveh. Repentance restored David. Repentance would have perpetuated the light of the Ephesian church and permitted its candlestick to remain in place forever. Apparently they did not repent and do the first works because the church in Ephesus is no more.

It is a serious thing for a church to be ignored by our Lord. If He cannot have our love, He will not use a light which attempts to lead lost men to God by religious efforts or dead works. It is our love for Christ and our "lifting Him up" that draws men to the Father. If this love is missing, whatever else we are doing in the name of Jesus is really just doing for ourselves. It is a sacrilege and serious offense to further our egotistic ambitions in the name of religion and of Christ. When this happens, He must come "quickly" to remove this fraudulent light. There is an urgency here, because this false beacon will guide men to the rocks of destruction and their ship will sink. This light must be extinguished at once!

7. Promise: "...To him that overcometh will I give to eat of the tree of life, which is in the midst of the paradise of God" (Rev. 2:7).

Do not order your spiritual meal from the menu of Nicolas. This world provides fare only for the flesh, leaving the soul emaciated, weak, and sick. Jesus alone has water which will slake your thirst and bread "which comes down from heaven" (John 6:38) to strengthen and satisfy forever. "Blessed are they which do hunger and thirst after righteousness, for they shall be filled" (Matt. 5:6).

The thrice-planted tree of life is seen by John in the midst of the street and on both sides of the river (Rev. 22:2)—three identical trees with twelve manner of fruits on them, fresh every month. The leaves are for the health of the people; the blight of unfaithfulness and other loves can never afflict us here. These leaves are a perpetual healing against all of the works of Satan. The serpent can never enter this garden of God.

All our Lord asks of us is our first love in exchange for His first and last and everlasting love. His love includes not only the tree of life, but all things which "eye hath not seen, nor ear heard, neither have entered into the heart of man, the things which God hath prepared for them that love him" (1 Cor. 2:9)!

II. SMYRNA, THE SUFFERING CHURCH
(Revelation 2:8-11)

1. Place and People: "Unto the angel of the church in Smyrna write...I know thy works, and tribulation, and poverty..." (Rev. 2:8-9).

Smyrna was a great city, a rival to Ephesus, and is still thriving today. It had the greatest harbor in the world. Homer, the Grecian poet, was born here. The chief god was Dionysus who claimed to have returned from the dead. Jesus wanted the people of Smyrna to understand that He alone can make resurrection claims and represented himself to them as the one "which was dead, and is alive

61

again." The time period represented by this church would be from about 170 A.D. to 312 A.D.

The minister of the church in Smyrna was Polycarp, who, like John, also suffered persecution. When word was spread about of the plans to martyr him, he fled and hid in the rocks. A little girl, who was told where he was hiding, took food and water to him daily. Observing this repeated routine, an enemy followed her. Unknowingly, the little girl led the enemy to the place where Polycarp was hiding. He was arrested and brought to trial where he was offered his freedom if he would renounce and curse Christ. He replied, "These eighty and six years have I served Christ, he has done me nothing but good, how then could I curse him now, my Lord and Savior." For this testimony, Polycarp was wrapped in skins, soaked in pitch and set on fire.

As for the people other than Polycarp, I can offer you no names. This is always the case with the poor, the faithful, the humble, and meek. Our Lord loves the poor and said of them, "Blessed are the meek: for they shall inherit the earth" (Matt. 5:5). In his song, "We Shall Shine As The Stars," J.W. Van Deventer writes:

We may tarry a while here as strangers,
Unnoticed by those who pass by;
But the Savior will crown us in glory,
To shine as the stars of the sky.

We may never be rich in earth's treasures,
Nor rise on the ladder of fame;
But the saints will at last be rewarded,
Made rich in Immanuel's Name.

We may live in a tent or a cottage,
And die in seclusion unknown;
But the Father who seeth in secret,
Remembers each one of His Own.

We shall shine as the stars of the morning,
With Jesus the crucified One,
We shall rise to be like Him forever,
Eternally shine as the sun.(2)

Although the names of kings, queens, generals, popes, and bishops are recorded in history books — and their pictures hang in halls of fame — we have no names of those who died for Christ in Smyrna. But they are recorded in "the book of life."

2. Personification: "...These things saith the first and the last, which was dead and is alive" (Rev. 2:8).

There is an immense volume of power and authority packaged in the words, "I am first, and last, was dead, and am alive forevermore." The author of eternity, creator of the universe, destroyer of death and giver of life steps into the midst of this suffering assembly and, with one short but awesome stroke of language, says everything this church needed to hear in their hour of trial. When you are being hated, hunted, abused, and molested by the ministering servants of Satan, you need a strong arm, a voice of authority, and a power like that of the "first and the last, who was dead and is alive forevermore," to give assurance of His presence and assistance.

Our Lord always comes through with the right word just on time. How the tears must have flowed from the eyes of this frightened congregation, when the implications of this comforting word quickened their understanding. Jesus fortified their trembling spirits by naming a few of His attributes. To hear Him say, "I am the first, the last, was dead and am alive forevermore," is the same as hearing Him say, "I am omnipotent, eternal and omnipresent." This was the word the church in Symrna needed that day!

We need never fear those who kill the body. Our souls belong to Him and they shall return to Him when our bodies return to that from which He created them. He has the first word and He shall have the last word. There is a judgment of rewards coming and the death we die for Him here will be remembered no more once the crown of life is placed upon our head. Once we behold Him and the beauties of heaven, to waste even a single unit of eternity's time recalling the suffering and miseries back on earth would be folly supreme. There will be far too many glories to be wondering about in our Father's house. When we see the signs of crucifixion upon our Savior's sinless body, we shall realize like never before that there was no reason why He should have suffered and died for sinners like us.

We shall understand forever that it was a grand privilege to suffer or perhaps even die for Him.

3. Praise:

It seems strange that a church in such distress should not be complimented by our Lord. But Jesus knew it was not praise they needed, it was comfort. There is a sense in which praise is to be found in the meaning of the word Smyrna which comes from the word myrrh, meaning bitter. There are three references made to myrrh in the Gospels: Matthew 2:11, Mark 15:23, and John 19:39. From these passages, we discover myrrh is an ointment with a pleasant fragrance and very expensive. The wise men brought myrrh as a gift to the Christ child. It was also offered to Jesus as a drink while He was dying upon the cross. Nicodemus included it among the spices he brought for the burial of Jesus. These Symrnians exemplified what Paul was talking about in 2 Corinthians 2:15 and Ephesians 5:2 when He spoke of believers literally offering themselves as "a sweet smelling savour unto God."

What we need to observe here is that when it comes to bitterness and myrrh, Jesus experienced it from the cradle to the grave and thus was able to say, "I know." He was aware of everything this church was going through. To hear the Master say, "I understand," is a kind of hidden, sympathetic praise which is more precious than any words of commendation He might have spoken. When Jesus said, "I know," He was praising and comforting them at the same time. His knowing about their plight went much further than reporting to them that He had witnessed their trials with His eyes. He was really saying, "My knowing about your poverty is not merely the result of my walking among the churches and thus discovering it. I know because I have experienced what you are experiencing."

Our Lord was acquainted with poverty. His cradle was a manger in a barn. His boat belonged to Peter. His money belonged to a fish. His cross belonged to the Romans. His grave belonged to Joseph of Arimathea. His food belonged to a little boy. When He says, "I know," in reality, He is saying, "I've walked in your shoes. I was whipped, spit upon, stripped naked, and crucified. I have not overlooked anything." It was praise enough for them to hear Him say, "I know." But did they really know they were actually sharing in His suffering and, by so doing, they would also share in His glory?

And now for the words of Revelation 2:9 that cause us to count it all joy, "...I know thy...poverty (but thou art rich)...." I do not know if this is a statement of praise or an assessment of their spiritual state — perhaps both. There are no better words that the child of God could hear from the Savior than "you are rich." When Jesus says, "You are rich," He means the kind of riches that do not rust and thieves cannot steal. These riches disclose our attainment of an eternal wealth, a superior worth reserved only for saints He regards as "precious in His sight."

When man says, "I am rich," in reality he is admitting, "I am spiritually poor, blind, and naked," just like those of the church of Laodicea. As far as the dedicated saints in Smyrna were concerned, all the gold, diamonds, jewels, money, and real estate properties that Smyrna could offer might just as well be in a bank in hell in Lucifer's name. To hear the Son of man say, "You are rich," strips the sham from any investment on earth, leaving man trying to cover his nakedness with a few filthy dollar bills.

> Love not the world, neither the things that are in the world. If any man love the world, the love of the Father is not in him. For all that is in the world, the lust of the flesh, and the lust of the eyes, and the pride of life, is not of the Father, but is of the world. And the world passeth away, and the lust thereof, but he that doeth the will of God abideth forever (1 John 2:15-17).

> ...A man's life consisteth not in the abundance of the things which he possesseth (Luke 12:15).

4. Problem: "I know thy...tribulation...and I know the blasphemy of them who say they are Jews, and are not, but are the synagogue of Satan" (Rev. 2:9).

The tribulation of the Smyrna Christians was one problem. One expression employed to connote tribulation is "to grind grain fine like with a millstone." The saints of Smyrna were driven from their homes and lived in subterranean galleries (catacombs), about ten feet wide and four feet high, which wound around for hundreds of miles beneath the city of Rome. Here they lived, died, and were buried. Jesus said of himself, "...The foxes have holes, and the birds of the air have nests; but the Son of man hath not where to lay his head" (Matt. 8:20).

The second problem was "blasphemy." The word blasphemy, as used in the King James Version of the Bible, does not altogether convey the full impact of the experiences of these Christians. Other translations use words like affliction, distress, pressing trouble, and slander, which all add a dimension which helps us to sympathize with them. The worst kind of tribulation is not being ground down by sinners, but being ground down by temple people, church people, other Christians, "...Those who say they are Jews and are of the synagogue of Satan."

Jesus says, "I know these people. They are the ones who condemned me to crucifixion."

In the temple is where most of the character assassination was hatched. When the chips were down, Judas betrayed Jesus and Peter denied Him and the rest of the disciples fled like wimps. Only a few women came on resurrection morning to take care of His burial. The child of God will learn, sooner or later in life, that the people who heap accolades upon you in public will also spear you in private.

There are times in life when you really need a friend. Generally, it is not those who talk a lot about how important it is to "build bridges of friendship" that actually cross the distance in order to help when your little ship is sinking. Rather, your true friends are those who built no bridges at all and have to swim to help rescue you from your distress. These are no hypocrites, cowards, or wimps — they are the ones, like Jesus, who will say, "I know. I have walked in your shoes."

5. Persecution: "...The devil shall cast some of you into prison that ye may be tried; and ye shall have tribulation ten days..." (Rev. 2:10).

The above Scripture reveals that the evil conduct of men comes from Satan. It wasn't so much Judas as it was Satan having entered into him that caused him to betray Christ. It wasn't so much the sinner in Smyrna as it was the synagogue that Satan occupied there that deluded the sinner into hating the saint. The devil has his saint slanderers and church destroyers in every congregation. Even the good church in Philadelphia was plagued with them.

I will have you thrown into prison is what the devil has said thousands of times to saints who loved the Lord. How we forget that God has so often used prisons to clear schedules for men who were otherwise too busy for holy priorities. From these dens of detention, men of God literally wrote most of the New Testament. Martin Luther translated the Bible into German. Many other men and women received visions, special revelation, and inspiration like John on the Isle of Patmos. Peter had an angel come and unlock the prison gates so he could escape. That angel must have laughed, as he was flying back to heaven, about men's prison padlocks. God shook the prison of Paul and Silas while its keeper cried out, "What must I do to be saved?" (Acts 16:30). Imagine, baptizing a convert at midnight in prison. Daniel slept better in the den of lions than did his prosecutor and persecutor in his bed of gold. God has surely had good laughs about men trying to imprison His people!

6. Prescription: "Fear none of those things...be thou faithful unto death..." (Rev. 2:10).

Fear is as old as man. When man heard the voice of God walking in the garden, he was afraid and hid himself. The reason he hid himself is because he was unfaithful. Being "faithful unto death" removes the fear of death. We must take special note that our Lord did not say to be successful unto death. Rewards will not be granted on the basis of how successful we were, but rather upon how faithful we have been.

7. Promises: "...I will give thee a crown of life...he that overcometh shall not be hurt of the second death" (Rev. 2:10-11).

When the Lord makes a promise, we can be sure it will be kept. He clearly told us, "Heaven and earth shall pass away, but my word (promises) shall not pass away" (Matt. 24:35).

"I will give thee" establishes the certainty of this promise. A crown of life illustrates the suitability of it. These Christians lived in a city where dying for Christ became commonplace. I cannot think of anything more appropriate as a reward for martyrdom than a crown of life, an incorruptible crown that shall endure forever. This crown will be worn for eternity to forever bear witness to the fact that "they loved not their lives unto the death" (Rev. 12:11).

The second promise is "You shall not be hurt of the second death." The second death is the death of deaths. The first death has a soft coffin in which to rest; the second death is a bed in flames where "they have no rest day or night" (Rev. 14:11). The first death offers hope for a resurrection; no one returns from the second death. The first death separates for a night; in the second death, morning never comes. The first death offers a comforting funeral service; in the second death, we hear the words, "Depart from me." The first death delivers from all suffering; the second initiates eternal suffering because "their worm dieth not, and their fire is not quenched." In the first death you are buried in the ground; in the second death you are buried in the wrath of God. The first death has friends to sympathize; the second death offers demons to terrorize.

The first death provides a grave in a cemetery; the second death is a "gulf" eternally fixed. The first death is brightened with flowers and wreaths; the second death brings chains of darkness. The first death frees from pain; in the second death, "the smoke of their torment rises forever." The first death separates from man; the second death separates from God and man.

James Montgomery had this to say about the second death:

There is a death, whose pang outlasts the fleeting breath,
Oh, what eternal terrors hang around the second death.
Lord of all grace and truth, teach us that death to shun
Lest we be banished from thy face, and evermore undone.(3)

III. PERGAMOS, THE COMPROMISING CHURCH
(Revelation 2:18-29)

1. Place and People: "And to the angel of the church in Pergamos write..." (Rev. 2:12).

Pergamos means "elevated" or a "tower in marriage." The Pergamos period of Church history begins with Constantine at 312 A.D. and continues on to 606 A.D. It was Constantine who decried the persecutions of the early Church and declared Christianity the state religion. This is interpreted by many church historians as a victory for the Church. On the contrary, it resulted in the stifling of her effectiveness because of compromise with the existing pagan Roman religion which originated from Babylon.

Pergamos was a proud, highly cultured, Hellenistic, well educated, and sophisticated metropolis. Pergamos enjoyed the distinction of being the political capitol of Asia Minor and, as such, was consort to high society and wealthy, fashionable people. Its library was second only to that of Alexandria.

A special section of the city was called the Nicephorium, or thank offering grove, which was reserved for an assemblage of temples of idols—Zeus, Athene, Apollo, Esculapius, Dionysus, and Aphrodite. Esculapius was the chief deity known as the god of medicine and healing with a serpent as an insignia. He was called "savior" and was worshiped as the sun god whose birthday was to have fallen on or near the twenty-fifth of December. He was recognized by the Roman senate under Tiberius as "having the right of sanctuary." Satan's image, the serpent, was sacred to him, and charms and incantations were among medical agencies at that time.

With this as a backdrop, we see in Pergamos an "open arms" policy to the devices Satan had in mind in undermining the Church of Jesus Christ. If the Church could not be physically destroyed, then she must be spiritually paralyzed. This was done by integrating the pagan practices of Rome into the early Church. The religion of Rome (originating from Babylon) was nothing less than the religion of Tammuz, the son of Nimrod, and his wife, Semerimus, who were the descendants of Ham and Cain.

Satan's plan in paralyzing the Church began when he succeeded in conquering Cain. Satan closely followed this vagabond, for he would need him again and again. In Genesis 4:16, we read the sad words, "And Cain went out from the presence of the Lord, and dwelt in the land of Nod, on the east of Eden." Here Cain's first son, Enoch (not the one who walked with God), built a city. Satan loves cities, but Jesus weeps over them. Four generations later, Lamech was born and became the world's first polygamist. He, like his great, great, great grandfather Cain, became a murderer when he killed two young men. The seeds of death planted by Satan through Cain now began spreading throughout the world.

After the flood, Satan needed another victim. He found him in Ham, the forefather of Nimrod whose name means "we will rebel." Since a curse was placed upon Cain and Ham, it should not be surprising to learn that one of their progeny should become a rebel. Nimrod married Semerimus and they had a son whom they named Tammuz. It is a well known fact that Nimrod built the tower of Babel which later was situated in the middle of Babylon. He also built Nineveh. Both of these cities were known as being exceedingly sinful.

Semerimus, Nimrod's wife, proclaimed herself to be "The Queen of Heaven," or the sun goddess. Tammuz was later claimed to be the fulfillment of Genesis 3:15; thus, statues of a woman holding a child in her arms became a very common sight in many ancient countries. Egypt, Phoenicia, Assyria, India, and China all worshipped gods similar to that of the Babylonians who worshipped Semerimus and Tammuz, the mother/child deity. In his book *The Two Babylons*, Alexander Hislop writes about this mother/child deity, saying:

> This son, thus worshipped in his mother's arms, was looked upon as vested with all the attributes and called by almost all the names of the promised Messiah. As Christ in the Hebrew of the Old Testament was called Adonai, The Lord, so Tammuz was called Adon or Adonis. Under the name of Mithras, he was worshipped as the Mediator. (4)

As civilization moved westward from Babylon to Rome, the teaching, regarding the mother/child sun god moved with it. According to Ezekiel 8:13-16, this teaching also affected Israel. It is this pagan religion which was integrated into the doctrines of the early Church. Semerimus was soon called the Virgin Mary. Tammuz, the sun god, became Jesus, the Son of God.

2. Problem:

> I know...where thou dwellest, even where Satan's seat is...thou hast there them that hold the doctrine of Balaam, who taught Balak to cast a stumbling block before the children of Israel, to eat things sacrificed unto idols, and to commit fornication. So hast thou also them that hold the doctrine of the Nicolaitans, which thing I hate (Rev. 2:13-15).

We come now to a very sad juncture in the history of the Christian Church. The spiritual record regarding the early Church from Constantine to the papacy is not good. The period of persecution, or the Symrna period, closes with the philosophy *If you can't lick them, join them.*

Because persecution was not successful in impeding the progress of Christianity, Constantine the Emperor proclaimed Christianity as the state religion. Here is where Satan wove his web in which he ensnared the early Church. This was the moment in history when he had to make his move. The plot and circumstances were perfect. The religious climate was compatible. Christians were walking on a liberated path, relaxing, and breathing free and easy after 200 years of fear, catacombs, bloodshed, tears, and death.

Christianity became famous when Constantine embraced it. The Church and pagan Rome were innocently joined in marriage. The Church did not realize that they were going to bed with the teaching from Babylon. Satan knew that the two religious systems were diametrically opposed, but they had enough similarities that a union of the two would go by virtually unopposed. The result of this marriage is called "fornication" by our Savior.

Semerimis was substituted for the Virgin Mary and Tammuz was substituted for Jesus. Esculapius, the god of healing and the sun god, became Jesus the "Son of Righteousness, with healing in his wings." Esculapius had a serpent for an insignia. When Jesus said, "As Moses lifted up the serpent in the wilderness, even so must the Son of man be lifted up (John 3:14)," He was saying the serpent was a prototype of Himself. The serpent insignia of Esculapius harmonized with what Jesus said about Himself, and the charms which Esculapius loved became the rosary.

Winter Solstice, or the birthday of the sun god, was celebrated from December 21-25. Since Christians did not know for certain on which night in April the shepherds were out in the fields watching their sheep when the angels announced the birth of the Messiah, they designated the twenty-fifth of December (the birthday of the Roman sun god) as the birthday of Christ.

3. Personification: "...These things saith he which hath the sharp sword with two edges" (Rev. 2:12).

Christ's representation of Himself with the sharp sword is not a friendly symbol. Our Lord is prepared to do battle. The religious system which was contrived at Pergamos and Rome has never ceased to exist. It is called "MYSTERY, BABYLON THE GREAT, THE MOTHER OF HARLOTS AND ABOMINATIONS OF THE EARTH" (Rev. 17:5). It is a monster which will fuse the mother church of Rome together with other religious systems (inferred as daughters of this mother) to become, in the last days, the world church under the headship of the false prophet.

Jesus is angry here because Satan succeeded in maneuvering history in such a way that the confusion of Babel and the religion of Babylon had paralyzed the workings of the Holy Spirit within His Church. The day is now drawing very near when Jesus will use His sword (as described in Rev. 19:1-3) to destroy the coming world religious system.

Jesus is further angry because the doctrine of Balaam was tolerated. Numbers 22 through 25 tells the story of Israel's confrontation with Balak, king of Moab. In order to avoid this conflict, Balaam, the spineless prophet of Israel, advised Balak to encourage his young men and woman to marry the sons and daughters of Israel. And so

> ...they called the people unto the sacrifices of their gods: and the people did eat, and bowed down to their gods. And Israel joined himself unto Baal-peor: and the anger of the Lord was kindled against Israel (Num. 25:2-3).

Because of this "joining" at Baal-peor, the judgment of God fell against Israel and 24,000 were slain. The message is clear: "Wherefore come out from among them, and be ye separate, saith the Lord, and touch not the unclean thing; and I will receive you" (2 Cor. 6:17). God will have absolutely no compromise or giving ground to the enemy. There was to be no "marriage" of His Church with pagan Rome or Babylon.

Jesus is further angry because the teachings of the backslidden deacon, Nicolas, from Ephesus had also reached Pergamos and found a following. Nicolas had one foot in the Church and the other in the world, and he just could not wean himself from the world. He loved the sun god religion and the drunken parties where all kinds of immorality was practiced. Jesus hated the deeds of the Nicolaitans then, and He still hates them today.

4. Praise:

> ...Thou holdest fast my name, and hast not denied my faith, even in those days wherein Antipas was my faithful martyr, who was slain among you, where Satan dwelleth (Rev. 2:13).

There are certain places on earth where Satan, during the course of time, has held his headquarters. Clarence Larkin, in his work *The Book of Revelation,* says:

> Pergamos is spoken of as 'Satan's seat'. When Attalus III, the Priest-King of the Chaldean Hierarchy, fled before the conquering Persians to Pergamos and settled there, Satan shifted his capital from Babylon to Pergamos. At first he persecuted the Church and Antipas was killed. But soon he changed his tactics and began to exalt the Church, and through Constantine united the Church and state, and offered all kinds of inducements for worldly people to come into the Church. Constantine's motive was more political than religious. He wished to weld his Christian and pagan subjects into one people, and so consolidate his empire.(5)

Considering the fact that Satan had his seat here, it is almost incredible that the Lord found any who were faithful to Him. His compliments are brief, but powerful, when He says, "I know thy works, and where thou dwellest, even where Satan's seat is, and thou holdest fast my name, and hast not denied my faith...." It would not be easy to "hold fast" His name and not deny the faith in such a city. The fact that Antipas was killed for this reason subjected the Church to constant fear and danger.

Antipas —I love that brother, even though no details of his life have been recorded. I have searched the writings of many scholars and all agree that not much is known about him, but there is one powerful detail that speaks volumes concerning him. Jesus called

73

him His "faithful martyr who was slain." Just a brief sentence, yet embodied in it lingers a great potential for a wonderful reward. When I get to Heaven, I will look him up.

We know that Polycarp was the bishop of Smyrna and that he was burned at the stake. This dear brother has no other known legacy. No one remembered to etch a sentence somewhere of how or why he was killed. I expect that on one of those first days in heaven, the Lord will rise to His feet upon His throne in glory and say, "My dear children, this is Antipas, my faithful witness." And like on that day long ago in Egypt when the brothers wept because they heard Joseph say, "I am your brother," so will we weep when we see the wounds of martyrdom that will attest to Antipas' faithfulness. Then shall we understand that holding fast His name where Satan dwells requires a faith that overcomes the world.

5. Prescription: "Repent..." (Rev. 2:16).

To repent or not to repent means to have eternal life or not to have it. The word repent is the remedy our Lord used most frequently for the healing of all our iniquities. Five of the seven churches were commanded by our Lord to repent. Repentance is the only cure for sin, and I know of no other word that will attract the attention of the mercy, love, and grace of God like the deed of repentance. There is no other act which will cause the blood of Christ to sympathize over the stain sin has made and wash it white as snow. It is the key that unlocks the door to salvation.

6. Punishment: "...I will come unto thee quickly, and will fight against them with the sword of my mouth" (Rev. 2:16).

The fact that Christ personifies Himself in this "sword" manner probably indicates that Antipas was killed with a sword. The Lord gave these solemn warnings: "...He that killeth with the sword must be killed with the sword" (Rev. 13:10) and, "...Vengeance is mine; I will repay, saith the Lord" (Rom. 12:19).

It will be a terrible day when all those who murdered the faithful servants of Jesus Christ must look into the face of an angry God. But the good news is that even they may find grace in the eyes of the Lord if they repent before that day dawns.

7. Promise:

> ...To him that overcometh will I give to eat of the hidden manna, and will give him a white stone, and in the stone a new name written, which no man knoweth saving he that receiveth it (Rev. 2:17).

The hidden manna, the white stone, and the new name are each a reward to "him that overcometh." Antipas, Christ's faithful witness, must have been very much on the mind of Jesus when He made this promise. Our search for the interpretation of these symbols must be found in the loyalty of Antipas.

Somehow, I cannot help but hear our Lord saying to Antipas, the overcomer:

> Because you refused to eat of the meat sacrificed to idols, I will therefore give to you (in the place of that sin-stained, devil-dedicated fraud) the pure, clean, white manna which was "hidden" from the eyes of your killers, or else they would have had second thoughts about slaying you.

Second Corinthians 4:3-4 declares that:

> ...if our gospel be hid, it is hid to them that are lost: in whom the god of this world hath blinded the minds...lest the light of the glorious gospel of Christ...should shine unto them.

Esculapius, the sun god, blinded their eyes so that they could not see the manna sent from heaven which is Jesus Christ, the Son of righteousness.

Could it further be that Antipas was handed the black stone by the judge at his trial? This was the manner in which a guilty verdict was pronounced so that no one in the court room but the judge and the accused would know the verdict. Is Jesus here saying, "I know what the verdict was and in exchange I will give you 'a white stone' and a 'new name' which nobody knows but you and I" ?

The white stone was an ancient contract of friendship. It was called the "Tesera Hospitalis." Close friends would break a white stone in half, each would write his name on his half and then they exchanged stones. This meant that if ever there was a time they needed lodging or food, all they needed to do was produce their half of the stone which guaranteed them hospitality. Jesus is saying, "My name is on your half and your name is on my half." Jesus honored that kind of friendship, for He needed a home like that in Bethany. He also said, "If any man hear my voice, and open the door, I will come in to him, and will sup with him, and he with me" (Rev. 3:20).

He further stated in John 15:13-15:

> Greater love hath no man than this, that a man lay down his life for his friends. Ye are my friends if you do whatsoever I command you. Henceforth I call you not servants; for the servant knows not what his lord doeth: but I have called you friends; for all things that I have heard of my Father I have made known unto you.

Could it be that the secret new name of a faithful witness like Antipas is no longer servant, but FRIEND?

I should like to think that being called "a sinner saved by grace" is more than what we deserved. But to think that Jesus Christ would so humble Himself as to identify as our friend is more than what the mortal mind can comprehend.

IV. THYATIRA, THE IMMORAL CHURCH
(Revelation 2:18-29)

Before we give consideration to this next church, we must pause to put things into perspective. We have reached the middle point in these messages to the churches. A political and spiritual marriage through the decree of Constantine has taken place. However, persecution and killing as seen in the martyrdom of Antipas (who probably was the minister of the church) have not yet been abolished. Christianity and Babylonianism (the religion of Pergamos and Rome) obviously were not getting along too well. In spite of the fact that Christianity and Babylonianism were on opposite ends of the spectrum and diametrically opposed to each other, they were in some respects surprisingly similar.

It was not only in Pergamos that the doctrines of the Christian Church and pagan Rome seemed to be similar, this has been true everywhere at any time in history. There is not a thing in the economy of God that Satan does not mimic. Every religion in the world has enough truth and similarity to Christianity in it to make it appear equal with Christianity. But every religion in the world also has enough concealed falsehood to make it completely opposed to Christianity. The unenlightened are therefore easily deceived. What might we expect history to disclose under such arrangements?

Nothing changes as we make the transition from the Pergamos to the Thyatira church period. Changes in history take place gradually. As we move with history, we must not allow the distraction of transferring from one church to another to disrupt our continuity of thought.

In order to enforce a moratorium on persecution, we begin to see more compromise between religion and politics. Greater attempts to harmonize Christianity with the heathenish state religions were made so as to foster unity. As a result, Christianity as the first religion of the state enjoyed more power and experienced less stress and duress in matters relating to law and governmental policies. Strange doctrines and practices were bound to surface because of the heathen influence in the membership of the Church. With the kind of unequal yoke in marriage that took place, a divorce not too far down the road was inevitable.

Politics and true Christianity are not compatible. They have different purposes and goals. One seeks to rule the world, the other to evangelize it. One seeks to put men in subjection to it, the other endeavors to free them. One seeks an insatiable luxurious lifestyle, while the other is satisfied with subsistence. With such opposing forces cruising down the religious freeway, there was bound to be a Christian/political pileup.

1. Place: "And unto the angel in the church in Thyatira write..." (Rev. 2:18).

The city of Thyatira had a population of only 17,000. Like Ephesus, it had a temple of Diana, called Artemis. Their chief deity was Tyrimnas; but because he was also a sun god, it is believed Tyrimnas was simply another name for Esculapius. The period of history covered by this church is from about 606 A.D. to 1520 A.D. Thyatira means "continual incense."

2. Personification: "...These things saith the Son of God, who hath his eyes like unto a flame of fire, and his feet are like fine brass" (Rev. 2:18).

In most of these churches, our Lord's dissatisfaction is expressed in a twofold manner. The first is hidden in the symbolism of His personification representation. The second is openly verbalized and articulated with the preamble, "Nevertheless I have somewhat against thee." I have been dealing with these two aspects of Christ's dissatisfaction under the captions "Personification" and "Problem."

In this instance, Christ's hidden dissatisfaction has a threefold dimension. The first has something to do with an affront to His position as the Son of God. The second must have something to do with a sin they are trying to hide, because the power and intelligence of His eyes are announced. The third is an expression of the severity of the sins, as symbolized by the judicial nature of His feet.

In this pronouncement, we observe that Christ's title as the "Son of man" (utilized to this point in the book) has been suddenly replaced by the title of the "Son of God." The humanity of Christ is removed and immediately we sense that the intimacy brought about through the incarnation is beyond reach. He seems to have put a distance between himself and that church. Intuition hints that an estrangement has taken place.

We should not be surprised at this rift, for it is in this period that the early Church had gone from praying until the "place was shaken" to incense continually burning upon the altar. This is what the heathen as well as the Jews were accustomed to doing in their temples. What's wrong with incense? Incense is an impersonal symbol representing the very personal and intimate exercise of prayers continually arising to God. The close fellowship that God desired from the time of Eden was gone. Incense may be a symbol of prayers ascending, but God does not want our smoke, He wants our friendship.

During this period, the first official pope, Gregory I, was installed. History tells us he was a good man. However, as Arthur I. Brown writes in *Into The Clouds*:

On the crown of the pope we find these words, VICARIUS FILII DEI, which means, "The substitute of the Son of God", or as Pirolo puts it, and as Catholics are accustomed to say: "God is in heaven, and the pope is on earth."(6)

What the Church regarded as quite acceptable was here being accosted by Christ with flaming eyes of fire and judicial feet of molten brass, blazing with warning flashes of judgment. He was saying, "I am the Son of God, and I need no one to take my place." Not only is the exhalation of the pope a problem to Christ; the position that the common priest assumed is also a problem. First Timothy 2:5 states, "For there is one God, and one mediator between God and men, the man Christ Jesus."

Halley, in his *Pocket Bible Handbook*, gives the following information:

> The darkest period of the papacy was introduced by Adrian II, John VIII and Marinus, 870-1050. The 200 years between Nicolas I and Gregory VII is called by historians the "Midnight of the Dark Ages". Bribery, corruption, immorality and bloodshed within the papacy make it just about the blackest chapter in the entire history of the church.(7)

By this time in history, both Babylonianism and what the early Church stood for was, for the most part, a thing of the past. That is usually the case in a religious union. The original sources with their doctrines and standards disappear and something quite different from what was hoped emerges. I am sure the early Church was convinced that joining with the religion which was brought from Babylon was an opportunity to win them all to the Lord. But remember that Paul warned that "a little leaven leaveneth the whole lump" (1 Cor. 5:6). Leaven does not refer to something good, as some suppose, but rather to evil.

The Church needs to heed the true story about an eagle whose claws became deeply embedded in the carcass he was feeding on as it gently floated down an icy river. He was getting a free ride, while he drifted carelessly with the stream, and enjoying a free meal as a bonus. But in the meantime, his claws froze solidly into his fare. Suddenly, the eagle heard the sound of the waterfalls. Unable to free himself from the deadness he had been feeding upon, it was too late for anyone to rescue him. The eagle plunged to his death upon the rocks below, still clamped to his pleasure.

The Christian Church was enjoying all of the advantages of being yoked with the deadness of pagan Rome as well as being consort with government officials. Time testifies that the deadness the Church tried to influence and vitalize became her bondage, and spiritual destruction was imminent.

3. Problem:

> ...Thou sufferest that woman Jezebel, which calleth herself a prophetess, to teach and to seduce my servants to commit fornication, and to eat things sacrificed unto idols...all the churches shall know that I am he which searcheth the reins (kidneys) and hearts...unto the rest...which have not known the depths of Satan...I will put on you none other burden (Rev. 2:20, 23-24).

Jesus is saying, "Your marriage to the pagan religion at Pergamos and Rome is a counterpart to what happened when Ahab King of Israel married Jezabel." As Jezabel was the daughter of the king of Tyre and Sidon, Ahab rationalized that a political advantage was to be gained by such a union. But what he failed to realize was that in addition to becoming a queen and wife, she was also a teacher and worshipper of Baal, which was a filthy, adulterous, and licentious religion. He had no idea that after his death she would control the "steering wheel" behind the corrupt rule of her two sons, Ahaziah and Jehoram, bringing the displeasure of God upon Israel.

She continued her scheming and brought about the marriage of her daughter Athaliah to Jehoram (son of Jehoshaphat and king of Judah) who brought idolatry into Judah. And so "Jezabel caused all Israel to sin" (1 Kings 16:29-33). She was not satisfied in just establishing her religion, but tried to destroy the prophets of God in the process. The bloody story of Jezabel I and her husband Ahab ended with a heathen's arrow in his back and dogs eating her body, but refusing to eat her sin-stained hands.

Jezabel II, of Thyatira, was also a harlot. During this period, popes had mistresses. Sergius III "had a mistress, Marozia. She, her mother Theodora, and her sister filled the papal chair with their paramours and bastard sons, and turned the papal palace into a den of robbers. This is known in history as the Pornocracy or Rule of the Harlots." (8) This quite graphically describes the Jezebelean era, against which our Savior has filed a complaint. This is a chapter in history which the Church has tried desperately to hide.

"I search the reins and hearts" is a fascinating expression. Reins are used to control horses. However, while there could be an interesting discussion regarding this idiom, a close consideration of it from other translations conveys a somewhat different idea. The German translation uses the word "*Nieren*" (meaning kidneys) instead of "reins." This is a shocking revelation.

I have a niece who for many years was on dialysis until my brother Bill, her father, gave her one of his kidneys. It was during that time that I learned how important the function of the kidneys actually was. The process of dialysis is to purify the blood. It goes without saying that kidneys do the same thing. Jesus is saying to this period:

> *Your heart has not been faithful to me. You are married to the world; as a result you have impure blood flowing in your veins. Your blood line is not of pure pedigree. You have substituted Jerusalem for Babylon, Jesus Christ the Son of Righteousness for Tammuz the sun god, Mary the virgin for Semerimis the harlot and Queen of Heaven, and Holy Communion for meat sacrificed to idols. I have examined your kidneys and they can never purify your blood. If Jezebel, your prophetess, does not repent and change her teaching and you do not get rid of her, judgment will come and you will become very sick. "I will cast her into a bed, and them that commit adultery with her," and you and all your children will die.*

Jesus also employs the expression "the depths of Satan." It is easy for us who possess the records of history to see what this means. For the people in the church at Thyatira, as well as those living in the papal Thyatirean period, it was not so. The depths of Satan can only mean his entire plan as to how he would go about paralyzing the Church of Jesus Christ, beginning with Cain and ending with his harlot Babylon as described in Revelation 17.

Only Jesus Christ fully understands the depths of iniquity embodied in that plan. To bring this plan to fruition requires disobedience, murder, pride, licentiousness, adultery, lying, stealing, profanity, idolatry, deceit, witchcraft, demonism, drunkenness, drug addiction, pornography, abortion, commandment breaking, sacrilege, and every imaginable evil. God have mercy on him who graduates from the course known as "The Depths of Satan."

4. Punishment: "Behold, I will cast her into a bed, and them that commit adultery with her into great tribulation...(and) will kill her children with death..." (Rev. 2:22-23).

Three methods of judgment are described in this statement: a bed, great tribulation, and the killing of her children. The bed here certainly does not imply rest as the words "tribulation" and "kill" are involved in this judgment. This must mean a sick bed and eventually a death bed because of spiritual kidney failure, sleeping sickness, and blood poisoning brought about by the sin of compromise. There is no antibiotic or dialysis for this sin; only repentance can heal, but this church never did repent. This is a sad commentary and conclusion to a church that was wide awake at Pentecost and could not tolerate even a single lie in its fellowship.

Not only is this church to be cast into a sick bed, but also "them that commit adultery with her." Who are they? We discover this in the Scriptures which describe their judgement, Revelation 17:1-2:

...Come hither; I will shew unto thee the judgment of the great whore that sitteth upon many waters: with whom the kings of the earth and the inhabitants of the earth have been made drunk with the wine of her fornication....

The entire seventeenth and eighteenth chapters of Revelation are devoted to telling the sad story of her final chapter. Instead of preaching the gospel, this church was busy doing business with the kings of the earth. Revelation 18:13 declares that she traded away the souls of men for worldly merchandise.

Also included in this judgment are "her children." How can a church have children? J.A. Seiss, in his book *The Apocalypse*, says: "It is characteristic of popery to enforce celibacy upon the clergy, holding them to be married to the church, and hence teaching all her sons and daughters to call them 'fathers'."(9) In Matthew 23:9, our Lord comes down hard upon such demands. He must have known that this would happen, because He said, "Call no man your father."

Any church found in a spiritual state similar to that depicted by the church in Thyatira will miss the rapture of the prepared and faithful Church. They will consequently suffer the horrors of the tribulation.

5. Prescription: "And I gave her space to repent of her fornication; and she repented not" (Rev. 2:21).

The Church age depicted by the Thyatirean period was the lowest spiritual ebb the Church has ever experienced. But even in this deplorable state, repentance would have healed her. But according to verse 21, she did not repent.

The Lord provided a special extension of time for repentance for this church, inferred by the words, "I gave her space to repent." The word "space," in addition to referring to an extension of time, probably includes a special opportunity as well. The opportunity given would most likely be the pre-reformation ministry of Peter Walden which began about 1165 A.D. According to Gustav Just, in his book *The Life of Luther*, Walden and his adherents, called Waldensians, taught that:

> In all questions pertaining to our salvation we dare trust no man or book, but must believe the Holy Scriptures only. There is but one mediator; the saints must not be worshiped; purgatory is a fable invented by men. There are but two sacraments, baptism and the Lord's Supper. "The life of the Waldenses conformed so well with their doctrine," that King Lewis of France exclaimed, "These heretics are better than I and all my people. They lead a purer life than other Christians. They do not swear, except necessity demands it, and beware of taking God's name in vain. They keep their promises faithfully; they are truthful in their words and live peacefully together in brotherly love." (10)

The Waldenses were mercilessly treated by the church of Rome. About a million of them were slain in continuous wars of persecution. Seven thousand were slaughtered in a church at one time. A

judge in Spain had ten thousand of them burned alive, and imprisoned ninety-seven thousand more who perished, enduring the most
frightful tortures. These men and women gave their witness for
Christ at the end of the Thyatirean period of the Church age. Through
their preaching and witness, they provided ample opportunity and
"space" for repentance.

God does not make a prescription for any church that is beyond
anyone's reach. Money, status, education, or anything else are not
requirements for qualification. These words, "...A broken and a con-
trite heart, O God, thou wilt not despise" (King David in Ps. 51:17),
have always been, are now, and shall always be the only requirement
necessary.

6. Praise: "I know thy works, and charity, and service, and faith,
    and thy patience, and thy works; and the last to be more than
    the first" (Rev. 2:19).

God has never left himself without a witness. After all the evil
and debauchery that has been disclosed about this era, and in spite
of those dark days of Church history, there were nevertheless those
who lived through it all and earned this high praise from our Lord.
This is also true of the Church at the eve of its destruction as described
in Revelation 18:4; where the call goes forth, "...Come out of her, my
people...."

The works Jesus enumerates here are basically the fruit of the Spirit. Love, ministry, faith, and patience are special grace gifts dispensed
by the Holy Spirit. These are the outgrowth of a Spirit-controlled life
and the potential for tangible evidence as expressed through the ministry exemplified by the Waldensians.

Love is the queen of all grace gifts. First Corinthians 13 gives us
a wonderful résumé of things love will and will not allow you to do.
Jesus explained how all of the ten commandments are contained in
just one, "...Thou shalt love the Lord thy God with all thy heart, and
with all thy soul, and with all thy strength, and with all thy mind;
and thy neighbor as thyself" (Luke 10:27).

In this respect, Thyatira was better off than the Ephesian church
which had left its first love. Love in the lives of a few members in
this church was not a coincidence, it was a way of life. Love in the
Church of Jesus Christ is like perfect timing to the engine. If the ig-

84

nition fires before the piston reaches dead center top stroke, the engine will backfire. If you lived in those days when we cranked engines, you probably know of men who lost their lives or were seriously hurt because of this malfunction. Instead of you cranking the engine, the engine cranked you. Love in the Church never allows it to backfire.

Ministry was another of the grace gifts demonstrated by the faithful at Thyatira. When love is the driving force, what kind of outward manifestations in ministry might one expect? The Lord does not list any special achievements, but we can be sure that in any congregation where love flows spontaneously, good things are bound to happen.

Did they build an orphanage or senior citizens' home? Were they sending out and supporting missionaries? Were souls being saved every Sunday? We really do not know, but I doubt that their group was strong enough to be engaged in any great ministry enterprise. The fact that the Lord says to them, "That which ye have hold fast (Rev. 2:25)," would indicate that their goodness was to be found in their determined perseverance to "hold fast to their faith" in the midst of iniquity. The spiritual climate was dark, discouraging, and hopeless, and they struggled for spiritual survival. The Lord classifies their works as "His works." Blessed is the church that is found doing "His works" when He comes.

The Lord acknowledges the faith of these believers. If love is the driving force, then faith is the daring force. Loving people will accomplish little without a daring faith. Love constrains you to want to do something; faith will not allow you to be restrained from doing it. Love keeps your eyes upon the will of God for your life; faith empowers you to execute that plan.

These people not only dared to confront the evils of their time, they spoke out against them. They suffered torture, imprisonment, and death. Their experiences were similar to those Jesus had while here on earth. That is why He calls their works "His works."

Patience was also noticed by Jesus. Patience is to possess the spirit of peace under pressure. Patience is the virtue that keeps you positive and going forward, even when progress and success evade you after you have exercised faith. Patience is a quality that calms all the people around you when everything is chaotic. Patience is nourished and nurtured by faith, which never insists on an answer right now.

It took a lot of patience for the faithful at Thyatira to remain faithful. There was much darkness, sin, corruption, compromise, and fraud and this kind of spiritual environment is hardly conducive to producing much fruit. However, the best wheat always grows in the valleys, and a rose is never so fragrant as when it is crushed. Our Lord was satisfied with the faithful at Thytira "who had not the doctrine of Jezabel," nor had known "the depths of Satan." These were the evils responsible for the darkness that existed.

Christ's expression, "And the last to be more than the first (Rev. 2:19)," suggests that the faithful at Thyatira were not an "on-and-off" congregation. This statement suggests a continual progress in their lasting endurance. The German transliteration, *Und das du je laenger, je mehr thust,* means "the longer you endure in your work, the more you accomplish." There is a ray of hope expressed for the Church in this statement. I hear the Lord saying, "It is not as dark now as it was at the beginning of your era; things are improving." The faithful witness of Peter Walden and his followers prepared the way and was a forerunner to the Reformation.

The church in Thyatira was indeed a paradox. In it was to be found the best and the worst.

7. Promise: "...I will put upon you none other burden...he that overcometh, and keepeth my works unto the end, to him will I give power over the nations...I will give him the morning star" (Rev. 2:24, 26, 28).

It must have been a consolation for this congregation to hear that the burdens they were carrying were actually given to them by their Lord. The burden becomes much lighter when we know the Lord wants us to bear it on His behalf. Burdens imposed upon us by man, were it not for the Lord, would surely crush us. His statement, "I will put none other burden upon you," seems somehow to imply, "I know you have all you can carry; just faithfully carry your present burden. Take up your cross and follow me and I will give unto every one of you according to his works."

The second promise our Lord gives to these faithful ones is, "I will give (you) power over the nations." His saints shall be kings and priests and reign with Him a thousand years in the millennium ahead. I do not wonder that there are many of God's children who cannot grasp this. The world laughs in derision at the very suggestion of it, but I smile at the truth of it.

The concluding promise is, "I will give him the morning star." Somehow, there is a reality in this promise that I have not yet fathomed or understood. There seems to be some kind of mysterious glory that keeps evading my imagination, but let me share with you what I see through a glass, "darkly."

When I was a teenager working on the farm with my father, I often worked in the field clear through the night. The darkest time of the night was just before the dawn when the last star, the morning star, would be seen still shining when all the others had gone out. When I saw the morning star, I knew that in about half an hour the eastern sky would begin to turn crimson and the blazing rim of the sun would begin to rise on the horizon to announce a brand new day.

Jesus calls Himself the "morning star" (Rev. 22:16). To these faithful saints He is saying, "Your long dark night will soon be over." Jesus, the morning star, speaks to us of hope and the dawning of a new day where the sun and moon will not be needed. His light will be the light of the holy city. His coming into the world was signaled by a star which shone to guide wise men to Bethlehem. His presence always brings light, for He is the Light of the World. He gave Israel a light to guide them through their wilderness. When "darkness reigned over the face of the deep," He spoke and there was light.

Darkness has no power over light, for light always dispels darkness when it is engaged. In this same manner, our Lord has power over Satan and the darkness he has brought into the world is sure to disappear when we see the "Morning Star."

V. SARDIS, THE CHURCH WITH A NAME, BUT DEAD
(Revelation 3:1-6)

1. Place:

Sardis was the capital of the Roman province of Lydia. In 600 B.C., it was the richest and most powerful city in the world. Ruins of huge temples and amphitheaters reveal that the architecture of Sardis was among the finest the world has ever known. The city was fortified by very steep and strong walls. During the reign of Tiberius, the city was nearly destroyed by an earthquake. Today, just a poor small village called Sart marks its memorial. Sardis means "escaping one." The time period represented by the Sardis church would probably cover the period from 1520 A.D. to 1750 A.D.

2. Personification: "...These things saith he that hath the seven Spirits of God, and the seven stars..." (Rev. 3:1).

Christ informs this congregation of the availability of His special means of grace, which leads us to conclude that the era which the Sardis church typified had need of them. He offers a twofold provision for the solution to their problem: "the seven Spirits of God" and "the seven stars." The seven Spirits, already discussed in chapter one, represent the fullness of His power. Isaiah, in prophesying about the coming of Jesus, said,

> And the spirit of the Lord shall rest upon him, the spirit of wisdom and understanding, the spirit of counsel and might, the spirit of knowledge and of the fear of the Lord...(and) with righteousness shall he judge... (Isa. 11:2-4).

The seven stars, of course, are the ministers of the churches whose counsel is also available.

This period of Church history includes the Reformation under Martin Luther. From what is generally perceived about the Reformation, it appears that the description of the spiritual condition of this Church age as annunciated by Christ seems to be incongruous with the Reformation. Protestant historians have left the impression that the Reformation was a great spiritual revival. An honest evaluation of the Reformation, and what it actually achieved, does not support such a perception.

The Reformation was basically a protest against the corruption of the Church of Rome. It succeeded in creating a world consciousness and awareness of certain abuses which existed, and instilled a considerable opposition into the minds of the people against the Church of Rome. However, to successfully win a battle against certain evils is not to presuppose that a spiritual revival has taken place. As a protest against abuses, the Reformation was successful. As touching the deeper things of the work of the Holy Spirit in the life of the believer through the new birth and sanctification, this church was appropriately classified by Christ as being "dead."

There were many abuses by Rome which Martin Luther opposed. Basically, it was Tetzel's sale of indulgences which provoked Martin Luther to nail his famed ninety-five theses to the church door at Wittenberg on October 31, 1517. Henry H. Halley, in his *Halley's Pocket Bible Handbook* defines an indulgence this way: "An indulgence was a lightening of the pains of Purgatory, that is, a remission of the punishment for sin according to Romanist teaching. Purgatory is very much the same as Hell, only it does not last as long, but all have to pass through it."(11)

In the same book, Halley writes about John Tetzel's actions. Halley explains, "John Tetzel came through Germany selling certificates, signed by the pope, offering pardon of all sins to buyers and their friends without confession, repentance, penance or absolution by the priest."(12) Halley goes on to write, "[Tetzel] said to the people, 'As soon as your coin clinks in the chest, the souls of your friends will rise out of Purgatory into Heaven.' This horrified Luther."(13)

This basically is what the Protestant Reformation was about. The people of Germany protested against having to pay money to the pope in order to release the souls of their loved ones from Purgatory. Because of this protest, the pope declared a war against the Germans which lasted nine years (from 1546 to 1555), ending with the peace of Augsburg.

A nine-year war against the pope is bound to catch the attention of the world. The Church age as represented by Sardis thus became recognized by Christ as having a "name, but dead."

Martin Luther did not forsake many of the questionable teachings of Rome. The doctrine of transubstantiation and baptismal regeneration continued to be necessary to salvation. The Reformation was not a spiritual revival, rather it was a religious protest. A revelation that "the just shall live by faith" is very good, if the faith by which the just are to live has been imparted by the new birth. To belittle the courage of Martin Luther would be inappropriate. Just because the Reformation in reality was not what we may have perceived it to be, that is not to say that what Luther accomplished was anything short of being a very noble thing.

The church at Rome had become very corrupt. All kinds of indulgences were invented to instill fear and bondage into the hearts of the people. For example, the church held a firm grip upon the forgiveness of sin and eternal life. The pope, or papa, was supreme, and only by the purchase of indulgences could the graces of God become operative within the heart of a layman. Luther, Wycliffe, Huss, Savonarola, Staupitz, and Frederick the Wise were some of the great enemies of the pope. Openly, they declared that the pope was no greater than any ordinary minister and that he could not withhold eternal life. They also declared that Purgatory was an invention of men.

The Reformation was a battle against Rome, with its worship of saints, withholding the Bible and the cup from the laity, penances, monkery, the sale of indulgences, statues and relics, pomp and pageantry, masses, the confessional, Mariolatry, and papal infallibility. Many other practices and doctrines of Rome were denounced and a simpler form of worship instituted.

3. Problem:

> ...I know thy works, that thou hast a name that thou livest, and art dead. Be watchful, and strengthen the things which remain, that are ready to die: for I have not found thy works perfect before God...If therefore thou shalt not watch, I will come on thee as a thief, and thou shalt not know what hour I will come upon thee (Rev. 3:1-3).

The zeal, courage, and action of the reformers gave them the "name" that they were alive. A church can become very popular, acceptable, and exciting and yet be "dead," having works not "perfect before God." What are these imperfect works?

To prove the pope fraudulent, meaning almost certain excommunication and death, was courageous. To nail ninety-five theses to the castle church door at Wittenberg, and thereby win many followers to a better form of worship, was courageous, but not "perfect." What is the Lord trying to say when He offers this church the fullness of the seven Spirits and the seven stars who were the reformers?

The answer is to be found in the word "watch." Peter was ready to pull the sword and let the ears fly in the garden of Gethsemane, but he was not willing to "watch" even one hour. The reformers were winning court battles, wars, and debates, and multitudes were joining their ranks. They had badly clawed Rome in the face and defamed and denigrated the indulgence tax system. These reformers had exposed the pope to all of Europe. But the Lord was looking on and saying, "I have not found thy works perfect."

The conquering force at Pentecost was not the same force that was doing the conquering at Sardis. The "more perfect way" which superseded all of the spiritual gifts, the way of love, was missing. This was a time of animosity, strife, and bloodshed. It was not the way the Lord fought His battles while still in the world. One of the last words that our Lord left us with is "watch." This injunction is repeated many times in the Scriptures.

The Christian has a living hope that embodies a "watching" for the return of our Lord Jesus Christ. The reformers, in their zeal against Rome, the formulation of new doctrines, the writing of the Augsburg confession, and a multitude of other reforms, somehow overlooked the importance of the message of Christ's return and the indulgence of "watching." Christianity without "watching" and waiting for the return of Jesus Christ is a dead exercise.

4. Prescription: "Be watchful, and strengthen the things which remain, that are ready to die...remember therefore how thou hast received and heard, and hold fast, and repent..." (Rev. 3:2-3).

Watching and praying are faith's sentinels which guard the sanctity of the soul. Prayer produces a healthy, intimate relationship with Christ which brings peace, assurance, strength, and happiness. A happy, contented Christian bears all kinds of spiritual fruit and is very useful to the Master.

"Strengthen that which remains." The hatred, violence, and bloodshed generated by the Reformation gave the church of Sardis a severe "shaking down." Many of its adherents lost faith and confidence and felt victimized and swindled, consequently forsaking the Sardis church. Our Lord is here admonishing this church to "strengthen" that which remains. No Christian can survive long on dead ritual and meaningless pomp and ceremony which pleases the eye only as long as it lasts. Real worship happens in the heart and changes the entire life. The Sardis era inaugurated a fresh approach to worship, providing less for the eyes and more for the heart.

The expression "ready to die" suggests a spiritual malnutrition and a near-to-death condition. When a church tries to exist by making a name for itself, it will die. When we become more concerned about our reputation in Sardis than favor with God in heaven, the spiritual blessings of bread and water will be cut off. Feeding upon the praise and accolades of men instead of our Father's blessing will ensure spiritual starvation.

"Remember how thou hast received and heard." Remembering is the first step to repentance. Peter remembered, wept, and then repented. Many married couples have revived a dead marriage by sitting down and remembering the love of their youth. The Sardis church is admonished to recall how they first "received and heard" the message at Pentecost. There was a reason why the Lord was adding to His Church daily such as were converted. God will again bless His Church, even today, when we go to the upper room and stay there until we hear and feel the breezes of the Holy Spirit blowing once more. When this happens, we will never need to be told to "strengthen the things which remain, that are ready to die."

"Repent" of your unwatchfulness. Watching, waiting, and hoping for the return of Jesus Christ is not only a blessed hope, it is also a purifying hope. Listening for the trump of God to sound every day will keep us faithful. Looking up not only assures the onlooker that we truly believe our redemption is drawing nigh, but it will keep our eyes away from the world and fixed upon the author and finisher of our faith.

According to our Lord's admonition, it is a serious thing for a Christian not to be thinking of His return. If we could only grasp and perceive the reality that the Church is indeed the bride and Christ is the bridegroom in the greatest wedding to ever take place, then the thought of His coming would truly excite us.

5. Penalty: "...I will come on thee as a thief, and thou shalt not know what hour I will come upon thee" (Rev. 3:3).

"I will come." That is a complete and settled promise. However, there's a big difference between the arrival of a thief and a bridegroom. A thief comes to take what you have if you are not watching over it. A bridegroom comes to bring all that he owns to bestow upon his bride. One brings sorrow and loss, the other brings joy and blessing and treasures. One loves himself, the other loves his bride. The first one impoverishes, the second makes rich.

Being robbed is a very unpleasant experience and you want to ask, "What have I done to have someone so abuse me?" Being robbed by this world's meanest is one thing. To have the Lord come and take away your reward and give it to someone else is almost unimaginable.

6. Praise: "Thou hast a few names even in Sardis which have not defiled their garments; and they shall walk with me in white: for they are worthy" (Rev. 3:4).

The faithful in Sardis are recognized only as "a few names." The important thing to note here, though, is that their names are recorded in the Book of Life. If you want a name, then honor His name. If you want to be known as being alive, live His life. If you want Him to confess you and pronounce your name in heaven, then confess His name here on earth.

The Sardis period in history has many notable names on their memorial roll. I believe we can begin with Martin Luther, his predecessors, and his contemporaries: Wycliffe, Huss, Savonarola, Staupitz, Wise, and Zwingli. They and many others will "walk with me (Jesus) in white" and not in the long black robes of the dead church or the deceptive white robe of its leader. They will wear pure white linen "which is the righteousness of the saints" (Rev. 19:8).

Selfishness, murder, pride, greed, and arrogance can never remain hidden under a white robe decorated with beads and crosses. One day God will rip it away and the whole world will see the heart within. "For from within, out of the heart of men, proceed evil thoughts, adulteries, fornication, murders, thefts, covetousness, wickedness, deceit, lasciviousness, an evil eye, blasphemy, pride, foolishness" (Mark 7:21-22).

7. Promise: "...I will not blot out his name out of the book of life, but I will confess his name before my Father, and before his angels" (Rev. 3:5).

Membership books in this world do not impress God. Excommunication from a dead church is no tragedy. Mary Kidder wrote these words in her song *Is My Name Written There:*

> Lord I care not for riches, neither silver nor gold,
> I would make sure of heaven, I would enter the fold.
> In the book of Thy kingdom with its pages so fair,
> Tell me, Jesus my Savior, is my name written there? (14)

To be certain that my name is recorded in the Book of Life is what is important. I am a no-name Christian here on this earth. Never in my life has anyone applauded me. My picture has never appeared in the local paper. I have never held high official positions. My work has been in seclusion. I teach a class of bad boys in a small Sunday school room in the church basement. Most of the people in the church are not aware of how much I love and pray for those rascals. But I am happy. I am happy most of all because He knows and because He has written my name in His book. That Mary Kidder understood what I am saying is clear from some of the other lyrics in her song. She wrote:

> O that beautiful city with its mansions of light
> With its glorified beings in pure garments of white;
> Where no evil thing cometh to despoil what is fair,
> Where the angels are watching,
> Yes, my name's written there. (15)

You may be unknown and appear to be a nameless entity, but you are alive or you would not be reading this. That is a much better report than, "You have a name that you live, and art dead." What a tragedy it would be if all the world knew my name, but no one in heaven knew my name. This world will pass away soon. Heaven is forever. Jesus knows my name; He has written it into the Book of Life and He has told His Father about me. Hallelujah!

VI. PHILADELPHIA, THE CHURCH THAT JESUS LOVED
(Revelation 3:7-13)

1. Place:

Philadelphia means brotherly love. The Turks call it *Allah Shehr* or "city of God," literally transliterated as "beautiful city." The people of Philadelphia were known for their congeniality and friendliness. This clean and neat city was situated twenty-eight miles southeast of Sardis and most of its citizens were Christians. The same earthquake which destroyed Sardis during the reign of Tiberius also ruined Philadelphia. When it was rebuilt, a strong tall pillar was erected where the church once stood. The pillar is still intact today. This must surely be a symbolic response to our Lord's promise that "I will make him a pillar in the temple of my God (Rev. 3:12)." The period of history that this church symbolizes is from about 1750 A.D. to the present.

2. Personification: "...These things saith he that is holy, he that is true, he that hath the key of David, he that openeth and no man shutteth; and shutteth, and no man openeth" (Rev. 3:7).

The language in this personification is friendly. There is no restless walking about like in the Ephesus church. There are no eyes as flames of fire, or feet like molten brass, as in the message to the church in Thyatira. Neither does He represent Himself as having a sword with two sharp edges, as was the case with the Pergamos church. He is assuredly firm and yet cordial and kind. The message to this church contains no rebuke, so we may speculate that no serious problem existed.

Nothing derogatory is being said, yet questions are broached and issues are implied which are not so complimentary. There must be a reason why He confronts them with His attributes of holiness and truth, His authority (having the key of David) and as being the opener and closer of doors. He is also annoyed with the "synagogue of Satan." What is "the word of my patience"? Why does He bring up the subject of the New Jerusalem and its "marked" citizens?

3. Problem: "... (Those who say) they are Jews and are not, but do lie..." (Rev. 3:9).

In trying to decipher the problems posed, we must focus our attention upon the period of Church history here exemplified. Keep in mind that the above implications made by Jesus also address post-Reformation days. What might one expect to happen in the Church as a result of the work of Luther and the reformers?

History testifies that Rome killed tens of thousands of the followers of Peter Walden. A nine-year war, as well as a thirty-year war, was waged against Protestants by Rome. It is obvious that Rome was trying to put the lid on something. The Holy Roman Empire was in a panic over losing its millennium of political rule. The only way it could retain some semblance of power was through its religion. Eternal life is very important to everyone. If you can convince the world that you control and dispense eternal life, you have a very powerful religious weapon at your disposal.

The key to understanding the problem is to be found in the words, "...(They who say) they are Jews, and are not, but do lie." Jesus accuses them of belonging to "the synagogue of Satan." The message of Jesus for the literal church in Philadelphia was this: Do not believe them when they say that the true people of God are those who observe all the religious traditions of the Jews: circumcision, holy feasts, sacrifices, and all that went with Judaism. They are lying when they say you must do these things in order to belong to the chosen people of God. My death, resurrection, ascension, and Pentecost has fulfilled all of that.

To the period of history that Philadelphia typifies, Jesus was saying: Do not believe them when they tell you that the only people who are the true people of God are those who obey the pope and go through all the rituals the Church of Rome imposes upon its adherents. Do not believe that this church holds the keys and the power to dispense or withhold eternal life.

Jesus' statements now begin to take on meaning and purpose. He was telling them: I am the Holy One and the only Father of God's people. There can be no other 'holy father'. I speak the truth when I say I am the way. There is no other way to heaven — no man or church can withhold eternal life from those who will come to me. I hold the 'keys of David' and the next millennium of true righteous rule will come when I sit upon my throne in Jerusalem. Peter does not hold the keys to the kingdom, neither can he lock or unlock the door. There is only one city of God — the new Jerusalem — and all of its subjects will have the name of God and the name of the city of my God written upon them.

The Philadelphia era of Church history demonstrated a bold stand against Rome. Protestantism saw many revivals and people were converted by the thousands.

4. Proof: "...I will make them (of the synagogue of Satan) to come
   and worship before thy feet, and to know that I have loved thee,
   because thou hast kept the word of my patience..." (Rev. 3:9-10).

Protestantism saw much opposition from Rome during the post-
Reformation days. The "word of patience" alluded to here by our
Lord must be tribulation. Paul, in Romans 5:3, said, "Tribulation wor-
keth patience," and history bears out that these people endured severe tribulation. They just kept on conquering as they kept on
suffering and dying. The well known adage, "The blood of the martyrs is the seed of the Church," which was born out of the Smyrna
era, was true here as well.

Protestantism today leaves a lot to be desired spiritually. However, numerically Protestantism does authenticate the fulfillment of
the prophecy of Jesus that many from the "synagogue of Satan," (who
were their murderers, persecutors, and haters) did bow down at their
altars and were born again.

5. Potential: "I know thy works: behold, I have set before thee
   an open door, and no man can shut it: for thou hast a little
   strength, and hast kept my word, and hast not denied my
   name" (Rev. 3:8).

This open door is known as the evangelistic and missionary period of the Church when the Pietists, Puritans, and Methodists appeared. Great men and women of prayer and fasting were used of
God as messengers of the cross. Knox, Whitfield, Wesley, Finney,
Moody, Sunday, Spurgeon, Graham, Maxwell, Carey, Paton, John
and Betty Stam, Kilborne, and thousands of others like them crossed
oceans and mountains and rivers to build printing presses, Bible
schools, and seminaries. The gospel spread from Europe to America and great conviction of sin fell upon men as the Lord, through His
Holy Spirit, honored their sacrificial service.

6. Protection: "...I also will keep thee from the hour of temptation, which shall come upon all the world, to try them that
   dwell upon the earth" (Rev. 3:10).

As the transition from one church to another takes place, little change is detected. History takes its time as it moves forward. Likewise, certain characteristics of the Philadelphia church would carry over into the Laodicean church period. The faithful Christians of the Philadelphia era do not just disappear because the Laodicean period, known as the lukewarm era, is introduced.

The hour of temptation is expressed in the Greek as being "the hour of trial," or better known as the great tribulation. Because of faithfulness, the Church will be rewarded by being spared from this storm by what is known as the rapture of the Church. This Church age overlaps into the Laodicean period and actually takes us very near to the second coming of Christ, as verified by the announcement: "Behold, I come quickly." That the great tribulation is here alluded to is clear. What other hour of trial can we point to that will come upon *all* the world?

7. Promise:

> Him that overcometh will I make a pillar in the temple of my God, and he shall go no more out: and I will write upon him the name of my God, and the name of the city of my God, which is the new Jerusalem, which cometh down out of heaven from my God: and I will write upon him my new name (Rev. 3:12).

With regard to the pillar in the temple, the Philadephians understood this better than we do today. Their Church was memorialized by a pillar which went deep into the heart of the earth and remains standing today. The Lord here is using the pillar as an example of how firm our position is with Him. "They shall go no more out." Pillars must not go out or the building will collapse. The figure of the saints being part of heaven's permanent structure is not uncommon. Revelation 21:12 and 14 indicate that the gates of the city are named after the twelve tribes of Israel and the foundation stones bear the names of the apostles.

Men love to have their names inscribed upon the walls of the halls of fame. In this case, the names written upon the pillars representing the faithful are "the name of my God," "the name of the city of my God," and "my new name." These names are not the same as the name promised to the people of Pergamos. Theirs was simply "a new name." In this instance, the name is His "new name." What His new name will be, we cannot speculate. Revelation 19:12 simply states that "he had a new name written, that no man knew, but he himself." Heaven will be full of many "new" things, for Jesus said He would create a new heaven and a new earth, He would make every thing new and a new song would be sung.

With great excitement, we anticipate moving into a new home here on earth. To try explaining with this world's vocabulary what our home in heaven will be like is impossible, for, "...Eye hath not seen, nor ear heard, neither have entered into the heart of man, the things which God has prepared for them that love him" (1 Cor. 2:9). Human speech cannot attach an earthly name to heavenly things we have never seen.

VII. LAODICEA, THE NAUSEOUS CHURCH
(Revelation 3:14-22)

1. Place:

Laodicea was a prominent banking center, proud of its wealth, beautiful with resplendent temples and theaters, noted for its manufacture of rich garments made of black glossy wool and the seat of a medical school which made a powder for the treatment of eye troubles. Our Lord thus draws from their affluence the parallel of the "riches," "garments," and "eyesalve."

Paul, in writing to the Colossians, had a special reason to ask that the Colossian letter also be read to the church at Laodicea (Col. 4:16). Paul expressed a desire earlier in this letter that the hearers would seek true riches and treasures hidden in Christ (Col. 2:1-3). He knew the people of Laodicea were proud of their riches, wisdom, and culture, worshipping the mysteries of the world of spirits, angels, and new moons (Col. 2:15-18). This period of Church history will conclude the activity of the Church on earth and witness the return of Christ.

2. Personification: "...These things saith the Amen, the faithful and true witness, the beginning of the creation of God" (Rev. 3:14).

In this personification, Jesus employs three metaphors which are to serve as a prod to jab the Laodiceans awake. Let us try to understand the mind of our Master with regard to this last Church age, for it is directed especially at us today.

The first metaphor Jesus employs is, "These things saith the Amen." Three times in the powerful first chapter, Jesus uses the word "amen." It is a word that has been used in the Church for centuries to emphasize a certain conviction or belief. In modern vernacular, we would use phrases like, "You can say that again...you'd better believe it...that's for sure" and other similar idioms. The word "amen" means "so may it be." It is a powerful assertion of the veracity and integrity of a premise or claim presently articulated. There was something in the church at Laodicea as well as the Church age it represents that caused our Savior to give such emphasis.

The Laodicean church did not take seriously who Jesus Christ actually was, what He stood for, and the truth He represented. This church was setting its own rules, making its own doctrines, and living by its own opinions. This we deduce from Jesus' words, "Thou sayest..." The Laodicean Christians did not obey the promptings of the Holy Spirit who testified to them that Jesus Christ was the Son of God. Thus a conflict between what they were saying and what He was saying is here disclosed.

At the transfiguration, Moses and Elijah were talking with Jesus. The voice which spoke from heaven said, "This is my beloved Son, in whom I am well pleased, hear ye him" (Matt. 17:5). God's voice from heaven notified the disciples that what Moses, Elijah, or anyone else had spoken was now merging into one supreme message. Jesus, the Word, is the fulfillment of that message.

In Revelation 1:5, John employs these words in his salutation: "And from Jesus Christ, who is the faithful witness...." In this message to the Laodiceans, Jesus adds the word "true" to this same salutation, thus strengthening the quality, substance, and character of His witness. I seem to hear Him saying, "Why can't you believe and obey and recognize and respect my words?" In Revelation 19:11, Jesus is called "Faithful and True." Here the words are capitalized which means they are proper nouns or actual names like Jesus, Master, or Lord. When Jesus said He was the Faithful and True witness, He not only meant it, He had a very specific reason for saying it.

The Book of Revelation begins with an assertion, "faithful" (Rev. 1:5), and it closes with a double assertion, "faithful and true" (Rev. 22:6). One of the conclusions that characterizes this last Church age is that the Church is not paying attention to what He, the True and Faithful witness, is saying. The Church is paying more attention to the opinions and rationalizations of men and women who, for the most part, are neither true nor faithful.

Jesus has patiently asserted again and again who He is: "The beginning of the creation of God," "the Alpha and the Omega," "the first and the last," "the first begotten from the dead," "he which is, which was and which is to come," "he who was dead and am alive forevermore," and other similar phrases. This is a wicked rebellion against the innate intuition which God has placed into every human breast that He indeed does exist and is the creator of all things.

Revelation 21:8 places the unbeliever nearly at the top of the list of those who shall forever be consigned to the lake of fire. The words of Jesus when He said, "I will spew thee out of my mouth," express divine disgust at the spiritual taste of the Laodicean church and the Church age it represents today. His words, "Thou art lukewarm," also express a strong statement of disapproval.

When Paul wrote his letter to the Colossians some thirty years before the Book of Revelation was written, he gave instructions "that this epistle also be read to the church of the Laodiceans" (Col. 4:16). The Colossian letter affirms:

> (Jesus) who is the image of the invisible God, (is) the first-born of every creature: for by him were all things created, that are in heaven, and that are in earth, visible and invisible, whether they be thrones, or dominions, or principalities, or powers: all things were created by him, and for him: and he is before all things, and by him all things consist (Col. 1:15-17).

It should not surprise anyone that we find our Lord deeply disappointed with the Laodiceans for ignoring this tenet of truth. Obviously, they had not taken very seriously the instructions that Paul gave the Colossians.

3. Problem: "...Thou sayest, I am rich, and increased with goods and have need of nothing..." (Rev. 3:17).

There is no hint of deterioration in leadership or false teaching in this church. There seems to be no Nicolaitans, Jezabelites, or Balaamites. What we do find is a generally conceited self-assessment and opinion of who the members of the Laodicean church thought they were. "We are rich. We are increased with goods. We have need of nothing." What a tepid (lukewarm) spiritual offering to those who were hungering and thirsting after God. How hungry would you have to get to stomach this? No wonder that Jesus said, "I would spew thee out of my mouth."

But wonder of wonders, the Lord stands at the door of this very church saying, "If you can hear me in there, and someone opens the door, I will come in. I will set before you a table and turn host and spread a meal that will give you a burning with your heart (Luke 24:28-34) like that of the Emmaus disciples who invited me to come in. They realized the day was far spent and the night was coming. After I supped with them, their eyes were open and they knew who I was."

Today men build cathedrals with stained glass windows, install organs that can provide music for neighboring churches a mile away, and design water fountains to spurt a hundred feet into the air. They insist on only well bred, university graduate preachers who tell you that you can be anything you want to be by "possibility thinking." But the Lord will never be satisfied with man's possibility thinking. He has provided a faith which supernaturally makes things happen because He is the Creator and a man or woman has placed their absolute trust in Him.

God did not send us into all the world to entertain or impress it. He is not smiling down from heaven as we proudly strut through our temples, conducting grand tours while we boast about our beautiful worship services, the exclusiveness of our membership, and the millions it cost to bring all of this about. These churches think they are "rich, and increased with goods, and have need of nothing." But if they were to arrange for a week of evangelistic services or a missionary convention, the attendance would be an embarrassment.

So many strange new "so called" theologies have been conjured up: positive confession, positive thinking, possibility thinking, self-image, unfortunate childhood, self-esteem, new age movement, inner healing, being slain of the Spirit, the church universal and triumphant, and scores of other new ideas and teachings all sounding quite convincing to the average listener. When analyzed, they are all centered in self, extolling the intelligence and independence of man. Self-help techniques promise health, wealth, well being, happiness, security, and everything else that is sure only to make their promoter succeed. These techniques and methods teach that your destiny is in the power of your mind. Ask what you will and it can be yours simply by turning your fantasies into realities through positive mind power.

All of this is a far cry from Christ's words to take up our cross and follow Him. This is a far cry from being crucified with Christ. In all of these new "doctrines," the sacrifices Jesus calls us to make are curiously absent, and the tribulations we are to have in this world are never talked about. Of course they aren't. Such statements will not attract new members to the church that makes them.

We need to be very careful that in our positive spiritual meditation we do not wander too far back into our inner self and find that the devil is there waiting for us. Ancient religions have been doing this for a long time, and the Eastern religions are becoming increasingly attractive to those today who are not willing to pay the price of genuine discipleship and faith in God. This is exactly what the devil is trying to achieve.

This is how Adam and Eve were trapped. In essence Satan told them, "Don't be negative, be positive. Did God positively say you can't eat of the tree of the knowledge of good and evil? The problem is that God knows if you eat of this tree, your eyes will be opened and you will be as gods." Satan is using this act of deception today in persuading people that they actually became gods back then when they ate of the tree of knowledge. He insists that all you need to do is go far enough back in your sub-conscious god-being and you can become anything you want to become with this new-found power.

Positive is in. Negative is out. Yet Paul, John, Peter, and all of the New Testament writers warn us against sin and damnation in what appears to be a negative manner. John admonishes us to stick to that which we "have heard from the beginning." In other words, if it is a new concept theologically, check it out very carefully. Jesus warned that in the last days "false prophets would come" (Matt.

24:24). Paul said there would be those who "would depart from the truth, giving heed to fables and doctrines of devils" (1 Tim. 4:1).

4. Plight: "...And (thou) knowest not that thou art wretched, and miserable, and poor, and blind, and naked" (Rev. 3:17).

I am sure some anguish must have surprised and bewildered that comfortable congregation in Laodicea. Some must have said, "This letter has been sent to the wrong address." Everything that the Master indicted them with was the exact opposite to what they thought they were. Jesus' complaint here must have sent their ego into next week as their chief goal as a church was to impress others. How some men struggle themselves into oblivion, while others forget themselves into immortality. The greatest sadness about their state is "they knew it not." There is no deception that is more deceitful than he who deceives himself.

The aftershock of this "church-quake" left many of its members with unanswered questions. How could the Lord actually accuse them of being wretched, miserable, poor, blind, and naked? They were the only church in Asia that could afford slaves to carry their burdens. They were a highly educated people, and their city was the envy of all Asia. The sword of the Master was very painful.

How bad is wretched? My thesaurus suggests synonyms like deplorable, lamentable, pathetic, despicable, inferior, and unworthy. Only a wound from the sword that proceeds out of the mouth of the Son of man can bring down the proud, for pride does not bleed easily. I cannot help but feel this church was severely wounded by the words of our Lord.

How bad is miserable? The thesaurus suggests synonyms like flawed, shabby, sorry, and worthless. That is certainly not what the people who toured and admired the church at Laodicea were saying. This church was renowned throughout the whole world. Tourists came here and probably purchased the ancient equivalent of postcards depicting the beautiful Laodicean church.

How bad is poor? Here the synonyms are threadbare, deficient, inadequate, meager, destitute, and down-and-out. There is a poverty which wealth creates that makes men miserable, and this was the misery of the Laodicean church. There are riches which poverty creates that makes men very happy, as found in the happiness of the church at Smyrna. True happiness can only be found in the riches experienced by the "poor in spirit." No doubt this church boasted of a large bank balance in a city which was known to be the banking center in Asia Minor. Yet the Lord called them "poor and miserable" because their riches were not true riches.

How bad is blind? It means to be sightless, unconscious of light, begging for aid, and having no vision. This comment hurt them deeply. To be spiritually thrust through with the sword and bleeding badly is insulting, but here the Lord gives the sword a twist to the right by calling them blind. Spiritual beggars sitting in the dark — poor, miserable, and naked — is how the Lord viewed them. This was almost more than what they could bear. They must have cried out, "How can you accuse us of having no vision? People from all over the world come here to buy our eye powder which has healed the eyes of thousands."

How bad is naked? Words to describe this condition are bare, exposed, uncovered, and stripped. Spiritual nudity means we have not been adorned with the wedding garment. In the parable told by Jesus, the man without a wedding garment was cast into outer darkness. This is the same condition as that of Adam and Eve who, after sinning, found themselves naked and then were cast out of the garden.

In Revelation 16:15, Jesus said, "...Blessed is he that watcheth, and keepeth his garments, lest he walk naked, and they see his shame." Spiritual nakedness in the sight of God is not acceptable, because Jesus died naked upon the cross so that we might be clothed in His righteousness.

5. Prescription:

> I counsel thee to buy of me gold tried in the fire, that thou mayest be rich; and white raimant, that thou mayest be clothed, and that the shame of thy nakedness do not appear; and anoint thine eyes with eyesalve, that thou mayest see (Rev. 3:18).

Three things appear on this spiritual shopping list recommended by Jesus: gold, white raiment, and eyesalve.

Gold is the most precious of all metals. It takes a lot of paper currency to buy just a few ounces of it. Men have gone on long expeditions, endured danger, crossed oceans, and persevered under untold hardships as they dug into the earth in search of it. In the days of the gold rush, many men died of starvation and disease as they fought off enemies and endured the elements while trying to get their hands on a little of this precious prize.

This is not the gold Jesus is talking about. The gold Jesus counsels them to buy is prayer. Gold is a symbol of prayer. It is associated with the golden censer in which prayers are kept and the golden altar upon which prayers are offered with the continual burning of incense (Rev. 8:3). As gold is the most precious of all metals, then prayer must be the most precious spiritual material with which we may build our spiritual house (see 1 Cor. 3:12). This is probably what Paul had in mind when advising the Corinthians to use gold in building upon their foundation in Christ, for the results of their building would be tried by fire. The gold Jesus instructed the Laodiceans to buy had also been "tried in the fire."

I know of nothing that will purify and refine the child of God like prayer. And nothing will allow such spiritual deterioration to set in, like that found in the Laodicean church, as a lack of prayer. Jesus must have felt alienated from this church as a result of the lack of prayer, or else He would not have said, "Behold, I stand at the door and knock." Prayer is visiting with God. Jesus was standing outside the door of this church wanting to sup with them if they would only invite Him to enter.

White raiment is a symbol of the righteousness of Christ. Jesus is openly exposing the awful truth that this wonderfully proper church had not made provision for the covering of sin. They were walking around in spiritual shame, not covered with white raiment. Their own fig-leaf doctrines and opinions regarding the deity of Christ, the separated Christian life, and the forgiveness of sins were nauseating to Jesus.

God can do a lot of things, but He cannot remove sin. That may shock you, but no one can remove sin. When a sin is committed, there is no angel, demon, or man who can change what has been done. God can forgive you of that sin, but He cannot remove it. He promises to forget that sin and remove it from His remembrance, but He cannot obliterate it. There are some things that are irrevocable.

106

David will always be remembered because of his adultery even though he was forgiven and called "a man after God's own heart." Peter will always be remembered for his denial. Judas will forever be the betrayer. God has not obliterated the sins of any one of these men.

God washes our sin in the blood of His Son and turns the stain into the righteousness of Jesus Christ. So what was once death through sin has now become eternal life through the blood, for there is life in the blood. What was once impure is now pure. What was once uncovered and exposed is now covered with the robe of righteousness (Ps. 32:1, 85:2; Rom. 4:7).

The people of Laodicea were not born again and, consequently, had no covering for their sins. No wonder Jesus said:

> *You turn my stomach by your solace in a beautiful church build-ing and your manmade philosophies regarding what is right in the eyes of God. Your beautiful shiny black, Persian lamb robes can never cover the stains of sin. What you need is the "fine white linen which is the righteousness of the saints." (Rev. 19:8)*

Eyesalve is a symbol of new birth enlightenment. The powder medicine which the whole world knew could be purchased in Laodicea could never provide the kind of sight Jesus was talking about. The wonderful thing about new-birth Christianity is that you are made aware of it immediately. Your eyes are suddenly opened, and there is an assurance in your heart that you have been born again.

You need not tell a mother when the baby has been born. No one needs to tell you when you have been born again, for "His Spirit bears witness with our spirit, that we are the children of God" (Rom. 8:16). Signing a decision card does not prove you are a Christian. Baptism, communion, church membership, penance, mass, indulgences, confession, or keeping the ten commandments can never save you and make you a child of God. You can do all of these things and still be as spiritually blind as the Loadiceans.

I fear that in many gospel preaching, evangelical churches today there are many people who have never come to eyesalve salvation. The light has never dawned upon them. They do everything they are taught to do, jumping through all the religious hoops. But the joy of the Lord and the love which baptizes the believer at the initiation of the new birth has never been experienced. Illumination, revelation, and breakthrough with a sure certification of salvation is not their experience. But Jesus has given the solution to a procedure that will heal spiritual blindness.

6. Procedure: "As many as I love, I rebuke and chasten: be zealous therefore, and repent" (Rev. 3:19).

There is hope for this church. Jesus reminds them that His hard words against them were uttered only because He loved them. If He had not loved the church at Laodicea, He would have left her alone. He said of the Ephesian church, "You have left your first love...remember from whence thou art fallen." The church of Laodicea didn't have much love to leave and didn't have far to fall. But in spite of their deplorable condition, you still find the Lord saying things like, "I stand, I knock, I will come in, I will sup with him, and I will grant him to sit with me in my throne."

Of this church it can be said that they were faithfully faithful and faithfully unfaithful. The married relationship which is a type of Christ and His Church exemplifies this truth. They were faithfully faithful in providing shelter, food, clothing, money, clean clothes, clean home, and everything else that belongs to the duties of a husband and wife. Yet at the same time, they were faithfully unfaithful when it came to love, tenderness, intimacy, and everything else that really is the crown of the married relationship. Love is the ingredient which gives meaning to all temporal faithfulness.

The Lord might have been very proud of this church just as it was if they would have been as faithful to Him as they were to each other. If only they would have loved Him as they loved their comfortable situation. If only they would have included Him in all of their fellowships as they included each other. If only they would have worshipped Him as they worshipped what they had built.

How sad, as He stands at the door knocking and saying, "If any man hear...." He is not asking for a deacon, a minister, a Sunday school teacher, or any church official. He would be satisfied with "any man" from the church to be His friend.

In my office, I have a large picture by Holman Hunt entitled "The Light of the World." The artist depicts Jesus as described in Revelation 3:20, standing at a church door and knocking. He is carrying a lantern and its soft glow lights up the door to the church which is covered with tall weeds. This must mean that not too much spiritual activity is going on inside, because no one has gone out of it to evangelize for a long time. It must be night time, or He would not be carrying a lantern.

The letters to the seven churches announce at the outset that the Church itself is to be the candlestick and light bearer in a dark world. In Revelation 1, Jesus is also described as walking among the different churches and having free access to all of them. After 2,000 years of Church history have transpired, Christ approaches the Church and finds that the latch is on the inside which must mean He is not welcome. In this work of art, Jesus is wearing a crown of thorns and His eyes are very sad. It is not easy to study this painting for any length of time.

7. Promise: "...to him that overcometh will I grant to sit with me in my throne, even as I also overcame, and am set down with my Father in his throne" (Rev. 3:21).

There is great reward for zealous overcoming. There is also great sacrifice and suffering. There are many mountains to scale, rivers to swim, and oceans to sail until this promise can be claimed. How did Jesus overcome? His ascent to the throne led Him down the Via Dolorossa (the way of suffering) and to the cross. If there is no battle, there is no victory. If there is no victory, there is no crown. If there is no suffering, there is no reward. If there is no reward, there is no promotion or throne.

"...Be zealous therefore and repent" (Rev. 3:19). The Greek does not use the word zealous, rather the expression "be hot therefore." This must mean burning with a love for the Lord and hot with a compassion for lost men. It must mean on fire for God with a flaming testimony, touched with coals from off the altar and endowed with a flaming tongue of Pentecostal power. Our world today needs people like that!

"He that hath ears to hear, let him hear what the Spirit saith unto the churches." Seven times our Lord uttered these words, as we have seen as we studied these seven churches. Six times I have ignored them. Is not that exactly the very nature of man? How many times have we heard messages about the seven churches and how many times has the Spirit admonished us regarding some personal fault revealed in the process? How many times have we procrastinated in acting upon the promptings of the Spirit? The Lord will deal with us in the same manner that He dealt with these churches.

Let me close the forty-nine pronouncements about the Church with the words of the saintly old Julianna Pahl of Hanna Alberta, Canada, who is now in heaven. She could not understand the English language, but was always first to arrive at the worship services. I asked her one winter evening as she sat in the darkness of the church waiting for the people to come, "If you cannot understand the English language, why do you come to an English service?"

She replied (in German), "*English is a language which my ears do not understand, but there is another language which I hear with my heart while you preach English. That I listen to all the time.*" The language she must surely have been talking about was "the spirit bearing witnesses with her spirit."

"He that hath ears to hear, let him understand with the heart and obey what the Spirit saith unto the churches" (author's paraphrase).

CHAPTER THREE

The Laodicean era of history brings to a close the activity of the Church here on earth. Chapters four and five of the Book of Revelation disclose pre-tribulation judgment preparations. The scene about the throne of God in heaven resembles a court room with the witnesses, jury, and every necessary element in place. A "little book" seen in the hand of God becomes the prime exhibit. This little book contains the final three and one half years of judgment as symbolically revealed in the seven seals.

The actual drama of the three and one half years, known as the great tribulation on earth, are played out in chapters six through nineteen. However, chapters four and five reveal the necessary judicial system which sanctions every judgment to be executed on earth. Permission is granted only from the throne.

The judgments of the three-and-a-half-year great tribulation and the final forty-five days of the wrath of God will all but annihilate civilization. But before any judgments are executed upon the world, a special tribunal in heaven must give its consent. Chapters four and five reveal who these jurors will be and the careful manner in which details of justice are observed at the throne before the storm of God's wrath lashes out against the universe.

Before we consider this select jury and the forty-nine pronouncements concerning them, notice must be given to the seven preceding details seen in the first two verses of Revelation 4.

SEVEN PRELIMINARY DETAILS

(1) The Detail of the Time

Chapter four begins with the words, "After this...." This begs the question, after what? The answer must be, after the Church age. When "the times of the Gentiles be fulfilled" (Luke 21:24) or, as Paul puts it, when "the fullness of the Gentiles be come in" (Rom. 11:25). Then judgment will come.

God's next great act in the redemption of man will be focused upon the Jews, His chosen people. When the Jews crucified Jesus, God turned to the Gentiles. When the time of the Gentiles' abuse of Jesus is fulfilled, ("crucifying him in their hearts"), God will again turn to the Jews.

(2) The Detail of the Place

The scene shifts from the Isle called Patmos to heaven. John is transformed into spirit and allowed to see the very throne of God through a door opened in heaven.

The entire chronological sequence of tribulation judgements, as symbolized by the seven seals, seven trumpets, and seven vials, proceed from this throne. The execution of the judgments represented by these symbols are preceded by either voices, thunderings, lightnings, or an earthquake. These are God's messengers marking out the trail of a chronological order for us, making it possible to follow a step-by-step progression of tribulation happenings.

(3) The Detail of the Voice

...And the first voice which I heard was as it were of a trumpet talking with me; which said, Come up hither, and I will show thee things which must be hereafter (Rev. 4:1).

The first voice referred to here is that of Revelation 1:10. Because John was taken to heaven from the Isle of Patmos, our Lord needed to be certain that John would not become confused about the conti-

112

nuity of the vision because of the sudden change in surroundings. John verbally acknowledges that he recognized the voice he was hearing in heaven as being the first voice he heard on the Isle of Patmos. Our Lord was satisfied that John was aware that the subject, purpose, and person of the vision were a continuation of what started on earth on the Isle of Patmos.

(4) The Detail of the Invitation

The words, "Come up hither," are not simply a singular invitation for John to come up into heaven. Before the tribulation begins, God will remove the Church. This invitation to "come up hither" includes the Church and will subsequently be called the "pre-tribulation thief rapture."

When the mystery regarding Israel and her conversion through the trials of the tribulation has been completed, God will remove her in a cloud in a second "come up hither" as seen in the ascension of the two witnesses (Rev. 11:12). This event will subsequently be referred to as the "post-tribulation trump rapture." Israel's rapture will clear the way for the forty-five days of the pouring out of the vials of God's wrath which are known as "that great and terrible day of the Lord" (Joel 2 and 3).

(5) The Detail of the Disclosure

...I will show thee things which must be hereafter (Rev. 4:1).

According to Revelation 1:19, we note that the things John was to record are divided into three sections. First, "the things which thou hast seen" refers to the vision of the Son of man as portrayed in chapter one. Second, "the things which are" deals with the seven churches that existed at that time as recorded in chapters two and three. Third, "the things which shall be hereafter" deals with the things which are to happen after the rapture of the Church as recorded in chapter four on through the end of the Book of Revelation.

(6) The Detail of John's State

And immediately I was in the spirit... (Rev. 4:2).

This means John was in a trance. There is no other way that a mortal can enter into the presence of God. This is the same state that John found himself in while still on the Isle of Patmos when he turned to see the voice that spoke with him (Rev. 1:10-12).

(7) The Detail of the Throne

...A throne was set in heaven... (Rev. 4:2).

The word throne is used twelve times in the eleven verses of chapter four. This is the throne of thrones from which all of the tribulation verdicts and judgments will be announced. This throne is still in place at the end of the tribulation as seen in Revelation 19:4. The only throne in heaven is the throne of God.

FORTY-NINE PRONOUNCEMENTS
REGARDING THE SEVEN TRIBULATION JUDICIARIES

I. THE ONE SITTING ON THE THRONE
(Revelation 4:2-3)

And immediately I was in the spirit: and, behold, a throne was set in heaven, and one sat on the throne. And he that sat was to look upon like a jasper and a sardine stone...

There can be no doubt about the identity of this one sitting upon heaven's throne. It is the judge, God the Father, the creator and sustainer of the universe. He alone has the authority to judge the world of sin.

1. His Righteousness, Holiness, and Purity: "(His appearance was)...like a jasper and sardine stone..." (Rev. 4:3).

Ezekiel and Daniel both saw a throne with the same personage upon it. Their descriptions of this throne speak of intense brightness

114

and fire (Ezek. 1:26-28; Dan. 7:9). This is the brilliance of a jasper stone. In describing the holy Jerusalem, John says, "...Her light was like unto a stone most precious, even like a jasper stone, clear as crystal" (Rev. 21:11). The nature of God is symbolized here by the pure, clear, crystal composition of the jasper stone.

Precious stones, like a jasper, are ground into multi-angular cuts, creating many facets flashing their brilliance. God is depicted as a celestial jasper, omni-faceted, with infinite brilliance in His righteous and holy attributes. This judge is the essence of true justice and righteousness, stirring himself to do a new thing in the world. He will overlook nothing. He is about ready to settle the score with the fallen Lucifer whose days as "prince of this world" are numbered to but forty-two months at this point.

2. His Justice, Impartiality, and Wrath: "(God is also likened to) ...a sardine stone..." (Rev. 4:3).

The sardonyx is red. Isaiah, some 800 years before this Revelation was written, saw the great day of God's vengeance. He saw one whose garments were red, whose visage and disposition were characterized as being angry.

God is "slow to anger, and gracious in mercy," but here His patience, longsuffering, and love have worn thin. We delight in talking about the love of God. But if the frightfulness of God's wrath is to be perceived proportionately to the delightfulness of His love, then it is indeed a "fearful thing to fall into the hands of an angry God (Heb. 10:31)." The cup of God's wrath is full. Man cannot continue in his ridiculous justification of criminalistic acts without suffering the consequences.

Abortion is the equivalent of murder, for it is the termination of a soul and body made in the image of God. I would not want to be found interfering with the creative mysteries and wonders of life which are only to be terminated by the giver of life who is called the "first and the last, the beginning of the creation of the world." Homosexuality is not a lifestyle. Romans 1:27-32 calls it "unrighteousness...worthy of death." Pre-marital sex and adultery are not free love. Revelation 21:8 declares that "...whoremongers...shall have their part in the lake which burneth with fire and brimstone...."

The red sardine stone proclaims that the judge upon the throne is angry. Surely, if it were to be known, His hands must be gripping the arm rests of the throne with a posture which suggests He is about to stand to His feet to say something.

3. His Faithfulness, Mercy, and Love: "...And there was a rainbow about the throne, in sight like unto an emerald" (Rev. 4:3).

The color of an emerald is a pure transparent green. God gave the rainbow to Noah after the flood as a sacred covenant that He would never again destroy the world with a flood. The rainbow we see on earth is a half circle. A rainbow as seen from heaven is a full circle and speaks to us of the unending mercy, love, and grace of our covenant-keeping God.

The rainbow is a guarantee that the same justice which brought the great flood will of a certainty be invoked in the judgments of the great tribulation. God does not make idle threats. The rainbow is a messenger saying, "God will carry out His warnings regarding the tribulation".

4. His Voice:

God speaks several times from this throne during the tribulation through either "lightnings, thunderings, voices, or an earthquake." These demonstrations are intonations that a stern decree and verdict that has been agreed upon by the heavenly tribunal is about to be executed.

Lightning and thunder, as recorded in the Revelation, are not simply symbols of the voice of God; they are the voice of God. This can be seen in Revelation 10:4, where seven thunders utter their voices. John must have understood their rumblings, for he was about to write when God said, "...Seal up those things which the seven thunders uttered (other translations use the word "said"), and write them not." John heard audible words which he was about to record, evidence that thunder as symbolized in the revelation is the voice of God. (See also: Exod. 9:23-28, 19:16; I Sam. 7:10, 12:17-18.)

The seven lamps named in connection with the voice are the sevenfold ministrations of the Spirit of God which are "the spirit of wisdom, understanding, counsel, might, knowledge, fear of the Lord, and righteous judgment (Isa. 11:1-4). Considering the momentous decisions which need to be made by the seven judiciaries, it is imperative that the Holy Spirit be in continual operation (as typified by the words "burning before the throne") giving perpetual wisdom to the jurors.

The Holy Spirit is not named as being one of the seven participants among the judiciary. He was not sent to execute judgment, but rather to warn of "judgment to come." Since the tribulation has to do with the wrath of the Lamb and the wrath of God, the Holy Spirit does not participate. His work during the Church age was "to convince the world of sin, of righteousness and of judgment to come" (John 16:8). He is present here in this universal tribunal as a witness against the world which grieved Him as it ignored His invitation to partake of righteousness.

5. His Mysterious Document: "...I saw in the right hand of him that sat on the throne a book written within and on the backside, sealed with seven seals" (Rev. 5:1).

Circumstantial evidence is not the best kind of evidence in courts of law. Eyewitnesses and documented, tangible exhibits are regarded as reliable and credible evidence. This is the kind of evidence the jury or judge cannot ignore.

God sent Daniel to John on the Isle of Patmos to deliver the message of a coming tribulation (Rev. 1:1). John did not know that the angel was actually Daniel. Overwrought by such a presence, John actually desired to worship him, but the angel forbade John to do so because he was the prophet Daniel who bore "testimony of Jesus" (Rev. 19:10, 22:9). This testimony of Jesus was sealed in a book by Daniel hundreds of years before this. The book is now seen in the hand of the judge as evidence that civilization from John's day (when the seals were opened) to our day has known about the judgments of God for nearly 2,000 years. This mysterious little book has created more curiosity, generated more controversy, and spawned some of the wildest eschatological fabrications imaginable.

Matthew 24 contains the account of the disciples taking Jesus aside and privately asking Him two questions: "When shall these things be and what shall be the signs of thy coming?" Jesus addressed the second question first by stating that false prophets and wars and rumors of wars would be the initial signs, but He hastened to add that "the end is not yet."

Then He continued by listing four more signs: "Nation shall rise against nation, and kingdom against kingdom and there shall be famines, and pestilences, and earthquakes, in divers places." Then He warns that "all these are the beginning of sorrows." Jesus continued listing still further signs of persecution, much iniquity in the world, false prophets, and the gospel of the kingdom finally being preached in all the world.

"Then," He said, "shall the end come."

There is one specific sign which follows and marks the beginning of the tribulation. Jesus expressed it in this way, "When ye therefore shall see the abomination of desolation, spoken of by Daniel the prophet, stand in the holy place, (whoso readeth let him understand)" (Matt. 24:15). An image of the antichrist erected in the temple in the middle of the seven-year treaty is the signal that the early hours of tribulation terrors are about to begin.

Daniel 9:27 indeed confirms that the antichrist or a leader of a European Confederacy will make a covenant with the Jews for one week, which translates into seven years. Among other things, this covenant will include military protection and freedom to worship and make sacrifices in the temple in Jerusalem. However, in the middle of the week or after three and a half years, the antichrist will break the covenant, prohibit the daily sacrifices, and erect his statue in the temple which is called "the abomination that maketh desolate" (Dan. 12:11).

The specifics of time were given to the prophet in two different ways. First, the man on the waters informed Daniel that from the time these wonders (regarding the tribulation) begin and until they end would be a time, times, and half a time or 1,260 days (Dan. 12:6-7). Second, from the time the abomination which maketh desolate is erected until the end would be 1,290 days (Dan. 12:11).

What makes this image so abominable? The answer is that it is replacing the daily sacrifices made to God in the temple. Revelation 13:14-15 explains that compulsory worship of this image will be instituted. Paul perceived the antichrist's arrogant action of electing himself to be God as a very sacrilegious act (2 Thess. 2:3-4). These things are an abomination to God, enraging Him to the point that He allows the desolation caused by the tribulation to begin.

Daniel was told to seal the contents of the book (of which he appeared to know very little) until "the time of the end." The end begins with Revelation 5 where the book reappears prior to the tribulation and is taken by Jesus from the hand of God to execute its seals.

There seems to be little doubt that the book which Daniel sealed in Daniel 12 is the same book which Jesus claims in Revelation 5. As Ezekiel saw a wheel within a wheel in Ezekiel 1, likewise we have here a book within a book. The little book of Revelation5 contains a consecutive chronological order of symbolical messages contained in seals, trumpets, and vials woven in between visions of tribulation participants. When we understand that the little sealed book contains the future unfolding of the great tribulation and that the seven tribulation participants seen by John in separate visions are actually responsible for creating the tribulation, we spare ourselves many hours of trying to fit the seals somewhere into past history.

6. His Worshipers:

A judge must always be respected. When he enters the chamber, everyone must rise to their feet. The judge of the Revelation is highly revered by the worshipers here enumerated as the four living ones, the four and twenty elders, the raptured Church, the angels, and every creature in the universe.

7. The Worship He Receives and Its Implications:

Revelation 4:8-11 and 5:8-14 record the worship the Lord receives. Of the twenty-five verses contained in chapters four and five, eleven of them are devoted to worship. It is interesting to note that the theme of worship centers around Him as Creator, the one who always was and who will be alive forevermore. This theme is being rejected by many today.

He is the judge above all judges, having already judged the world at certain times in the past. He is the Holy God of Israel. Before these chapters conclude, all heaven and earth will have bowed to worship Him.

II. THE FOUR AND TWENTY ELDERS
(Revelation 4:4)

And round about the throne were four and twenty seats: and upon the seats I saw four and twenty elders sitting, clothed in white raiment; and they had on their heads crowns of gold.

1. Their Identification:

These personages are called "elders." The fact that they wear clothes and crowns and can sit, fall down, worship, sing, play harps, speak, think, and are redeemed from every tribe, kindred, and nation unquestionably makes them glorified men in heaven.

These glorified men are probably twelve elders of Israel and the twelve apostles of Jesus. Much is said in the Scriptures as to the place that these two classes are to occupy in the kingdom of Christ. Matthew 19:28, Luke 11:47-50, Ephesians 2:20, and Revelation 19:12-14 and 20:4 all indicate that God has chosen certain men to sit with Him in judgment. We conclude that the twelve from the Old Testament represent the wife of Jehovah, the nation of Israel, and the twelve from the New Testament represent the bride of Christ, the Church.

2. The Nature of Their Domicile:

King James chose the word "seats" to describe the twenty-four objects around the throne of God. I have researched several other translations including the German and Greek interlinear and find the word "thrones" being used most of the time. This is very important.

A casual visitor would sit upon a seat which could be found nearly anywhere. A throne can be occupied only by an official of high status, and only a few select humans would be allowed to ascend it. These thrones reveal that these elders are to function as judiciaries or advocates.

3. Their Posture:

The twenty-four are "sitting" upon a throne, presupposing promotion, trust, and grave responsibility. Revelation 5:5 describes one of them as comforting John while revealing profound knowledge regarding the one who was "worthy to open the book." We will discover how these twenty-four are allowed to influence God to proceed with the predetermined judgments.

4. Their Attire:

The white raiment speaks of purity and honesty. History has taught us that not all judges and jurors can make this claim. This jury's judgment will be altogether absolute and just.

5. Their Ministry of Worship:

Out of the twelve times the twenty-four elders are mentioned in the Book of Revelation, five times they are intensely involved in worship (Rev. 4:10-11; 5:8-10, 14; 11:16; 19:4). Their worship is directed either to God, who is honored as the Creator, or to Christ who was slain. These tenets of truth are a powerful theme throughout the Book of Revelation and proclaimed by the elders many times, certifying the Father and the Son as worthy of the honor and authority ascribed to them.

6. Their Priestly Ministry:

> And when he had taken the book, the four beasts and four and twenty elders fell down before the Lamb, having every one of them harps, and golden vials full of odours, which are the prayers of the saints (Rev. 5:8).

The prayers of the saints will affect the tribulation world. In Revelation 6:9-17, the souls under the altar cry out, "How long, O Lord, holy and true, dost thou not judge and avenge our blood on them that dwell on the earth?" Terrible natural calamities follow. Likewise, in Revelation 8:3-5, an angel pours the prayers into the world and there were "voices, and thunderings, and lightnings, and an earthquake." During ordinary times, prayer would be regarded a blessing. During the tribulation it becomes a source of judgement.

God is quite sensitive to His praying people. The prayers of the saints do indeed move the heart of God. It is the priestly duty of the twenty-four elders to preside over these prayers and conserve them in golden vials.

7. Their Music:

I love music. In the Book of Revelation, two new songs are recorded, one in 14:1-3 and the song that the twenty-four elders sing (Rev. 5:9) about Christ being worthy to take the book and "open the seals thereof." The fact that so much attention is given to this sealed book affirms the truth that its contents are of momentous import. Heaven sings one more song on the evening of the great tribulation.

III. THE FOUR BEASTS
(Revelation 4:6-8)

...And round about the throne, were four beasts full of eyes before and behind. And the first beast was like a lion, and the second beast was like a calf, and the third beast had a face as a man, and the fourth beast was like a flying eagle. And the four beasts had each of them six wings about him; and they were full of eyes within: and they rest not day and night, saying, Holy, holy, holy, Lord God Almighty, which was, and is, and is to come.

This phenomenon can best be discussed while keeping the seven pronouncements regarding these four beasts constantly in mind. The following characteristics constitute their scriptural description in Revelation 4:

1. THEIR NUMBER (v. 6)
2. THEIR EYES (v. 6)
3. THEIR APPEARANCE (v. 7)
4. THEIR WINGS (v. 8)

5. THEIR PERPETUAL SERVICE (v. 8)
6. THEIR MESSAGE (v. 8)
7. THEIR OFFICIAL JUDICIAL AUTHORITY
    (Rev. 6:1, 3, 5, 7; 15:7)

Bible translators have had difficulty deciding which Greek word to use in describing these beings. These "four beasts" as they are called in the King James translation are very important players in the execution of tribulation judgments. It is imperative that an accurate representation and identification be made concerning them.

Other translators call them "four living creatures" and "four living ones." Menge, in his German translation, calls them *vier lebewesen,* meaning four "living somethings." *Cassell's German-English Dictionary* defines the word *wesen* as "being, existence, creature, living thing, that which is essential or the substance of a book."(1)

When considering the above, it is not difficult to understand how these opinions in translation have evolved. Their appearance as being like a lion, calf, man, and eagle is so diverse that classifying these beings is nearly impossible which, in turn, makes their identification difficult. After considerable research, I have come to the conclusion that Menge's *lebe wesen* meaning "living somethings" and Cassell's definition of *wesen* as "the substance of a book" need to be taken seriously.

Observe first that they are not beasts, as they have wings. They are not birds, because they have six wings. They are not angels, because angels are not redeemed from every tribe. They are not men, because they rest not day or night. But they are indeed "living somethings." What are these "living somethings" which can praise God day and night and never require rest (Rev. 4:8)?

Every court needs a judge, here portrayed as God sitting upon the throne. Every court needs a jury; they are the twenty-four elders. Every court needs witnesses, and this is what we have in the four beasts. If the correct translation indeed is "four living somethings...as the substance of a book," then these four could well represent the four Gospels.

It is a well known fact that Matthew represents Christ as man, Mark represents Him as the lion, Luke as the ox (calf), and John as the eagle. It can hardly be coincidental that the four living somethings should be characterized in both the Gospels and the Book of Revelation in the same manner. It needs also to be remembered that the tribulation judgments have something to do with the full spectrum and scope of creation as seen by the participation of all creatures (Rev. 4:11; 5:13). Paul in Romans 8:19-22 declares that all creatures wait for their deliverance which will come with the redemption of the sons of God.

In addition to characterizing the four representations of Christ as portrayed in the Gospels, the four beasts also represent the four kingdoms of the creature domain: the lion, wild animals; the ox, domesticated animals; the eagle, birds; and man. All are waiting for their deliverance.

Regarding His Word, Jesus said, "Heaven and earth shall pass away, but my words shall not pass away" (Matt. 24:35). The four Gospels speak of the fulfillment of the law and the prophets and they contain the solution to the problem of sin. The four Gospels bring together all of the prophecies in the Scriptures concerning the life, death, resurrection, and return of Jesus.

The message of the plan of salvation as recorded by the four Gospel writers will be present at this universal court in the persons of Matthew, Mark, Luke, and John as symbolized by the four beasts. They bear witness that God has done His best in providing the information essential to salvation through the Gospels into which merge all the sacred writings of Scriptures.

These living creatures are filled with eyes, before and behind, which suggests that the Gospel writers saw both ways. They could see the Old Testament Scriptures being fulfilled in the life of Jesus and they were shown the Scriptures into the future which were yet unfulfilled. Ezekiel was shown a similar vision (Ezek. 1:4-28; 10:1-22). He saw the same "living ones," each with four faces for a total of sixteen faces. It seems apparent that the sixteen prophets of the Old Testament are being depicted in the sixteen faces of Ezekiel's vision.

Eyes speak of intelligence. John's "living ones" had eyes not only in their faces and behind their heads, but also within (under their wings). I understand this to mean that the four living beings possessed a cognizance that qualifies them to not only understand, but to also speak on behalf of the prophets, Moses, and the Psalms (including all poetry). These manifold eyewitnesses represent every word spoken by God through men and women who wrote according to the inspiration of the Spirit.

In 1 John 5:7 we read that "there are three that bear record in heaven, the Father, the Word, and the Holy Ghost...." Two persons of the trinity are named by their usual names. Why should Jesus be called the Word? Because that is what God said He was. That is also John's description of Him in Revelation 19:13. Jesus is the very essence and heart of the message of every Biblical messenger. It is this Word "in heaven" as depicted by the "living somethings" that will testify against mankind at this great trial.

The living thing which praises God day and night is "the word of God, which 'liveth' and abideth forever (1 Pet. 1:23). It is God's perpetual servant with no limitations. Psalm 19 is a beautiful poem explaining how the heavens have a language all of their own, affirming the veracity of the Word of God. This Word is not simply a book which we read on earth — it has a voice which is heard in heaven. Jesus said "heaven and earth would pass away (which would include all Bibles), but my word shall not pass away." God's Word is much more than a book which we call the Bible.

If the altar can speak, as in Revelation 9:13, why is it inconceivable that the Word of God can be audible? These "living somethings" (the Gospels) speak with great authority, as the Word of God often does. In Revelation 6, they are heard giving commands.

At the outset of the forty-five days designated for the pouring out of God's wrath, they stop speaking. One of them actually hands the seven vials of God's wrath to the seven angels (Rev. 15:7). I understand this to mean that God has nothing more to say. The irrevocable and point of no return has been reached.

Each of these "living somethings" has three sets of wings, a total of twelve sets. This must be a quad-triune reminder of Jesus' cry from the mount of Olives on Palm Sunday: "If only you would know what belongs to your peace, how often I would have gathered you as a hen gathers her little chicks under her wings. But you would not let me (Matt. 23:37)." The time of protection has also expired.

IV. A STRONG ANGEL
(Revelation 5:2)

And I saw a strong angel proclaiming with a loud voice, Who is worthy to open the book, and to loose the seals thereof?

In addition to a judge, jury, and witnesses, every court also needs a court clerk. This strong angel assumes this position and function. Let us consider the import of his mission.

1. His Identity:

It may not be important to know who this strong angel actually is, but it is important to recognize his power. This angel is probably Gabriel, whose name means strong, the attribute ascribed to this angel. Gabriel's function is announcer. In Daniel 8:16, he announced God's future judgments to Daniel. He also announced the births of John the Baptist and Jesus Christ.

In 2 Enoch 24:1, Gabriel "sits at the left hand of God." In 1 Enoch 40:3, he is depicted as "looking down from heaven." In 2 Enoch 21:3, he is called "one of the Lord's glorious ones." In 1 Enoch 20:7, Gabriel is referred to as "one of the holy angels," and 2 Enoch 40:9 declares "he is set over all powers." Do not think it strange that I should quote Enoch who was not included as a canonical writer. In Jude 14 and 15, Enoch is quoted as saying; "Behold, the Lord cometh with ten thousands of his saints to execute judgement upon all...." If we are talking about judgment, it is appropriate to quote an expert on the subject.

2. His Voice: "...Proclaiming with a loud voice..." (Rev. 5:2).

In the Scriptures, whether it be a trumpet, thunder, singing, or voices, the intensity of a signal exemplifies the gravity of the message. This is the reason why John was compelled to write that the voice was "loud."

3. His Question: "...'Who is worthy to open the book and to loose the seals thereof?'" (Rev. 5:2).

The nature of this question presupposes perfection and holiness as necessary to approach the book. This is a holy document that cannot be trifled with by ordinary people, an inward sanctification being necessary before touching this sacred writ. The question itself is a warning that the qualifications for touching seem unreachable by humans.

4. The Search Pursuant to the Question: "And no man in heaven, nor in earth, neither under the earth, was able to open the book, neither to look thereon" (Rev. 5:3).

The search was for a man and not an angel. Yet all men are born in sin and therefore disqualified from matters having to do with the final deliverance and redemption of man, beast, and everything that is in the world.

5. The Sad Response to the Results of the Search: "And I (John) wept much, because no man was found worthy to open and to read the book, neither to look thereon" (Rev. 5:4).

The weeping of the prophet gives evidence that failure to find the one who qualified for the execution and delivery of the contents and substance of the book would result in a very sad state of affairs for the universe. The many tears of John are a harbinger of the sorrow and grief awaiting a world where weeping would never end if no one was found worthy to open the book.

6. An Unnamed Elder: "And one of the elders said unto me, Weep not..." (Rev. 5:5).

In every court room, you will find not only a judge, jury, witnesses, and a court room clerk, you will usually also find a key witness. This elder is a key witness.

If we are talking about elders of Israel, then the patriarchs Abraham, Isaac, and Jacob must be among the twenty-four elders seated upon these thrones. Hebrews 11 records a list of those who are called elders, and Jacob is among them. This certain elder could very well be Jacob. Genesis records the account of Jacob's death and his last instructions to his sons:

> Judah is a lion's whelp: from the prey, my son, thou art gone up: he stooped down, he couched as a lion, and as an old lion; who shall rouse him up? The sceptre shall not depart from Judah, nor a lawgiver from between his feet, until Shiloh (Jesus) come; and unto him shall the gathering of the people be (Gen. 49:9-10).

127

As he was dying, Jacob saw Jesus and witnessed to his family concerning Him. He saw Jesus, whom he called "Shiloh," as a "crouching lion" coming out of the tribe of Judah. It is not a coincidence that, in comforting John, the unnamed elder says, "Behold the Lion of the tribe of Judah, the Root of David, hath prevailed to open the book, and to loose the seven seals thereof" (Rev. 5:5). The similarity between the scene in Revelation and that of Genesis could be recognized only by one who is familiar with both scenes. Up to this point, Jacob is the only one who had seen the Lion of Judah. Who but Jacob could possibly have recognized Him at the throne?

Jacob would be very interested in what would happen to his last generation. He knew much sorrow, and tears had marked a trail from his father's house when he fled from his brother's wrath to Bethel and then to Haran where his uncle Laban deceived him. He had an unreconciled past with his brother Esau and an unbearable life with his crooked uncle Laban. His unhappy surroundings and broken heart drove him back to Bethel. As he traveled, he again encountered an angel who must have been Gabriel, the announcer. Jacob fought with this angel until his hip was out of joint. It was here that Gabriel announces Jacob's new name was Israel and was told that, as a prince, he had power with God and man.

Jacob reconciled with Esau and renewed his vows with God. He then settled in Mamre were twelve sons were born. Death robbed him of his beloved Rachel and he lost his favored son, Joseph, through the deception of his own sons. His family ended up in Egypt as slaves. The wilderness wanderings, the conquest of Canaan, the battles with the surrounding heathen nations, captivity to Babylon and Assyria, and the final defeat, destruction, and dispersal by Rome is a very sad story about Jacob and his descendants.

Jacob's life was indeed filled with tears, but the worst is yet to come. The great tribulation is known in Scripture as the time of Jacob's trouble (Jer. 30:7). Tears and more tears are ahead for Israel.

7. The Encouragement He Gives to John: "Weep not, behold, the Lion of the tribe of Judah, the Root of David, hath prevailed to open the book, and to loose the seven seals thereof" (Rev. 5:5).

The weeping apostle begins to wipe the tears from his eyes. The celestial air is charged with an omnipotent electricity, for something is about to happen. There is new hope for an old problem. The darkness, sadness, and weeping of Israel will be exchanged for effervescent light and exuberant joy. Every Jew has heard about the Lion of Judah, and John was one of those Jews who knew the Lion was Jesus. John lifts his eyes to look, reacting to the words of the elder Jacob, "Behold the Lion," and instead he beheld the Lamb.

V. A LAMB
(Revelation 5:6-7)

And I beheld, and lo, in the midst of the throne and of the four beasts, and in the midst of the elders, stood a Lamb as it had been slain, having seven horns and seven eyes, which are the seven Spirits of God sent forth into all the earth.

In every court room, there is not only a judge, jury, witnesses, court room clerk, and key witness, there must also be an offended party. I hope God never lets us forget that we are responsible for the death of His Son, "the Lamb."

1. His Person:

The Lamb is Jesus. Every Jew has heard about Him, but not every Jew believes in Him. But John believed, for as he had stood beside the Jordan and heard John the Baptist say, "Behold the Lamb of God, which taketh away the sins of the world...And John himself bare record (of it)" (John 1:29, 32).

A personage with the power and courage of a Lion, yet tempered with the tenderness of a Lamb, is exactly what it will take to set things right in this world and to wipe away the tears. This personage was the Lion (who could eat a lamb) who became the Lamb who was slain and is symbolically eaten when His broken body is remembered in the Eucharist.

2. His Position:

> Wherefore God has highly exalted him, and given him a name which is above every name: that at the name of Jesus every knee should bow, of things in heaven, and things in earth, and things under the earth (Phil. 2:9-10).

3. His posture: "...Stood (as) a Lamb..." (Rev. 5:6).

Standing is not the posture the Lamb usually assumes. "He ascended into heaven, and sitteth at the right hand of God the Father Almighty" is what we affirm in the creed. There are, however, certain times when His love and pity for His people takes preference over the honor of being seated at the right hand of the Father. He will rise to His feet in honor of His suffering child as He did when Stephen was being stoned, for He knows what it means to suffer.

4. His Appearance: "...A Lamb as it had been slain..." (Rev. 5:6).

This is not a pretty picture. As a boy, I helped in the slaying of lambs. And the thing that would keep me awake at night is the fact that the lamb made absolutely no attempt to free itself. There was no fight. It simply surrendered in complete trust that its master would do it no harm.

One of the greatest prophecies concerning Jesus in the Bible declares, "...He is brought as a lamb to the slaughter, and as a sheep before her shearers is dumb, so he openeth not his mouth" (Isa. 53:7).

5. His Horns: "...Having seven horns and seven eyes, which are the seven Spirits of God, sent forth into all the earth" (Rev. 5:6).

The horns speak of the completeness of His power. He declared upon leaving this world that "all power was given unto Him. Who else can you trust with such power? In these two chapters, the twenty-four elders, the four beasts, the thousands of angels, and the many creatures all laud him for His power.

In addition to the completeness of power God vested in His Son, it needs to be pointed out that the seven horns also represent the seven angels described in Revelation 15. These are His angels, for they wear His pure white robes and golden girdle. These horns called "the seven Spirits of God sent forth into all the earth" are His angels, special cherubim or seraphim to whom will be given the awesome task of pouring the last seven vials of the wrath of God upon the world.

6. His Eyes: "...Having... seven eyes, which are the seven Spirits of God sent forth into all the earth..." (Rev. 5:6).

His seven eyes speak of His sevenfold endowment of the spirit of wisdom, understanding, counsel, might, knowledge, fear of the Lord, and judgment. These seven eyes also speak of His ability to penetrate the four horizontal directions — north, south, east and west — as well as the three vertical directions — down into earth, down into the sea, and up into the heavens.

7. His Authority: "And he came and took the book out of the right hand of him that sat upon the throne" (Rev. 5:7).

Christ's fearless approach to the throne, which was ablaze with burning white light, speaks silent volumes about His sinless perfection, worthiness, and favor with the one occupying the throne. Would not thirty-three years of faithful service and perfect obedience to His Father's will, culminating in crucifixion and death, qualify Him for such an act of authority? The angels certainly believed it did.

VI. THE MANY ANGELS
(Revelation 5:11-12)

And I beheld, and I heard the voice of many angels round about the throne, and the beasts and the elders: and the number of them was ten thousand times ten thousand, and thousands of thousands; saying with a loud voice, Worthy is the Lamb that was slain to receive power, and riches, and wisdom, and strength, and honor, and glory and blessing.

Every court needs not only a judge, jury, witnesses, court room clerk, key witness, and offended party; it also usually has spectators. Who are the spectators here? Revelation 5:9 says:

And they sung a new song, saying, Thou art worthy to take the book, and to open the seals thereof: for thou wast slain and hast redeemed us to God by thy blood out of every kindred, and tongue, and people, and nation.

These redeemed ones are the raptured Gentile Church in heaven who were taken out of the world before the storm strikes. Let us consider this unrehearsed, spontaneous, sevenfold doxology sung by 10,000,000 plus still thousands of thousands more.

WORTHY IS THE LAMB THAT WAS SLAIN, TO RECEIVE:

1. POWER
2. RICHES
3. WISDOM
4. STRENGTH
5. HONOUR
6. GLORY
7. BLESSING

Anything that kings, queens, presidents, prime ministers, premiers, politicians, actors, common people, or uncommon people have ever sought after is here articulated. Wealth, fame, popularity, power, praise, honor, luxury, or whatever else you might wish, are all a part of our Lord's exaltation.

Vainly men go about seeking after these things, believing they can be obtained without taking up their cross as did our Savior. His people will be surprised one day to learn they have inherited all of this with Him by just faithfully loving and serving Him, never thinking about the rewards while in the world.

Heaven is too small to contain the worship and praise which is about to erupt. An omnipotent electrical wave of worship and praise spills over the battlements of heaven. Every nerve created by the Alpha and Omega is energized unto His praise. A contagious spontaneous concert of praise bursts into the stratosphere. A tidal wave of worship now fills the universe. Joining the celestial is the terrestrial, which includes every creature.

VII. THE UNIVERSAL PRAISE EVENT
(Revelation 5:13-14)

And every creature which is in heaven, and on the earth, and under the earth, and such as are in the sea, and all that are in them, heard I saying, Blessing, and honour, and glory, and power, be unto him that sitteth upon the throne, and unto the lamb for ever and ever.

1. HEAVEN RESPONDS
2. PRAISE FROM THE TERRESTRIAL AND SUBTERRANEAN
3. REACTION FROM THE WATERS
4. BLESSING BESTOWED UPON THE LAMB
5. HONOUR ASCRIBED TO GOD
6. ACCOLADES OF GLORY GIVEN HIM
7. ACKNOWLEDGMENT OF POWER

What is the meaning of this universal spiritual jubilation? The celestial colliding with the terrestrial in a thunderous discharge of praise: "Shalom, Shalom, Praise Jehovah and the Lamb, Hallelujah, Hosanna, Peace on Earth, Amen, Amen", is what they say. This, my friends, is the drama of universal deliverance being played out according to the foreknowledge of God. This is what Paul talked about when he said,

> For the earnest expectation of the creature waiteth for the manifestation of the sons of God...For we know that the whole creation groaneth in pain waiting for the REDEMP-TION!" (Rom. 8:19- 23, author's translation).

The whole creation has been waiting for this redemption and deliverance!

Isaiah records his similar vision:

> The wolf and the lamb shall feed together, and the lion shall eat straw like the bullock: and dust shall be the serpent's meat. They shall not hurt nor destroy in all my holy mountain, saith the Lord (Isa. 65:25).

IT STARTED IN A GARDEN, IT WILL END IN A GARDEN!

God did not give these pronouncements to convince the twenty-four elders, the four living Ones, the strong angel, the unnamed elder, the 10.000,000 + thousands of thousands of angels, or every living creature in heaven, on earth or in the sea, that He is the everlasting God and Creator of the universe and that His Son is the Redeemer. He did not give these pronouncements to convince any of these named above that His Son is the Redeemer and that both He and His Son are worthy of worship. These chapters are given to those who were not included in this the greatest praise event. This message is being sent to men on earth who are the object and reason for all that has transpired.

Man needs to understand that judgment is coming and that Christ the Lamb intends to set everything straight. Satan needs to understand that his domain and princehood over this world are almost over. God has pronounced to the universe that the Lamb will be the universal King.

The antichrist, about to emerge on the scene in Europe will not be the greatest leader the world has ever known. Neither will his eighteen-nation confederacy about to be formed through the European Economic Community be the greatest kingdom.

God always has the last word. The greatest leader the world will ever know is JESUS CHRIST, who will reign over the greatest kingdom that man has ever seen. Under the reign of the Lord Jesus Christ, the world will enjoy peace for 1,000 years.

In the mind of God, the universal court and tribunal are in place. God has informed man of all of this for nearly 2,000 years. Every detail for justice has been provided. Seven divinely selected participants will give their consent to the conquests of Christ over Satan. The Bible, which has always been the most widely circulated book in the world, is available for all to ponder over these things. God is already stirring Himself in the heavens as the signs of His coming multiply and intensify. The warning: "Prepare to meet thy God."

From this point on, we must carefully keep our eyes upon the little book within the Book of Revelation whose seals we must interpret. Its contents cover the three and a half years of Jacob's trouble that is known as the great tribulation and the forty-five days when the vials of God's wrath will be poured out, the period of time known as THAT GREAT AND TERRIBLE DAY OF THE LORD!

WHAT THE WORLD WILL BE LIKE PRIOR TO THE TRIBULATION

The New World Order

There is a great deal of excitement on the continent of Europe today. The reunification of Germany, the collapse of communism in Eastern Europe with the nod for democracy to replace it, and many of the Baltic states gaining independence are all signals that major changes are imminent. The infant Commonwealth of Independent States is experiencing political claustrophobia as unrest with fears of civil war are closing in upon it. These conditions, along with others, are captivating the political imagination of New World Order-thinkers today.

The European Economic Community (E.E.C.), with its political, economic, and other manifold complexities, is struggling to achieve a workable blueprint for economic unity by the end of 1992. That there is an urgency about this ambition cannot be denied. Leaders like Margaret Thatcher, who was not so enthusiastically inclined about rushing into this kind of unified arrangement, had to be removed so that this obsession could be realized. The day will come, perhaps sooner than imagined, that many will regret her resignation and wish they had heeded her reservations as the negative implications of the new world order actually become a reality.

The formation of the European Common Market, known as the "Treaty of Rome" which was created in 1957, now has a membership of twelve countries. The term "European Economic Community" is a hot phrase in Europe today, and it illustrates the spectrum of cultures which the community must one day unify. COMUNITA' EUROPEA, EUPQIIAIKH KOINOTHE, EUROPAEISKE FAEL-LESSKAB, EUROPAEISCHE GEMEINSCHAFT, COMMUNAUTE' EUROPE'ENNE, EUROPESE GEMEENSCHAP, COMUNIDAD EUROPEIA, COMUNIDAD EUROPEA and EUROPEAN COMMUNITY are the various ways the term is pronounced. Belgium, Denmark, France, Great Britain, Greece, Ireland, Italy, Luxembourg, Holland, Portugal, Spain, and Germany are the nations currently constituting the membership of the E.E.C.

Euorpeans Surveyed

Recently, my wife Ruth and I made a trip to Europe. The prime purpose was to conduct a survey and collect data for this manuscript. One of the twenty questions on the survey was, "Do you think the E.E.C. will be good for Europe? Why or why not?" Every response was positive. The following are some of the responses I received:

- "The E.E.C. will create a Europe without internal borders or restrictions."
- "A Europe where war is virtually an impossibility."
- "A more successful Europe."
- "Lower prices."
- "Less unemployment".
- "No shortages."
- "Unrestricted trade."
- "Better social health programs."
- "Open opportunities for work in other countries".

- "Stiffer competition with the U.S.A. and Asian countries."
- "Relaxed freedoms."
- "A safer continent."
- "No more drug smuggling."
- "A better future for our children."
- "Less expenditures for armaments."
- "An irresistible, super super-power that will keep all other nations from fighting with each other."

Other questions on the questionnaire were:

- Do you feel a common currency must be in place in order to have a workable financial system in operation? Most answered favorably, with a few of the more knowledgeable respondents saying, "There already is such a system in place called ECU (European Currency Unit)."

- Do you expect, if a united Europe would ever become a reality, that it would be necessary to have just one leader? By far, the majority answered, "NO." They greatly resented the innuendo that they might lose their autonomy.

- Have you ever heard of the antichrist? Only a few answered, "YES."

- Have you ever heard of the number 666? Most of the answers were, "NO." A few said, "YES, it is the devil's number."

- Have you ever heard of the battle of Armageddon? Most answered "NO".

- Do you think there will ever be a nuclear war? Most answered, "NO," but several answered, "YES, in Asia."

- Do you think the world will come to an end some day? Most answered, "NO." A few said, "YES, in millions of years when the sun burns itself out." A few said, "YES, when Jesus Christ returns."

- Do you believe in Christ's return?   The majority answered, "NO."

Biblical Truths

As you continue reading, you will discover that the Bible declares the following:

- Although the European Economic Community was organized by democracies, in the final analysis it will become the most ruthless dictatorship the world has ever known, ultimately evolving into the New World Order spoken about today.

- While the E.E.C. has designs for a peaceful world, it will eventually find itself in a colossal conflict because of Israel, culminating in the battle of Armageddon.

- The people of Europe assume that each of their countries will remain autonomous and self-governing. Eventually, they will discover that expediency will necessitate the appointment of one leader over this European Confederacy. The Scriptures describe him as the "antichrist," the "beast" or the "son of perdition" who will rule Europe and many other countries of the world,

- Liberty is considered to be the hallmark of the E.E.C., and freedom of worship will be assumed automatic. The final reality will be compulsory worship of this leader. Those refusing to comply to such homage will be killed.

- The people of Europe cannot foresee a world church or a religious world leader emerging. Eventually, they will discover that a religious world leader will become a powerful associate of the antichrist as well as a key player in politics.

- Europeans believe that the monetary system called ECU (European Currency Unit), now in place, will serve as the medium of commercial exchange and trade. However, the Bible reveals that a mark (or the symbolic number 666) on the right hand or forehead will replace the ECU and become the mandatory currency expression necessary to conduct trade and commerce in much of the world. Those refusing to accept this mark will be killed.

- Europeans cannot perceive that Israel will play much of a role in future world politics. But it will be their own leader, the antichrist, who will sign a seven-year peace treaty with Israel. The terms of the treaty will include a guarantee to protect Israel from military attack and freedom to worship in their newly built temple. However, in the middle of the seven years, the leader will break his pact with Israel and enthrone himself in the temple, declaring himself to be God. This sacrilegious act will ignite the three-and-a-half-year period known in the Scriptures as the great tribulation and it will culminate in the battle of Armageddon and the end of the world!

Before proceeding with Revelation 6 and the execution of the seals of the book that the Lamb has taken from the Father's hand in Revelation 5, we need to determine where we are in history. In Matthew 24:15 Jesus instructs us that Daniel has pertinent information that relates to this specific time.

In the last chapter of Daniel, we encounter the archangel Michael, standing as the protector of Israel, for "there shall be a time of trouble, such as never was since there was a nation" (Dan. 12:1). Later in the chapter, the question is asked, "How long will it be to the end of these wonders (vs. 6)?" In other words, how long will Michael be required to protect Israel and how long will this time of trouble persist?

The answer is given in these words, "It shall be for a time (one year), times (two years) and an half (six months)" (Dan. 12:7). The last part of this verse implies that it will take the antichrist three and a half years to scatter the power of Israel. This will end Michael's vigil, "finishing" whatever history was sealed in the book.

A second record of this important historical time reference point is given in Revelation 12, where it is again called a "wonder." Israel is depicted as a pregnant woman, and Michael is again seen as defending her. The duration of her protection is recorded as "a thousand, two hundred and threescore days" (Rev. 12:6). In comparing these two Scriptures, it is clear they speak about the same personages and the same period of time. Whatever is to transpire during these 1,260 days is what Daniel was commanded to seal in a book.

Daniel was given very precise time information in 12:11-12. The disclosure is that from the day the contract is broken and the image of the antichrist set up in the temple to the end of Michael's vigil (the 1,260 day tribulation) will be 1,290 days. What are we to make of the thirty day difference between the two accounts, 1,260 versus 1,290? The first 30 days of the 1,290 days are given to Israel as an ultimatum and response time to worship or not to worship the image. These thirty days are not regarded to be a part of the three-and-a-half-year tribulation. This harmonizes with the action of Darius when a similar situation existed regarding dictator worship. Daniel remembered this experience very well, for because of it he was cast into the den of lions (Dan. 6:7).

Israel's trouble ends after 1,260 plus 30 days (1,290 days) when the contents of the sealed book are exhausted, as seen in Revelation 10:6-8. Then, Israel is raptured away as seen in Revelation 11:12-18 and 15:2 (also referenced in Matt. 24:29-31). The additional 45 days (Dan. 12:11-12), from 1,290 to 1,335 days, are known as the wrath of God or "that great and terrible day of the Lord" from which Israel is spared. Jesus refers to this period as the "shortened days" (Matt. 24:22).

According to Daniel 9:27, the breaking of the contract takes place in the middle of the week (after three and a half 'day years' have expired). The breaking of the covenant is the signal that there are only 1,335 (1,260+30+45) days to Armageddon.

Having established that Israel's troubles begin with the setting up of an image of the antichrist in the temple, we are prepared to pursue the explosive situation created by such a sacrilegious act. To this point, I have asked you to assume that the antichrist who sets up his image in the temple will be the leader of the European Economic Community. I must now proceed in qualifying this assumption.

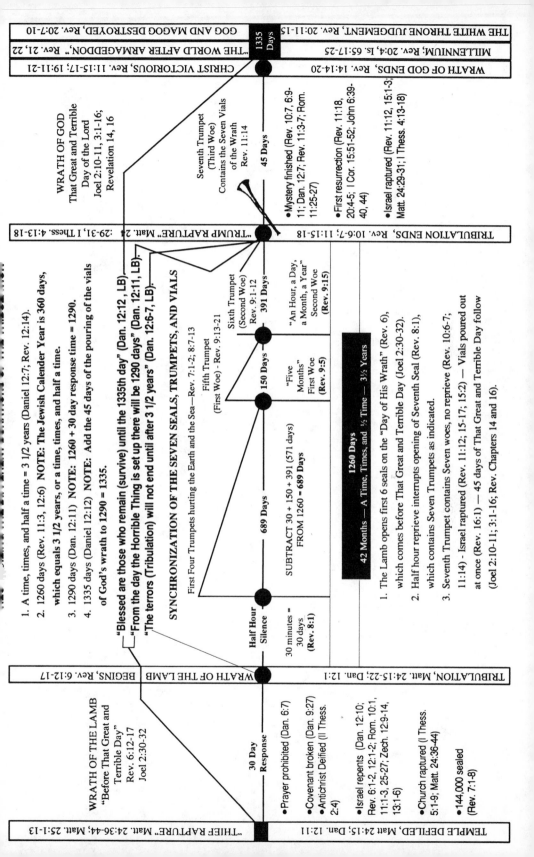

SYNCHRONIZATION OF THE SEVEN SEALS, TRUMPETS, AND VIALS

GOG AND MAGOG DESTROYED, Rev. 20:7-10

THE WHITE THRONE JUDGEMENT, Rev. 20:11-15

"THE WORLD AFTER ARMAGEDDON," Rev. 21, 22

MILLENNIUM, Rev. 20:4, Is. 65:17-25

CHRIST VICTORIOUS, Rev. 11:15-17; 19:11-21

WRATH OF GOD ENDS, Rev. 14:14-20

1335 Days

WRATH OF GOD
That Great and Terrible
Day of the Lord
Joel 2:10-11, 3:1-16;
Revelation 14, 16

Seventh Trumpet
(Third Woe)
Contains the Seven Vials
of the Wrath
Rev. 11:14

45 Days

- Mystery finished (Rev. 10:7; 6:9-11; Dan. 12:7; Rev. 11:3-7; Rom. 11:25-27)
- First resurrection (Rev. 11:18, 20:4-5; I Cor. 15:51-52; John 6:39-40, 44)
- Israel raptured (Rev. 11:12, 15:1-3; Matt. 24:29-31; I Thess. 4:13-18)

"TRUMP RAPTURE" Matt. 24:29-31, I Thess. 4:13-18

TRIBULATION ENDS, Rev. 10:6-7; 11:15-18

1. A time, times, and half a time = 3 1/2 years (Daniel 12:7; Rev. 12:14).
2. 1260 days (Rev. 11:3, 12:6) NOTE: The Jewish Calender Year is 360 days, which equals 3 1/2 years, or a time, times, and half a time.
3. 1290 days (Dan. 12:11) NOTE: 1260 + 30 day response time = 1290.
4. 1335 days (Daniel 12:12) NOTE: Add the 45 days of the pouring of the vials of God's wrath to 1290 = 1335.

"Blessed are those who remain (survive) until the 1335th day" (Dan. 12:12, LB)
"From the day the Horrible Thing is set up there will be 1290 days" (Dan. 12:11, LB).
"The terrors (Tribulation) will not end until after 3 1/2 years" (Dan. 12:6-7, LB).

First Four Trumpets hurting the Earth and the Sea—Rev. 7:1-2; 8:7-13

Sixth Trumpet
(Second Woe)
Rev. 9:1-12

"An Hour, a Day, a Month, a Year"
Second Woe
(Rev. 9:15)

391 Days

Fifth Trumpet
(First Woe) - Rev. 9:13-21

"Five Months"
First Woe
(Rev. 9:5)

150 Days

689 Days

SUBTRACT 30 + 150 + 391 (571 days) FROM 1260 = **689 Days**

1260 Days

42 Months — A Time, Times, and 1/2 Years — 3 1/2 Years

1. The Lamb opens first 6 seals on the "Day of His Wrath" (Rev. 6), which comes before That Great and Terrible Day (Joel 2:30-32).
2. Half hour reprieve interrupts opening of Seventh Seal (Rev. 8:1), which contains Seven Trumpets as indicated.
3. Seventh Trumpet contains Seven woes, no reprieve (Rev. 10:6-7; 11:14) - Israel raptured (Rev. 11:12; 15-17; 15:2) — Vials poured out at once (Rev. 16:1) — 45 days of That Great and Terrible Day follow (Joel 2:10-11; 3:1-16; Rev. Chapters 14 and 16).

Half Hour
Silence

30 minutes = 30 days (Rev. 8:1)

TRIBULATION, Matt. 24:15-22, Dan. 12:1

WRATH OF THE LAMB BEGINS, Rev. 6:12-17

WRATH OF THE LAMB
"Before That Great and Terrible Day"
Rev. 6:12-17
Joel 2:30-32

30 Day Response

- Prayer prohibited (Dan. 6:7).
- Covenant broken (Dan. 9:27).
- Antichrist Deified (II Thess. 2:4).
- Israel repents (Dan. 12:10; Rev. 6:1-2, 12:1-2; Rom. 10:1, 11:1-3, 25-27; Zech. 12:9-14; 13:1-6).
- Church raptured (I Thess. 5:1-9; Matt. 24:36-44).
- 144,000 sealed (Rev. 7:1-8).

"THIEF RAPTURE," Matt. 24:36-44, Matt. 25:1-13

TEMPLE DEFILED, Matt. 24:15; Dan. 12:11

CHAPTER FOUR

FORTY-NINE PRONOUNCEMENTS REGARDING THE SEVEN TRIBULATION PARTICIPANTS

1. THE BEAST OUT OF THE SEA
   (Revelation 13:1-10)
2. THE BEAST OUT OF THE EARTH
   (Revelation 13:11-18)
3. THE BEAST CARRYING THE MOTHER OF HARLOTS
   (Revelation 17)
4. THE WONDER OF THE PREGNANT WOMAN
   (Revelation 12)
5. MICHAEL AND THE DRAGON
   (Revelation 12:7-17)
6. THE 144,000 FAITHFUL WITNESSES
   (Revelation 7:1-8; 14:1-5)
7. THE TWO WONDER-WORKING WITNESSES
   (Revelation 11:3-12)

Revelation 6 introduces a systematic study of the Book of Revelation. The little book with seven seals covers the tribulation chronologically; however, the continuity is broken many times as the apostle periodically sees separate visions of the seven tribulation participants interjected between the seals, trumpets, and vials.

143

Before we can understand the seven seals, we must first understand the meaning of the interjected visions regarding the seven tribulation participants. These participants have an important commonality. As all of them have a three-and-a-half-year tenure, this can only mean they are contemporaries.

The two witnesses prophesy for three and a half years (Rev. 11:3). The woman is preserved for three and a half years (Rev. 12:6). The beast's tenure is limited to three and a half years (Rev. 13:5). The 144,000 are sealed before the storm (tribulation) begins (Rev. 7:1-3) and appear again after the tribulation ends (Rev. 14:1-5; 15:1-2), which is three and a half years later. The dragon pursues the woman and her seed for three and a half years (Rev. 12:6). The false prophet is always present with the antichrist (Rev. 13:11-16) and is captured with him at the end of the three and a half years (Rev. 19:20). While the mother of harlots is described as having a long history of killing apostles and prophets, she is depicted riding the beast of Revelation 13 during his three-and-a-half-year rampage and is then destroyed at the end of the tribulation (Rev. 17:16; 19:2).

As we consider each of the above participants in detail and observe the constant struggle between them because of Israel, we clearly see they are players in the same drama. I invite you to a front row seat as we watch each participant entering the stage of tribulation drama.

I. THE BEAST OUT OF THE SEA (Revelation 13:1-10)

This thirteenth chapter depicts an evil trinity viciously fulfilling the wishes of Satan during the tribulation. The first beast with the seven heads and ten horns represents the antichrist and the kingdom over which he presides. The beast with the two horns like a lamb is the false prophet. The dragon is Satan (Rev. 12:9). Expect nothing good from this wicked triumverate.

> And I stood upon the sand of the sea, and saw a beast rise up out of the sea, having seven heads and ten horns, and upon his horns ten crowns, and upon his heads the name of blasphemy. And the beast which I saw was like unto a leopard, and his feet were as the feet of a bear, and his mouth as the mouth of a lion: and the dragon gave him his power, and his seat, and great authority. And I saw one of his heads as it were wounded to death; and his deadly wound was healed: and all the world wondered after the beast. And they worshipped the dragon which gave power unto the beast: and they worshipped the beast saying, Who is like unto the beast? Who is able to make war with him?
>
> And there was given unto him a mouth speaking great things and blasphemies; and power was given unto him to continue forty and two months. And he opened his mouth in blasphemy against God, to blaspheme his name, and his tabernacle, and them that dwell in heaven. And it was given unto him to make war with the saints, and to overcome them: and power was given him over all kindreds, and tongues and nations. And all that dwell upon the earth shall worship him, whose names are not written in the book of life of the Lamb slain from the foundation of the world (Rev. 13:1-8).

The beast with ten horns and seven heads described in the above passage typifies the European Economic Community (soon to become known as the New World order) and its leader. Watch for a very clever, popular, young man, probably a Jew and possibly thirty years of age, who will rise up out of the E.E.C. to emerge as its leader.

According to Ezekiel (chapters 38 and 39), there will be a war between Israel and Russia which Israel will win. It could very well be

145

that at this point the leader of the newly formed E.E.C. will come to the aid of the weakened and now vulnerable nation of Israel to sign the seven-year peace treaty with them. Protection against aggressors would be guaranteed and freedom to build and worship in their new temple assured. How can we identify this leader and the kingdom over which he will preside?

1. The Ancient Origin of the European Economic Community:

Some of the Scriptures describing the beast employ a figure of speech known as a synecdoche, meaning the whole is referred to as a part or a part as the whole. For example, in Revelation 13:1, John sees the beast in terms of a plurality with his seven heads and ten horns. At the same time he is referred to in the singular as being the "eighth" (Rev. 17:11). The beast may be spoken of as a singular person, the antichrist. On other occasions, because of the synecdochial nature of the text, references may allude to the kingdom he controls.

In tracing a family tree, you usually begin with the most distant ancestor at the top of the family tree structure and then proceed downward, filling in the names of his progeny. Following this procedure, we can determine the origin of the beast. We would begin with the mouth at the top which John said was that of a lion. The branches are his legs and feet which John said were those of a bear. The body is that of a leopard. The ten horns and seven heads represent ten monarchs and seven dictators. The mystery of his origin is to be found in his lion-like mouth, bear-like feet, leopard-like body, and ten-horned head. Daniel records a similar vision of four beasts, a lion, a bear, a leopard, and a dreadful beast with ten horns all rising up out of the sea (waters of humanity) in Daniel 7:1-7.

Scholars generally agree that the lion represents Babylon (612-539 B.C.), the bear represents Medo-Persia (539-331 B.C.), the leopard represents Greece (331-63 B.C.), and the ten-horned beast represents the Roman Empire (63 B.C.-1453 A.D.).

The link between the two ten-horned beasts of Daniel and Revelation is found in the little horn that sprouted out from among the ten. This little horn had eyes and a mouth speaking great things. A careful study of Daniel 7 reveals that this horn shall become great in the last days and his tenure is to be three and a half years (Dan. 7:25). This little horn with the "big mouth" is also called a beast (Dan. 7:11). No doubt this "little horn" beast is the one John sees centuries later with the distinguishing features of a lion, bear, and leopard. It also had ten horns which represent the revival of the old Roman Empire after 1,500 years of dormancy (Rev. 13:1-5).

The fact that Christ is destined to destroy Daniel's big-mouthed beast (Dan. 7:11-14), as well as John's beast with the big mouth (Rev. 13:5; 19:20), verifies they are the same personage. Further, Daniel's beast persecutes the Jews in the last days for three and a half years (Dan. 7:24-25), as does John's beast (Rev. 13:5-7). It is obvious the leader of the E.E.C. will not be on good terms with Israel.

The boundaries of the E.E.C. will extend over a large section of the world, more specifically the land mass over which Rome presided at its apex. This will include Israel, the Mediterranean rim, and much of the Arab world. According to the imagery depicted by the two prophets, it seems quite clear that the European Economic Community is a political and geographic evolution originating with Babylon, continuing on with Medo-Persia, Greece, and finally Rome. Its boundaries will be basically the same as those of the Old Roman Empire.

2. His Personal Diabolical Origin:

Jesus Christ, the Son of God, was conceived by the Holy Spirit and born of a virgin. The antichrist, the son of Satan, will probably be conceived by Satan himself. The Bible clearly teaches that the dragon (Satan) will give the beast his power (Rev. 13:4). In Genesis 3:15, God says, "I will put enmity between thy seed (Satan's) and her seed (Eve's). This certainly suggests some kind of Satanic genetics. It must always be remembered that the antichrist will be a deceiver and will himself be exploited by the devil. A miraculous birth like Jesus' birth would be a very advantageous springboard that Satan could use to introduce the antichrist to the world.

We have seen how Saddam Hussein is exploiting religion to deceive his people. The language of war is increasingly being wrapped in verbal packages that are passionately religious. The real impostor will appear on the scene employing what will be perceived by the world as the miraculous power of God. Can you think of a better way to deceive the Jews into thinking the antichrist is the Messiah than by claiming spirit conception and calling fire down from heaven like Elijah did (Rev. 13:13)?

The antichrist will be meticulously versed in the four Gospels. He will know more about the details of Christ's life than the average Christian. His ability to mimic the miracles of Christ will catapult him into the limelight in a very short time.

Most of us are familiar with the Scripture which says, "And I will put enmity between thee and the woman, and between thy seed and her seed; and it shall bruise thy head, and thou shalt bruise his heel" (Gen. 3:15). We know that the seed of the woman spoken of here is Christ as it is He who will bruise Satan's head. "Thy seed" speaks of Satan's seed, which means that Satan has a son. Who else could it be but the antichrist?

Ezekiel knew about this hundreds of years ago when he recorded a message of God for the prince of Tyrus in Ezekiel 28:1-10. There can be little doubt that Ezekiel was speaking of the antichrist. God also had a message for the king of Tyrus in Ezekiel 28:11-18, who is obviously Satan. If the king of Tyrus is Satan, then the prince (who must always be a king's son) has to be the antichrist. It is a terrifying thing to discover that the man who will govern much of the world, probably within the next decade or two, will be the son of the devil.

3. His Ultra Deceptive Character:

The antichrist will be a living enigma who visibly presents himself as a benevolent and well intentioned charismatic leader. In his heart, however, he will be a deceiver and liar just like his "father." He will be very effective in presenting himself as a properly religious person (Dan. 11:38). In reality, he will be a blasphemer of Jehovah God (Rev. 13:16). Of this we can be certain: he will deceive the masses by both his benevolence and his evil deeds. The Scriptures declare that "he shall work deceitfully" (Dan. 11:23). Paul warns that he will come "with all deceivableness of unrighteousness" (2 Thess. 2:10).

He will be a man of convincing eloquence, obtaining "the kingdom by flatteries" (Dan. 11:21). Daniel and John both made special note of the antichrist's communication skills (Dan. 7:8, 11, 25; Rev. 13:5-6) with expressions like: "A mouth speaking great things," "because of the voice of the great words which the horn spake," "he shall speak great things against the most High," "a mouth speaking great things and blasphemies," and "he opened his mouth in blasphemy

148

against God...." Whether he uses his mouth in boasting about his accomplishments or to impress the wicked by how eloquently he can blaspheme God, it is always for the purpose of deception.

The Psalmist describes the antichrist's words as being "smoother than butter, but war was in his heart: his words were softer than oil, yet were they drawn swords" (Ps. 55:21). In Isaiah 14:13-14, he makes five boasts beginning with "I will": "I will ascend into heaven...I will exalt my throne above the stars of God...I will sit upon the mount of the congregation on the sides of the north...I will ascend above the heights of the clouds...I will be like the most High."

Isaiah 14:12 is frequently understood to be referring to Satan because Lucifer is named. However, look closely at what the text is saying: "How art thou fallen from heaven, O Lucifer, son of the morning." The fact that the word son is used would support other translations which do not mention Lucifer but refer instead to "his son." In the Menge translation, this son is called "son of the morning redness." Isaiah 14:16 says further that those who look upon him will say, "Is this the man that made the earth to tremble, that did shake kingdoms?" As Satan is not a man (he is a fallen angel), the reference here to a "man" would have to be regarding his son, the antichrist.

The eyes of antichrist were also noticed by the prophet Daniel, who spoke of seeing "...eyes like the eyes of a man..." (Dan. 7:8). Eyes speak of intelligence, and Daniel went on to say that he was a "...king of fierce countenance, and understanding dark sentences..." (Dan. 8:23). This has to do with soothsaying, witchcraft, and other diabolical predictions originating from the kingdom of darkness. The antichrist will overwhelm the populace with sensationalism as he "...forecast(s) his devices against his strong holds, even for a time" (Dan. 11:24). He will do this by going on television and radio to broadcast accurately what he will do one year ("...a time...") in advance. This will greatly impress his citizens.

4. Europe, a Model for World Government:

Just prior to the rapture, the world will be very dangerous. Thousands of missiles (armed with nuclear, chemical, biological, and conventional warheads) will be in constant readiness for deployment from the land, air, and seas around the world. Sophisticated electronic weaponry will be on alert everywhere. Millions of ground forces will stand ready. Countries who can scarcely feed their own people will be spending billions on defense.

A solution, albeit robed in death, will come on the horizon as the antichrist, with his slick tongue and deceitful character, and convinces the world that he is the man for the hour. Prophetic Scriptures such as "he shall come in peaceably...obtain(ing) the kingdom by flatteries" (Dan. 11:21-24) are now on the threshold of being fulfilled. He will flirt with the religions of the world through his alliance with a religious world leader (the false prophet), confusing and deceiving many. The miracles this duo will perform through satanic power will attract millions.

The Jews have always insisted on a miracle as evidence that Jehovah is on their side. A satanic miracle will change things overnight and the Jews will be indisputably convinced that this is the Messiah they have long awaited. They will be won over by his religious demeanor, saying, "The only way the world can possibly be safe is if a single man controls the war arsenals of all the world. This is the man we have waited for."

Many will exclaim:

> ...Who is like unto the beast? Who is able to make war with him...he doeth great wonders, so that he maketh fire come down from heaven on the earth in the sight of men and deceiveth them that dwell on the earth by the means of those miracles...(Rev. 13:4, 13-14).

The first three and a half years of the antichrist's reign will impress the world for "through his policy also he shall cause craft to prosper in his hand..." (Dan. 8:25). He will be wonderfully creative, with many new electronic and mechanical wonders emerging up under his administration. With the coming of new inventions, factories will spring up everywhere, creating wide-spread employment which will generate contentment, pleasure, and well-being. Unemployment will probably be non-existent.

The antichrist will be very wealthy (Dan. 11:28). He will introduce a monetary system mysteriously based on the number 666 which will somehow be affixed to the hand or forehead of individuals either as a tattoo or minuscule sub-skin computer chip (Rev. 13:16-18). Coins, bills, cheques, credit cards, and other mediums of exchange will be eliminated. A tattoo, computer chip, or laser impression (exclusively registered to its wearer) would have many benefits. Robbery of money and the murder associated with it would be eliminated. Drug traffic, bootlegging, gambling, and prostitution would be hard pressed to improvise a mechanism whereby they could survive financially. This would greatly reduce crime and, consequently, the cost of servicing it as well.

However, the mark presents two problems. First, in order to receive it, one must worship the image of the beast (Rev. 13:15). Homage to the beast invokes the wrath of God upon the worshipper with no possibility of forgiveness and an automatic sentence to an eternity in hell (Rev. 14:9-11). Second, the Scriptures forbid the application of a tattoo upon God's people (Lev. 19:28). God alone, through the rite of circumcision for the Jews and baptism for Christians, reserves the right to place a mark or seal of ownership and covenantal responsibility upon those who identify with Him.

The first three and a half years of the seven-year contract with Israel will yield phenomenal successes. To many it will appear that the announcement by the angels on the night of Christ's birth, "...On earth peace, good will toward men," has finally come to pass (Luke 2:14). Europe will be the most affluent continent on earth, the model and envy of mankind. However, there is a very sad story yet to be told.

The story ends with the decimation of Europe and with it the entire world, terminating at Armageddon. This should bring back a few memories to those short-sighted Conservative parliamentarians who were concerned only about their political futures, while another saw a dangerous world ahead. She dared to stand firm in her convictions, even if it cost her position as Prime Minister of Great Britain. Her opposers will regret the day they voted Margaret Thatcher out of office because she insisted on saying, "No! No! No!"

5. His Names - the Origin of His Person - the Source of His
   Power:

The various writers of the Scriptures have depicted the character of the antichrist, either directly or by inference, as a double crosser,

151

bloody, and deceitful (Ps. 55:20-23); a king of fierce countenance (Dan. 8:23); the man of sin, son of perdition, wicked (2 Thess. 2:3, 8); the antichrist (1 John 2:18, 22); the beast (Rev. 13:1-8); from the pit (Rev. 17:8); and the one who comes in his own name (John 5:43).

As to the origin of his person, we encounter a sad possibility. Judas Iscariot, the disciple who betrayed his Lord, is also referred to in the Scriptures by some of the above names. I ask you to carefully consider these tragic implications. The Jewish expectation for the Messiah presupposes him to be a "son of David." Matthew went into great genealogical detail to convince the world that Jesus is the Christ (Messiah) because of His Davidic extraction (Matt. 1:1-17).

While the Bible does not specifically state that the antichrist must be of Davidic genealogy, it is commonly agreed that Jews would not acknowledge him as the Messiah unless he was. Their Palm Sunday cry (Mark 11:10) was, "Blessed be the kingdom of our father David, that cometh in the name of the Lord: Hosanna in the highest," which revealed the common consensus of Jews.

Judas Iscariot, the man from Kerioth and the only disciple from Judea, is the son of Simon Iscariot who was a descendant of David. The prophecies regarding the birth of the Messiah are that He will be a descendant of David, born in Bethlehem of Judea. As touching the origin of his person and birthplace, Judas accommodates prophecy in that he is a Jew of the line of David and was born in Judea.

The antichrist must also meet the demands of the law met by Jesus, namely circumcision. In the record regarding the assassination of the antichrist, there is an interesting sentence which reads, "Thou (antichrist) shalt die the deaths of the uncircumcised by the hand of strangers..." (Ezek. 28:10). The inference is that even though he was a circumcised Jew, this will not avert his ignoble death in dying like an uncircumcised Gentile. As touching the demands of the law regarding circumcision, both antichrist and Judas qualify.

The process in identifying the antichrist oscillates around a triangle comparing Jesus, Judas, and the antichrist. A guiding principle in recognizing the antichrist will be his ability to repeat the miracles, signs, and wonders performed by Jesus during His earthly mission. While the Bible draws attention to the false prophet (the second beast) as being the miracle worker, there is a statement in Revelation 13:12

that he will "[exercise] all the power of the first beast." This implies that the first beast (the antichrist) was able to perform the same miracles.

Nowhere in Scripture are we prohibited from attempting to identify the antichrist. On the contrary, our intelligence is challenged to decipher his person by these words: "Here is wisdom. Let him that hath understanding count the number of the beast: for it is the number of a man; and his number is Six hundred threescore and six (666)" (Rev. 13:18).

The following Scriptures are prophecies concerning the Messiah. These are the evidences the Jews will be looking for in their Messiah:

> The blind receive their sight, and the lame walk, the lepers are cleansed, and the deaf hear, the dead are raised up, and the poor have the gospel preached to them (Matt. 11:5).

> The spirit of the Lord is upon me, because he hath annointed me to preach the gospel to the poor; he hath sent me to heal the brokenhearted, to preach deliverance to the captives, and recovering of sight to the blind, to set at liberty them that are bruised, to preach the acceptable year of the Lord (Luke 4:18-19 [Isa. 61:1 paraphrased]).

The works surrounding the ministry of Jesus on earth were performed primarily so the world would know He is the Christ (Messiah), the Son of God. His miracles and deeds of love certainly give evidence to His messianic qualifications.

In attempting to identify the antichrist, we must look for one who will mimic the things that Jesus was, stood for and did. Jesus, the true Messiah, was called a deceiver in Matthew 27:63. When the real deceiver appears, people will ask, "Who is like unto the beast?" He will be wonderfully successful in deceiving the Jews.

At about 90 A.D., when the Book of Revelation was written, John was told that the solution to identifying the mysterious beast would be found in the four clues of Revelation 17:8. This Scripture says the beast:

- Was (lived and died before John wrote the Revelation);
- Is not (his physical body was not visible in the world at that time);
- (His spirit) shall ascend out of the bottomless pit (when he enters the antichrist either at his birth or resurrection);
- (He will) go into perdition (after he is defeated at Armageddon [Rev. 19:20]).

The truth of his ascending out of the pit is further substantiated in Revelation 11:7 where we are told that it is the beast from the pit who kills the two witnesses.

Judas lived before the Revelation was written (he was); he committed suicide (he is not); he went to his own place (Acts 1:25) which probably is the bottomless pit; and he must again ascend out of the bottomless pit. Judas is also called the son of perdition (John 17:12) as is the antichrist (2 Thess. 2:3). If the antichrist's pretense as the Messiah of Israel is to be successful, then an incarnation and resurrection are necessary.

If my conjecture that the antichrist will be conceived of the devil is not true, then we must give serious consideration to the possibility that when antichrist is assassinated and raised from the dead by the false prophet (Rev. 13:12, 14), the spirit of Judas (into whom Satan entered (Luke 22:3) will incarnate his dead body at that time. This would explain the complete and sudden change in the personality of the antichrist after he is raised from the dead.

Titles and names attributed to Judas are similar to those listed earlier about the antichrist: The son of perdition (John 17:12); a conspirator (Mark 14:11); a devil (John 6:70); entered by Satan (Luke 22:3); a betrayer (Mark 14:44); a thief (John 12:6).

Before his death (the first three and a half years of his reign), the antichrist will seem to be the most wonderful man in the world — like Jesus in many respects. Our Lord warned that it would be possible "that they (the false prophet and antichrist) shall deceive the very elect" (Matt. 24:24). This means that the Jews will actually mistake him for the Messiah.

After his resurrection, the antichrist will become very proud and set up an image of himself in the temple and demand worship. This action is referred to by Biblical scholars as "the desecration of the Tem-

154

ple." Jesus and Daniel refer to it as "the abomination of desolation" (Matt. 24:15; Dan. 11:31; 12:11). Refusal to worship this image will result in death (Rev.13:15).

Finally, consider the source of the antichrist's power. Paul said we wrestle not against "flesh and blood, but against principalities, against powers, against the rulers of the darkness of this world, against spiritual wickedness in high places" (Eph. 6:12). The antichrist will have access to all of these diabolical forces. John wrote that the "dragon (Satan) gave him (the beast) his power, his seat, and great authority" (Rev. 13:2). This is also substantiated by the words of Daniel that "his power shall be mighty, but not by his own power..." (Dan. 8:24).

It would be foolish to belittle the power of Satan; he has a following of one-third of all the angelic host (Rev. 12:4). Ezekiel 28:11-19 contains several startling sentences about Satan:

> Thou sealest up the sum, full of wisdom and perfect in beauty...thou hast been in Eden...thou art the annointed cherub that covereth; and I have set thee so: thou wast upon the holy mountain of God...I will cast thee to the ground.

From these statements, we learn that Satan enjoyed an exalted position at the throne of God. Pride caused him to rebel against God and he was cast out of heaven. However, nothing is said of him having lost any of his power because of the expulsion.

Revelation 12:7-12 records a war in heaven between Michael and his angels and Satan and his angels. Michael prevails, and Satan is cast into the world. John then hears the words, "Woe to the inhabiters of the earth." The word "woe" tells us that Satan's expulsion from heaven into the world will be a tragedy for man.

When God removed the hedge of protection from Job, Satan wrought all kinds of havoc. He helped the Sabeans steal Job's oxen and asses and kill the servants. He caused fire to fall from heaven and burn up the sheep and the servants. He gave the Chaldeans success in stealing the camels and killing the servants. He commanded a storm to destroy the eldest brother's house, killing the sons and daughters of Job who were in it.

155

It is hard to know exactly what Satan will do after God removes the hedge (the Church and the Holy Spirit) and no measures of restraint stand in his way. The world will be free to commit every evil the Church has ever fought against. When the Church has opposed evil, it has been accused of standing in the way of progress. The world has yet to learn what a devastating effect evil will have upon the world when Satan is given full leash.

In the affairs of world government, there is a science called "geopolitics." The *Encyclopedia Britannica*, under the heading of geopolitics, states:

- He who rules Europe, commands the Heartland (the Middle East).
- He who rules the Heartland, commands the World-Island (Israel).
- He who commands Israel, commands the world.(1)

The *Encyclopedia Britannica* continues on by quoting Sir Halford Mackinder:

If the world-Island (Israel) be inevitably the principal seat of humanity of this globe, and if Arabia, as the passage-land from Europe to the Indies and from the northern to the southern Heartland, be central in the World-Island, then the hill citadel of Jerusalem has a strategic position with reference to world realities. (2)

I cannot help but wonder if the "seat" that Satan confers upon the antichrist (Rev. 13:2) is the same seat that Mackinder refers to as being Israel. Mackinder is correct when he says that Jerusalem is the "hill citadel" and strategic with reference to world realities. This is exactly what Ezekiel declares God said in the Bible, "This is Jerusalem: I have set it in the midst of the nations and countries that are round about her..." (Ezek. 5:5). Jerusalem is situated in the middle of the world and will be the capital from whence Christ shall reign for 1,000 years. It is in the temple in Jerusalem where the antichrist sets up his image of worship. This is the "seat, and great authority, and power" which Satan gives antichrist and which he will defend until the blood flows in the valley of Armageddon.

6. His Pseudo-Theocratic and Polytheistic Defiance:

> And he shall speak great words against the most High, and shall wear out the saints of the most High, and think to change times (the calendar) and laws (oaths)..." (Dan. 7:25).

This God-hater will not be able to bear the thought of acknowledging Christ every time he writes a letter. The appellation of A.D. (after the death of Christ) will certainly be targeted as an object for obsolescence. I cannot imagine the Bible surviving in our courts under his administration. His defiance of Christ is expressed by these words: "...By peace (he) shall destroy many: and he shall stand up against the Prince of princes (Jesus); but he shall be broken without hand" (Dan. 8:25).

What kind of insanity would drive any human to confront the one with "eyes as flames of fire, and the sharp two-edged sword in his mouth"? The "breaking without hand" referred to by Daniel means that Christ will not so much as lay His hand upon the antichrist. The sword of His mouth will consign him to the lake of fire (Rev. 19:15, 20).

Paul expressed the antichrist's opposition to Jehovah with the words, "Who opposeth and exalteth himself above all that is called God, or that is worshipped; so that he as God sitteth in the temple of God, shewing himself that he is God" (2 Thess. 2:4). The antichrist will not only oppose the worship of almighty God, he will oppose the worship of any god. His hatred is polytheistic in scope. The Living Bible says, "He opposes himself against every so called god, or object of worship." By this we deduce that every religion will be in jeopardy.

It seems almost incomprehensible that the antichrist will be able to summon every worshipper of every religion to himself. Yet there seems to be evidence that even God will help Satan in achieving this goal. The mysterious words of Paul need to be taken seriously that "God shall send them (the worshippers of the antichrist) strong delusion, that they should believe a lie" (2 Thess. 2:11). Instead of "a lie," the Greek renders the meaning as "the lie" which changes the grammatical construction from a verb to a noun. This means that it's not "a lie" (false words) by which they will be deceived, but by "the lie" (false person).

Under the administration of the antichrist, the practicing of all religions, even false religions, will be strictly forbidden. Even the world church will be hated and eventually destroyed by part of the E.E.C. alliance (Rev. 17:16). It is probable that the antichrist will destroy Christian book stores, Bible colleges, seminaries, church buildings, shrines of false deities and anything else that might be a threat to him.

7. His Extreme Anti-Semitism (Semitic meaning the offspring of Shem, specifically the Jews):

Israel's refusal to worship the antichrist is the spark which will ignite the fiery trials of the great tribulation. This will be the spiritual siren that will awaken Israel to realize that they have been deceived by the antichrist. The world has never known a hatred like that which the antichrist will display against Israel. Jesus instructed the Jews that when they see the abomination (image), spoken of by Daniel, standing in the temple,

> Then let them which be in Judea flee into the mountains: let him which is on the housetop not come down to take any thing out of his house: neither let him which is in the field return back to take his clothes. And woe unto them that are with child, and to them that give suck in those days! But pray that your flight be not in the winter...behold I have told you so (Matt. 24:16-20, 25)

At this point, Moses and Elijah will appear and begin their witness of Jesus to the house of Jacob. Millions of Jews will repent and finally turn to their true Messiah, disobeying the edict to worship the beast. This will precipitate an uncontrollable fury on the part of the antichrist to completely annihilate them.

The devil tried unsuccessfully to destroy the Messiah of Israel at His birth in Bethlehem. The Messiah is now about to be born spiritually to Israel as typified by the pregnant woman of Revelation 12. The time of Jacob's trouble, when "he shall wear out the saints of the most High" (Dan. 7:25), will be upon them.

- "...When he shall have accomplished to scatter the power of the holy people, all these things shall be finished" (Dan. 12:7).

- "And it was given unto him to make war with the saints and to overcome them..." (Rev. 13:7).

- "...How long O lord, holy and true, dost thou not judge and avenge our blood on them that dwell on the earth" (Rev. 6:10).

- "...These are they which have come out of great tribulation..." (Rev. 7:14).

- "And I saw them...that had gotten the victory over the beast, and over his image, and over his mark, and over the number of his name..." (Rev. 15:2).

All of these Scriptures proclaim a baptism of blood for Israel. A fierce battle between the Jews and the antichrist looms on the horizon. The most powerful weapon he will use against Israel is money. Daniel 11:43 tells us that "he will have power over the (treasuries)...." There will be a common currency, and, in order to obtain currency or engage in industry and commerce, one will have to accept the mark of the beast (Rev. 13:16-17). The repentant Israel will refuse the mark and many will be killed.

Another weapon the antichrist will use against Israel is world opinion. The leaders of the world are working overtime trying to bring about peace in the Middle East. The Bible says there will be a time "when they shall say peace and safety," but it shall not last. For "...sudden destruction cometh upon them, as travail upon a woman with child; and they shall not escape" (1 Thess. 3:5). Israel will be blamed for the peace treaty's failure and the antichrist will convince the world that the Jews are refusing to cooperate with his financial plans, thereby creating difficulty for his entire kingdom.

According to Zechariah 12:9 and 14:2-3 and Revelation 16:14-21, the armies of the world will be brought against Israel. So, it is obvious that the antichrist's propaganda machine will have been successful. World opinion will turn so overwhelmingly against themthat the destruction of Israel is almost inevitable.

II. THE BEAST OUT OF THE EARTH (Revelation 13:11-18)

And I beheld another beast coming up out of the earth; and he had two horns like a lamb, and he spake as a dragon. And he exerciseth all the power of the first beast before him, and causeth the earth and them which dwell therein to worship the first beast, whose deadly wound was healed. And he doeth great wonders, so that he maketh fire come down from heaven on the earth in the sight of men, and deceiveth them that dwell on the earth by the means of those miracles which he had power to do in the sight of the beast; saying to them that dwell on the earth, that they should make an image to the beast, which had the wound by a sword and did live.

And he had power to give life unto the image of the beast, that the image of the beast should both speak, and cause that as many as would not worship the image of the beast should be killed. And he causeth all, both small and great, rich and poor, free and bond, to receive a mark in their right hand or in their foreheads: And that no man might buy or sell, save he that had the mark, or the name of the beast, or the number of his name.

Here is wisdom. Let him that hath understanding count the number of the beast: for it is the number of a man; and his number is six hundred threescore and six (Rev. 13:11-18).

The beast described in this passage will be the leader of the world church. He will deceive many through the miracles (like calling fire down from heaven) that he and the antichrist will perform (Rev. 13:14). The fact that the fire descends from "heaven" will delude and convince men it was sent by God like in the days of Elijah.

1. His Title:

At the time of his capture, he is called the false prophet. "And the beast was taken, and with him the false prophet that wrought miracles with him..." (Rev. 19:20). This duo will probably be the most sensational pair the world has ever known. They will try to out perform Moses and Elijah in an attempt not only to deceive the people, but to win disciples. False prophets are nothing new. Ancient kings like Nebuchadnezzar, Belshazzar, Ahab, and many others had prophets, soothsayers, or witches whom they consulted in critical times. The antichrist has his prophet who will reveal the future for him.

It has been a long time since miracles like those performed by Jesus have been seen in the world. People today are very gullible when it comes to sensationalism.

2. The Miracle of Elijah:

Moses and Elijah will be performing all sorts of miracles (Rev. 11:5). In the days when Elijah was battling with Jezabel and her prophets of Baal, the test of deity was to be certified by the God capable of answering by fire. The Jews know all about Elijah's ancient encounter with the prophets of Baal on Mount Carmel. The false prophet and antichrist will pass this fire test in a way dramatic enough to deceive many people into believing they are the prophets sent by God.

3. The Miracle that Defies:

The miracle of raising the dead has always been exclusively reserved as proof of the power of Jehovah God. Men like Elisha and Paul raised the dead, but they were quick to acknowledge the miracle to be by the power of God. It is understood from this passage that the false prophet not only brings the slain antichrist (first beast) back to life, but that he gives life to an image built in honor of the resurrected beast. To restore life to a body not yet buried is one thing. To give life and speech to an inanimate object of earthly materials is quite something else. Some believe that the speaking image which John sees in Revelation 13 will be a large television screen. I don't think so. In today's terms, a large screen is no longer a miracle and would not deceive the people. I understand this image to be a replica of the antichrist, perhaps made of wax, brass, wood, or maybe even gold. Its composition and substance are not important. The fact that the false prophet is able to give life and speech to this statue will absolutely stun the population.

4. The Symbol which Redeems:

In Revelation 5:6-9, the false prophet is represented as a lamb with two horns and the mouth of a dragon. We can know by this symbolism that something devious is being depicted. The figure of a lamb with a dragon's mouth is contradictory. The figure of lamb with horns is also a contradiction. This man, according to the symbolism, is a contradiction within himself, just like the antichrist and his father the devil.

Lambs are the meekest of all animals. This man, while he is represented as a meek and submissive lamb, cannot be judged by his outward appearance. He must be judged by his dragon mouth, for out of the mouth comes that which resides in his heart. Because Satan is represented as a dragon, we can conclude that the false prophet's dragon mouth personifies the mind and will of the devil.

5. His Origin:

The first beast, the antichrist, rises up out of the sea (many peoples as a kingdom). But as the spirit of a person, he ascends out of the bottomless pit. This second lamb-beast rises up out of the earth. Who is he? Here are many learned scholars' suggestions:

- Sir Isaac Newton - the Greek Church
- Galloway - the French Republic
- Fysh - the Jesuits

- Mulerius - the Roman theologians
- Hengstenberg - the earthly carnal wisdom of heathen philosophies, false doctrines and the like
- Waller - the evil which arises in the Church of Christ
- Stuart - the heathen priesthood
- Gebhardt - witchcraft, sooth saying and magic
- Seiss - a figure of the resurrection of Judas
- Many others - the Roman Papacy

If this two-horned, dragon-tongued lamb-beast represents the false prophet, then we know he is a man. The fact that he is a "false prophet" discloses that he is religious.

The expression "came up out of the earth" must not be overlooked. Again we encounter a synecdochical situation (the using of a part for the whole or the whole for a part). Genesis 2:7 says that "...the Lord God formed man of the dust of the ground, and breathed into his nostrils the breath of life; and man became a living soul." The imagery of "coming up out of the earth" tells us that this false prophet is a very earthly man. The only life he possesses is physical life, devoid of all Godly spiritual realities, because God has not breathed anything spiritual into him. He is controlled by the dragon as depicted by his mouth.

The second aspect of the synecdoche has to do with the kingdom or the devotees he controls. We know that there are several parables spoken by our Lord where the kingdom of God is being linked to the "earth." Matthew 13:24-30 depicts the kingdom of God as being vulnerable to enemies sowing tares into a "field" already sown with good seed. In Matthew 13:31-35, the kingdom is likened to a mustard seed sown into a field of the "earth." In Matthew 13:44, the kingdom is like a treasure hidden in a "field." These references all speak of the kingdom of God as the "earth" or "field."

The disciples said to the Lord, "Declare unto us the parable of the tares of the field." He replied:

> ...He that soweth the good seed is the Son of man; the field is the world; the good seed are the children of the kingdom; but the tares are the children of the wicked one. The enemy that sowed them is the devil; the harvest is the end of the world... (Matt. 13:36-43).

Satan has his tares growing among the wheat in the kingdom of God. The false prophet is depicted as a two-horned lamb that rises up out of the earth (the kingdom of God) where the wheat and tares grow together. He has hypocritically disguised himself as a lamb among them, but his mouth betrays him. No one informed John as to his identity, nevertheless, John recognized him immediately and called him the false prophet (Rev. 19:20). While the identity of the first beast is a mystery and it will require wisdom to decipher his number (Rev. 13:18), there seems to be no mystery about this second beast as far as John was concerned

Religion has always been in the world. Generally, mankind is religious, even though he may not always admit it. God has placed an intuitive awareness within every human breast that there is someone greater who must be appeased. There is not a people, regardless of how primitive and remotely removed from civilization, that does not worship something.

Governments and political leaders have always been in the world. Most frequently, the world's political leaders align with the religion that is in the majority. Sometimes political and spiritual leaders have been the same person. At other times, they were two people working in concert with each other. Such was the case with Rome for much of the time that she was in power. Rome has been vanquished as a world power, however, as a religious force she has always played a strong role in politics. The pope is actively engaged in travelling and visiting various countries in the interest of humanitarian causes, which are most always politically motivated. His is a strong voice and the world usually listens.

The last government of the world will probably be the eighteen European Common Market nucleus or founding nations (plus the "many" in Daniel 9:27) which are situated within the general boundaries of the old Roman Empire. Revelation 13 depicts the antichrist (as the leader of the E.E.C.) and false prophet (the leader of the world church) cooperating and orchestrating the affairs of the world in the name of religion.

One must not necessarily presume that the false prophet or religious world leader is the pope of Rome. However, the question must be asked as to whether or not the church of Rome, allied with many other religions, will accept anyone other than their pope as leader.

For that matter, would the world accept anyone other than the pope to be the leader of a world church?

The third of the tribulation participants, which we will discuss shortly, symbolizes the world church, called "...MYSTERY, BABYLON THE GREAT, THE MOTHER OF HARLOTS AND ABOMINATIONS OF THE EARTH" (Rev. 17:5). That the world church is called "the mother of harlots" predicates that she has daughters who will comprise the world church "harem." Nothing is said of her having a leader, yet we are told she sits on seven mountains (Rev. 17:9) and she is called "that great city" (Rev. 17:18).

Everyone knows that Rome is surrounded by seven hills. The city has also been given names like "queen city of the earth," "center of history," and the "eternal city." It would appear that the woman of Revelation 17 typifies the church of Rome and her daughters represent the many religions which will join her in creating a super world church. The idea of the false prophet being her leader would probably go by unchallenged.

6. The Source of His Power:

This lamb is represented as having two horns which are symbolic of two sources of power. This probably refers to his power over the religions of the world and his influence in politics because of his intimate relationship with the antichrist.

The first beast rises out of the sea which represents many people. His power is political. The second beast rises out of the earth "and he exerciseth all the power of the first beast before him, and causeth the earth (the world church kingdom) and them which dwell therein to worship the first beast" (Rev. 13:12). These two personages will control and manipulate the political and religious dominions of the world. This situation is volatile not only because so much power rests in their hands, but because it is Satan who confers these powers upon them.

7. Democracy/Dictatorship for Europe:

Europe envisions an incredible super-democracy through the E.E.C. The sad reality will be the emergence of the cruelest dictatorship the world has ever known. It will, in fact, be a double dictatorship with two men keeping time with Satan's metronome while the people march to its enslaving rhythm.

Note the power this false prophet possesses. He orders the people to build a statue in honor of the beast and they build it. He commands them to fall down in worship and they prostrate themselves. He demands that those who refuse allegiance to the beast be killed and they are killed. He orders everyone to receive an irreversible "mark" of unpardonable sin against God, forever condemning their souls to an eternal Hell as affirmed by the Scriptures:

> And I saw another angel fly in the midst of heaven, having the everlasting gospel to preach unto them that dwell on the earth, and to every nation, and kindred, and tongue and people, saying with a loud voice, Fear God, and give glory to him; for the hour of his judgement is come: and worship him that made heaven and earth, and the sea, and the fountains of waters (Rev. 14:6-7).

> And the third angel followed them, saying with a loud voice, If any man worship the beast and his image, and receive his mark in his forehead or in his hand, the same shall drink of the wine of the wrath of God, which is poured out without mixture into the cup of his indignation, and he shall be tormented with fire and brimstone in the presence of the holy angels, and in the presence of the Lamb: And the smoke of their torment ascendeth up for ever and ever: and they have no rest day nor night, who worship the beast and his image, and whosoever receiveth the mark of his name (Rev. 14:9-11).

Life on earth during this reign will be dreadful. Imagine a dictator:

- Who is "wiser than Daniel" (Ezek. 28:3)
- Who has "a mouth speaking great things" (Dan. 7:8)
- Who opposes God by sitting "in the temple of God, showing himself that he is God" (2 Thess. 2:4)
- "Whose coming is after the working of Satan with all power and signs and lying wonders" (2 Thess. 2:9)

166

- Who curses God and everyone who dwells in heaven (Rev. 13:6)
- Who is glorified by the world church which is headed by a leader who forces people to submit to and worship him (Rev. 13:15)
- Whose "god" is the devil who is furious because Michael ejected him from heaven (Rev. 12:9-12)

Under such a leader/dictator, the future will indeed be grim.

III. THE BEAST CARRYING THE MOTHER OF HARLOTS
(Revelation 17:1-18)

And there came one of the seven angels which had the seven vials, and talked with me, saying unto me, Come hither; I will shew unto thee the judgment of the great whore that sitteth upon many waters: with whom the kings of the earth have committed fornication, and the inhabitants of the earth have been made drunk with the wine of her fornication. So he carried me away in the spirit into the wilderness: and I saw a woman sit upon a scarlet coloured beast, full of names of blasphemy, having seven heads and ten horns.

And the woman was arrayed in purple and scarlet colour, and decked with gold and precious stones and pearls, having a golden cup in her hand full of abominations and filthiness of her fornication: and upon her forehead was a name written, MYSTERY, BABYLON THE GREAT MOTHER OF HARLOTS AND ABOMINATIONS OF THE EARTH. And I saw the woman drunken with the blood of the saints, and with the blood of the martyrs of Jesus: and when I saw her, I wondered with great admiration. And the angel said unto me, wherefore didst thou marvel? I will tell thee the mystery of the woman, and of the beast that carrieth her, which hath the seven heads and ten horns.

The beast that thou sawest was, and is not; and shall ascend out of the bottomless pit, and go into perdition: and they that dwell on the earth shall wonder, whose names were not written in the book of life from the foundation of the world, when they behold the beast that was, and is not, and yet is.

And here is the mind which hath wisdom. The seven heads are seven mountains, on which the woman sitteth. And there are seven kings: five are fallen, and one is, and the other is not yet come; and when he cometh, he must continue a short space. And the beast that was, and is not, even he is the eighth, and is of the seven, and goeth into perdition.

And the ten horns which thou sawest are ten kings, which have received no kingdom as yet; but receive power as kings one hour with the beast. These have one mind, and shall give their power and strength unto the beast. These shall make war with the Lamb, and the Lamb shall overcome them: for he is Lord of lords, and King of kings: and they that are with him are called, and chosen, and faithful.

168

And he saith unto me, The waters which thou sawest, where the whore sitteth, are peoples, and multitudes, and nations, and tongues. And the ten horns which thou sawest upon the beast, these shall hate the whore, and shall make her desolate and naked, and shall eat her flesh, and burn her with fire. For God hath put in their hearts to fulfill his will, and to agree, and give their kingdom unto the beast, until the words of God shall be fulfilled. And the woman which thou sawest is that great city, which reigneth over the kings of the earth (Rev. 17:1-18)

What is the meaning of this double-entendre vision? What is this scarlet blasphemy graffitoed, polycephalous, decamerous-horned creature? Who is this purity-impoverished, sinful, blood-red murderous prostitute, destitute of goodness, humility, and love? She is none other than the matriarch of the house of whores and spiritual abominations of the "EARTH." She is the bride of Satan whose children have sprung up from the "tares which were sown in the field" of the kingdom of God. Her leader is the false prophet (who is also her progeny) disguised as a lamb in the sheepfold of God, even as the tares are disguised as genuine wheat. But this lamb has two vicious horns (religion and politics) which he will use to gore her patrons to death.

In opposition to him is "the Lamb of God which taketh away the sins of the world" (John 1:29). This Lamb is the true prophet sent from God who was planted into the earth as a corn of wheat. He "arose out of the earth" on the third day to announce to the world that His Father had vested Him with all power and authority. Then He instructed His disciples to wait in the upper room where they would receive, not the forked tongue of a dragon, but cloven tongues of fire. These went forth into all the world to build the true Church "without spot or wrinkle, or any such thing" (Eph. 5:27).

Revelation 17 and 18 are difficult chapters to talk about. They speak of the Church being lured into compromise with Constantine in 313 A.D. The early Church mounted the beast of power and politics and, by so doing, resigned herself to a life of spiritual fornication and harlotry. All of this was under the guise that Christianity could prevail if it became the state religion.

The kingdom of God was never designed to be a state religion which would be legislated down from a political throne to the people. The Church was never intended to become a cloak to cover political and religious corruption, but it did. The period which followed is called "the dark ages" by historians and "a falling away" by Paul . (2 Thess. 2:3). This is precisely what John was seeing in this vision of Revelation 17 and 18. Let us then consider the seven pronouncements regarding the beast and his harlot.

1. Identifying the Beast:

In attempting to ascertain his identity, we have his scarlet hue, seven heads and ten horns, the blasphemous names, and the three tenses indicating the pluralistic eras of his existence (was, is not, and shall). These are symbolical characteristics providing us with adequate clues.

At the time John wrote the Book of Revelation, this beast already had existed, did not then exist, but would reappear again. Embodied in these expressions we have a past (was), present (is not), and future (shall ascend) dimension (Rev. 17:8). We need to remember that this vision is another synecdoche, meaning that the Scriptures may be speaking of the beast as a political force, like a grouping of countries, in one place and referring to him as its leader in another place.

Attention quickly shifts from the beast being a singular person to its seven heads which (according the Scriptures' own explanation) represent a hierarchical sequence of five fallen kings. Of the remaining two heads, we are told that one "is," which must refer to the king in Rome reigning in John's day. The other one, who "is not yet come" (Rev. 17:10), is futuristic. This one, in all probability, is the antichrist, because he is to emerge "from the bottomless pit."

Finally, attention is directed at the ten horns. These are obviously future because "they have received no kingdom as yet" (Rev. 17:12). These ten horns cause the harlot a lot of woe (Rev. 17:16).

The key symbol here was never intended to be the beast, rather the woman riding upon it. The only reason the beast is mentioned at all is to draw attention to the fact that the woman has been riding upon it for a long time and will still be riding upon it when she is destroyed by its ten horns during the tribulation. The five ancient fallen kings (countries) at that time were Greece, Egypt, Assyria, Persia, and Babylon. These countries have been Israel's enemies through the centuries. Their chief religion was the mother/child worship as instituted by Nimrod and his wife, Semerimus, who deified their son, Tammuz (Ezek. 8:13-16).

This was the religion of Babylon which found its way even into the holy city of Jerusalem. The blasphemous names covering the beast certify that it is an anti-God system embraced by these five fallen countries. This system has been adapted by Rome to make it compatible with Christianity, and it is still in existence today.

God was careful to retain the original characteristics of this ancient beast so we would recognize it to be the same as that which John saw in Revelation 13. This beast is not only distinguishable by his seven heads and ten horns, but primarily by his blasphemy (Rev. 13:5; 17:3). Blasphemy occurs when someone or something is put in place of God and worshipped or when God is abused by speech or other profane acts. This beast's religion is anti-God. His scarlet hue aligns him with the red dragon, Satan (Rev. 12:9; 13:4).

The beast represents the empires of this world. These began with Babylon and follow the historical delineation of victories and defeats, culminating with the last great empire, the revived Roman Empire, or the European Economic Community. The E.E.C. is associated with ancient Babylon through its religion as typified by the woman. These ten horns were observed by Daniel centuries before John's day (Dan. 7:8-11). It is out of these ten horns that a little horn grows, becoming great and evolving into the modern beast which John sees with crowned horns (Rev. 13:1). The beast which was, and is not, and ascends from the pit is the spirit of Judas which will be incarnate in the leader of the E.E.C. who will go into perdition at his defeat (Rev. 19:20).

Within a relatively short time, we will be seeing the E.E.C., with a membership of eighteen nations, signing a peace treaty with Israel, creating a new monetary system and appointing a dictator over the entire constituency. The total composite of the beast with his seven heads and ten horns, plus his body (Rev. 17:11), equal eighteen. These are the eighteen nations that will be the nucleus of the E.E.C.

171

2. Identifying the Woman:

> And upon her forehead was a name written, MYSTERY,
> BABYLON THE GREAT, THE MOTHER OF HARLOTS
> AND ABOMINATIONS OF THE EARTH... (Rev. 17:5).

We have assumed that the whore (the world church) represents this world's final religious systems which appear to have originated from Babylon. Not yet having established that the whore is indeed a church, I wish to now verify this.

Since we do have a description of the bride of Christ (the true Church), then a juxtapositional comparison of the known (the bride of Christ) with the suspicious (the whore, the bride of Satan) should produce a paradox. The unknown identity of who the whore is may be established by the known identity of the Lamb's wife. We know that the Lamb's wife is a pure Church; of necessity, the whore must be an impure church.

The Residence of the Whore:

> And there came one of the seven angels which had the seven
> vials, and talked with me, saying unto me, Come hither; I
> will shew unto thee the judgment of the great whore that
> sitteth upon many waters (Rev. 17:1).

> So he carried me away in the spirit into the wilderness: and
> I saw a woman sit upon a scarlet coloured beast, full of
> names of blasphemy... (Rev. 17:3).

The Residence of the Bride of Christ:

> And there came unto me one of the seven angels which had
> the seven vials full of the seven last plagues, and talked with
> me, saying, Come hither, I will show thee the bride, the
> Lamb's wife. And he carried me away in the spirit to a great
> and high mountain, and showed me that great city, the holy
> Jerusalem, descending out of heaven from God (Rev. 21:9-
> 10).

The opposite nature of their residences is established by comparing the whore and the bride as a "wilderness" to a "high mountain." The opposite environmental atmosphere which exists places the two on opposite ends of the spectrum.

The Attire of the Whore:

> And the woman was arrayed in purple and scarlet colour, and decked with gold and precious stones and pearls, having a golden cup in her hand, full of abominations of the earth and filthiness of her fornication (Rev. 17:4).

The Attire of the Bride of Christ:

> And to her was granted that she should be arrayed in fine linen, clean and white: for the fine linen is the righteousness of the saints (Rev. 19:8).

The two churches are as different as "purple and scarlet" are from "fine linen, clean and white." The whore represents the "abominations of the earth" and the bride represents "the righteousness of the saints," which are direct opposites. The bride, the Lamb's wife, is the redeemed Church. The harlot, who must be Satan's bride, is a false religious system.

Other opposites in the study of the two women reveal that both are identified as cities. Babylon is remembered by Jews as the place of their exile and captivity. They longed to return to Jerusalem as their home. Both cities have a relationship to light. Babylon has its light and candles extinguished (Rev. 18:23). It is said of Jerusalem that its light never goes out (Rev. 21:23). The harlot has the name Babylon on her forehead (Rev. 17:5) which is "the habitation of devils, and the hold of every foul spirit" (Rev. 18:2). The bride of Christ has His name in her forehead (Rev. 22:4). Babylon exploited the nations (Rev. 17:5), but the bride brings healing (Rev. 22:2). The harlot offers a cup full of abominations and filthiness (Rev. 17:4). The bride prohibits them (Rev. 21:27).

Most eschatological scholars agree that Revelation 17 speaks of a false religious system, but there are many opinions as to the interpretation of Revelation 18. Most agree that the destruction of a city is here described. A rebuilt Babylon, London, New York, and many others are suggested. This cannot be the case.

The error arises from a failure to recognize the carry over of the subject (the judgment of the whore) from chapter seventeen to eighteen. John is told that he will be shown "the judgment of the whore" (Rev. 17:1), but he is not shown this judgment until chapter eighteen (which is entirely devoted to it). In Revelation 18, the woman is no longer depicted as a whore, she is called a city. In Revelation 17:18, John is told that the woman is a city.

If Rome is the city, why call her Babylon? For the same reason that Jerusalem is spiritually called Sodom and Egypt in Revelation 11:8. This analogy was not only to inform us of the place where the two witnesses are to be killed, but to also give Christ's spiritual estimation of the condition of Jerusalem by comparing her to "Sodom and Egypt." Likewise, in the use of the name Babylon (Babel means confusion) for Rome, we are given Christ's spiritual estimate of Rome as the capitol of the world church.

We are warned that this is a "mystery." The symbolic fact that John "was carried away in the spirit into the wilderness" sends a signal that we are to understand this from a spiritual perspective. Therefore, the mystery of the wilderness, the woman and her name are to be interpreted in a spiritual framework. The symbolic "wilderness" is used to express the spiritual wilderness where the world church will find herself. Her name "Babylon" represents confusion. Her character as "harlot" connotes unfaithfulness and impurity.

Finally, in identifying the woman, the words in 1 Peter 5:13 should be considered. Peter is sending greetings from the church in Babylon, yet no one has any evidence of Peter ever having been in Babylon or that a Christian church ever existed there. It seems certain that he was writing from Rome, as Jews do commonly refer to Rome as Babylon.

3. Her Ancient Origin (Also see Isaiah 47):

Alexander Hislop, in his book *The Two Babylons*, says this:

> The chief feature of the religion of Babylon was the cult of Mother-child worship. This system was instituted by

174

Nimrod's wife, Semerimus, who claimed that her son Tammuz was the fulfillment of Genesis 3:15. She symbolized this notion with a mother holding a child up in her arms, which is the figure seen in much of Eastern religious literature. Furthermore, she adopted the title of "Queen of Heaven" (which is also the claim of the church of Rome, and boasted of by the harlot of Rev. 18:7), and taught ancient Babylonians that salvation was administered only through her.

This religion appeared in one form or other in Phoenicia, Pergamos, Egypt, Greece, Rome, and was reported to have been discovered as far away as India.(3)

Jezabel brought this teaching with her when she married Ahab. In Jeremiah 44:16-25, the prophet chastises Israel for their sin of offering incense unto the "queen of heaven." Jeremiah 44:18 discloses that the expression "queen of heaven" existed long before there was a Roman church. Rome inherited the name from Babylon. Note further that Ezekiel 8:6-14 must surely be speaking of the confessional when he describes the "hole in the wall." This practice is being described as an "abomination" with which the mother of harlots is indicted (Rev. 17:5).

Many of the rituals and practices of the church of Rome are not original with her, nor did she learn them from Christ or the apostles. These are religious elements and practices which originated from Babylon and existed in pagan Rome when Christianity was declared the state religion. Constantine, like all Roman Emperors, was also the high priest when Christianity was sanctioned as the state religion in 312 A.D. He introduced the mother/child worship. The early Christians, along with the pagan Romans, worshipped Semerimus and Tammuz until 381 A.D. when the worship of the virgin Mary and her child, the Christ, was instituted.

The new church continued "cutting the cloth to fit the carcass" by incorporating Babylonian holy days into the new system. For example, the Easter spoken of in Acts 12:4 had nothing to do with the resurrection of Christ. Easter was a high and holy pagan celebration when the goddess Ishtar was honored. The word "Easter" actually originated from the word "Ishtar," one of the titles of the Babylonian queen of heaven.

Our modern Christmas celebration is an adaptation of the December 21st birthday of the Babylonian sun-god. It was believed that the actual lengthening of days did not begin to happen until December 25th. The pagan festival known as Winter Solstice, in honor of the birthday of their sun-god, became known as Christmas. Jesus Christ is called the "Sun of righteousness" in Malachi 4:2. The adaptation from worshipping the sun-god to the "Sun of righteousness" required only a slight modification with small concern that Jesus was probably born in April when it was warm enough for the shepherds to watch their sheep in the fields by night.

Another symbol which spilled over from ancient Babylon was the cross. Long before Rome introduced the cross as a Christian symbol, it had existed in ancient Egypt. It was known as the mystic *TAU*, which came from the letter "T" which is the initial for Tammuz. History reveals that the pagan religious symbol of the cross existed long before Christ was crucified.

The rosary was also revised from Babylonian ceremonies. Religious practices like "Celibacy, Tonsure and The Order of Monks and Nuns" have nothing to do with the Church of Pentecost. These are nothing more than imitations of the vestal virgins of pagan Rome. These are the things which the prophet Ezekiel calls "abominations" (Ezek. 8:15-16). They were in existence long before there was a church of Rome.

Empires, kings, queens, presidents, and governments come and go. Religion comes, but it does not go. Some of the most ancient religions which seemed irrelevant to our modern mind just a few years ago are being introduced and propagated in all the world today. Islam and Catholicism, which have never been compatible, are showing signs of religious tolerance.

The religion of Babylon was the very first religion. It had its beginning at Babel (Babylon) which means confusion. It was the religion of Cain and his progeny, Nimrod. It was also the religion of the city of Nineveh which Nimrod built. Both names, Babel and Nineveh, when totaled in Hebrew letter values equal 666. This does not necessarily connect them with the antichrist, but it does cast suspicion on them. The religion which started in ancient Babylon, plus the addition of eastern religions like Islam, will be incorporated into the religion and practices of the soon-emerging world church.

4. Money, Power, Investments and Politics:

A distinguishing factor of the newly formed E.E.C. will be the role that religion will play in politics. The antichrist and the false prophet will be the main players, but they will not trust each other. Daniel 11:27 declares their "hearts shall be to do mischief, and they shall speak lies at one table."

The two "kings," the antichrist and false prophet, cannot both rule. One will have to go. As the great tribulation comes to a climax, the ten horns of the antichrist will destroy the false prophet's headquarters which is also the seat of the harlot (Rev. 17:16-17). Cathedrals (albeit spiritually dead) and churches will be destroyed. The burning described in Revelation 18:8 and 18 will be catastrophic. It needs to be pointed out that, while the rift in the E.E.C. may be largely responsible for this disaster, God's destructive equation of judgment must also be considered. The following Scriptures would support this truth:

> ...Babylon is fallen, is fallen, that great city, because she made all nations drink of the wine of the wrath of her fornication (Rev. 14:8).

> And a mighty angel took up a stone like a great millstone, and cast it into the sea, saying, Thus with violence shall that great city Babylon be thrown down, and shall be found no more at all (Rev. 18:21)

> For true and righteous are his judgments: for he hath judged the great whore, which did corrupt the earth with her fornication... (Rev. 19:2).

> ...For God hath put in their hearts to fulfill his will... (Rev. 17:17).

The purpose God intended the Church to fulfill is the preaching of the gospel. If she departs from this mission, she invokes the anger of God upon herself. This is the picture painted of the world church in Revelation 17 and 18. The following statements are indictments against the self-centered indulgences of the world church and will bring certain judgment:

> (She committed fornication)...with the kings of the earth... (Rev. 17:2).

> ...The merchants of the earth are waxed rich through the abundance of her delicacies (Rev. 18:3).

> How much she hath glorified herself, and lived deliciously, so much torment and sorrow give her, for she saith in her heart, I sit a queen... (Rev. 18:7).

> And the fruits that thy soul lusted after are departed from thee, and all things which were dainty and goodly are departed... (Rev. 18:14).

> The merchants of these things, which were made rich by her, shall stand afar off...weeping and wailing...saying Alas, alas...every shipmaster, and all the company ships...weeping and wailing...saying, Alas, alas, that great city wherein were made rich all that had ships in the sea by reason of her costliness... (Rev. 18:15-19).

This is the obituary of the early Church which ignored the great commission of Matthew 28:19-20 and was busy with the mammon of this world.

In the encyclopedia, *Our Wonderful World*, we find an account of the extent of Rome's commerce and trade, an account that gives the reader an eerie sense that he or she might be reading Revelation 18. The account reads:

> In the days of the Roman Empire when ancient commerce reached its peak, large ports along the circumference of the Mediterranean had regular schedules for shipping to the great capitol of Rome. Wheat, jars of oil and wine, salt fish, luxury goods of all sorts, silks, Greek statues, incense for altars, olive oil, gaily painted pottery, dishes and other kitchen wares, cotton, Sicilian wine, Spanish silver, Italian iron,

rare woods, ivory, oriental rugs, tapestries, perfumes, rare table delicacies, ebony, beryl, pearls cinnamon and above all pepper. (4)

Compare the above with Revelation 18:12-13:

The merchandise of gold, and silver, and precious stones, and pearls, and fine linen, and purple, and silk, and scarlet. and all thyine wood, all manner vessels of ivory, and all manner vessels of most precious wood, and of brass, and iron, and marble, and cinnamon, and odours, and ointments, and frankincense, and wine, and oil, and fine flour, and wheat, and beasts, and sheep, and horses, and chariots, and slaves, and the souls of men.

In listing her commercial trade, the "souls of men" are included as being traded along with horses, sheep, wheat, etc. When the Church exchanges the call of Christ for the call of riches, it wanders into a spiritual wilderness of materialism, committing spiritual fornication and invoking the wrath of God upon herself. A separated life cannot serve God and mammon. There cannot be two kings vying for the same throne. One of them has to go and when it Is Christ who goes, so does blessing, happiness, and contentment.

Therefore shall her plagues come in one day, death, and mourning, and famine; and she shall be utterly burned with fire; for strong is the Lord God who judgeth her (Rev. 18:8).

It is not surprising that our Lord calls the world church a harlot. When the Church (the bride of Christ) begins to forsake prayer, praise, song, and fellowship with Christ (the bridegroom) in order to spend her time flirting with kings and merchant men in the pursuit of riches, she will be implicated with spiritual fornication.

5. Blasphemy, Blasphemy, Blasphemy, Blasphemy:

Profanity and obscenity are carved into the nature and character of this beast. His inherently religious and political personality has not bettered itself through the process of time. What he was when

179

he cast the three Hebrew children into the fiery furnace, because they refused to worship his image, is what he will still be when he reappears.

John both heard and saw the beast's blasphemy. In Revelation 13:6, John heard the beast open his mouth and vent his hatred of God, His tabernacle and those who dwell in heaven. In Revelation 17, John sees this venomous hatred expressed in blasphemic hieroglyphics. This is a different kind of blasphemy as that of Revelation 13.

Blasphemy, in addition to speaking with an obscene mouth, has a second dimension. This is what John was seeing in the graffito which covered the scarlet-colored beast the woman was riding. It was not blasphemous or obscene "words," but blasphemous "names" which covered this beast. It is my impression that John saw actual names of men, women, religions, or gods who have contrived against God by forcing idolatry upon the worshipping public down through the centuries. There are, no doubt, names like Nebuchadnezzar, Darius, Belshazzar, Antiochus Epiphanes, some of the popes, and Hitler written upon this scarlet beast.

Religion just prior to the return of Christ will be exactly like that symbolized in Revelation 17. Blasphemy, whoredom, fornication, and abominations will be quite acceptable. When most of the world's major religions become one church, there will be nothing left that resembles Christianity. Paul saw the behavior of man in this way:

> ...In the latter times some shall depart from the faith, giving heed to seducing spirits, and doctrines of devils. Speaking lies in hypocrisy; having their conscience seared with a hot iron. Forbidding to marry, and commanding to abstain from meats... (1 Tim. 4:1-3).

> But you must realize that in the last days the times will be full of danger. Men will become utterly self-centered, greedy for money, full of big words. They will be proud and contemptuous, without any regard for what their parents taught them. They will be utterly lacking in gratitude, purity and normal human affection. They will be men of unscrupulous speech and have no control of themselves. They will be passionate and unprincipled, treacherous, self-willed and conceited, loving all the time what gives them

pleasure instead of loving God. They will maintain a facade of religion, but their conduct will deny its validity (2 Tim. 3:1-7, Phillips).

One of the signs of the end of the world is the rise of many false Christs, prophets, and religions. It is disgusting to hear these egotistic bigots arrogantly affirming they are Jesus. In Matthew 24:23-27, our Lord warns about such people, instructing believers to "believe it not" when someone says such.

The Scriptures describing the rapture of Israel (Zech. 14:4; Acts 1:11; 1 Thess. 4:16; Rev. 1:7) make it clear that our Lord will not return to a secret chamber or the desert. Every eye shall see Him when His feet stand that day upon the Mount of Olives. These will be the signs of the true Messiah of Israel. If someone invites you to come see any other, "believe it not!"

Another sign for the coming of Jesus will be a light shining out from the East and crossing the earth clear to the West. Our Lord specifically gave us this sign because Satan will mimic such a coming in a similar fashion. Luke 10:18 discloses the fact that Satan "shall fall as lightning from heaven." When the people left on earth during the tribulation see this phenomenon, they will cry out, "Jesus is coming back again." (Note: If the light falls, it is Satan. If the light comes out of the East and crosses the earth to the West, it is Jesus.)

In a recent popular talk show, three would-be false Christs sat side by side arguing earnestly why one was and the other was not the Christ. There are actually people who are willing to believe and become their followers.

These are just little irreligious whirlwinds stirring up a little dirt here and there. When the real deceivers, the antichrist and the false prophet, team up on international television, the nations will be glued to the tube day and night. The world will believe "the lie." These are the days the Bible describes as "perilous times."

6. The Blood that Spills God's Cup of Wrath:

The Bible says, "Be not deceived, God is not mocked, for what a man soweth that shall he also reap" (Gal. 6:7). The balances will one day be level. God will strike back and when He does, there is not a mountain big enough in this universe to hide men from His wrath.

181

The harlot has a long history of theologically brainwashing people. Revelation 17:2 tells us that "the inhabitants of the earth were made drunk with the wine (teaching) of her fornication." The fornication referred to is spiritual, because John was taken by the Spirit to discover her in the wilderness (spiritual confusion). She is also implicated with being the habitation of Satan (Rev. 18:2).

This harlot has a history of killing good people. Anyone who would try to expose her had to be eliminated. "...The woman (was) drunken with the blood of saints, and with the blood of the martyrs of Jesus" (Rev. 17:6; 18:6).

The time in history when these atrocities were committed is limited to the apostolic era. Only those men who saw Jesus, who were eyewitnesses to His works and who were called by Him for special service can qualify as an apostle. There were no apostles before Christ's appearance upon earth and there have been none since the death of John.

Rome and the apostles were contemporaries and the woman who killed the apostles can only be Rome. Rome crucified the Lord; Rome killed Peter and Paul; Rome killed Polycarp, Flavius, Clemens, Jesus' brother Simon, Ignatius, Justin Martyr, Bladina, Leonidas, Perpetua, Felicitus, and Cyprian, as well as multiplied thousands of other saints. Christ was scarcely born, in the days of Caesar Augustus, when thousands of boy babies, two years and under, were killed in an effort to kill Him. The history of the ten Roman emperors is soaked in blood. Rome's favorite entertainment was feeding good people to the lions.

These are the deeds that will undo the harlot when the cup of God's wrath will finally run over. God has heard the prayer, "How long O Lord, wilt thou not avenge our blood upon them that dwell on the earth," and will answer it. Heaven will rejoice when He does.

> ...Many people in heaven, saying Alleluia...for true and righteous are his judgments: for he hath judged the great whore, which did corrupt the earth with her fornication, and hath avenged the blood of his servants at her hand (Rev. 19:1-2).

7. The Three Babylons:

There are three Babylons referred to in the Book of Revelation. The historical, ancient Babylon, symbolized by the head and mouth of a lion (Rev. 13:1-2), is the first one. The spiritual Babylon, or the world church headquartered in Rome as symbolized by the harlot (Rev. 17:5), is the second one. The third Babylon is the future (presently non-existent), soon-to-be built ultra-modern city which will be destroyed by God at the close of the tribulation (Rev. 16:19).

Ancient Babylon has already been judged. Her horn, one of the ten seen by Daniel, has been plucked up by the roots and her name has been obliterated from the geography of the modern world. Her ruins are buried deep in river mud, the favorite digging pit of many archaeologists.

Spiritual Babylon has her appointment with the ten horns who will destroy her, thereby fulfilling the will of God (Rev. 17:16-18).

The future Babylon used to make me raise an eyebrow, but not anymore. When the Bible says it, believe it! It is no secret that Saddam Hussein has dreams of rebuilding the city of Babylon. I removed a clipping from the October 18, 1987, issue of *The Edmonton Journal*, entitled, "Resurrected Babylon Rallying Cry Uniting Iraq." The writer, Uli Schmetzer, states how millions of dollars are being spent trying to determine as nearly as possible the original layout of the ancient city of Babylon. Plans are in the works to build hotels, palaces, and even the hanging gardens. The foundation of the original Tower of Babel is still intact. A posh hotel is to be erected in its place.

I believe Uli Schmetzer is sniffing at the heels of something that is not only possible, but indeed very probable. The scriptural basis for the above belief comes from Revelation 16:19:

> And the great city (Jerusalem) was divided into three parts, and the cities of the nations fell: and great Babylon came in remembrance before God, to give unto her the cup of the wine of the fierceness of his wrath.

In this instance, nothing is implied of a "spiritual" connotation and we must therefore take it at face value. This great Babylon must be the city Nebuchadnezzar was boasting of in Daniel 4:30 when he said, "Is not this the great Babylon which I have built...." In other words, this is the Babylon that took Israel captive in 586 B.C. for seventy years; the Babylon that plundered the temple in Jerusalem, carrying away the holy golden vessels to use them for drunken orgies; the Babylon where the Tower of Babel was built and used by the Ziggurats who "...labored (with sorceries and astrology) from your youth...Let now the astrologers, the stargazers, the monthly prognosticators stand up, and save thee from these things that shall come upon thee" (Isa. 47:12-13).

This is also the newly-rebuilt Babylon which will reside on the site of the ancient Babylon from whence the religion of Nimrod, Semerimus, and Tammuz defiled the whole world. This is an ancient location as hinted at by the expression, "Babylon came in remembrance before God." When the contractors from around the world start their bidding on various structures at this location, do not forget that the Bible told you so.

More astounding than this is a second consideration prophesied in Zechariah 5:8-11:

> ...This is wickedness...Then lifted I up mine eyes, and looked, and, behold, there came out two women, and the wind was in their wings; for they had wings like the wings of a stork: and they lifted up the ephah between the earth and the heaven. Then said I to the angel that talked with me, Whither do these bear the ephah? And he said unto me, to build it an house in the land of Shinar (Babylon): and it shall be established, and set there upon her own base.

I do not pretend to fully understand this passage, but I do know that the house alluded to is a house of worship. The land Shinar is named, which is indeed Babylon. The wickedness expressed has something to do with the house to be built. The two women referred to are no doubt two powerful religious systems of the last day. One of the popes of a few centuries ago was asked by a Muslim leader if he would ever permit a mosque to be built near the Vatican. He replied, "Whenever you permit us to build a cathedral in Mecca, I will permit a mosque to be built near the Vatican."

During a recent religious telecast, I heard a Muslin minister asking people to send donations to him which were to go towards the construction of a mosque near the Vatican. One can only conjecture whether the two women alluded to could be Catholicism and the Muslims. The implications are that a temple will be built in modern Babylon, compatible to the teachings of both women (churches). If so, the entire Eastern Islamic world will be enlisted to join the religions of the West in membership of this religious monstrosity.

This great museum city with its compromising temple will become the world's greatest tourist attraction. The construction will attract some of the world's best architects as the world's biggest contractors converge on its site. The city will be built in a very short time with trillions of dollars from investors with mega-fortunes. It will become one of the wonders of modern civilization. However, it will be destroyed even quicker than the time it took to build it. God has a score to settle with Babylon and the world will know when it happens that retribution has taken place.

The word "remembrance" tells us that God has not forgotten the heartbreak and loss Babylon has inflicted upon His people, the Jews. Babylon is the heart of the world's first civilization and the vicinity of the Garden of Eden. Here is where Satan deceived Adam and Eve, where Abel was murdered and where the tower of Babel was erected. Babylon was the inventor of astrology, witchcraft, and many other sorceries and idolatry. God has not forgotten all of this, and He will give to her "the cup of the wine of the fierceness of His wrath."

Iniquity started in Babylon and iniquity will end in Babylon!

IV. THE WONDER OF THE PREGNANT WOMAN
(Revelation 12)

And there appeared a great wonder in heaven; a woman clothed with the sun, and the moon under her feet, and upon her head a crown of twelve stars: and she being with child cried, travailing in birth, and pained to be delivered. And there appeared another wonder in heaven; and behold a great red dragon, having seven heads and ten horns, and seven crowns upon his heads. And his tail drew the third part of the stars of heaven, and did cast them to the earth: and the dragon stood before the woman which was ready to be delivered, for to devour her child as soon as it was born. And she brought forth a man child, who was to rule all nations with a rod of iron: and her child was caught up unto God, and to his throne (Rev. 12:1-5).

And when the dragon saw that he was cast unto the earth, he persecuted the woman which brought forth the man child. And to the woman were given two wings of a great eagle, that she might fly into the wilderness, into her place, where she is nourished for a time, and times, and half a time, from the face of the serpent. And the serpent cast out of his mouth water as a flood after the woman, that he might cause her to be carried away of the flood. And the earth helped the woman, and the earth opened her mouth, and swallowed up the flood which the dragon cast out of his mouth. And the dragon was wroth with the woman, and went to make war with the remnant of her seed, which keep the commandments of God, and have the testimony of Jesus Christ (Rev. 12:13-17).

The wonder of the sun-clad pregnant woman is expressed in symbolical language. The fact that John saw this wonder in "heaven" means that it must be understood in a figurative, spiritual way. This is not a pretty picture as Satan is portrayed to depict his true vicious character. All of his ambitions to destroy the Christ and Israel are here represented. What kind of being would be so depraved and savage as to attack a pregnant woman in labor and ready to give birth? This woman is struggling and writhing in pain before a vicious beast ready to devour her child.

186

How truly evil and devoid of mercy this red dragon is. Satan is here caught and exposed in the full blaze of a maternal sun surrounding the weeping woman. He stands, in the presence of a state of being that begs for privacy, ready to prevent Israel from finally giving spiritual birth to their Messiah. Israel's remorse, repentance, and acceptance of Jesus as their Messiah infuriates the antichrist and he unleashes all that hell can mobilize against God's holy people. His wrath ignites the fires of the great tribulation which is known as Jacob's trouble (Jer. 30:7).

A study of the juxtapositional, cross-referenced chart, which compares Revelation 12 with other Scriptures, reveals that the sun-clothed, moon-mounted pregnant woman is Israel. She is not a harlot. She is the original blood mother of the man-child whom she bore at Bethlehem who will rule the world with a "rod of iron." She is also the spiritual mother of the Church, "the daughter of Zion," (Micah 4:8). Jesus died that she might live. This is probably the saddest scene in all of the Bible, not just because Satan is here standing waiting to devour the child as soon as it would be born. It is immensely sad because this is the second time that Israel is going through the pangs of Messiah labor.

This second spiritual birth produces a sorrow vastly more intense and excruciating than the pains of a natural birth. There is a painful memory lingering in the consciousness of this weeping woman. She remembers the day two millenniums ago when false witnesses were summoned to condemn her Son, the Messiah, to hang on a Roman cross until He was dead. Her heart is broken with deep grief. Memories of bribed Roman centurions reporting a fabricated story surrounding her Son's resurrection also haunt her. While sobbing, bearing down, and panting in pangs of spiritual birth, she must drink the bitter dregs of a murderer's grief and guilt, pronouncing her own sentence as she condemns herself as the mother who crucified her own Son, the Messiah (Zech. 12:10).

1. The Sorrow of Salvation Squandered:

When the antichrist sets up his image in the temple and demands worship, the eyes of the house of Israel will become ablaze with spiritual understanding. The "veil" will be lifted from Israel's eyes as

VERIFICATION BY JUXTAPOSITIONAL COMPARISONS AND TERMINOLOGY DUPLICATION THAT THE WOMAN OF REVELATION CHAPTER TWELVE TYPIFIES ISRAEL AND NOT THE CHURCH.

CHAPTER 12

And there appeared a great wonder in heaven; a woman clothed with the sun[a], and the moon under her feet, and upon her head a <u>crown</u> of twelve stars:

2 And she being with child cried, travailing in birth[b], and pained to be delivered[c].

3 And there appeared another wonder in heaven; and behold a great red dragon, having seven heads and ten horns, and seven crowns upon his heads.

4 And his tail drew the third part of the stars of heaven, and did cast them to the earth: and the dragon stood before the woman which was ready to be delivered, for to devour her child as soon as it was born.

5 And she brought forth a man child[d], who was to rule[e] all nations with a rod of iron: and her child was caught up unto God, and *to* his throne.

6 And the woman fled into the wilderness[f], where she hath a place prepared of God, that they should feed her there <u>a thousand two hundred *and* threescore days.</u> [g]

7 And there was war in heaven: Michael and his angels fought against the dragon; and the dragon fought and his angels,

8 And prevailed not; neither was their place found any more in heaven.

9 And the great dragon was cast out, that old serpent, called the Devil, and Satan, which deceiveth the whole world: he was cast out into the earth, and his angels were cast out with him.

10 And I heard a loud voice saying in heaven, Now is come salvation, and strength, the kingdom[h] of our God, and the power of his Christ: for the accuser of our brethren is cast down, which accused them before our God day and night.

11 And they overcame him by the blood of the Lamb[c], and by the word of their testimony; and they loved not their lives unto the death.

12 Therefore rejoice, *ye* heavens, and ye that dwell in them. Woe to the inhabiters of the earth and of the sea! for the devil is come down unto you, having great wrath, because he knoweth that he hath but a short time.

13 And when the dragon saw that he was cast unto the earth, he persecuted the woman which brought forth the man *child*.

14 And to the woman were given two wings of a great eagle, that she might fly into the wilderness, into her place, where she is nourished for a <u>time, and times, and half a time</u>, from the face of the serpent.

15 And the serpent cast out of his mouth water as a flood after the woman, that he might cause her to be carried away of the flood.

16 And the earth helped the woman, and the earth opened her mouth, and swallowed up the flood[i] which the dragon cast out of his mouth.

17 And the dragon was wroth with the woman, and went to make war with the <u>remnant</u> of her seed, which keep the commandments of God, and have the testimony of Jesus Christ.

a. THE SIGN OF THE "SUN," "MOON," AND "STARS" identifies her as the family of Jacob, the father of Israel, as interpreted by Joseph's dream: "And he dreamed yet another dream... the sun moon and the eleven stars made obeisance to me ... What is this dream? ...Shall I and thy mother and thy brethren indeed come to bow ourselves to thee?... His father observed the saying (Gen. 37:9-11).

b. ISRAEL AND NOT THE CHURCH IS DEPICTED AS "TRAVAILING IN BIRTH." "Ask ye now and see whether a man (Jacob called Israel) doth travail with child?" (Jer. 30:6). "Be in pain, and labor to bring forth O daughter of Zion, like a woman in travail (Micah 4:10).

c. THE TRAVAIL TYPIFIES ISRAEL'S SPIRITUAL RE-BIRTH. "He will give them up until the time that she which travaileth hath brought forth" (Micah 5:3). "God hath not cast away his people ... blindness in part is happened to Israel ... (But) all Israel shall be saved" (Rom. 11:2, 25). "And I will pour upon the house of David ... the spirit of grace and supplications; and they shall look upon me whom they have pierced, and they shall mourn for him as one mourneth for his only son" (Zech. 12:10). "In that day there shall be a fountain opened to the house of David and to the inhabitants of Jerusalem for sin ... And one shall say unto him, What are these wounds in thine hands? Then he shall answer, those with which I was wounded in the house of my friends" (Zech. 13:1, 6).

d. THE CROWN REPRESENTS REGALITY. THE PROMISE IS THAT ISRAEL WILL BE GIVEN THE KINGDOM. "And the kingdom and dominion, and the greatness of the kingdom under the whole heaven shall be given to the people of the saints of the most High, whose kingdom is an everlasting kingdom" (Dan. 7:27).

e. THE MAN CHILD COMES OUT OF ISRAEL AND NOT THE CHURCH. "Out of thee shall he come forth unto me that is to be ruler in Israel" (Micah 5:2) ... "She (Israel) was delivered of a man child" (Isa. 66:7). "I saw ... one like the Son of man came with the clouds of heaven ... and there was given him dominion, and glory and a kingdom ... which shall not pass away" (Dan. 7:13-14).

f. THE CHURCH IS UNIVERSAL AND COULD NOT POSSIBLY FLEE INTO THE WILDERNESS. THIS CAN ONLY REFER TO ISRAEL. "And I will bring you into the wilderness" (Ezek. 20:35).

g. THIS IS THE 3 1/2-YEAR TRIBULATION OF ISRAEL. "Alas that day is great, so that none is like it: it is even the time of 'JACOB'S TOUBLE'; but he shall be SAVED OUT OF IT" (Jer. 30:7). "And he shall ... wear out the SAINTS of the most High ... and they shall be given into his hand until a time, times and the dividing of time (Dan. 7:25). "... There shall be a time of trouble such as never was ... It shall be for a time, times and an half ... when he shall have accomplished to scatter the power of the HOLY PEOPLE (Israel - Dan. 12:1, 7).

h. THE WOMAN IN TRAVAIL THAT "HALTETH" CANNOT BE THE CHURCH. "I will make her that halted a remnant, and her that was cast far off a strong nation ... The kingdom shall come to the daughter of Jerusalem ... Why dost thou cry out aloud? ... Pangs have taken thee as a woman with child ... be in pain and labor to bring forth O DAUGHTER OF ZION" (Micah 4:4, 9, 10). "And... as the sun rose upon him, he HALTED upon his thigh" (Gen. 32:28, 31).

i. THE FLOOD TYPIFIES MANY PEOPLE (A great army) WHO COME AGAINST ISRAEL. "Now also many nations are gathered against thee (Micah 4:11). "... I will seek to destroy all nations that rise up against Jerusalem (Zech. 12:9). "For I will gather all nations against Jerusalem" (Zech. 14:2; Joel 3:9-16).

she sees the wounds in His hands for which she was responsible. She will look upon Him whom she pierced and every family in Israel will return home to mourn and weep alone.

> ...If thou hadst known, even thou, at least in this thy day, the things which belong unto thy peace! But now they are hid from thine eyes (Luke 19:42).

> O Jerusalem, Jerusalem, thou that killest the prophets, and stonest them which are sent unto thee, how often would I have gathered thy children together, even as a hen gathereth her chickens under her wings, and ye would not"(Matt. 23:37)

The sun-clad woman in travail, the moon, and the stars, as recorded in Revelation 12, are a paradigm of the family of Jacob. This is confirmed by the dream of Joseph:

> ...Behold I have dreamed a dream more; and, behold, the sun and the moon and the eleven stars made obeisance to me. And he told it to his father, and to his brethren: and his father rebuked him, and said unto him, What is this dream that thou hast dreamed? Shall I and thy mother and thy brethren indeed come to bow down ourselves to thee to the earth? (Gen. 37:9-11)

Jacob, (Joseph's father) though angry at the dream, nevertheless must have wondered about the implications of it. The sun-clad woman represents Rachel (the mother), the moon is Jacob, and the twelve stars are the sons of Jacob. Joseph's star to which the family bows to worship represents Jesus Christ, the Messiah, of whom Joseph is a prototype.

2. The Sorrow of a Second Spiritual Rebirth:

This vision represents a dual panorama of the two births of Christ to Israel. Isaiah 66:7 records that "before she travailed, she brought forth; before her pain came, she was delivered of a man child." How can the man child be born before the pains of birth? Christ's first

190

birth in Israel brought no pain to her as a nation. Only Mary experienced the pain of labor. Basically the prophet is saying, "A man child (the Messiah) will be delivered to Israel without her knowledge of it."

The real travail will be the spiritual birth of Christ to Israel as portrayed through the pregnant woman of Revelation 12. This is confirmed in Isaiah 66:8 where the prophet asks:

> Who hath heard such a thing? Who hath seen such things? Shall the earth be made to bring forth in one day? Or shall a nation be born at once? For as soon as Zion travailed, she brought forth her children.

Israel's deception by the antichrist, as the impostor Messiah, and her revelation of Jesus, as the true Messiah, will result in a national spiritual revival. Bitter tears will flow because of how they treated Him when "he came unto his own, and his own received him not" (John 1:11).

3. The Sorrow Over Their Suffering:

> And I will pour upon the house of David, and upon the inhabitants of Jerusalem, the spirit of grace and of supplications: and they shall look upon me whom they have pierced, and they shall mourn for him, as one mourneth for his only son, and shall be in bitterness for him, as one that is in bitterness for his firstborn. In that day shall there be a great mourning in Jerusalem, as the mourning of Hadadrimmon in the valley of Megiddon...the land shall mourn, every family apart...and their wives apart...In that day there shall be a fountain opened to the house of David and to the inhabitants of Jerusalem for sin and for uncleaness...And one shall say unto him, What are these wounds in thine hands? Then shall he answer, Those with which I was wounded in the house of my friends (Zech. 12:10-14; 13:1-6).

Zechariah saw Israel on its knees, crying out to Jehovah for the forgiveness of the crime of crucifying His Son. The prophet calls their sorrow "a great mourning in Jerusalem, as the mourning of

Hadadrimmon in the valley of Megiddon." Every Jew knows about the mourning over Josiah who became king at the age of eight. At the age of sixteen, he began to seek after the God of David, his father. After thirty-one years as king, he was wounded in a battle against Pharaoh Necho of Egypt in the valley of Meggido. He was carried from Hadadrimmon, but died before they reached Jerusalem. Josiah was buried with every honor.

Annually, the Jews would gather at Hadadrimmon to weep over Josiah, so they understood the reference to this story. Jerusalem's mourning, spoken of by Zechariah, will be much greater than the sorrow over Josiah. The prophet says that wives and husbands shall lose interest in each other and mourn separately over Christ whom they killed (Zech. 12:12-14).

The world has never heard such moaning and groaning. The world has never seen such rivers of tears, not even in Egypt when the first-born were killed, nor in Jerusalem when all boy babies under two years of age were slaughtered in an attempt to get the Christ child, nor in Germany where millions of Jews were exterminated. The cries of a nation on their knees will be heard in heaven. God, who gives Israel many second chances, here opens the fountain of Calvary for the second time (Zech. 13:1) and indeed a nation shall be born in a day.

Elijah's intercession for Israel will be answered (Rom. 11:2). Paul's "heart's desire and prayer to God for Israel...that they might be saved" will be heard (Rom. 10:1). Paul's steadfast faith and assurance "that all Israel would be saved" will become a reality (Rom. 11:26-27). The entire redemption of the world hinges upon the salvation of the Jews.

4. The Sorrow of her Scattering:

The mass conversion of Israel to Jesus Christ incites the wrath of the Devil and the antichrist. Israel is forced to flee (Rev. 12:6, 13, 17). Zechariah 13:7 tells how Israel will be scattered like sheep whose shepherd has been killed. There are hard times ahead for Israel. The Palestine Liberation Organization and Iraq are not the only ones trying to drive Israel into the sea.

Israel's restraint, as demonstrated in not retaliating against Iraqi agitation and aggression, will gain only temporary world approval. Unforeseen circumstances will turn world opinion against her. Russia will invade and fight a bloody battle with her (Ezek. 38 and 39). Israel will win the battle and, consequently, become a threat to the world, just as Saddam Hussein was a threat to peace in the Middle East. There is, however, a great difference. Iraq had an ambition to occupy Kuwait, Saudi Arabia and to control all of the Arab States. Israel will fight against Russia for her own survival, not to conquer new territory.

Israel just wants to be left alone in peace where she is now situated, but this will be misunderstood. Eventually, all the world will meet in the battle of Armageddon in an attempt to annihilate her, but this "holy war" will be different. It will not be Allah who is to save, as was the case with Iraq. The world will be facing "THE KING OF KINGS, AND LORD OF LORDS" (Rev. 19:16).

5. Her Sorrow Reaps Second Opportunities:

Not only will Israel experience a second birthing process, but she will also experience a second Pentecost. Zechariah 12:10 declares that God will pour His spirit upon the inhabitants of Jerusalem. In Joel 2:28-32, we are told that He would pour His spirit upon "all flesh" which actually means only the people of Israel. Verse 32 states that "whosoever shall call upon the name of the Lord shall be delivered..." and then restricts this deliverance of "whosoever" and "all flesh" to those residing "in mount Zion and Jerusalem" where this deliverance is to take place.

I am aware that there are brothers and sisters in the faith who insist that the Bible teaches there will be a great spiritual revival in the last days. I sincerely hope they are right. They see a universal implication in the expression "all flesh." The Bible does sometimes appear to imply universal implications that do not apply. For example, when Christ was born, "A decree went out that all the world should be taxed." But "all the world" referred only to the citizens of the Roman Empire and not to the entire world. Likewise, the "all flesh" referred to here means only Israel.

Israel will not only experience a second birth of Christ and a second Pentecost, but a second ascension as well. The statement that "...her child was caught up unto God, and to his throne" (Rev. 12:5) has a spiritual connotation. This symbolic spiritual ascension is made to assure Israel that their Messiah, in whom they now trust, inhabits a throne where no dragon can touch Him, and He will return to earth to "rule with a rod of iron."

Christ's second ascension announces to heaven that Israel has been freed by the fountain opened to the house of David for sin. Satan is promptly ejected from heaven. He is no longer allowed admission near the throne where, up until now, he has accused "the brethren" (Jews) of sin before God day and night. The Jews have overcome the devil by their "testimony" and "the blood of the Lamb" (Rev. 12:10-11)

Satan is furious when he is hurled out of heaven to the earth beneath, knowing "he hath but a short time." He lost the inhabitants of Sheol when Christ ascended the first time (Eph. 4:8). He lost the Church at the rapture before the tribulation (Matt. 24:36-41). Now he loses Israel through her repentance which is verified by the proclamation that the "brethren (the Jews)...overcame him (Satan) by the blood of the Lamb, and by the word of their testimony."

Finally, being born again unto Christ will result in a second rapture for the Jews. The first rapture is for the Church at the outset of the tribulation as implied by the invitation, "Come up hither..." (Rev. 4:1). The second rapture, which is for the Jews and the two witnesses after the tribulation, is again accompanied by the invitation to "Come up hither" (Rev. 11:12). This is the "post-tribulation trump of rapture" spoken of in Matthew 24:29-31 and 1 Thessalonians 4:16-17. This is almost always confused as the rapture of the Church.

Israel's "trump of God" rapture has no similarities with the "thief in the night" Church rapture spoken of in Matthew 24:36-42 and Luke 17:34-37. This will be discussed in detail just prior to the opening of the first seal in Revelation 6 and again at the sounding of the last trumpet (Rev. 10:6-8).

Because of her remorse for crimes committed against her Messiah, Israel will be delivered from her long captivity of legalistic blindness. The scales will fall from her eyes to see and understand that her deliverance was accomplished through the glorious gospel of Jesus Christ. The Church, after enduring many trials and suffering, will be rescued from the tribulation by the rapture. Israel, after she passes through the three and a half years of Jacob's trouble, will be caught up unto God before the vials of the wrath of God are poured out. She will be spared the judgments which will follow the sounding of the seventh trumpet. The duration of the seventh trumpet judgments are the forty-five days Daniel speaks of when he says, "Blessed is he that waiteth, and cometh (survives) to the thousand three hundred and five and thirty days" (Dan. 12:12). These will be discussed in detail with the seventh trumpet.

6. The Seeds of Sorrow:

On October 9, 1990, it was reported that nineteen Palestinians were killed at the wailing wall over a dispute regarding Israel's plans to build their temple near the Muslim mosque. After this incident, Saddam Hussein warned Israel that he had missiles capable of delivering chemical warheads right into Tel Aviv.

More recently, Israel assassinated the pro-Iranian Hezbollah leader, Sheik Abbas Musawi. Shiite guerrillas retaliated by firing rockets from Katyusha rocket launchers into Israel. In return, Israel crashed through U.N. barricades to storm into towns and villages in southern Lebanon, trying to flush out Katyusha launchers and terrorist nests. Sheik Hassan Nasrallah (Musawi's successor) issued a maximum alert of all the mujahedeen Islamic holy warriors. This kind of activity does not improve relations in the Middle East. Many countries, including the United States and Canada, expressed their displeasure against Israel's aggression.

A strange foreboding fills the air, and chaos and disaster are imminent as the seeds of destruction are being sown every day. The bombing of a bus or the shooting of a Palestinian soldier cannot go on without retaliation. Multiplied incidents will be used as propaganda to blackmail and discredit Israel until the world's opinion and good will turn against her. She will soon be forced to square off with Russia as prophesied in Ezekiel 38 and 39 and her victory will raise political eyebrows everywhere. Plans will be conjured up to greatly weaken or completely obliterate her. The rationale of the day will be: "A nation strong enough to defeat Russia could possibly take on the world; something needs to be done!"

A seven-year treaty will be agreed upon, which will then be broken by the antichrist, the leader of the E.E.C. who will represent the New World Order. However, the seeds of destruction have been sown to produce a full harvest of sin as described in Revelation 14. Armageddon will be the greatest harvest Hell has ever garnered.

7. The Church is Safe:

It would not be charitable to my brothers and sisters who insist that the pregnant woman symbolizes the Church to simply ignore them. It has never been my intent to tell the world why most everybody is wrong. Let me just ask a few questions (for which I do not claim to have all the answers) and leave it at that:

• If the pregnant woman symbolizes the Church and the Church is "a chaste virgin" (2 Cor. 11:2), is it not highly inappropriate for her to be found pregnant before the marriage supper of the Lamb? This symbol is not inappropriate for Israel, however, since Jehovah is her husband (Jer. 31:32).

• If the pregnant woman is the Church and the Church is the bride, then how can Christ — the bridegroom — also be the child she births?

• How can the man-child be born of the Church when the child is older than the Church? And how can we reconcile the fact that we, the Church, are born again of Christ? In the case of Israel, we know that Christ came from the root of Jesse, a son of David. Israel, His mother, is older than His coming in the flesh.

• If the woman is the Church and the twelve apostles are the twelve stars of her crown, then was Paul wrong when he said in Phillipians 4:1 that the Church (not the apostles) was his crown? If the Church begat the apostles, then they are her crown. But if the apostles brought the Church into being, then the Church is their crown.

• How could the Church flee into the wilderness and be protected for three and a half years when the Church is universal? Israel has already spent forty years in the wilderness and it should be no problem for this small nation to flee into the wilderness again.

Many nations in the world will regret how they have treated Israel! I am not a Jew, but I do know the Word of God. The Bible is full of disastrous consequences for those in history who have abused the chosen people of God:

...The Lord said to Abram...I will make of thee a great nation...and I will bless them that bless thee, and curse him that curseth thee: and in thee shall all families of the earth be blessed (Gen. 12:1-3).

V. MICHAEL AND THE DRAGON (Revelation 12)

And there appeared another wonder in heaven; and behold a great red dragon, having seven heads and ten horns, and seven crowns upon his heads. And his tail drew the third part of the stars of heaven, and did cast them to the earth: and the dragon stood before the woman which was ready to be delivered, for to devour her child as soon as it was born (Rev. 12:3-4).

And there was war in heaven: Michael and his angels fought against the dragon; and the dragon fought and his angels, and prevailed not; neither was their place found any more in heaven. And the great dragon was cast out, that old serpent, called the Devil, and Satan, which deceiveth the whole world: he was cast out into the earth, and his angels were cast out with him.

And I heard a loud voice saying in heaven, Now is come salvation, and strength, and the kingdom of our God, and the power of his Christ: for the accuser of our brethren is cast down, which accused them before our God day and night. And they overcame him by the blood of the Lamb, and by the word of their testimony; and they loved not their lives unto the death. Therefore rejoice, ye heavens, and ye that dwell in them. Woe to the inhabiters of the earth and of the sea! For the devil is come down unto you, having great wrath, because he knoweth that he hath but a short time (Rev. 12:7-12).

1. His Identity:

There are no hidden secrets or mysteries regarding the identity of the red dragon. The statement that "the great dragon was cast out, that old serpent, called the Devil, and Satan..." (Rev. 12:9) requires no further interpretation.

The dragon's seven crowned heads link him with the seven blasphemous heads of the beast which rises out of the sea. His red color links him with the other red or scarlet members of Satan's crew: The red horse (Rev. 6:4), the scarlet beast (Rev. 17:3) and the scarlet harlot (Rev. 17:4).

In addition to being called a dragon, he is known by many other names in the Scriptures, which include: Accuser, adversary, Beelzebub, Belial, deceiver, dog, god of this world, king of Babylon, leviathan, liar, Lucifer, murderer, prince of darkness, prince of the world, serpent, tempter, tormenter, and wolf.

2. The Reason for His Wrath:

Satan's chief ambition has always been to rule the world. Because his is a spiritual kingdom, this regency can only be realized through the subjugation of humans. For centuries, Satan has been called the "prince of this world" (worldliness), having tricked multitudes into acquiescing to his domination. Every satanic enterprise he has fostered has tried to bring separation from God, a state that yields eternal death. The first humans, Adam and Eve, were deceived by Satan and consequently every member of the entire human race has been vulnerable to his schemes. But Satan has been a loser in every battle fought against our Lord. Christ's victory over death, His ascension, and His promise to return to subdue and destroy the works of the devil and establish His kingdom of peace on earth are the reasons why Satan is filled with such great anger.

Satan's wrath will reach the boiling point when Israel, the pregnant woman, gives her allegiance to Jesus, her Messiah. The statement, "They overcame him by the blood of the Lamb, and by the word of their testimony; and they loved not their lives unto the death" (Rev. 12:11), reveals at once that Satan will lose his grip upon Israel's subjugation to him. Israel's refusal to bow and worship the antichrist's image, choosing rather to die, becomes the ultimate spiritual slap in the face of Satan. His son (the antichrist) is rejected and God's Son (the Christ) is chosen in his place.

The bondage of sin is broken when the blood of Christ cleanses Israel. They will find freedom and bear testimony of it. This will be Israel's finest and most perilous hour, for allegiance to Christ never comes without a price. There has never been, nor will ever be, a greater decision in the history of mankind than Israel's messianic trust in Jesus Christ and the staking of their nationhood upon faith in Him. God will greatly reward them for it. The capitol of the world will be the holy Jerusalem from which Jesus shall reign. Though Satan rages, his son will be defeated "...and they shall take away his dominion, to consume and to destroy it unto the end" (Dan. 11:26). Jesus will be King and the saints and Israel will rule the whole world!

> And I saw in the night visions, and, behold, one like the Son of man came with the clouds of heaven, and came to the Ancient of days, and they brought him near before him. And there was given him dominion, and glory, and a kingdom, that all people, nations and languages, should serve him: his dominion is an everlasting dominion, which shall not pass away, and his kingdom that which shall not be destroyed...but the saints of the most High shall take the kingdom, and possess the kingdom for ever, even for ever and ever...And the kingdom and dominion, and the greatness of the kingdom under the whole heaven, shall be given to the peo-

ple of the saints of the most High, whose kingdom is an everlasting kingdom, and all dominions shall serve and obey him (Dan. 7:13-14, 18, 27).

It has been God's intention from the beginning that His Son should rule the world. It has been Satan's intention to stop Him and install the antichrist as ruler. Satan endows the antichrist with all of the power he has at his disposal. All of Satan's hopes of defeating Christ and becoming the tyrant of this world will rest upon this one man. The devil knows this is his last opportunity.

Satan is frustrated, angry, and getting nervous. The mighty warrior from heaven is staring at him and the final showdown is inevitable. Satan knows he has never yet won a battle against Him.

3.   The Power at His Command:

As we approach the end of the world, it will become increasingly evident that the final conflicts are spiritual. It will not be Jew against Arab, Russia against Jew, or Jew against the world — the unseen battle will be Christ against Satan. The warring leaders of the world have never executed their strategies by their own genius, rather by a world of darkness and demonic power. War comes from the murderer and father of lies, Satan.

In the final analysis, however, it is God who will decide at whom the gun is to be pointed and when the trigger is to be pulled. God will use the blundering efforts of Satan to bring about a true world order where neither the Devil nor war will be present, and the world will experience peace for one thousand years. This will be Christ's world order, not the one which is being dreamed about by present-day world leaders.

In the meantime, the battle lines are being drawn. Satan, his one-third of all created angels, and the wicked spirits from Hell and the bottomless pit are arrayed against the forces of good. These evil spirits will take on locust-like forms to torment men for five months during the tribulation. Satan also has four angel generals bound in the Euphrates with 200,000,000 spirits of wicked men who will ride out on fire-spitting, lion-headed horses to kill one-third of the world's population (Rev. 9:11-21). And finally, three frog-like demons will come out of the mouth of the dragon, the beast and the false prophet to convince the world's kings to bring their armies to the battle of Armageddon. This battle will result in a blood river 160 miles long and as deep as the horse's bridles (Rev. 16:14-16; 14:20).

When all of these evil forces are unleashed against the weakened, child-bearing woman Israel, her only hope will be the power of the warrior of Revelation 19:11-21.

4. Michael Returns:

In her helpless posture of giving birth, the woman seems to be a sure victim for the dragon. But He "that keepeth Israel, neither slumbers nor sleeps" and He brings Michael and his angels onto the scene again. The devil has fought with Michael before. When Moses, the champion of Israel, died on Mount Nebo on the ridge called Pizgah, Satan was right there to try to claim his body. He accused Moses of sinning before God in striking the rock in anger instead of addressing it.

But the mighty Michael was also present when Moses died (Jude 9). He is the defender of Israel and especially concerned when one like Moses, the greatest leader Israel has ever known, is involved. Moses will reappear during the tribulation along with Elijah and bear his witness of the transfiguration, death, resurrection, and ascension of Jesus as recorded in Revelation 11. These two prophets will be the unmaking of antichrist. Satan tried his best to eliminate Moses long ago, but Michael came to his rescue.

In Daniel 10:13-21, we find Michael and Jesus strengthening Daniel, the man "greatly beloved" who was the prophet of God and of Israel. Daniel 12:1 and Revelation 12:7 could well be regarded as twin prophecies of Michael defending Israel. Daniel calls him "the great prince which standeth for the children of thy people (Israel)."

Recently a post-tribulation advocate has declared that Michael is the restraining power which must be taken out of the way before the man of sin can be revealed (2 Thess. 2:7-8). I have researched many translations of the Bible and none of them suggest that Michael "will step aside" and allow the devil and the antichrist to do with Israel as they please. On the contrary, Scripture asserts that Michael will "stand up" to fight and defend Israel during the tribulation.

It will be impossible for Satan to destroy Israel because Michael's chief office is to defend her. The battle between the dragon and his angels and Michael and his angels appears to be brief, decisive, and final. The Bible simply states that "the dragon fought and his angels, and prevailed not; neither was their place found any more in heaven. And the dragon was cast out, that old serpent called the Devil, and Satan..." (Rev. 12:7-9).

This will be Satan's second fall, and he will not take the defeat lightly. The advantages of being near the throne of God and being in the heavenlies will both be lost and he will be demoted to an earthling. But his next plunge will be much deeper and devastating.

5. God is Still on the Throne:

God's manner of assuring Israel of His presence and protection has most always been through a miraculous sign. In Revelation 12, we see that while Israel was fleeing from the dragon, "the serpent cast out of his mouth water as a flood after the woman, that he might cause her to be carried away of the flood" (Rev. 12:15). There is no dragon capable of spewing out enough water to flood away half a nation. The water is a symbol and is explained in Daniel 9:26 as an army (called a flood) which pursues Israel. Israel knows all about being pursued by heathen armies. Pharaoh sent his army to capture and return Israel to Egypt when they were attempting an escape at midnight. His army was swallowed by the Red Sea.

The dragon's army will be swallowed up by the earth which is nothing new for Israel. In Numbers 16:23-35 ,we have the account of Korah, Dathan, and Abiram, who rebelled against Moses and Aaron. Their judgment came swiftly when the earth opened her jaws and swallowed them and their families alive. The miracle of the earth swallowing the pursuing army will convince Israel that God is on their side, just as He was on the night they left Egypt enroute to Canaan. The eternal city promised to her fathers has been long in coming, but it is sure to come (Heb. 11:16). The real Canaan cannot now be far away.

There is a definite Old Testament correlation here between the enemy being swallowed up and the woman being given "two wings of a great eagle" (Rev. 12:14-15). In Exodus 19:4, we read, "Ye have seen what I did unto the Egyptians, and how I bare you on eagles' wings, and brought you unto myself." When Israel again gets on the side with God (and His Christ) as she did in the day of Moses, her march to the eternal Canaan cannot be impeded. All enemies will have to yield the right of way, even as when Israel fled from Egypt.

6. Blind Attack:

The escape of the woman and the suffocation of an entire division of his army infuriates the dragon even more. He now turns his fury upon the remnant of her seed, those in Israel who could not escape or perhaps the soldiers who stand guard (Rev. 12:17). Satan is beginning to experience real claustrophobia with the passing of each day. Fear of an ominous and humiliating defeat will drive him as he is about to go down for the third time.

Intimidation will be no deterrent to his final thrust. His last remembrance of Heaven will be the words, "Now is come salvation, and strength, and the kingdom of our God, and the power of his Christ" (Rev. 12:10). Yet there is no shred of decency to be found in him. He is devoid of feeling and conscience, completely incapable of remorse, shame, or intimidation.

Insult will be no deterrent. These same angels, which shout out the imminent victory of the Messiah, also proclaim, "For the accuser of our brethren is cast down." But he has no shame and he completely ignores their refrain.

A deadline is no deterrent. Normally, those on death row call for a clergy man to have an opportunity for repentance. The last hours before their appointment with death are spent in communion with the Almighty, seeking His grace and forgiveness. Satan is far too proud to pray or call upon God for forgiveness for his attempted coup. To him, knowing his time is short means he must deceive as many as he possibly can in what remains.

Loss is no deterrent. He will witness the suffocation of a division of his army as the Almighty opens a cleft in the earth to swallow the men who try to capture the woman. Death has always been his trophy and delight.

Disrespect and indignity are no deterrent. He will do whatever it takes to inflict destitution and desolation. Prisons, hospitals, mental asylums, and various holding institutions are filled with those who bear witness to the devastation wrought by his deeds. Here we see him in pursuit of the last of that which is good in the world: "The remnant of her seed."

Military suicide is no deterrent. Silhouetted against the eastern sunrise at the front battlelines of the little "remnant" will be the one sitting on a white horse with a sword in His mouth. Following Him upon white horses are the armies of heaven. They will win the war without a drop of blood splattered on their pure white robes, for it will be King Jesus who will fight. His word is sharper than any one's sword. The Lamb is angry, and Satan's preposterous stand against Him means certain suicide.

There is a side about our Lord Jesus Christ that the world has never yet seen. Man's perception of Him is as a penniless Galilean — a homeless, merciful, disease-healing, mankind-loving Savior. And so He is. But He will not forever pray to the Father, "Forgive them for they know not what they do." When God's great love has been offended, hurt, and provoked, it finally becomes the wrath of God. He is to be pitied, who falls into the hands of "a living God" (Heb. 10:31).

Victories of past history are no deterrent. God's most spectacular victories have been in the face of sure defeat. David and Goliath, Gideon and his 300 men, Samson with the jaw-bone of an ass as his weapon against hordes of Philistines, are just a few examples. The supreme mistake of Satan is in his attacking the defenseless pregnant woman and remnant of the woman's seed. Micah 4:6-13 tells the consequences of those who attempt to hurt the one in travail. God will literally thresh out the wicked that come up against her that "halteth." He will destroy those who will attempt to "defile her that is in travail."

Our Lord will not sit by in the hour of Israel's deepest need. She will be surrounded by enemies, but they shall not prevail. Just about the time that Satan feels he has destroyed her will be precisely the point at which he will go down for a ten-century count.

Confrontation with omnipotence is no deterrent. There is absolutely no strategy that will wipe Israel off the face of the earth. Neither the Palestine Liberation Organization, Iraq, Iran, Libya, Russia, nor any other nation in the whole world, will or can defeat her. Just a single word spoken by the one with the sword in His mouth is all that is necessary to decimate the enemies of Israel.

7. No Light at the End of the Tunnel:

The second to the last scene in the drama of Satan's defeat is recorded in Revelation 20:1-3:

And I saw an angel coming down from heaven, having the key of the bottomless pit and a great chain in his hand. And he laid hold on the dragon, that old serpent, which is the Devil, and Satan, and bound him a thousand years, and cast him into the bottomless pit, and shut him up, and set a seal upon him that he should deceive the nations no more....

I do not know what this "bottomless pit" really means. I have often wondered if it might signify eternity. If it does not, then I hope it is so deep and so dark that Satan can never come into contact with a human again. I hope its depth and darkness are compounded of the misery, anguish, and grief of the many he has crushed. I hope the word "bottomless" denotes an utterly deplorable circumstance, proof that Satan will be so removed as never to be remembered. When that day arrives, justice will be satisfied.

VI. THE ONE HUNDRED AND FORTY-FOUR THOUSAND FAITHFUL WITNESSES (Revelation 7:1-8; 14:1-5)

And after these things I saw four angels standing on the four corners of the earth, holding the four winds of the earth, that the wind should not blow on the earth, nor on the sea, nor on any tree. And I saw another angel ascending from the east, having the seal of the living God. And he cried with a loud voice to the four angels, to whom it was given to hurt the earth and the sea, saying, Hurt not the earth, neither the sea, nor the trees, till we have sealed the servants of our God in their foreheads. And I heard the number of them which were sealed: and there were sealed an hundred and forty and four thousand of the tribes of the children of Israel...(twelve thousand from each of the following tribes: Judah, Reuben, Gad, Ahser, Nephtali, Manasseh, Simeon, Levi, Issachar, Zebulon, Joseph and Benjamin) (Rev. 7:1-8).

And I looked, and lo, a Lamb stood on the mount of Zion, and with Him an hundred forty and four thousand, having his Father's name written in their foreheads. And I heard a voice from heaven, as the voice of many waters, and as the voice of a great thunder: and I heard the voice of harpers harping with harps: and they sung as it were a new song before the throne, and before the four beasts, and the elders: and no man could learn that song but the hundred and forty and four thousand, which were redeemed from the earth. These are they which were not defiled with women; for they are virgins. These are they which follow the Lamb whithersoever he goeth. These were redeemed from among men, being the firstfruits unto God and to the Lamb. And in their mouth was found no guile: for they are without fault before the throne of God (Rev. 14:1-5).

In the "theological camp" of the 144,000, we discover a few religious bigots wandering around, envying this holy class of God's specially selected servants. There are several forms of religion whose leaders and teachers believe they have a revelation from God that they represent this specially selected class. They are somehow overlooking the fact that those who were "sealed were an hundred and forty and four thousand of all the tribes of the children of Israel" (Rev. 7:4).

The Scriptures do not tell us that these 144,000 are a mystery or a number that needs to be understood spiritually. This is not a symbolic number or a figure of speech, this is a simple fact. The 144,000 are Jews! Following is the scriptural data available to us:

- They are "servants of our God" (Rev. 7:3). The Greek calls them "slaves." The Amplified Bible employs the term "bond servants."

- They are sealed "in their foreheads...having his Father's name written in their foreheads" (Rev. 7:3; 14:1).

- The time of this sealing is established as being just before the winds (which four angels are now holding back) are released (Rev. 7:1-3). The four winds represent judgments that will "hurt" the earth, sea, and trees. This hurting and releasing of the winds takes place shortly after the half-hour silence has expired and constitutes the execution of the first three trumpets of the seventh seal (Rev. 8:1, 7-11). The precise time of this sealing is very near the beginning of the tribulation, when the first three trumpets are sounded.

- Their identity as being Jews is certified in the direct naming of the twelve tribes of Israel, with twelve thousand being sealed from each of the tribes named (Rev. 7:4-8).

- We observe that two tribes, Dan and Ephraim, are omitted from this list, and that Joseph and Levi take their place. These are Jews who believe in the messianic Jesus, "They which follow the Lamb whithersoever he goeth" (Rev. 14:4).

- They are honored by a celestial harp choir and the raptured Church (many waters) which sings "a new song" (Rev. 14:2-3).

- Their high and holy character is typified by their being "redeemed from the earth" (worldliness) and "from among men" (separated unto God) (Rev. 14:3-4).

- They are saints of the purest order. Not being defiled with women does not necessarily mean they are not married. A man or a woman who has known only his or her matrimonial partner and has never been unfaithful to that partner will forever be regarded by God as a virgin, for the "marriage bed is undefiled" (Heb. 13:4).

- They are disciples of the highest order, for "in their mouth was found no guile: for they are without fault before the throne of God" (Rev. 14:5).

- "They are firstfruits unto God, and the Lamb" (Rev. 14:4), meaning they were the first to believe in Christ after the antichrist set up his image for compulsory worship in the temple.

With the above data at hand, it is clear to see why the antichrist will run into very heavy sledding. These 144,000 Jewish witnesses of Jesus will turn many Jews to Jesus Christ around the world. Many in Israel will not bow the knee to antichrist because of their powerful message. Let us qualify this by considering the following seven pronouncements regarding them:

1. They are Anti-Antichrist:

- Because they are called "the servants of our God."

- Because they stand with the Lamb on mount Zion.

- Because they have refused the mark 666 and in its place bear the name of Jehovah. Jesus said in John 5:43, "I am come in my Father's name, and ye receive me not; another will come in his own name, him ye will receive." By rejecting the mark, they indicate their willingness to die for Christ, exemplifying great love for their Master.

- Because of their pure, holy, righteous, and redeemed estate.

2. They are Tribulation, Messianic, Global Missionaries:

Proclamation of the gospel is accomplished by the Church and the Holy Spirit. Because both of these means will have been removed before the tribulation, God will revert back to Old Testament methods of employing prophets and angels to convey His messages.

The mission of evangelizing the world will be difficult. An intense conflict over the mastery of the souls of God's people, the Jews, will ensue. This is Israel's last call and God's final invitation. The 144,000 are sent to take the place of the Church and the Holy Spirit. They, along with angels and the prophets, Moses and Elijah, will carry the message of the kingdom to the lost sheep of the house of Israel.

In Zechariah 12:10-14 and Revelation 7:9-17, we see that the message indeed reaches every tribe of the children of Israel. How God does this, I do not know, for Israel is scattered all over the world. I would not be surprised to learn that there are many peoples of the earth who are Jews and unaware of it. God, however, knows, and He has solved greater problems than this.

Israel will experience, as previously stated, a second birth, a Pentecost, ascension, and rapture. The 144,000 of Revelation 7 represent the second post-Pentecost scattering. I believe these 144,000 Jews are a type of the fourteen nations who were present on the day of Pentecost. There are fourteen tribes of Israel involved in Revelation 7, the twelve who are named and the two who are omitted, Ephraim and

Dan. This omission would not mean that these two tribes will be excluded from being evangelized by the 144,000. It only means they were not worthy to be included as evangelists.

Consider the aggregate number of Christians who went everywhere preaching the gospel:

- The 3,000 converted on the day of Pentecost recorded in Acts 2:41
- Those added daily to the Church in Acts 2:47
- The 5,000 of Acts 4:4
- The adding and multiplication of Acts 5:14
- The multitudes of Acts 5:16
- The converts of Acts 5:42
- The multiplied group of disciples of Acts 6:1
- The increasing of the Word of God and the great multi plying of the Church in Acts 6:7
- Philip's converts (Acts 8:6)
- The preaching of Acts 8:25
- The converts of the Ethiopian eunuch (Acts. 8:27)
- The preaching at Azotus and other cities (Acts. 8:40)
- The ministry of Saul (Acts 9:22)
- The preaching of Peter (Acts 9:35)
- The revival at Joppa (Acts 9:42)
- The Gentile converts of Acts 10:45 and 11:18
- The success at Antioch (Acts 11:26)
- Plus the many whom Paul, Barnabas, Peter, Mark, Silas, Timothy, John, and others brought into the Church.

I believe the early Church missionaries and their mission, as listed above, could quite possibly total 144,000, a prototype of the 144,000 tribulation missionaries. The enemies of the early Church were emperors like Nero. The enemy of the 144,000 servants of God is the antichrist. I see in this a type of Pentecost and a second scattering for the purpose of proclaiming the message of the kingdom to all the world.

Matthew 24:29-31 states that after the tribulation God will send His angels into all the world and they will gather His elect (the spiritual fruits of the 144,000 and of Moses and Elijah) from the four winds of heaven. Here is evidence of how faithfully these "servants of God" proclaimed this message on a global scale. I suppose the answer to their faithfulness lies in their obedience in following the Lamb "whithersoever" He calls them.

3. They are Scrupulously Selected:

God has a good memory. After centuries have rolled by, He remembers the sins of Dan and Ephraim. In 1 Kings 12:25-30, we have the record of how Jeroboam built altars in Dan in the tribe of Dan and at Bethel in the tribe of Ephraim. They made two golden calves and then said, "Behold thy gods, O Israel, which brought thee up out of the land of Egypt" (1 Kings 12:28).

God warned Israel that any man or woman or family or tribe whose heart turned away to serve other gods would be separated from among the tribes of Israel (Deut. 29:18-21). This is exactly what happened. Dan and Ephraim have been excluded from the list of the twelve tribes chosen for this special task and in their place we find the names of the righteous Joseph and Levi.

The Psalmist knew the high expectations God has for those who proclaim His Word. In Psalm 24:3, David asks the questions, "Who shall ascend into the hill of the Lord? Or who shall stand in his holy place?" The answer is revealed in verse 4, "He that hath clean hands, and a pure heart; who hath not lifted up his soul unto vanity, nor sworn deceitfully."

These 144,000 are without fault. They will come from every corner of the world - black Jews, Asian Jews, Russian Jews, German Jews, and all kinds of other Jews. There is not a country in the world to which they have not been scattered. But the Lord's promise is that He "...will gather them out of all countries" (Jer. 32:37).

This is the only reference to end-time spiritual revival that I find. It is a duplication of Joel 2:28-32, a dual prophecy concerning the first Pentecost resulting in the evangelization of the Gentiles here being repeated as typified by Ezekiel's valley vision of the resurrection of dry bones (Ezek. 37). The Gentiles do not appear to be included in this revival. The Bible teaches in Romans 11:25-26 that Israel will be blind until the time of the Gentiles is come in, but "all Israel shall be saved."

Both Jews and Gentiles who give allegiance to the antichrist will be smitten with discernment failure. "God shall send them strong delusion, that they should believe a lie, that they all might be damned who believed not the truth, but had pleasure in unrighteousness" (2 Thess. 2:11-12). May God have mercy upon every one who is squandering his day of grace, for he will surely be stricken with the divine delusion spoken of by the apostle.

4. Their Seal, a Signet of Safety:

It should be regarded as a miracle that all of the 144,000 will survive the tribulation as seen in Revelation 14:3-4. The demons of the fifth trumpet are restricted to hurting only "those men which have not the seal of God in their foreheads" (Rev. 9:4). It would appear reasonable to conclude that if God protects the 144,000 from this first woe, they would likewise be protected from all of them.

5. They are Especially Favored Because of Past Service:

At the outset of the tribulation John sees "under the altar the souls of them that were slain for the word of God, and for the testimony which they held" (Rev. 6:9). These slain ones are, no doubt, the first converts of the 144,000 before they were sealed. The 144,000 will no doubt be the first to recognize that the antichrist is not the Messiah, and they will immediately sound the alarm.

Matthew 24:24 says that it is possible that the "very elect" could be deceived by the antichrist. These mentioned here must have been acquainted with the Scriptures which tell about the deceiver. They are called "first fruits" which means they were the first to believe in Christ and the first to win converts for Christ. The statement that "these were redeemed from among men, being the first fruits (first converts) unto God and to the Lamb" (Rev. 14:4) certainly seems to indicate this.

6. Heaven Honors Them with a Song That Only They Can Learn:

The people of God are known by the songs they sing. God's greatest triumphs are always celebrated with songs. Exodus 15 records the songs

211

of Moses and Miriam after God delivered them from Egypt. In Numbers 21:17, we find the song Israel sings after God provides water for them. The Psalms, the Song of Solomon, and the Books of Isaiah and Jeremiah are famous for their songs. Paul and Silas sang songs at midnight while in prison. During His darkest night here on earth, our Saviour met with His disciples in the upper room, sang a song, and then went to the garden to pray. God will give a song to His faithful ones even during the tribulation (Rev. 5:9; 14:3; 15:3).

Satan is no musician and the lake of fire, the bottomless pit, and Hell have no choirs or organs in them. The only sounds heard in Hell will come from drums beating time to the endless suffering of the lost. True music and melody can be found only in the heart at peace with God. The joys of salvation generate songs of praise. The majesty and greatness of God cause all of creation to break forth with song. I hope God allows us to at least hear the song of the 144,000, even though we can never learn it.

7. They Reap a Great Harvest:

> After this I beheld, and, lo, a great multitude, which no man could number, of all nations, and kindreds, and people, and tongues, stood before the throne, and before the Lamb, clothed with white robes, and palms in their hands; and cried with a loud voice, saying, Salvation to our God which sitteth upon the throne, and unto the Lamb.

> And all the angels stood round about the throne, and about the elders and the four beasts, and fell before the throne on their faces, and worshipped God, saying, Amen: blessing, and glory, and wisdom, and thanksgiving, and honour, and power, and might, be unto our God for ever and ever. Amen.

> And one of the elders answered, saying unto me, What are these which are arrayed in white robes? And whence came they? And I said unto him, Sir, thou knowest. And he said to me, These are they which came out of great tribulation, and have washed their robes, and made them white in the blood of the Lamb. Therefore are they before the throne of God, and serve him day and night in his temple: and he that sitteth on the throne shall dwell among them.

They shall hunger no more, neither thirst any more; neither shall the sun light on them, nor any heat. For the Lamb which is in the midst of the throne shall feed them, and shall lead them unto living fountains of waters: and God shall wipe away all tears from their eyes (Rev. 7:9-17).

There are three very visible elements about this multitude. First, they are time-oriented. Because they "washed their robes" during the great tribulation, their tenure is limited to but three and a half years.

Second, they come "out of great tribulation." Pre-tribulationists insist that the tribulation spoken of here includes all of the tribulations the Church has endured during her history. I have researched many translations of the Bible and none of them give any indication that this is the case.

Martin Luther, in his German translation, says, *Aus grossen truebsal.* These words translate into "out of great tribulation" which does not necessarily mean the great tribulation. Menge renders the same words, *Aus der grossen truebsal,* which means "out of the great tribulation." The Amplified, Living, and Revised Standard versions (as well as others) agree with Menge's translation. The Greek interlinear employs the words "out of the affliction great." There seems to be little doubt that the tribulation here intended is "Jacob's trouble" or the great tribulation.

The third visible element is the expression, "A great multitude from every tribe, kindred and nation." This statement has created a problem for scholars who hold that the Church will not be going through the tribulation because they have failed to identify Israel as being the "great multitude." The reference to all nations, kindreds, people, and tongues, "seems" to describe the Church, but instead is describing the regathered Israel.

A proper understanding of the magnitude of Israel's dispersion sheds new light on the identity of this "great multitude." I recall, reading somewhere in the footnotes of Ryrie's Bible, one historian describing the "diaspora" as being so absolute that "there is not a corner in the world where a Jew cannot be found." The scattering of Israel was not just a happening, it was a direct judgment from God. When God scatters something, it will take angels to gather it up again.

Immediately after the tribulation of those days shall the sun be darkened, and the moon shall not give her light, and the stars shall fall from heaven, and the powers of the heavens shall be shaken. And then shall appear the sign of the Son of man in heaven: and then shall all the tribes of the earth mourn, and they shall see the Son of man coming in the clouds of heaven with power and great glory. And he shall send his angels with a great sound of a trumpet, and they shall gather together his elect from the four winds, from one end of the heaven to the other (Matt. 24:29-31).

It should not be difficult to identify those for whom our Savior comes after the tribulation. The words "tribes of the earth" are certainly not descriptive of the Church, rather they are descriptive of Israel. The entire context of Matthew 24 employs Jewish connotations like holy place (in the temple - vs. 15), sabbath day (vs. 20), and Judea (vs. 16).

The prophet Ezekiel records a graphic vision of Israel's regathering and spiritual revival. He sees a valley filled with dry bones and is commanded to call the four winds to breathe upon them. Imagine how amazed Ezekiel must have been when he heard the rattle of dry bones coming together, taking on flesh, and then standing to their feet until they were an "exceeding great army." The prophet was told the vision typified the regathering of Israel from the ends of the earth (Ezek. 37:1-14).

The following are just some the Scriptures regarding Israel's dispersion:

- I said, I would scatter them into corners... (Deut. 32:26 - this is where the angels gather them from in Matt. 24:31).

- ...I have cast them far off among the heathen, and ...scattered them among the countries... (Ezek. 11:16).

- And I will bring you out from the people, and will gather you out of the countries wherein ye are scattered, with a mighty hand, and with a stretched-out arm and with fury poured out. And I will bring you into the wilderness of the people... (Ezek. 20:34-35)

See also: Leviticus 26:33, 1 Kings 14:15, Nehemiah 1:8-9, Psalm 106:26-27, Jeremiah 30:11, Zechariah 7:14, Deuteronomy 30:3-4, Joel 3:2, and Isaiah11:11-12. Israel does indeed qualify as "all kindreds, nations, tongues and peoples."

The Church has never looked or waited for a Messiah. We are sure that Jesus Christ, who was crucified, is the Messiah. We look for the Son of God to return from heaven. The people with palms in their hands in Revelation 7:9 are the converts of the 144,000 and of Elijah (John the baptist, who preached the gospel of the kingdom as a witness to all the world [Matt. 24:14]). Having come out of the great tribulation, they (along with the two witnesses Moses and Elijah) hear the call of "come up hither" and are themselves the cloud in which the two witnesses ascend into heaven. This is the second rapture recorded in the Book of Revelation (11:12). These Jewish converts are also those seen in Revelation 15:2 who escape the last forty-five days called the shortened days in Matthew 24:22, when the wrath of God is poured out upon an unbelieving world.

VII. THE TWO WONDER-WORKING WITNESSES
(Revelation 11:3-12)

And I will give power unto my two witnesses, and they shall prophesy a thousand two hundred and threescore days, clothed in sackcloth. These are the two olive trees, and the two candlesticks standing before the God of the earth. And if any man will hurt them, fire proceedeth out of their mouth, and devoureth their enemies: and if any man will hurt them, he must in this manner be killed. These have power to shut heaven, that it rain not in the days of their prophecy: and have power over waters to turn them to blood, and to smite the earth with all plagues, as often as they will.

And when they shall have finished their testimony, the beast that ascendeth out of the bottomless pit shall make war against them, and shall overcome them, and kill them. And their dead bodies shall lie in the street of that great city, which spiritually is called Sodom and Egypt, where also our Lord was crucified. And they of the people and kindreds

215

and tongues and nations shall see their dead bodies three days and an half, and shall not suffer their dead bodies to be put in graves. And they that dwell upon the earth shall rejoice over them, and make merry, and shall send gifts one to another; because these two prophets tormented them that dwelt on the earth.

And after three days and an half the Spirit of life from God entered into them, and they stood upon their feet; and great fear fell upon them which saw them. And they heard a great voice from heaven saying unto them, Come up hither. And they ascended up to heaven in a cloud; and their enemies beheld them (Rev. 11:3-12).

God is quite serious about rescuing Israel from the hand of the antichrist. He brings two ancient prophets back from the dead to perform all the miracles that the false prophet and antichrist perform to convince Israel and the world that they are impostors.

1. The Identity of the Two Wonder-Working Witnesses:

There are three names ascribed to these two prophets: "My witnesses," "the two olive trees," and "the two candlesticks." These names, plus the miracles they perform, are really all we need to establish their identity.

In order for the two men of Revelation 11 to fully meet the prerequisites to be witnesses of Jesus, it is essential that they must personally have witnessed the death, resurrection, and ascension of Jesus. Moses and Elijah fulfill these prerequisites. Just a few days before His death, Jesus took Peter, James, and John onto a mountain where He was transfigured before them. They saw Him talking with Moses and Elias (Elijah) and heard God's voice saying, "This is my beloved Son in Whom I am well pleased; hear ye Him" (Matt.17:5).

As the two prophets talked with Jesus, I believe Jesus instructed them that He was the Messiah of whom the prophets had written and informed them of His impending death, resurrection, and ascension. I believe it is here that He commissioned these two as witnesses for Him during the tribulation some 2,000 years hence. Not only did He commission them during this moment in time, He also in-

216

structed them to be present on the day He died, the day He arose, and the day He ascended into heaven.

- On the day that Jesus died, there was an earthquake, the veil was rent in twain, the rocks were shattered and graves were opened. The Word of God says that during those days, saints which slept arose and went into Jerusalem (Matt. 27:52-53). I think Moses and Elijah were among them.

- On the day of Christ's resurrection, I believe it was these two men (not angels) who were waiting for the women at the tomb to witness of Jesus' resurrection (Luke 24:4; John 20:12).

- On the day that Jesus ascended into heaven, two men (not angels) appeared and said, "This same Jesus, which is taken up from you into heaven, shall so come in like manner as ye have seen him go into heaven" (Acts 1:11). I firmly believe these two men who witnessed the death, resurrection, and ascension of Jesus are Moses and Elijah (John the Baptist). Both of them miraculously escaped death as infants for this special ministry.

When (in the very near future) the antichrist, or leader of the E.E.C., sets up his image in the soon-to-be-built temple in Jerusalem, Moses and Elijah will appear in Jerusalem, dressed in sackcloth. They will tell the people in Israel that 2,000 years ago, just a few days before His crucifixion, they met Jesus, the Jewish Messiah, on the mount of transfiguration. They heard the voice of Jehovah from heaven saying that Jesus was His Son. They will recount how, in spirit, they saw Him dying on a cross and then stood by the sepulcher as the earth shook and He, with wounded hands and feet and side, walked forth from the tomb. They will relate how forty days after He arose from the dead, they stood on the mount of Olives at Bethany and saw Him ascending into heaven.

This will send shock waves throughout the world. The Jews will be terrified and confused. Over in one end of Jerusalem, the false prophet and the antichrist are calling fire down from heaven in an attempt to deceive the people into believing the antichrist is the Messiah. In the other end of Jerusalem, Moses and Elijah will be saying the Jews crucified the true Messiah some 2,000 years ago. In order for Moses and Elijah to establish their credibility, the Jews will demand a sign. Moses and Elijah will prove their legitimacy by the power Jehovah has vested in them.

2. The Witness of Elijah:

I can imagine Elijah opening the Jewish scroll and reading:

Behold, I will send you Elijah the prophet before the coming of the great and dreadful day of the Lord (Mal. 4:5, KJV).

His preaching will bring fathers and children together again, to be of one mind and heart, for they will know that if they do not repent, I will come and utterly destroy their land (Mal. 4:6, Living Bible)

I can envision him saying, as he rolls up the scroll, *I am Elijah of old; and I will verify this claim by withholding rain for the next three and a half years. To further demonstrate God's power in me, fire from my mouth will destroy my enemies with the words of God. I will also do many other miracles.* Prophecies regarding these acts are recorded in Revelation 11:5-6.

God not only thought it necessary for Moses and Elijah to witness His Son's death, resurrection, and ascension, but also His baptism and the early days of His ministry. This was done through John the Baptist. Second Kings 1:8 describes the appearance of Elijah in the same manner that Matthew 3:4 describes the appearance of John the Baptist. In Matthew 11:10, Jesus speaks of John with the same words used regarding Elijah in Malachi 4:5-6. Jesus declares in Matthew 11:14, "If ye will receive it, this (John) is Elias (Elijah), which was for to come."

The words in Luke 1:17 record the prophecy given to Zacharias (John's father) by an angel, "And he (John) shall go before him in the spirit and power of Elias...." Elias (Elijah) walks from Gilead where he was called the Tishbite, to Aenon where he was called the baptizer, to Jerusalem where he is called a witness and candlestick, and, finally, to the day when the antichrist will murder him in "Sodom and Egypt" (Rev. 11:3-8). I do not believe in reincarnation, but I do believe that God can plant whatever seed He wishes into the womb of a woman He chooses to bring forth whatever He wills. This He did in the case of Jesus and, I believe, in the case of John as well.

What was so special about John that God found it necessary to send Gabriel to announce his birth and his name to Zacharias? Jesus' birth was supernatural because He was born of a woman who knew not a man. John was "miraculously" born of a woman who was both barren and past child-bearing age. John's unique birth and life was prophesied in the following sentences:

> Many shall rejoice at his birth...he shall be great in the sight of the Lord...he shall drink no wine or strong drink...he shall be filled with the Holy Ghost, even from his mother's womb...he shall go before him in the spirit and power of Elijah...for with God nothing is impossible...Zacharias wrote on a tablet, his name is John, and his mouth opened, and his tongue was loosed, and fear came upon all that dwelt round about them...and all that heard it, said, What manner of child shall this be? (Luke 1)

John, and everything Jesus said about him, was a duplicate of Elijah. In Matthew 11:14, Jesus said, "If ye will receive it, this is Elias, which was for to come." I believe Jesus is saying here, "I know it will be hard for you to accept, but though you see the body of John, the spirit and soul are Elijah's." God needed Elijah incarnate in John to baptize the Messiah so that he would hear, for the second time (for by the mouth of two or three witnesses all things are established), "Thou art my beloved Son, in whom I am well pleased."

It has always seemed strange to me why John, while in prison before he was executed, needed to be assured regarding Jesus' messianic identity (Matt. 11:3). He sent disciples to ask Jesus, "Art thou he that should come, or look we for another?"

Jesus answered John with the following messianic prophecies:

> The blind receive their sight, and the lame walk, the lepers are cleansed, and the deaf hear, the dead are raised up, and the poor have the gospel preached to them (Matt. 11:5).

John and Elijah are inseparable. Both men were evangelistic prophets and both men were hated by queens. John died because of a birthday wish whispered by a vindictive harlot queen to satiate the fickle whims of her half-naked dancing daughter. In Matthew 17:11-13 Jesus declared,

> Elias truly shall first come, and restore all things, but I say unto you, That Elias is come already, and they knew him not, but have done unto him whatsoever they listed. Then the disciples understood that he spake unto them of John the Baptist.

Not only has God given the Jews a second birth of Christ, Pentecost, ascension, rapture, and global scattering, He has also given them a second Elijah in John the Baptist. He is also called "the two candlesticks" (Rev. 11:4).

We are told in Revelation 1:20 that a candlestick represents a church. Elijah himself is a type of the Church in that he was translated or raptured away and did not see death. He represents the Gentile Church, which will by this time have been translated or raptured away, and the Jewish Church which is born during the tribulation.

Jesus said that when Elijah came, he would "restore all things" (Matt. 17:11). Although Elijah will be a thorn in the side of the false prophet and antichrist, he will also be a man of great prayer who will weep many tears for Israel during the three and a half years of tribulation. And God will answer his prayers like he did in the days of Ahab and Jezabel. Elijah will have the joy of seeing thousands of Jews heeding his witness of the baptism, miracles, death, resurrection, ascension, and soon return of Jesus, the Messiah of Israel and of the whole world!

3. The Witness of Moses:

Moses represents the two olive trees. Both Elijah and Moses represent dual dispensations and must be depicted in this dual manner. Because the original ministries of the two prophets were quite dissimilar, two different symbols are employed. Paul (in Rom. 11:13-26) goes into detail to explain this double olive tree. There is really only one tree and it symbolizes Israel. Its two appearances at separate times in history portray it quite differently. In its first appearance, the tree bears evidence of having been badly mutilated. Its original branches, because of having rejected and crucified their Messiah, were broken off and regrafted with wild olive branches.

These wild olive branches represent the Gentile Church which takes sustenance and life, which comes from God, from the trunk and roots of the tree. Paul predicts that one day the original branches, which were broken off, will again be grafted in again to give the tree a much different appearance. This process typifies the spiritual rebirth of Israel.

As spiritual leader and national figurehead, Moses represents the Israel whose branches were broken off when they rejected and crucified their Messiah. He also represents Israel as the tree that is healed when the branches are grafted back in after they reject the false Messiah and repent of their crime of crucifying the true Messiah. Not only does Israel experience a second birth of Christ, a second pentecost, a second ascension, a second rapture, a second scattering, a second John the Baptist in Elijah, a second Moses, and a second witness of the baptism, miracles, transfiguration, death, and resurrection of Christ — it also experiences a second Church.

The first tree with the broken-off branches is referred to as the five foolish virgins who were not ready when the bridegroom came at midnight (Matt. 25:1-13). When they returned from filling their lamps with oil, the door was shut and the time for weeping (known as the tribulation) began. Through the trials of the tribulation, her branches are restored, and, through repentance and faith in Jesus, she "hath made herself ready" (Rev. 19:7).

Moses' principle concern for Israel is to get her into the Promised Land. He has his eyes on Canaan and the city "whose builder and maker is God" (Heb. 11:10). Moses has never forgotten the bush which burned, but was not consumed. He knows this everlasting burning bush is a symbol of the nation of Israel — tormented, persecuted, scattered, hated, but never consumed. When Moses appears this second time, he will once again pick up the rod that was a serpent and complete the journey (interrupted when God took him away on mount Nebo) into the eternal Canaan.

Moses and Elijah will arrive on the scene after the antichrist breaks the seven-year treaty and sets up his image in the temple. They will see the antichrist sitting on the temple throne, with people going in and out to worship him. Moses and Elijah will comfort Israel by assuring them that they do not need the temple anymore. Salvation is not to be found in animal sacrifices, but only in Jesus Christ, their true Messiah and the Lamb of God. The desecration of the temple will have a counter-productive effect upon the schemes of the antichrist. Satan's compulsory worship plan will fail. The Jews will see they have been deceived and turn to Christ by the thousands.

As we approach the end of the world, things will happen rapidly. The news of a second prophet rising from the dead will hit the air waves of the worlds' communication systems. Everyone will seem to accept the fact that Moses has actually come back from the dead because of his "power over waters, and to turn them into blood" (Rev. 11:6). The false prophet and the antichrist will be smitten with panic, hurriedly putting on sensational exhibitions of magic and wizardry. But their crowds will get smaller while the crowds of Moses and Elijah swell. Assassination attempts on the lives of the two prophets will be made, but their assailants will be burned to a crisp from the fire which issues out of their mouths. This awesome defense will give tremendous credibility to their mission.

Zechariah 3:8-10 is a prophecy that was made of Moses after he was dead. The stone which was laid before Joshua is Moses, through whom, the Lord says, "I will remove the iniquity of that land in one day."

4. Their Death:

Satan is good at shooting himself in the foot. He couldn't select a less beneficial time in which to send his son, the antichrist, out to kill the witnesses than when they "have finished their testimony" (Rev. 11:7). It will be too late for damage control then, irreparable damage will have already been done. Satan will have lost his grip on the pregnant woman who has now given spiritual birth to a Son, her Savior and her Lord. The 144,000 faithful slaves and the two witnesses, Moses and Elijah, will have done their work well.

Then Satan will shoot himself in the other foot. In Israel, there was no greater humiliation and indignity than to leave a dead body in the street without a proper burial. Crucifixion was one thing, but to leave a body unburied was quite another. Exodus 33:11 declares that "God spoke with Moses as to a friend." Deuteronomy 34:10 says, "And there arose not a prophet since in Israel like unto Moses, whom the Lord knew face to face." Of John the Baptist, who was also Elijah, Jesus said, "Of all born among women, there hath not arisen (any-one) greater...."

You cannot subject friends of God like Moses and Elijah to the shame of letting their bodies rot in the streets for three and a half days without having to face the judgment of God. You cannot extinguish one of God's brightest lights without finding yourself in great danger. Beware of God's move "after three and a half days."

5. God's Turn:

Nothing is really over when it is done. If only it were! Julius Caesar said, "The evil that men do lives after them." Satan will suppose victory to be his when there is no one to harass or hinder his murdering anymore. As they who "dwell upon the earth shall rejoice over them, and make merry, and shall send gifts one to another...(Rev. 11:10)," there will be blood-curdling screams and shrieks in the streets of Jerusalem. God's three and one half days expire and the two witnesses will suddenly stand to their feet. The people will run in every direction, instantly sensing that the word "retribution" is written across Israel's skies. It is a terrible thing to fall into the hands of an angry God.

6. Deliverance at Last:

A loud voice crying, "Come up hither," will be heard from heaven. And from everywhere they will come — the East, the West, the North, and the South — the blood-washed candlesticks of Israel. The bride, the Church (Israel), "has made herself ready" by enduring the trials of the great tribulation. The dead in Christ will rise with the redeemed out of the tribulation to become the cloud that accompanies Moses and Elijah to meet the Lord in the air (Matt. 24:31; 1 Thess. 4:16-17). They disappear while their enemies watch them go:

> And I heard as it were the voice of a great multitude, and as the voice of many waters, and as the voice of mighty thunderings, saying, Alleluia: for the Lord God omnipotent reigneth. Let us be glad and rejoice, and give honor to him: for the marriage of the Lamb is come, and his wife hath made herself ready (Rev. 19:6-7).

This event can only be felt with the heavenly heart. Such celebration, joy, and delight are the atmosphere of heaven.

7. The Last Converts of Moses and Elijah:

> And the same hour was there a great earthquake, and the tenth part of the city fell, and in the earthquake were slain of men seven thousand: and the remnant were affrighted, and gave glory to the God of heaven (Rev. 11:13).

These who glorified God only after 7,000 were dead are the last converts this world will ever know. There appear to be no converts during the last forty-five days known as "that great and terrible day of the Lord." This remnant gives "glory to the God of heaven" just in time, for the seventh angel is prepared to sound his trumpet which means "time shall be no longer" (Rev. 10:6-7).

The killing of the two witnesses is what Daniel calls the "breaking" and "scattering" of the power of the holy people (Dan. 12:7); this killing takes place at the end of the tribulation. Israel will have endured much torment and be almost decimated. The power which they possessed in Moses and Elijah (Rev. 11:3-6) will have been taken from them. Daniel states that when this happens, "All these things shall be finished."

This "finished" becomes a very crucial reference point in understanding the many prophetical turn-overs taking place. "There shall be no further delay" in pouring out the vials of God's wrath upon the world, because "the mystery of God should be finished, as he hath declared to his servants the prophets" (Rev. 10:7). The finished mystery is God's completion of the redemption and rapture of Israel (Rom. 11:25-26; Rev. 11:12; 15:2-4)). This is the mystery which Daniel said "he understood not" (Dan. 12:7-13).

The completion of the redemption and rapture of Israel clears the way for the great and terrible day of the Lord. The book is seen open (Rev. 10:8), meaning everything in it has been executed and Jacob's trouble is over. The seventh trumpet is about to sound (Rev. 10:7-8; 11:15) when the vials of God's wrath will be poured out during the last forty-five days of history for planet earth.

That the rapture of Israel is meant by the words, "Come up hither" (Rev. 11:12), can scarcely be questioned. What follows in succeeding verses is what one would expect to happen following such a rapture. Christ promptly assumes His position as King (Rev. 11:15), the dead are resurrected and the righteous rewarded (Rev. 11:18). The victorious disciples of Moses (the overcomers of the beast) rejoice over their raptured state (Rev. 15:2-3). All of this takes place in heaven, confirming the fact that Israel's rapture was embodied in the words, "Come up hither."

From the "finished" in Revelation 10:7 to the "it is done" in Revelation 16:17, there are forty-five days from which Israel is spared. They are the same forty-five days Daniel speaks of that follow the 1,290 days, totalling 1,335 days. The Word says that any who survive these days can consider themselves blessed. These are also the days which Jesus calls the "shortened days" which have been subtracted for Israel's sake. This will be further discussed with the seventh trumpet.

This completes the forty-nine pronouncements regarding the tribulation participants. Before proceeding to Revelation 6, there is a supernatural phenomenon to be considered that plays an important part in making the world what it shall be at the outset of the great tribulation.

THE RAPTURE OF THE CHURCH OR THE "THIEF RAPTURE"

Jacob's trouble, the great tribulation, is not the same period of time as "that great and terrible day of the Lord." The Church escapes the great tribulation and Israel escapes the great and terrible day of the Lord. This basic Biblical premise (heretofore overlooked) has spawned several eschatological teachings that are fraught with Scriptural misrepresentations.

There are at least four theories in eschatology regarding the rapture:

- Such a phenomenon will not take place and is not taught in the Bible
- The Church must go through half of the tribulation
- The Church will be raptured away before the tribulation
- The Church must go through the tribulation.

That the Bible does not teach a rapture is a position that must simply be rejected. The Scriptures which explain the three remaining positions affirm that there will indeed be a rapture of the Church and of Israel.

The teaching regarding the Church rapture occurring in the middle of the tribulation comes about because of an inaccurate understanding of the duration of the tribulation. Many scholars simply assume that the seven-year tenure of the antichrist's covenant (Dan. 9:27) with Israel is all tribulation. This is not so. The Bible teaches a three-and-a-half-year tribulation. Daniel 9:27 clearly teaches that the antichrist will break the seven-year covenant and set up the image of abomination in the temple in the middle of the week (seven-day period). This is the point at which the tribulation begins.

The following Scriptures address the two remaining theories regarding not only the rapture of the Church, but also the rapture of Israel.

MY BASIC PREMISE

The fact that a controversy exists between reputable Bible scholars as to whether the church does, or does not go through the tribulation, is in itself conclusive evidence that a rapture exists before and after the tribulation.

1. Jesus' Description of the Rapture of the Church (The Pre-TribulationThief Rapture):

   But of that day and hour knoweth no man, no, not the angels of heaven, but my Father only. But as the days of Noe were, so shall also the coming of the Son of man be. For as in the days that were before the flood they were eating and drinking, marrying and giving in marriage, until the day that Noe entered the ark, and knew not until the flood came and took them all away; so shall also the coming of the Son of man be. Then shall two be in the field; the one shall be taken, and the other left. Two women shall be grinding at the mill; the one shall be taken, and the other left. Watch therefore: for ye know not what hour your Lord doth come (Matt. 24:36-42 [See also Matt. 25:1-13; 17:22-37]).

2. Jesus' Description of the Rapture of Israel (The Post-Tribulation Trumpet Rapture):

Immediately after the tribulation of those days shall the sun be darkened, and the moon shall not give her light, and the stars shall fall from heaven, and the powers of the heavens shall be shaken: and then shall appear the sign of the Son of man in heaven: and then shall all the tribes of the earth mourn, and they shall see the Son of man coming in the clouds of heaven with power and great glory. And he shall send his angels with a great sound of a trumpet, and they shall gather together his elect from the four winds, from one end of heaven to the other (Matt. 24:29-31).

An honest evaluation of the above Scriptures reveals that the first event Jesus describes in Matthew 24:36-44 and Luke 17:34-37 is not the same as the second event He describes in Matthew 24:29-31. The first event takes place at night, during peace time (sleeping in bed, grinding at the mill, working in the field) and "at such an hour as ye think not," secretly "as a thief."

The second event takes place during the day when they can "see" the sign of the coming of the Son of man. It happens at the end of Jacob's trouble, "immediately after the tribulation of those days," and just before that great and dreadful day of God's wrath when the sun and moon shall be darkened (Matt. 24:29; Rev. 16:10). It is not "thief-like" because it is heralded by the blast of a trumpet and Christ is seen in the heavens accompanied by angels who gather the "elect" (Jews) from the four corners of the world. Jesus is describing two different raptures.

3. Paul's Description of the Rapture of the Church (The Pre-Tribulation Thief Rapture):

But of the times and the seasons, brethren, ye have no need that I write unto you. For yourselves know perfectly that the day of the Lord so cometh as a thief in the night. For when they shall say, Peace and safety; then sudden destruction cometh upon them, as travail upon a woman with child; and they shall not escape. But ye, brethren, are not in darkness, that that day should overtake you as a thief. Ye are all the children of light, and the children of the day: we are not of the night, nor of darkness. Therefore let us not sleep, as do others; but let us watch and be sober. For they that sleep sleep in the night; and they that be drunken are drunken in the night. But let us, who are of the day, be sober, putting on the breastplate of faith and love; and for an helmet, the hope of salvation. For God hath not appointed us to wrath, but to obtain salvation by our Lord Jesus Christ (1 Thess. 5:1-9).

4. Paul's Description of the Rapture of Israel (The Post-Tribulation Trumpet Rapture):

Behold, I show you a mystery; We shall not all sleep, but we shall all be changed, in a moment, in the twinkling of an eye, at the last trump: for the trumpet shall sound, and the dead shall be raised incorruptible, and we shall be changed (1 Cor. 15:51-52).

For the Lord himself shall descend from heaven with a shout, with the voice of the archangel, and with the trump of God: and the dead in Christ shall rise first. Then we which are alive and remain shall be caught up together with them in the clouds, to meet the Lord in the air: and so shall we ever be with the Lord (1 Thess. 4:16-17 [See also 2 Thess. 2]).

Again, an honest evaluation of the Scriptures quoted by Paul reveals that the two events are not the same. The first event is referred to as "the times and seasons (not a certain known specific day)" and takes place during the night, secretly, as the attack of a thief. It comes during peace time ("when they say peace") and precedes the tribulation ("sudden destruction" or travail of the woman, Israel, Rev. 12). It comes when they will be "eating and drinking" (1 Thess. 5:7). Paul refers to the Church when he says "we are not appointed unto wrath."

Paul's description of the rapture of the Church is very similar to Jesus' description in Matthew 24:36-42. Statements like: "eating and drinking as in the days of Noe," "no man knoweth the day or the hour," "a thief in the night," and "working in the field, sleeping in bed, grinding at the mill" (time of peace) are the express language of

Paul. The conclusion is that both Paul and Jesus are speaking of the same rapture.

The second event described by Paul takes place during the day when you can "see" the clouds into which they are caught. This event is not a secret, rather it is heralded by Christ's visible appearance, the blast of a trumpet, and the resurrection of the dead. It happens on a specific day "at the last trump." This coming is for the Jews who survive the tribulation. It is referred to by Paul as "our gathering together unto him" (2 Thess. 2:1).

It is not coincidental that Paul's description of the Jewish rapture harmonizes with the statements by Christ: "Immediately after the tribulation," "see the Son of man," "a great sound of a trumpet," and "gather together his elect." Jesus and Paul are speaking about the same event.

There is one event that Paul mentions which Jesus omits. It is the resurrection of the righteous dead. However, in John 6:40 and 11:25 we learn from Jesus that this resurrection is to take place at "the last day." The last day is announced by the angel in Revelation 10:6 when "time shall be no longer" after the tribulation (Jacob's trouble) and just before the angel sounds the "last trump" (Rev. 10:7; 11:15). This last trumpet includes the resurrection of the saints as seen in Revelation 11:18. This harmonizes with Paul's teaching of the resurrection of the righteous at the "last trump." Conclusive evidence that Israel is raptured away after the tribulation is seen in Revelation 15:2-4 where Moses' tribulation converts are safe in heaven before the vials are poured out.

The Church has known centuries of having to choose one of the eschatological "theories" and then defend it. Contradictions have been inevitable when the mind set has been that there could only be one rapture, when all the while the Scriptures are describing a rapture for the Church and a rapture for Israel.

I have always been convinced that the Church was not going through the tribulation, even though some Scriptures required bending in order to make them describe such a rapture. I was willing to live with this bent situation because no other more convincing options were available. Let me share some of the hurdles that I recognized as accompanying that position.

Jesus clearly states that He would return after the tribulation (Matt. 24:29-31). I attempted to understand this to mean He came secretly the first time to rapture the Church (Matt. 24:36-42) and here He is coming back the second time to establish His kingdom after the tribulation of Israel. However, what should we make of "the sun and moon being darkened, and the universe shaken" when the tribulation is supposed to be over? These conditions hardly bespeak the initiation of Christ's millennial kingdom.

This passage is not speaking of the establishment of a kingdom, rather a gathering of the elect after the three and a half years of tribulation. Israel's rapture prepares the way for "that great and terrible day of the Lord" which is heralded by the darkening of the sun and moon (Joel 2:31; Rev. 16:10).

Another hurdle was Paul's expression, "at the last trump" (1 Cor. 15:51-52). If this Scripture speaks of the rapture of the Church, then this last trump had better not refer to the last of the seven trumpets (Rev. 10:7; 11:15) or the Church will have to go through the tribulation. In order to defend the position that this will not happen, something had to be done about Paul's "last trump." One solution was to find all of the different trumpets used in Israel's religious ceremonies and decide this must be the last trumpet that will ever be blown for any such occasions. This did not satisfy me.

Paul's "last trump" (1 Cor. 15:51-52; 1 Thess. 4:16), and Jesus' "last trump" (Matt. 24:31; Rev. 10:7; 11:15) are the same. The mystery Paul speaks of in 1 Corinthians 15:51-52 does not refer to either rapture; it refers to the dead who will be raised at the "last trump." Because Israel is raptured at the sounding of the "last trump," both the resurrection of the righteous and the rapture of Israel take place at that time.

The notion that the Church is raptured here comes because of an incorrect understanding of 1 Thessalonians 4:13-17. If one wrongly concludes that it is the Church which is raptured here (when the dead in Christ rise), one will also wrongly assume the Church will be raptured in 1 Corinthians 15:51-52 where the dead are raised at the "last trump." There is no resurrection of the righteous mentioned at the rapture of the Church in Matthew 24:36-42 because none takes place. The Church is raptured away because God intends to spare her from the tribulation. The dead cannot be hurt by the tribulation, so they remain in the grave until after the tribulation, when they will rise first to be caught up with Israel to meet the Lord in the air.

Another Scripture which has brought confusion is Revelation 20:4, where the resurrection of the righteous is called the "first resurrection." If 1 Thessalonions 4:16-17 speaks of the rapture and resurrection of the Church before the tribulation, then this would have to be the first resurrection. However, Revelation 11:18 and 15:2 speak of a resurrection after the tribulation which would have to be the second. Revelation 20:4 clearly states that the resurrection of the righteous which takes place after overcoming the beast is the first, and the resurrection of the wicked is inferred as being the second. There is only one resurrection of the righteous, and it takes place after the tribulation at the rapture of Israel.

CHAPTER FIVE

FORTY-NINE PRONOUNCEMENTS ABOUT THE SEVEN SEALS
(What the World Will Be Like During the Tribulation)

PRELUDE TO THE SEVEN SEALS

The political and spiritual climate at the outset of the three and a half years of tribulation will not be compatible. The world will be filled with tension and fear because the antichrist has become very belligerent and proud. He is a man possessed of the devil, supported by a blindly trusting religious consortium under the guise of the world church. At the head of this facade of holiness is a "false" prophet empowered by Satan to deceive the world into worshipping the antichrist. The false prophet affirms the antichrist as the Messiah, offering proof by the miracles they perform.

The seven tribulation participants focus their attention upon Israel, depicted as the pregnant woman. The antichrist, the false prophet, the world church, and Satan seek to destroy her. Michael, the 144,000 sealed servants of God and Moses and Elijah stand in her defense, which causes a fierce conflict to develop. Hostility between these seven participants ultimately ends in the tragedy of Armageddon.

Evidence that God is about to make His move in the affairs of the world will be verified by the miraculous rapture of the Church. Shock will be worldwide as every nation's newspapers confirm the strange disappearance of a class of people known as Christians. The world will recall how the missing used to talk about a rapture of the Church which was soon to take place. Fear will grip the hearts of many who were once half-believers. Psychologists, psychiatrists, and support groups will not be able to respond to every cry for help. The false prophet will, no doubt, have a special explanation for this phenomenon in an attempt to allay the fears of the peoples of the world.

When is this to happen? If Peter's prophecy in 2 Peter 3:7-13 suggests a time, it would be embodied in these words, "One day is with the Lord as a thousand years" (vs. 8). God created the world in six days, nearly 6,000 years ago. If the six days of creation are a counterpart to the history of civilization and each day of God's creation week represents a thousand years, then the six thousand years God has assigned to civilization is almost spent. We know that a thousand years are reserved as the millennium, or God's Sabbath day of rest, which will take place on the seven day or seven-thousandth year.

If the budding of the fig tree spoken of by Jesus in Matthew 24:32-34 represents the reinstatement of Jewish nationhood and if this prophecy was fulfilled in 1948 and if a generation time span represents fifty or sixty years, then indeed, His return is "even at the doors."

Jesus has informed us that no man can know the day or the hour when the Church will be taken away. However, those missing the rapture can know that from the day that the abominable image is set up in the temple to the day when the Jews will be raptured away will be 1,290 days. From Israel's rapture until the last day of "that great and terrible day of the Lord" (during which the vials of God's wrath are poured out), will be forty-five days (Dan. 12:11-12). God has not left us completely in the dark regarding the times and the seasons.

The Book of Revelation follows a very deliberate, time-oriented, systematic order, as will be observed in the opening of the seals, the sounding of the trumpets and the pouring out of the vials. Interjected between the seals, trumpets, and vials are John's visions of the seven tribulation participants. When you isolate the chapters dealing with the seven tribulation participants, what remains of the Book of Revelation is almost a perfect chronological order of the judgments which are to be executed during the tribulation.

Prior to pursuing our study of the seven tribulation participants, we were preoccupied with the little book (a book within a book) which originates from the Book of Daniel. We now continue with the rest of the Book of Revelation which depicts, in symbolical language, the judgments executed during the great tribulation.

I. THE FIRST SEAL (Revelation 6:1-2)

And I saw when the Lamb opened one of the seals, and I heard as it were the noise of thunder, one of the four beasts saying, Come and see. And I saw, and behold a white horse: and he that sat on him had a bow; and a crown was given unto him: and he went forth conquering, and to conquer.

1. And I Saw the Lamb:

The Lamb is Jesus. He will make the first move by executing the judgments of the first seal. Every move He makes from this point on will be designed to deliver the death stroke to the six persecutors of Israel for inflicting great pain and suffering upon her because she brought forth the man-child. John sees only the Lamb, but lurking in the shadows is the dragon who follows His every move. Prophesy and eternity merge when Christ, the Lamb, and Satan, the dragon, meet head-on in their final confrontation.

The Lamb is angry (Rev. 6:16-17) and the dragon is angry (Rev. 12:12). The point of no return has arrived, and the encounter Satan has evaded for centuries is about to erupt. Satan dreads the verdicts and judgments of the little book-within-the-book. In it is contained a complete description of the defeat he has sustained at every strategic move he makes in an attempt to retain mastery of the world. With each judgment, his grip grows weaker.

2. The First Seal:

Daniel died without understanding of the obscure and mystic message of the angel upon the water (Dan. 12:5-9). For centuries now, while resting and waiting for the end, he must have been wondering about the book which he was told to seal; the book that contained things "he understood not" (Dan. 12:4-13). He was told that in the end it would be opened and the wise would understand what it is all about.

In Revelation 5, Jesus (whom Daniel saw in a vision similar to what John saw on the Isle of Patmos) takes the book from the Father's hand and with great authority opens the first seal. A thunderous noise rolls forth.

3. The Noise of Thunder:

This thunder is an announcement of a storm the world shall never forget, for it contains the verdict of the Almighty upon Satan and his domain. Heaven and earth and the entire universe tremble at the magnitude of its unknown consequences. It is the harbinger of a storm so great that the cities of the earth will be leveled and the islands and mountains shall never be found again. When the voice from heaven announces, "It is done," Armageddon will flow with blood for 160 miles "as high as the horses bridles."

4. Come:

What is to come, the complete meaning of "Jacob's trouble," cannot be fully comprehended. The full impact of the Savior's words in

Matthew 24:21, "For then shall be great tribulation, such as was not since the beginning of the world to this time, no, nor ever shall be," are beyond our imagination. What is to come first is contained in the symbolism of the white horse.

5. White Horse:

The consequences of the white horse will stagger the planet with a great tribulation woe. We can only conclude that the message typified by it embodies a "power" so provoking to Satan that it drives him to unleash all the demonic forces available to him. Satan hates the mention of the blood of the Lamb and its power to cleanse sin and make a sinner "white as snow." Should we be searching for the meaning of this seal in the area of this holy provision?

There is one gracious clue which God gave Daniel regarding the sealed book and its message. Immediately after Daniel was told the book was sealed to "the time of the end," we find the words, "Many shall be purified, and made white, and tried" (Dan. 12:10). A similar message appears in Daniel 11:35, "...To purge, and to make them white, even to the time of the end...."

God opens the window to understanding the meaning of the white horse when He reveals to Daniel that this "making white" is to take place "at the time of the end." The answer is all but audible. In the end times when the antichrist's image is set up in the temple and he demands worship, the Jews will awaken to the fact that their Messiah was actually crucified 2,000 years ago. They will turn to Jesus Christ, their Messiah, whose blood will wash them white as snow.

The white horse seal announces the spiritual conversion of Israel as expressed in the words, "Many shall be made white and purified" (Dan. 12:10). The rider must be Christ himself who alone is able to convert and cleanse. In what manner is the spiritual conversion of Israel a judgment of God? It is the consequential phenomenon which brings to birth all other judgments that follow.

The worst possible scenario for the antichrist has materialized. To effectively gain Israel's allegiance, compulsory worship, and the acceptance of the monetary mark, a complete deterioration of faith and denial of their God would have to be effected. Precisely the opposite materializes. Their acceptance of Christ transforms them, body and soul. Their eyes will see and their hearts will understand the deception of antichrist and his real identity. An impossible obeisance to his demonic devices and schemes will become reality.

Israel is to become what everyone becomes when they accept Christ, "a new creature." In order for this to be effected, a complete new birth is necessary. Sin brings physical and spiritual death, and the only way life can be realized is by a new birth. This spiritual birth of Israel takes place as typified by the birth of the man-child (Rev. 12).

This transformation and national spiritual revival completely alienates Israel from the antichrist and they become fierce enemies. Because the antichrist (with a "mouth speaking great things") will be the ruler of most of the world, he will initiate a hate campaign against Israel through lying and deception that will turn world opinion against her. Persecution, slaughter, and sorrow follow, which results in the outpouring of the wrath of God upon those who harm His people.

The whiteness of this horse must surely symbolize something cleansed by omnipotence, purified by the blood of Christ, and sanctified by the Holy Ghost. The benign character of this first seal is further expressed by the arrowless bow in the rider's hand.

6. Bow:

No arrows were seen by John. The absence of them represents Christ's method of conquest, "Not by might, nor by power, but by my Spirit saith the Lord." The rider of the white horse is a bloodless conqueror, surely the fulfillment of Joel 2:28-32. The prophet, Joel, declares that a spiritual phenomenon in Israel is to take place "before that great and terrible day of the Lord." This is the spiritual phenomenon which ignites the tribulation and forces us to conclude that the white horse seal symbolizes it well.

The arrowless conquering bow also symbolizes the ministry of the 144,000 servants of God. They are the "first fruits," the first to believe on Jesus the Messiah. They are sealed with the signet of safety, and are the tribulation missionaries to the lost sheep of the house of Israel. The results of their labors are to be seen in the redeemed multitude of Revelation 7:9-17.

Finally, the bow also symbolizes the ministry of Moses and Elijah (Rev. 11). In Malachi 4:5, we are told that Elijah was to come "before that great and terrible day of the Lord." His mission was turn the fathers and the children to repentance and faith in God. The witness of Moses and Elijah is to span 1,260 days, and their testimony will be heard throughout the entire duration of the tribulation.

7. He That Sat Upon the White Horse Wearing a Crown:

The crown given Him is that which Jesus talked about in Matthew 28:18 when He said, "All power is given unto me in heaven and earth." It is God who vested Him with this regal power. John observes Him going forth conquering and to conquer in the same manner exhibited at Pentecost and the great spiritual revivals which have taken place during the Age of Grace. His is the most powerful weapon in the universe — love.

To a Jew, the possibility of a national spiritual revival in Israel with faith in Jesus Christ is incomprehensible. The spiritual phenomenon prophesied to take place in Israel subsequent to the desecration of the temple will be generated by the third person in the Trinity, the Holy Spirit (Joel 2:28; Zech. 12:10). It is He who convicts the world of "sin, righteousness and judgment to come." There is no force in the universe that can impede His purposes or intentions.

> And I will pour upon the house of David, and upon the inhabitants of Jerusalem, the spirit of grace and of supplications: and they shall look upon me whom they have pierced, and they shall mourn for him, as one mourneth for his only son, and shall be in bitterness for him, as one that is in bitterness for his firstborn (Zech. 12:10).

> In that day there shall be a fountain opened to the house of David and to the inhabitants of Jerusalem for sin and for uncleanness (Zech. 13:1).

> And one shall say unto him, What are these wounds in thine hands? Then he shall answer, Those with which I was wounded in the house of my friends (Zech. 13:6).

God gives Israel the best that He has. Here He extends to them a second crucifixion and a second fountain. "They shall look upon him whom they have pierced, and be in bitterness." This is not a literal crucifixion of Christ, but it will probably be more real to the Jews during the tribulation than it has ever been to any Gentile during the age of grace.

National fear will grip the hearts of Israel. The white horse seal speaks of all that happens in chapter twelve where the woman in travail gives birth to the Savior. The weeping, mourning, and bitterness will take place in every tribe. Wives and husbands will lose interest in each other. Their deception by the antichrist will overwhelm them as they finally see it all so clearly. They will look upon Him whom they have pierced. They will see the fountain opened to the house of David for sin. They will see their Messiah standing with wounds in His hands. Someone wants to make sure about His identity and asks, "What are these wounds in thine hands?" The answer is heart wrenching: "Those which I received in the house of my FRIENDS" (Zech. 13:6).

Israel, as if she were one body, falls to her knees in great travail and sorrow. Tears will flow over the faces of a deceived, humiliated, and offended nation. Their temple will be defiled and the covenant made with the one they thought would redeem Israel will be broken. World opinion will have turned against her, and "all nations" of the world shall come against Jerusalem" (Zech. 12:9; 14:2). The antichrist will manage to convince the world that if the Jews would just do as everyone else does (worship the image, and accept the monetary mark), there would be no problem.

The battle between Christ and Satan erupts. The 144,000, the first to accept Christ and be sealed with a mark of protection, fan out into the four corners of the world with an urgent message:

> ...If any man worship the beast and his image, and receive
> his mark in his forehead, or in his hand, the same shall drink
> of the wine of the wrath of God... (Rev. 14:9-10).

Accepting the mark and worshipping the beast assures everlasting doom in an eternal Hell.

Moses and Elijah will appear on the scene performing miracles in an attempt to convince Israel that their only hope of survival is repentance and faith in God and His Son. Pentecost, when compared with the spiritual tribulation-ingathering of the house of David, will appear as a whirlwind escorting a tornado into town. The false prophet will not be able to explain away the disappearance of the Gentile Church to the Jews. To them, this disappearance means they are the excluded virgins Jesus alluded to in Matthew 25:1-13.

The words of Isaiah 66:7-8 will become reality:

> ... She has delivered a man child. Who hath heard such a thing...shall the earth be made to bring forth in one day? Shall a nation be born at once? For as soon as Zion travailed, she brought forth her children." This will be the greatest spiritual harvest the world has ever known. Jesus "shall see his seed, and be satisfied.

The jilting of antichrist by Israel will reap terrible consequences. The conduct and actions of Darius, who issued an ultimatum, are here repeated. The Jews will be given thirty days to decide whether to bow in obeisance and accept the monetary mark or die (Dan. 6:7). The failure of Israel to comply will bring forth the next stage.

II. THE SECOND SEAL (Revelation 6:3-4)

And when he had opened the second seal, I heard the second beast say, Come and see. And there went out another horse that was red: and power was given to him that sat thereon to take peace from the earth, and that they should kill one another: and there was given unto him a great sword.

The four horses of the first four seals represent forces or conditions which shall persist throughout the tribulation. The spiritual revival symbolized by the white horse, the bloodshed symbolized by the red horse, the famine symbolized by the black horse, and the pestilence and disease symbolized by the pale horse will all persist throughout the duration of the tribulation.

That the four horses are one a consequence of the other is suggested by the common source commanding their execution. In each case, the four beasts (four living somethings), announce their arrival. All of them are ushered in by the same command.

1. Come:

The word "come" is usually an invitation. In this case, it is also an order. In the days of King Darius, a thirty-day royal statute was decreed that no one in his kingdom was allowed to make prayers or petitions to any god except the king himself. Anyone disobeying this order was to be cast into the den of lions. Daniel refused to obey the king and was consequently cast into the den of lions (Dan 6:7-17).

History and prophecy repeats itself. Much of the Book of Daniel was given as a prophecy up to and including the Roman Empire. However, what was prophesied regarding the Roman Empire was also prophesied regarding the empire of the antichrist. It appears that the thirty-day royal decree of Darius will be repeated during the reign of the antichrist. This accounts for the thirty-day differential in the duration of the tribulation existing between 1,260 and 1,290 days as recorded in Daniel 12:7 and 11.

Ultimatums are not uncommon. The Allied forces under George Bush set January 15, 1991, as the deadline for Saddam Hussein to withdraw from Kuwait. The antichrist will want to appear like a humane and considerate leader in allowing these thirty days as the come time to bow, worship, and receive the mark. Israel will not respond to the antichrist's ultimatum, and this enrages him. What follows in terms of persecution and bloodshed is symbolized by the red horse and its rider who wields a great sword.

This seal almost interprets itself. The color "red" and the statements, "power to take peace from the earth" and "to him was given a great sword," leave little to the imagination. The message is war and bloodshed. The instigators of these are the red dragon, the scarlet beast, the false prophet, and his scarlet harlot.

2. The Red Horse:

Having established that the red horse symbolizes war, persecution, and bloodshed, we now see far-reaching implications. These include the following tribulation participants:

The Red Dragon

It is not difficult to decipher the scent of the real warmonger. His trail of blood has stained the earth from Eden to Armageddon. He has lurked in the shadow of every crime commited on earth. He is the author of every conceivable woe.

From Revelation 12, we have already learned that the woman in travail represents the repentant Israel and the red dragon pursuing her is Satan. We would naturally expect that the white horse symbolizing Israel's actual cleansing from sin would be followed by the red horse who is driven by Satan and the antichrist in an attempt to destroy her as a nation. Why? Because the Word of God tells us the millennial kingdom, from which Jesus will "rule with a rod of iron," will be headquartered in Jerusalem.

The Scarlet-Colored Beast

This red beast symbolizes the antichrist, the rider of the red horse and the pawn of Satan. His weapon is a sword, and his influence upon the world is strife and unrest. Jesus breathed peace upon His disciples. This man who rides the red horse has the "power to take peace from the earth."

The Jews will not be the only ones persecuted by the scarlet beast. He makes a covenant with "many" (Dan. 9:27). This means he must also break the covenant with many. Daniel 11:21-45 gives the account of the conquests of the antichrist, which reveal that world conquest is very much on his mind.

The Two-Horned Dragon-Tongued Lamb

The symbolism used in Revelation 13:11-18 to describe the lamb contains a contradiction. Lambs do not have horns. The dragon tongue does not express the nature of a lamb. This beast represents a hypocrite, because outwardly he expresses himself in lamb-like qualities, but his dragon tonue betrays what lies in his heart. He is the false prophet, who exploits his position as a spiritual figurehead, leading his trusting followers to lend their support to the antichrist. Without him, it is doubtful that the antichrist would succeed.

The Scarlet Harlot

The harlot symbolizes the world church who is an accomplice and ally with the enemies of Israel. She and her leader, the false prophet will devise every means in an effort to annihilate Israel. She is spiritually blind. She did not buy gold tried with fire, nor did she anoint her eyes with eye salve as she was told in Revelation 3. She did not buy white raiment and put it on, so she will be stripped naked by the very brood she helped to hatch (Rev. 17:16; chapter 18). She forsook the Word of God which gives light and resorted to fables and graft-oriented doctrines, walking proudly in the spiritual darkness.

Many of her members are afflicted with the homosexual virus which manifests itself in a slow death. She knew it was sin, but ordained those who were practicing it, and blushed not in having them stand in the holy hill of God to proclaim, "Thus saith the Lord." She will not recognize the antichrist for what he is because God will send her strong delusion so that she too will believe the lie and be damned for her pleasure in unrighteousness.

The scarlet harlot is accustomed to shedding innocent blood, having killed many saints, prophets, and apostles. To pacify her guilty conscience and deceive her subjects, she then sainted, immortalized, deified, and idolized the very righteous ones she murdered.

In the red horse and its rider, we have the embodiment of every-thing Satan, the antichrist, the false prophet, the mother of harlots, and all her daughters are. What follows in the symbolism of the remaining seals is all one could possibly expect.

3. His Imposition:

Each of the four horse seals produce varying responses from John. At the opening of the first seal, John says, "I saw, and behold a white horse." After the opening of the third seal, he says, "And lo, a black horse." After the fourth seal is opened, he says, "I looked, and behold a pale horse." In the case of the second seal, nothing is said of him looking or beholding or seeing. John seems to have little time or opportunity to respond or give consideration to this seal. When it is opened, he immediately declares, "And there went out a horse that was red."

The deranged character of the antichrist is brazen, insolent, proud, and self-imposing. He has come to the place in his success as world leader that nothing or no one matters. He calmly sits upon the temple throne in Jerusalem declaring, electing, and appointing himself as God. He enacts the unthinkable and evokes the wrath of the Almighty upon himself, following the steps of his father, Satan, who was ejected from heaven for his pride.

Since Satan no longer has access to the throne in heaven, he has only one option available and that is the holiest place on earth — the temple of God. His desecration of the temple is met with opposition only from the Jews. The rest of the world sits by and watches to see what will happen. At this juncture, he has already so poisoned the minds of the world's population with anti-Semitism that nothing he invents against Israel will be opposed.

There is a fact borne out by history that Jew-haters have overlooked. No king, president, or dictator, including the antichrist, has ever been or is a match for Israel's God. Nebuchadnezzar, Belteshazzar, Pharaoh, Herod, Saul, Ahab, Hitler, Stalin, and thousands of others discovered that omnipotence is not to be trifled with. Their defiance of Him will consign them to oblivion's cemetery with an epitaph on their gravestone which reads: "Another fool who fought with God."

The words, "And there went forth a horse that was red," unleashes a force which has no braking power or forward thrust built into it. Before the rider of the red horse is captured at the end of the tribulation (Rev. 19:20), the death and destruction inflicted upon the world through the seven seals will be absolutely the darkest catastrophe the world will ever know.

The pile-up of planets, the cascading of mountains into the ocean, the flood of salt water covering great parts of the earth, the stink of rotting vegetation and flesh, the radioactive fallout, the oceans of blood, and the scorched earth will render the world uninhabitable. It is no wonder God said, "Behold, I create new heavens and a new earth" (Isa. 65:17).

It would be a dismal state of affairs if the tribulation was the only story there was to tell about the future. I am writing this book because beyond the bloody tribulation sunset there will be a most inexpressible sunrise. Its rays shall flood the universe with all the glories inherent in the Trinity. Its excellence will descend from the galaxy of many mansions and touch down above the mountains of Zion and they shall call it "the new Jerusalem."

The power of God will torch up the universe, making the sun and the moon obsolete. Holy angels will come to abide with us and with all of our departed loved ones who have chosen Jesus as Lord. The rest of the story is simply incredible!

So go ahead, "proud one," mount your scarlet steed and gallop out across the world. Let your hoofs be stained with blood. Gloat in the miseries you accomplish, for your "time is short." You have your appointment with divine destiny in a valley called Armageddon. You have been persecuting and killing Christians for centuries. Cowards kill Christians, because they never fight back. But it is almost over now, and the Church's rescue through the rapture is imminent. Then you cannot touch us, for we shall forever be with the Lord while you and your accomplices will have no rest day or night in the lake which burneth with fire and brimstone.

The message of this book is not primarily about the terrors that await the ungodly, but rather the divine provision that can rescue them. "For God so loved the world, that he gave his only begotten Son, that whosoever believeth in him should not perish, but have everlasing life" (John 3:16).

Sadness now surrounds Israel. They do not now believe in God's only begotten Son and, consequently, will miss the rapture. They will have a bitter path to everlasting life, but they may have it by exchanging their tribulation terrors for it. The cost will be a horrendous one, but through tribulation trials they will accept the Messiah of God who will appear on His white steed and confront the nations of the world gathered against Jerusalem. The white horse's hoofs are not stained with the blood of tribulation inhabitants, rather the rider's garments are stained with His own blood, which was shed at His crucifixion for their redemption (Isa. 63:1-7).

The red horse and its rider and his sword will be no match for the white horse and its rider whose sword is in His mouth (Rev. 19:11-16). The Messiah will not so much as raise His sword as a warning against His foe. If He could speak a word powerful enough to put the glories of outer space into orbit, He can reduce to ashes this devil-man called antichrist. The meeting between Christ and the antichrist will be very brief. Go to the abyss and ask Ananias, Sapphira, Dothan, Abiram, and Korah how long their meeting with supreme justice lasted. It would not be surprising to find their knees still knocking as a result of their encounter with omnipotence.

4. His Acquisition:

"The dragon gave him his power, and his seat, and great authority" (Rev. 13:2). To give a demon like the antichrist power to "take peace from the earth" and then place in his hand a "great sword" translates into certain tragedy. Add to this the satanic imperative that these gifts from the pit of iniquity are certified with a regal throne (seat) and great universal authority and it translates into destruction and catastrophe.

If the antichrist were an ordinary man given power to lead a great portion of the world, this alone would be great cause for concern. But he will not be an ordinary man; he is a devil-man. The manner in which he governs the world is prescribed by the devil himself. This is a terrible prospect!

5. Contrary:

The antichrist will have "power to take peace from the earth." The principal message of the angels on the night of the Savior's birth was,

"Peace on earth good will to men." One of Christ's final messages to His disciples before ascending into heaven was, "My peace I leave with you" (John 14:27; 16:33). The contrary character of this red horse rider leaves no doubt that he is indeed anti-Christ, for "to him was given power to take peace from the earth" (1 Thess. 5:3; Rev. 6:4, 16:13-14).

6. Contrary Again:

The sign the angels gave the shepherds by which they could authenticate and verify the discovery of the Messiah were his swaddling clothes or swaths of cloth. These swaths of cloth were the same garb with which He was wrapped in the tomb. In other words, the shepherds were to recognize the Messiah who was born in David's town by His grave clothes. The Messiah was born to die and give life. The antichrist was born to kill and take life.

The sign by which the antichrist will be recognized is his great sword. In modern terms, a person vested with a revolver or pistol represents authority. In John's day, a man carrying a sword represented authority. If it were possible, the antichrist would carry his sword in his mouth like our Lord. The sword in the mouth of Jesus and His name (the Word) are equal representations of His power and great authority. The sword is His word and His Word is the sword. By His Word everything came into being, because His Word is power. By wielding a great sword, the antichrist is trying to mimic the true Messiah. However, his "sword/word" authority creates nothing, gives life to nothing, and represents greed, dishonesty, pride, destruction, and death.

Revelation 13 describes the character of the antichrist in detail. Like others in the past who died on their own gallows or who were killed with their own sword, the antichrist likewise meets the same fate. Revelation 13:10 states that "he that killeth with the sword must be killed with the sword."

7. Civil War: "...That they should kill one another" (Rev. 6:4).

The worst kind of war is civil war. Yesterday's friend may be today's enemy. With his power to take peace from the earth and the fact that he is the world's biggest deceiver, the antichrist is capable of creating whatever climate he requires for any given situation. Every international television appearance made by him will result in a new kind of violence and terror. He will turn neighbor against neighbor. Anyone who dare speak a negative word regarding his administration will certainly be dead by morning.

Jesus said, "And then shall many be offended, and shall betray one another, and shall hate one another" (Matt. 24:10). While this is a fulfilled prophecy of the now defunct character of communism, it will also be the climate of the antichrist's reign.

In addition to the anitchrist's regal seat, great authority, power to take peace from the earth, and a great sword, "There was given unto him a mouth speaking great things" (Rev. 13:5). The fruits of hate propaganda, false accusations, innuendos, and suggestive questions will all be a part of his verbal arsenal.

Words are a powerful force. They have created friendships and broken them. They have accused and acquitted people. They have convicted and condemned, comforted and killed. Words influence, separate, unite, betray, praise, embarrass, encourage, and insult. Words impart wisdom or scatter folly. The Bible says, "With the mouth confession is made unto salvation." Your words will either insure eternal life and heaven or assure eternal death and Hell. The antichrist's "way with words" will result in his destroying the world and nearly wiping out its population.

> The tongue is a little member, and boasteth great things. Behold how great a matter a little fire kindleth! And the tongue is a fire, a world of iniquity: so is the tongue among our members, that it defileth the whole body, and setteth on fire the course of nature; and is set on fire of hell (James 3:5-6).

III. THE THIRD SEAL (Revelation 6:5-6)

> And when he had opened the third seal, I heard the third beast say, Come and see. And I beheld, and lo a black horse; and he that sat on him had a pair of balances in his hand. And I heard a voice in the midst of the four beasts say, A measure of wheat for a penny, and three measures of barley for a penny; and see thou hurt not the oil and the wine.

1. A Somber Syllable: "...Lo...."

The word "lo" is used at least thirty-eight times in the King James Version of the Bible and always prefaces an announcement. Its usage is intended To warn us that something of great import is about to be disclosed. It is with great respect that I proceed now to explain the meaning of this seal whose mystery is concealed in the seven pronouncements regarding it. Because the remaining six pronouncements are so interrelated, we must consider them as a whole, with the following captions in mind.

2. An Ominous Hue: "...A black horse...."

3. What is Your Name: "...He that sat on him...."

4. Did You Bring Your Coupons: "...He had a pair of balances in his hand...."

5. Heaven and Hunger: "...I heard a voice in heaven...."

6. It's My Turn to Eat Today: "...A measure of wheat for a penny...."

7. Prosperity Just Across the Street: "...Hurt not the oil and wine...."

I remember as a lad how excited I was the first time I read this sixth chapter of the Book of Revelation. I thought the Bible was a great book because I found these four horses in it. The white and red horses of the first two seals were a puzzle to me, but the black horse obviously had a story to tell. Being a farmer's kid, horses were very much a part of my life. The balances, barley, and wheat were every day language to me.

I quickly formed a mental image of this black horse. I imagined this scene taking place at the end of a long hot day. The sun was setting and the man had nowhere to go for the night with his very tired black horse. He had to buy wheat or barley because his horse was very weak and might soon die of starvation. I thought the rider was calling to the people along the way to help him find feed. He was telling them how much money he had in his pocket and how much he was willing to pay for the grain.

I saw the horse as one that was poorly cared for, in need of someone to love it. It was weak, sad-eyed, starved, and thirsty. I felt angry at its owner. How I wished the horse would run away from him and come to our farm so I could take care of it. I would wash it down, curry, and comb it. I would feed it well and bring it fresh water every day. I would let it rest in my dad's cool, stone barn for at least a week before riding it.

That childish image was not far from the message hidden here. When all of the elements embodied in this seal are integrated, an interpretation flows naturally. A rider upon a black horse, carrying a pair of balances as he announces an outrageously high price of wheat and barley, tells its own story to a farmer's son. Balances are used when an exact measurement is required for a minute quantity. Scales are used when measuring heavy loads. Balances are so sensitive that one kernel of wheat or barley would tilt them either way. The implication is that one kernel of wheat or barley will be very precious during the tribulation.

The black horse symbolizes famine and the balances speak of a shortage of grain. There are other Scriptures associating the color black with famine, but perhaps the most graphic are Lamentations 4:8-9 and 5:10:

> Their visage is blacker than coal; they are not known in the streets: their skin cleaveth to their bones; it is withered, it is become like a stick. They that be slain with the sword are better than they that be slain with hunger: for these pine away, stricken through for want of the fruits of the field...Our skin was black like an oven because of the terrible famine.

There are no winners in war. While it may be true that the victor takes home the spoil, the spoil is a miserable trophy for the price paid to acquire it. The wars of the antichrist, and his torture of Israel as seen in the red horse seal, inflict great loss and hardship upon the world. Men can neither plant nor harvest, because they are soldiers. The priority is the army, they are fed first while the civilian population starves.

In addition to shortages caused by war because of the preoccupation with fighting instead of sowing and reaping, it needs to be remembered that Elijah the prophet will appear at the outset of the tribulation (Rev. 11:6) and pronounce a three-and-a-half-year drought upon the world. This will be the second time Elijah has prayed and stopped the rain in Israel for three and a half years. The same calamity will again be used by God in an attempt to bring men to repentance.

The riders of the white and red horses represent personages. Their mission dictates that intelligence is a necessity. The crown worn on the head and the sword held in the hand suggests they are persons vested with authority.

The riders of the black and pale horses represent a condition. The record states that the name of the pale horse rider is death. Conditions surrounding the black horse presuppose the name of its rider to be hunger. The balances indicate that food will be carefully weighed because severe shortages will exist. Rationing will be the order of the day.

The old principle of supply and demand will adversely affect prices. The cry from heaven, "A measure of wheat for a penny, and three measures of barley for a penny," implies that inflation will be out of control. According to the Greek, a measure is one choenix (one and a half pints) and a penny is a denarius, the equivalent of a day's wages (Matt. 20:2). Imagine a father bringing home a pint and a half of wheat at the end of a day's work. If a day's wages during the tribulation is $100.00 (which would purchase one a half pints of wheat), a bushel (462 one-and-a-half-pint "units") of tribulation wheat would be worth $46,200.00.

The second statement from heaven is a command, "See thou hurt not the wine and oil." Many explanations have been espoused with regard to the wine and oil. They need to be understood literally, just like the wheat and barley, meaning that neither the supply of oil nor wine or their prices will be hurt. This is an ironic judgment from God. The children of Israel, while in the desert, were given quail until the flesh came out of their nostrils because they did not appreciate the essentials. In the tribulation, oil and wine (over which wars have been fought and blood shed) will be in abundance. But oil and wine will not feed the starving multitudes.

The obsession of many in the world is oil and the drunken lifestyle accompanying it. This will be a judgment of abundance with no ability to alleviate hunger. Drunkenness will be rampant, but sober men with minds to find answers will be few. Money will be plentiful, but its purchasing power is a mockery when the shelves are empty.

IV. THE FOURTH SEAL (Revelation 6:7-8)

And when he had opened the fourth seal, I heard the voice of the fourth beast say, Come and see. And I looked, and behold a pale horse: and his name that sat on him was Death, and Hell followed with him. And power was given unto them over the fourth part of the earth, to kill with sword, and with hunger, with death, and with the beasts of the earth.

We observe that while this seal depicts only one rider, the power to kill is shared with others as indicated by the word "them." The "them" spoken of here most certainly refers to the rider "Death" and his follower "Hell." The fact that the sword and hunger are employed, which are also the weapons of the red and black horse riders, confirms that the four horses represent forces which will persist through the tribulation. They are one a consequence of the other, thus merging with each other on the path to Armageddon.

There are seven pronouncements about this seal which provide valuable information in understanding its message.

1. His Putrid Color:

Bible translators seem to have varied opinions as to the third horse's hue. All of them are probably right, because the symbolism is fundamentally the same even though there appear to be differences in expression:

- King James calls the horse "a pale horse";
- Philips says he is "sickly green in color";

- Goodspeed says he is "the color of ashes";
- The Interlinear Greek English New Testament says he is "a pale green";
- Barclay translates the horse as being "the color of a face blanched with terror";
- The Amplified Bible says he is "an ashy pale horse" (black and blue, as if made so by bruising)";
- Moffat says he is "a livid horse, the bloodless color of a corpse";
- *Die Gutte Nachricht 's, ein Leichenfarbendes Pferd*, translates to mean he is "a cadaverous-colored horse"
- Menge translates it, *Leichen Farbe*, which describes this horse as having "to do with a corpse or the colors of a funeral".

The above opinions agree the color of this horse portrays flesh in a near-death state, ravaged by disease or malnutrition. Taking into account the murderings of the red horse rider and the starvation of the black horse rider, disease and pestilence resulting from unburied bodies would be an unavoidable consequence.

There is in this living, rotting, greenish-yellow horse a message which speaks to the morals of our day. "Free love" philosophies, unnatural sexual lifestyles, and perverted opinions cross over the median of God's one-way road of purity, chastity, and fidelity. There will be no homosexuality in heaven. The angels will not be handing out condoms to teenagers. There will be no abortion clinics there. This will not be because we are incapable of sex, but because these things are an abomination to God. The apostle Paul said:

> Because that, when they knew God, they glorified him not as God...but became vain in their imaginations, and their foolish heart was darkened. Professing themselves to be wise, they became fools...Wherefore God also gave them up to uncleanness through the lusts of their own hearts, to dishonour their own bodies between themselves...God gave them up unto vile affections: for even their women did change the natural use into that which is against nature: and likewise also the men, leaving the natural use of the woman, burned in their lust one toward another; men with men working that which is unseemly, and receiving in them-

selves that recompense of their error...they which commit such things, are worthy of death (Rom. 1:21-32).

Aside from God's displeasure as expressed in the Bible, the many diseases generated from unnatural and illicit sexual lifestyles reveal they are neither natural nor acceptable. In addition to the dying from direct or indirect consequences of war and famine, the pale horse is revealing that the tribulation will see a disease-smitten society such as the world has never witnessed.

Hospitals will be filled to overflowing. Cries of pain will be heard from every fourth house in the block and the dead will be too numerous for the living to bury. Funeral homes will run out of caskets and many corpses will be buried in boxes or bags. The magnitude of this epidemic may make mass burials in pits dug by bulldozers a necessity.

2. Death and Hell — An Unwelcome Presence with a Fearful Entourage:

As if the sights, sounds, and stench of death are not enough, following hard at the heels of the pale horse will be the entourage of a merciless Hell claiming its harvest. Whether John was seeing the flames of Hell at the heels of the pale horse or whether there is a fifth horse called Hell, we are not told. Whatever he saw, it was not good.

Except for the five months spoken of in Revelation 9:6, where "men...will desire to die, and death will flee from them," daily dying will be the rule, not the exception. The persistent horror of this dying is that death will end nothing. Man has a living soul and with Hell following to claim these souls, death becomes only a graduation into something far worse — eternal misery and suffering.

3. The Satanic Patrimony: "And power was given unto them over the fourth part of the earth."

Today's projection for world population by the year 2000 A.D. is six billion. The extent of this tragedy would number one and a half billion deaths. This translates into an equivalence of all the people of Europe, North America, and South America. The demonic gift of death "given" this rider comes from the same source as that of the red horse rider. This is the work of the Devil who exploits evil men and uses immorality, disease, and epidemics to carry out his devices. John 8:44 declares that Satan was a "murderer from the beginning."

4. The War Weapon: "...To kill with the sword...."

To describe Christ's thousand-year reign of peace, God told Isaiah the prophet to use this metaphor, "They shall beat their swords and spears into pruning hooks" (Isa. 2:4). The sword symbolizes war. The sword present with the red horse rider underscores the seals as being one a consequence of the other. What started with the red horse will only intensify with the execution of each succeeding seal.

5. Hunger, the Natural Weapon:

Again, this judgment is a continuation of the black horse seal. Ezekiel 14:21 calls the sword, famine, pestilence, and wild beasts, God's "four sore judgments." The starvation expressed by the black horse will also intensify as the tribulation progresses.

6. Plagues:

The word death is used in two grammatical forms with regard to this seal — as a proper noun when the rider's name is called "Death" and as a verb in conjunction with rider's judgments of sword, hunger, death, and wild beasts. The word "death" in The Amplified Bible is translated as "plagues." This would appear to be accurate. As the rider's name is "Death," to call one of his judgments by the same name seems redundant. Hosea 13:14 seems to support this view (in speaking of the tribulation) when it states, "O death, I will be thy plagues...."

The Amplified Bible translates Deuteronomy 28:22, 27, and 28 in the following manner:

> The Lord shall smite thee with consumption (wasting degenerative diseases)...fever and inflammation (communicable diseases)...tumors (cancer)...scurvy (deficiency and malnutrition diseases)...itch (sexually transmitted diseases which cannot be healed, such as herpes, AIDS, venereal diseases)...madness (psychological disorders and insanity)...blindness (birth defects)...dismay of mind (stress releated disorders, depression, and traumas).

It would appear that, in addition to the automatic consequences of the red and black horse seals, God will also use Moses (the plague expert of Egypt) to bring these plagues upon the people (Rev. 11:6, 10).

7. The Unnatural Weapon: "...To kill with the beasts of the field...."

I am not aware of any time in history when this has happened. While it is true that a beast can never be trusted and has been known to kill and gore people, this would be the exception and not the rule. Generally, man is the hunter and the beast the hunted. The law of nature that God placed into wild or domesticated beasts causes them to fear man.

In this pronouncement, there is a departure from the natural. It appears that the horrors of the four horsemen have so terrified the world that even the animals are driven to distraction. Perhaps they are smitten with some hallucinatory disease where they see and imagine people to be their common prey. Perhaps the famine and starvation are so severe that, being driven mad by hunger, beasts lose their natural fear of man. Or, God may simply reverse the order of nature so the beast becomes the hunter and man the hunted.

Whatever the case may be, it is not a pleasant prospect to think that your house cat might slash open your jugular vein while you are sleeping. Or that man's best friend, the dog, might tear out his throat. Or that a saddle horse might trample its rider into the ground. These are not mere gruesome speculations. When Jesus says the tribulation will be "a time of trouble such as never was, no, nor ever will be," the strangest fabrications of the imagination will fall short of the actual horrors of those days.

V. THE FIFTH SEAL (Revelation 6:9-11)

And when he had opened the fifth seal, I saw under the altar the souls of them that were slain for the word of God, and for the testimony which they held: and they cried with a loud voice, saying, How long, O Lord, holy and true, dost thou not judge and avenge our blood on them that dwell on the earth? And white robes were given unto every one of them; and it was said unto them, that they should rest yet for a little season, until their fellowservants also and their brethren, that should be killed as they were should be fulfilled.

Most Bible commentators seem to think that this fifth seal introduces a new subject, thus breaking the consecutive chronological order of exposition. This conclusion is seriously flawed. While it is true that the symbolic "substance" has changed from horses to an altar with souls under it, we have not encountered a change of subject. The place from which John saw the horses and the souls under the altar is Heaven, which has been his location since chapter four. There is no interruption in the continuous ongoing story of the tribulation on earth.

259

When I was a little boy, I used to go to a pond on a real calm day and try to throw a stone into the center of the placid water. I was intrigued by the splash of the stone creating a ring of ripple waves in the water that just kept multiplying until they reached the shoreline. The tribulation ripple waves are set in motion when the antichrist casts a stone into the middle of the seven-year peace treaty by setting up his image in the temple. This stone, called "the abomination which maketh desolate," is responsible for all of the ripples contained in the seals, trumpets, and vials.

The first disturbance caused by the stone is the refusal of Jews to bow to the image and their subsequent conversion to Jesus Christ, as symbolized by the white horse. The second ripple gets a little larger and more severe as world opinion turns against Israel because they refuse to comply to the order of the antichrist. The antichrist begins his killing campaign as symbolized by the red horse. The third ripple becomes still larger as Elijah pronounces a drought over the world, resulting in famine as symbolized by the black horse. The fourth ripple is even larger, as Moses pronounces his plagues of pestilence in epidemic proportion upon the world as symbolized by the pale horse.

This fifth seal is yet another ripple caused by the stone. The souls under the altar belong to Jews who were converted (as symbolized by the white horse) and subsequently killed by the antichrist "because of the word of God and the testimony they held." Their souls are here being preserved under the altar in heaven.

They are told to "rest for yet a little season" until the rest of their brethren, as decreed by God, are martyred. The fulfillment of this killing and the ongoing conversion of Israel is realized in Revelation 10:7, "But in the days of the voice of the seventh angel, when he shall begin to sound, the mystery of God should be finished (fulfilled) as he hath declared to his servants the prophets."

John, Isaiah, Daniel, Paul, as well as others, are the prophets who explain that the mystery spoken of here is Israel's acceptance of Jesus Christ (Isa. 66:8, Dan. 12:7; Rom. 11:25-26).

1. The Altar and the Souls Under It:

The altar under which these fifth seal martyrs are seen is in Heaven. This altar is the exegetical road map and prime object which links

260

the seals to the trumpets and the trumpets to the vials. Think it not strange to see souls under the altar in Heaven. The Bible declares that the soul returns to God who gave it (Eccles. 12:7). I cannot think of a more appropriate place for the safekeeping of a soul. If the prayers of the saints described in Revelation 8:3-5 can be preserved and kept on the altar, then why cannot the souls be kept under it?

These souls under the altar are the fruit of the labors of Moses, Elijah, and the 144,000 servants of God. They did not receive the seal of safety as did the 144,000. These were "purified and made white" and are the fulfilled symbol of the white horse rider and the trophies of the woman in travail (Rev. 12; Isa. 66:8).

Unfortunately, the killing does not end here, for the ripples the stone has created are not through multiplying. This is but the beginning of the tribulation, and more will be killed (Rev. 6:11 and 13:7). This underscores the fact that the conditions which are present at the beginning of the tribulation persist to the end.

2. Why Were They Killed:

The answer is given within the symbol of the seal, "...For the word of God, and for the testimony which they held...." To a Jew, the Word of God means the ten commandments given by God to Moses. Two of the ten commandments forbid the worship or the making of an image of another god. The testimony which these saints held is their witness of Jesus. The reason for their slaughter is because of these two tenets of faith which they embraced.

These are the saints whom the antichrist was "given power" to overcome (Rev. 13:7). They are also the saints "who keep the commandments, and the faith of Jesus" (Rev. 14:12). They are the saints the antichrist "prevails against" and "wears out" (Dan. 7:21, 25). These saints crying beneath the altar will rise and witness against those who martyred them (Rev. 15:2-4). They are the saints to whom the kingdom will be given (Dan. 7:18, 22, 27). It is obvious that these tribulation martyrs are Jews, because converted Jews "keep the commandments and the faith of Jesus" and the Jews will "sing the song of Moses and the Lamb."

These tribulation saints are of a dual spiritual economy. They are temple people, as well as those washed in the blood of the Lamb. The symbolism is Jewish. The altar is Jewish. The temple is Jewish.

The "brethren" in Revleation 12:11 are the same brethren, in Matthew 25:40, where Jesus the King administers judgment to the nations in proportion to how they treated His "brethren," the Jews, during the tribulation.

3. Their Cry: "...How long, O Lord, holy and true, dost thou not judge and avenge our blood on them that dwell on the earth?" (Rev. 6:10).

This company of martyrs is calling for justice and revenge upon the tribulation earth dwellers who are responsible for spilling their blood. God is not long in answering their prayer. In Revelation 8:1-5, these prayers offered upon the altar before God are cast as a judgment into the earth by an angel. This results in "voices, thunderings, lightening and an earthquake" which initiates God's first trumpet judgment.

There seems to be no room in this world for the Jew. While they are God's chosen people, they are the world's most abused people. There is no nation that has suffered like the Jews. They live in a little strip of land less than 100 miles wide (east and west) and less than 300 miles long (north and south). But it seems the world cannot leave them alone, even in this inadequate allotment. There is always someone making a claim to their land and vowing to drive them into the sea.

This struggle is not over the width, the length, or the richness of their land; this is a spiritual conflict. The Devil knows that Israel is the holy land, Jerusalem is the holy city, and the Jews are the holy people. It is in this holy land that the holy city of Jerusalem will become the capitol of all the world. From here, Christ shall reign as King over all the world for a thousand years. Satan has been struggling ever since he was expelled by God thousands of years ago to become the ruler of this world, but he is not included in God's equation for world rule. This will be the crux of the conflict and it will be bloody.

4. Their Attire: "...White robes were given unto every one of them...."

The "white robes" these martyrs wear, and their being "purified and made white" as spoken of by Daniel, is compatible with the interpretation that the white horse represents Israel's acceptance of Christ and repentance from sin. If perchance a Jew should read this book, let me assure you that these white robes are affirmation, evidence, and confirmation that your Messiah will forgive you for the crucifixion. He will forgive the lie your fathers fabricated regarding the disciples' stealing His body on the morning of the resurrection. He will forgive your forefathers for driving the resurrection-preaching Church out of Jerusalem. He will forgive all your sin, if you only ask Him.

5. Their Prayer Answered:

These white robed martyrs become the victorious, happy, and liberated crowd of Revelation 7:9-17. They come from every tribe and nation. One historian, when writing about the diasporsa, has said, "There is not a country or a sea where you cannot find a Jew."

In addition to their white robes, these saints also wave palms. This time the palms mean what they wanted them to mean two thousand years ago. The Messiah for whom they waited has come! God has heard and answered their prayers:

> ...I beheld, and, lo, a great multitude...clothed with white robes and palms in their hands...These are they which came out of great tribulation, and have washed their robes, and made them white in the blood of the Lamb... (Rev. 7:9, 14).

> And I saw...them that had gotten the victory over the beast, and over his image, and over his mark, and over the number of his name...And they sing the song of Moses the servant of God, and the song of the Lamb... (Rev. 15:2-3).

The judgments initiated at the outset of the tribulation (by which so many are "purified and made white" and subsequently martyred) continue to the end. Jews who overcame the beast by refusing the mark and laying down their lives for Christ are seen here, just before the vials are poured out.

6. What Withholdeth and Preventeth: "...Until your fellowservants and brethren are killed...."

The prayer for deliverance and revenge could not be answered until the fellowservants and brethren are also killed. Moses, Elijah, and thousands of converted Jews must die before deliverance can come. This is the finished scattering spoken of in Daniel 12:7. This is the finished mystery Paul speaks of in Romans 11:25-26. This is also the finished mystery of God (Rev. 10:7). When Moses and Elijah are killed, and the last Jew is saved, then can the prayer be answered.

7. Deliverance:

According to Revelation 14:1-3, the 144,000 are seen safe in Heaven. Moses, Elijah, and the Israel "cloud" are called up hither, or raptured away (Rev. 11:12). In Revelation 11:18, the prayer is finally answered. The dead are avenged against those who have shed their blood, by God's wrath, and Israel is safe with the Lord before the vials are poured out (Rev. 15:2-3). This prepares the way for the last forty-five days of God's wrath.

VI. THE SIXTH SEAL (Revelation 6:12-17)

And I beheld when he had opened the sixth seal, and, lo, there was a great earthquake; and the sun became black as sackcloth of hair, and the moon became as blood; and the stars of heaven fell unto the earth, even as a fig tree casteth her untimely figs, when she is shaken of a mighty wind. And the heaven departed as a scroll when it is rolled together; and every mountain and island were moved out of their places. And the kings of the earth, and the great men, and the rich men, and the chief captains, and the mighty men, and every bondman, and every free man, hid themselves in the dens and the rocks of the mountains; and said to the mountains and rocks, Fall on us, and hide us from the face of him that sitteth on the throne, and from the wrath of the Lamb: For the great day of his wrath is come; and who shall be able to stand?

The Lamb is angry. That seems incomprehensible, for the Scriptures have never characterized Jesus as possessing the attribute of wrath. He is angry because of the cry which has come from the souls under the altar, saying, "How long O Lord, holy and true, dost thou not judge and avenge our blood on them that dwell on the earth?"

Jesus is angry because the antichrist has made good his threat to kill all who refuse the mark. The cry heard is coming from His own "who received him not" at His first coming. Now they have received Him and their acceptance thrusts the omnipotent plan forward. These martyred ones shall rule the world with Him.

1. The Day of His Wrath Has Come:

The day of the Lamb's wrath is not the same as that "great and terrible day of the Lord." The "day" of the Lamb's wrath lasts for three and a half years, the same period of time He spent here on earth as a man who loved the world. The great and terrible "day" of the Lord, the outpouring of the wrath of God, lasts for forty-five days and ends with Armageddon.

The Lamb's wrath is prophesied in Joel 2:30-31:

> And I shall show wonders in the heavens and in the earth...the sun shall be turned to darkness, and the moon into blood, before that great and the terrible day of the Lord comes.

The day of the Lamb's wrath is described as a wonder, sign, or symbol which comes "before" and is a warning and harbinger of the coming of "that great and terrible day of the Lord."

The first six seals have very little or no time lapse between them and could all possibly begin on the same day. The white horse, representing the Jewish revival, covers three and a half years. The red horse, representing the antichrist, is given forty-two months or three and a half years. The black and pale horse seals are judgments pronounced by Moses and Elijah whose tenure is also three and a half years. The souls under the altar represent the atrocities of the red horse rider (forty-two months).

Essentially, the sixth seal is sent by God to bring about a hasty turning of yet unconverted Jews to Jesus Christ, as expressed by the praying from the dens and rocks and mountains. The prophet Joel associates this seal (the sun turning black, and the moon into blood) with the future Pentecost of Israel (Joel 2:28-32). That this seal involves the family of Jacob is further seen in the typology of the sun turning black (Rachael mourning), the moon turning to blood (Jacob's descendants being martyred), and the stars falling from the fig tree (the progeny of Jacob repenting), as interpreted in Joseph's dream (Gen. 37:9).

It is further symbolized by the woman in travail who is clothed with the sun, standing on the moon, and wearing a crown of twelve stars representing Israel in tribulation travail (Rev. 12:1). The fig tree (meaning Israel) "casting her untimely figs when she is shaken of a mighty wind" speaks of Israel being ripe for conversion when the storm strikes and is also compatible with Matthew 24:32. All of this takes place at the beginning of the tribulation, three and a half years "before" the day of God's wrath, and simultaneously with Elijah's appearance. Because the six seal judgments impact the same time frame, they are not only contemporaries, but their starting point would of necessity have to be simultaneous, or thirty days after the image is set up, when Jacob's trouble (the great tribulation) begins.

2. Hide Us From the Face of God: "It is a fearful thing to fall into the hands of the living God" (Heb. 10:31).

If the wrath of God is as great as the love of God, then you and I can never estimate or comprehend it. The people of Revelation 6:16 preferred being buried alive by the rocks and the mountains than to look into the face of God.

The account of the great white throne judgment is a dreadful scene. We see Heaven and earth fleeing from the presence of Him who sits upon the throne (Rev. 20:11). If John and Daniel felt like they had died in the presence of our friendly Lord, what might be the consequences of sinners looking into the face of an angry God?

The look of an angry God must be as embarrassing as a projection of all our deeds upon a huge movie screen hung for all of Heaven and earth to view. It must be as painful as open heart surgery to have everything hiding in the inner sanctum of the soul as if openly displayed. It must be as disgraceful as a mirror as large as the Atlantic Ocean standing upright to reflect every secret thought and deed done in the dark.

266

3. Nature's Seven Smitten Bodies:

The quaking universe, the black sun, the bloody moon, the falling stars, the rolled-up heavens, the crumbling mountains, and the sinking Islands are a seven-scened dramatic production starring God's created universe. The universe will demonstrate to the world that God is about to pull down the curtains on all of civilization because of their abuse of His holy people. The Lamb has become very angry, and the great and terrible day of the Lord is but 1,260 days off.

Visualize the entire universe quaking and shaking in fear as the sun veils her face with the black shawl of death. Mercy and love will stand far off in the distance, weeping over a world that would not respond to their overtures of grace, nor be entreated or persuaded to accept the redemption provided by the Lamb. What we read in the Scriptures seems to affect only the ethereal and the terrestrial. No lives appear to be lost, and there is no mention of cities being destroyed, which is quite the opposite to the executions of the great and terrible day of the Lord.

4. The Sevenfold Status Submission:

Kings, politicians, billionaires, tycoons, generals, and ordinary men will all be down on their knees crying out in futility. But their supplications will be to deaf mountains and rocks. In the days, when prayer to God was beneficial, they laughed and scoffed at the idea. In that day their hopeless petitions will be made to the mountains.

5. God's Last Invitation:

All of this upheaval and chaos will be God's last sermon to civilization. We've had the budding of the fig tree (the independence of Israel), earthquakes in many places, famine and starvation (Africa), pestilences like AIDS, wars and rumors of wars, an epidemic of crime, broken homes (exchanging in marriage),and a multitude of other signs prior to Christ's return. This phenomenon seems somehow to put an exclamation mark at the end of all of them saying, this is it!

I hope what I am about to say meets with divine approval. I feel, at this point, that it is not too late for the antichrist, false prophet, and scarlet harlot to repent. If these three tribulation participants would acknowledge their deceit and repent and be converted, perhaps God would cancel or call off the balance of the tribulation and establish His kingdom of peace at that point. Could it be that if all of the inhabitants of the world would fall on their faces before God and a universal spiritual revival were to erupt, that God would change His mind and annul the words of the prophets like He did the message of Jonah when Nineveh repented?

6. Still Hiding:

Man is incurably deceitful, trying to cover every crime. Even children are born with their little hearts set to hide, deceive, exaggerate, fib, and cheat. Adam and Eve started it all in the Garden of Eden at the dawn of creation when they tried to hide from God after disobeying and transgressing His command. Not much has changed after six millenniums as we approach the sunset of civilization. The Psalmist knew and expressed the futility of such an exercise when he exclaimed:

> Whither shall I go from thy spirit? Or whither shall I flee from thy presence? If I ascend up into heaven, thou art there: if I make my bed in hell, behold, thou art there. If I take the wings of the morning, and dwell in the uttermost part of the sea, even there shall thy hand lead me, and thy right hand shall hold me. If I say, Surely the darkness shall cover me, even the night shall be light about me (Ps. 139:7-11).

The people who prayed that God would "hide them from His face" were in fact themselves already hiding in the dens, rocks, and mountains. Their hiding apparently left a lot to be desired. Their prayer would have received a much better response if they would have prayed, "Rock of ages, cleft for me, let me hide myself in Thee. Let the water and the blood, from Thy riven side which flowed, be of sin the double cure, save me from its wrath and power."

7. Who Shall Be Able to Stand: "He that hath clean hands, and a pure heart; who hath not lifted up his soul unto vanity, nor sworn deceitfully" (Ps. 24:4).

Do not pray that you may die the death of the righteous if you live the life of the wicked. As the tree falls, so shall it lie. We do not abide in the land of the living, but in the land of the dying. It is not my dying I worry so much about, rather my living.

If John the beloved disciple could not stand and fainted dead away on the Isle of Patmos before his loving Lord, how then can one who is not a disciple at all stand in the presence of an angry God? If Paul, for whom our Lord had great plans for apostleship, was thrown from his horse and smitten blind on the way to Damascus, what will happen to those for whom God can make no plans because they insist on traveling the road to self-destruction?

VII. THE SEVENTH SEAL (Revelation 8:1-5)

And when he had opened the seventh seal, there was silence in heaven about the space of half an hour. And I saw the seven angels which stood before God; and to them were given seven trumpets. And another angel came and stood at the altar, having a golden censer; and there was given unto him much incense, that he should offer it with the prayers of all saints upon the golden altar which was before the throne. And the smoke of the incense, which came with the prayers of the saints, ascended up before God out of the angel's hand. And the angel took the censer, and filled it with fire of the altar, and cast it into the earth: and there were voices, and thunderings, and lightnings, and an earthquake.

The world will still be trembling from the awful experiences of the sixth seal when heaven observes the outcome of the seventh seal.

1. A Half-Hour Silence:

A half hour is thirty minutes. The thirty minutes referred to here probably means thirty days. The antichrist allows thirty days after setting up his image. God is also allowing thirty days after the spectacular warning of the sixth seal for reflection and decision.

The four living ones have spoken their "comes" and are now mute. The crying saints under the alter have been comforted and are silent. The angels stand with their wings folded and heads bowed in prayer. Grave concern and a sad foreboding fill the atmosphere of heaven now. This is surely the calm before the storm.

On the altar in the temple at Jerusalem sits the abomination that maketh desolate. On the altar in Heaven, the prayers of all saints are stirring themselves, contemplating the consummation of the realities in the great prayer:

> Our Father which art in heaven, Hallowed be thy name. Thy kingdom come. Thy will be done in earth, as it is in heaven. Give us this day our daily bread. And forgive us our debts, as we forgive our debtors. And lead us not into temptation, but deliver us from evil: For thine is the kingdom, and the power, and the glory, for ever. Amen (Matt. 6:9-13).

God is charitable, fair, and considerate. Preceding other great biblical judgments, He has allowed time for decision and reflection. Noah's generation had 120 years in which to decide to repent. Sodom and Gomorah had the days in which Abraham and God were bargaining over how many righteous were required to spare the cities. Pharaoh of Egypt suffered nine plagues (during which time he was to decide whether or not to let the people go) before the final midnight death stroke was administered. Nineveh was given forty days in which to repent.

2. In Heaven:

The scene has not changed. The souls are still under the altar. The fourth chapter tribunal is still responsible for whatever will happen on earth during the balance of the tribulation.

3. Seven Angels, Seven Trumpets:

John was never shown more than what he could absorb and record for the moment. Whenever he completed recording what he saw, the vision would unfold to the next scene. As this part of the vision unfolds, the court room has more tribulation participants added to it. John must have been startled when seven angels, each having a trumpet, appear. The blast of a trumpet symbolizes an announcement.

4. The Prayer Angel:

Incense burning upon the golden altar in the temple is a type of the prayers which arise to God continually. God has angels guarding children, water, trees, and everything He has created. He also has an angel guarding "all the prayers of the saints." Not one prayer is lost. The Jews write prayers on little pieces of paper and tuck them into crevices in the Wailing Wall. This is not necessary, for God has already deposited that prayer into the prayer censer in heaven.

Whenever I read about this prayer angel in heaven, something keeps telling me that this must be Elijah, the man of prayer, "who pleads with God on Israel's behalf" (Rom. 11:2, Phillips). We know that he and Moses will have a very vital role to play in executing the tribulation plagues. The dreadful thing about praying for a lost world is that one day men who were thus prayed for, but refused to accept God's Son, will have these prayers poured upon them as a judgment against them.

5. The Wealth of the Saints:

Paul, in admonishing the Christians in Corinth to grow in the grace of God, instructs them to build upon the foundation which he has laid, which is Jesus Christ. Paul further advises them to build with gold, silver, and precious stones. Because prayer would have to be regarded as the finest spiritual material with which to build for eternity, it would appear that the gold being alluded to is prayer. This idea is substantiated by the fact that the golden censer and golden altar are associated with prayer.

Heaven's bank contains no worldly currency. Our wealth in heaven will be determined by our giving, our love, our soul winning, and the amount of time we spent in prayer in the interests of His kingdom.

6. The Power of the Prayers:

In addition to the prayers of the saints of all ages being preserved upon the golden altar, God has not forgotten about the crying saints under the altar. The terrible happenings of the sixth seal has been God's response to those prayers, but it is not over. Seven judgment trumpets need yet to be blown, and seven vials of judgments need yet to be poured out.

Before proceeding with the trumpet judgments, these prayers must first be offered up before God and poured out upon the world as a judgment to men who scoffed at prayer. The result is a strong warning from heaven — voices, thunderings, lightnings, and an earthquake. The vibrations of the Lamb's wrath, and the tumult of the sixth seal just thirty days ago, are still very vivid in the minds of the people. And now the earth is shaking again. The prayer our Lord taught us, "Thy kingdom come," has moved one step nearer to reality.

7. Tragedy in the Winds: "The seven angels prepared themselves to sound."

The first four trumpet angels are those of Revelation 7:1 who were commanded to hold back the storm until the sealing of the 144,000 was accomplished. The judgments upon the earth, water, and trees, which the angels of Revelation 7 hold back, are the judgments which are here released by the first four of the seven trumpet angels.

This is the point at which the seventh seal merges and multiplies into seven trumpets. Likewise, the sounding of the seventh trumpet will usher in the seven vials (Rev. 11:15; 15:1, 5-8). In reality, the seventh seal incorporates seven trumpets and seven vials. These fourteen judgments which follow the half hour silence are the most severe of all of the tribulation plagues.

CHAPTER SIX

FORTY-NINE PRONOUNCEMENTS REGARDING THE SEVEN TRUMPETS

Only God knows what these fourteen judgments are all about. An inner foreboding numbs the mind's ability to believe in the possible realities embodied in them. There is a very dark chapter to man's history yet unwritten within these symbols.

The murderous society typified by the red horse, whose rider brandishes a great war sword, will have created hopelessness by "taking peace from the earth." Animals will be nothing more than walking skeletons searching for a blade of grass. Disease and the stench of death will fill the tribulation air. A sad sun, draped with death's shawl obscuring a third of its light, will reflect an eerie light. The moon will blush blood red at the tribulation crimes it witnesses every night. Sadness, sorrow, and despair will be everywhere. There will be nothing worth living for during any tribulation day or night.

Only God knows what will transpire in Heaven during the half hour or thirty-day silence. Could it be that, even in His wrath, God is remembering mercy? Might it be possible that even though the die is cast and the Lamb's cup of wrath is molten white, that His love is holding out just a little longer. Could He be not yet willing to let go and pour out its contents?

"There was silence in heaven for half an hour." How do we contemplate the implications of this? How can Heaven, this place of in-

273

expressible joy, jubilation, and song with so much to rejoice over, suddenly be silent for thirty days? Even the raptured Church, the bride of the Lamb, has ceased to sing the "new song." Instead, there is concern on every glorified face and apprehension fills the celestial air. Divine attributes will be in conflict; love, mercy, and grace will grapple with vengeance, justice, and wrath. This is God's final consideration over lost humanity's last dispensation and His first contemplation of ending His wrath at Armageddon.

Who are these angelic beings bearing trumpets (Rev. 8:2) and pitchers (vials Rev. 15:1)? Scripture tells us that angels are God's "ministering servants," powerful enough to shut lions' mouths, open prison gates, roll away stones from graves, touch men like Daniel and John to restore their strength, and enter Gethsemane to strengthen the Son of God as He languished with a broken heart.

Yet in Isaiah 37:36, we have the record of one angel destroying the entire Assyrian army. In Egypt, another angel (sometimes called the Death Angel) singularly killed all the first born of man and beast in one night. The Bible is filled with stories of the powers of angels. Lucifer was once one of them. Angels are not to be trifled with by humans.

I. THE FIRST TRUMPET - THE FIRE ANGEL
(Revelation 8:7)

The first angel sounded, and there followed hail and fire mingled with blood, and they were cast upon the earth: and the third part of trees was burnt up, and all green grass was burnt up.

1. A Voice Versus A Trumpet:

In announcing the tribulation judgments, the instrument of delivery progresses from a voice to a trumpet, which is intended to make us realize the progession of the severity of the judgments. The four horsemen are ordered into action by the word "come," spoken by one of the living ones. The trumpet judgment angels are commissioned to deliver their destructive ordinances by the blast of a trumpet. Similarly, when we come to chapter sixteen, the intensity again is accentuated by comparing the blast of a trumpet by an angel to the pouring out of the wrath of God from a vial by an angel. These are given to inform us that there is no hope for a better day to come during the tribulation.

2. Sources of Tribulation Judgments:

The fact that tribulation judgment commands come from heaven is conclusive enough that God has something to with their execution. It would appear that, as in times past, God will again allow man to destroy himself. By the same token, it needs to be understood that God does not need man to help Him execute judgement upon the world. He did not need him in the days of Noah, Sodom and Gomorah, or many other judgments.

God is the supreme source of tribulation judgments. These judgments must come as man has gone too far in his defiance of God's commands — the very commands that must be respected in order for the world to survive. Sin and obeisance to Satan has resulted in a bizarre behavior by mankind that is out of control. A new start must be made, for the world is no longer a place in which to live and be happy.

3. Environmental Warfare:

The burning up or, as the Greek says, "burning down" of one third of all trees and all green grass certainly falls within the capability of man. There are those who maintain that the world's nuclear weapons will never be used. According to the description John gives of tribulation judgments, not only will nuclear weapons be used, but biological, chemical, environmental, and every form of conventional warfare will be used as well.

It is not presumptuous to assume that man is here employing the use of environmental warfare. The fact that forests are bombed first, sparing heavily populated areas, seems to indicate that man is sending a signal to his enemy that the prospect of something more devastating is not beyond the realm of possibility.

4. Bigger Than Bombs:

Micah 7:16-17 speaks of the tribulation. God tells the prophet that plagues like those in Egypt will be experienced in the last days. We should not be surprised to note that the first trumpet plague is the same as the seventh Egyptian plague (Exod. 9:23-28). Here Moses stretches forth his rod, and thunder was heard, and hail and fire ran along the ground. Similarly, in the familiar encounter Elijah had with the prophets of Baal, fire fell from heaven consuming the water soaked sacrifices. If it happened during the days of Moses' and Elijah's first ministry, why not again?

5. Power Over Water and Fire:

Normally fire, hail, and blood are conflicting elements. Fire and water do not get along very well. However, there is nothing normal about the tribulation. Whenever God decides to use hail and blood to fan and spread fire, there's nothing the prophets of Baal or Pharaoh can do to stop it.

6. A Smoke-Filled World:

We cannot continue setting hundreds of oil wells ablaze (like Saddam Hussein has done) and burning down one-third of the beautiful oxygen producing rain forests — reducing meadows, grasslands, and parks into a black hinterland — without paying some horrendous environmental price for it. The destruction of forests and grasslands has far reaching implications. Think of all the living creatures that make these their home. Many animals and birds will be burned alive. It should not be surprising that the beasts turn on man as seen in the pale horse seal. They will be smitten with insanity and madness.

7. Oxygen Getting Thin:

Our world is powered by oxygen consuming conveniences. We need every tree and square foot of grass available to replenish our demands upon the oxygen supply. We can ill afford to lose one third of our forests plus all green grass. The oxygen producing ratio, compared to pollution emission content, is already dangerously near lethal in many parts of the world. It should not be surprising then that as the tribulation progresses, the pestilence and disease announced by the pale horse can only intensify because of pollution.

If all green grass is to be burned, what becomes of the animals which graze it? The black horse can only become more gaunt as it stalks the land in tribulation starvation.

II. THE SECOND TRUMPET - THE BLOOD ANGEL
(Revelation 8:8-9)

And the second angel sounded, and as it were a great mountain burning with fire was cast into the sea: and the third
part of the sea became blood; and the third part of the creatures which were in the sea, and had life, died; and the third
part of the ships were destroyed.

1. What Did John See:

The flaming mountain he saw is not an actual mountain. The
words "as it were" indicate it is "similar" to a mountain and is not
to be taken literally. Some scholars hold that this is a meteorite falling from heaven, burning all the way to earth. I doubt it.

Because this is the great tribulation and peace has been taken from
the earth, we need to look for the answer in something man in his
wrath can do against man. This is either an offensive missile armed with
an atomic warhead fired at Jerusalem from some eastern nation that over-
shoots its mark and accidentally strikes a great naval build-up in the Mediterranean Sea, or it is a defensive missile armed with an atomic warhead
fired intentionally by Israel at a large naval fleet approaching her from
the sea.

2. The Middle Sea:

The word Mediterranean means middle and the Mediterranean Sea
is indeed situated in the middle of the world. This burning "mountain"
falls into the sea. Since all tribulation wars are headed in the direction of
Armageddon in Israel, this can hardly mean any other sea than the Mediterranean.

3. Naval Holocaust:

The fact that John sees a colossal ball of fire as big as a mountain is in
itself evidence that this is an explosion of mega-magnitude. This could
be a large atomic, hydrogen, or neutron bomb. We can only deduce from
the destruction it produces that it is a very powerful destructive explosive device.

4. Bloodied Waters:

We can be sure that with the explosion of a nuclear bomb and the burning of ships, the reflection from such a fire storm at sea could cause the waters on the sea to be red. A second possibility is that an explosion of this magnitude in the waters would rip whales, sharks, and all living creatures in the sea to shreds for miles around, causing the water to turn red.

However, knowing what God is capable of, it is not safe to relegate such a phenomenon to the results of man's destruction alone. Simply remember that God has done this before. Perhaps Moses will stretch his rod over the Mediterranean and simply turn the waters to blood like he did in Egypt long ago (Exod. 7:20). This reminder to Israel will be an assurance to them that Canaan cannot be too far away.

5. Whose Ships:

A description is given of the Millennium in Isaiah 2. In verse sixteen, the "ships of Tarshish" are named as having been destroyed as they come against Israel. In Ezekiel 38:13, the "merchants of Tarshish with all the young lions thereof" have usually been taken to mean Great Britain is the lion and the young lions are her offspring or commonwealth English speaking peoples. It could be that many of these ships surrounding Israel in the last days, whether in defense of Israel or offense, will belong to Great Britain and her allies.

John was seeing an incendiary flying mass capable of setting ablaze possibly hundreds of ships. Such an explosion would make the Mediterranean look like a two or three hundred square mile gasoline refinery on fire. Ships, turning white hot under the intensity of radioactive fission, would be blown heavenward like erupting volcanoes as a result of secondary explosions caused by fuel reserves and conventional and nuclear arsenals on board. Demolished, they would melt away into the sea and create the biggest ship cemetery the oceans of the world have ever known.

6. Aquatic Catastrophe:

After the smoke and steam drift away, a most horrendous scene will greet and nauseate any survivors. The Mediterranean will be a heaving flotsam and jetsam of an atomic butchery of sea life. Woe to the beaches to which this marine carnage will be borne by the winds and waves. The stench and pestilence created by their rotting remains will only enlarge Death and Hell's procession of humans already following the pale horse. Hundreds of thousands of tons of decaying aquatic flesh, beached upon some unfortunate shore, will be a reminder that twelve even worse calamities are on the way.

7.   Famine Worsens:

Famine cannot hurt the oceans and seas of the world. A special omnipotent provision has always made fish available even during the fiercest famines. However, the countries surrounding the Mediterranean Sea will not be safe trying to consume fish taken from it. Radioactivity will so pollute the waters that sea life will continue dying daily for a long time from the consequences of it. Furthermore, people eating such flesh would surely be subject to more diseases like cancer, surrendering yet more victims to the black and pale horse riders. Hosea 4:1-3 explains a little about the judgments to come, revealing that even "the fishes of the sea shall be taken away." These are some of the sombre sounds of the second trumpet.

III.   THE THIRD TRUMPET - THE POISON ANGEL
(Revelation 8:10-11)

And the third angel sounded, and there fell a great star from heaven, burning as it were a lamp, and it fell upon the third part of the rivers, and upon the fountains of waters; and the name of the star is called Wormwood: and the third part of the waters became wormwood; and many men died of the waters, because they were made bitter.

This third trumpet angel is special because he bears the number of the Trinity. It should not be surprising that his judgment would have a spiritual connotation, having something to do with the powers of darkness which the Trinity has been in conflict with from time immemorial. The judgments of the first two trumpet angels come not from the upper stratosphere known as heaven, rather are cast from the sky, or the realm man knows something about, namely, the air space in which we travel and in which we fight wars.

This star is cast "from heaven," meaning we must approach this trumpet from an entirely different perspective. The devastation wrought by this single star cannot be the work of man. Rivers and fountains are represented in the plural. Man is not capable of producing a single toxic vehicle capable of poisoning the rivers and fountains scattered around the world with one delivery. If John would have seen a shower of falling stars, the possibility might exist. But this single star is a being with intelligence, like the Death Angel of Egypt.

1. Fell From Heaven:

A suggestive definition is provided in the words "fell...from heaven." This must mean he is from among those who belong to the powers of darkness and spiritual wickedness (Eph. 6:12). His abode is in the heavenlies, not the Heaven where God's throne is located, but rather between this earth and God's throne where prayers are hindered and accusations have been made against the saints. We can know he is a wicked angel because of his "falling" and his name, "Wormwood".

2. Of Ancient Origin:

This star is very old. He already bore this name when John received the revelation. In addition to being called Wormwood, a very bitter absinthe poison, his non-symbolical identity is envy and jealousy.

Numbers 5:11-30 gives a detailed account of a trial of jealousy. This passage reveals that jealousy comes as a result of adultery or, in the case of spiritual things, idolatry. Our God is a "jealous God." We learn from this passage that if God required an unfaithful woman to drink the bitter water of jealousy (resulting in a bloated belly and rotting bones), cannot this plague of bitter water as prescribed by the poison angel again be administered because of jealousy and envy?

The poison angel is against every plan and program the Trinity has for mankind. God has many ministering servants called angels and so does Satan. This wicked servant is in charge of all types of witchcraft, astrology, magicians, and soothsayers. The identifying fruits of people who fall into his bondage are of the "Wormwood and gall" variety which have bedeviled mankind ever since the day Cain killed his brother because of bitterness. This spirit was present in the days of Moses (Deut. 29:18), and was responsible for the root of bitterness that filled Esau's heart (Heb. 12:15). The spirit of bitterness has been a major tool in the arsenal of Satan to bring unhappiness into the Church of Jesus Christ. Many saints have allowed themselves, through their unsanctified personalities, to be poisoned by this star angel whom Paul admonished us to wrestle against with the whole armour of God.

In Revelation 9, we see a star fall from heaven having the key to the bottomless pit. This certainly is a personage, for he carries a key and knows how to use it. He does not own the key; Jesus owns the keys to Death and Hell. If the star of chapter nine is a fallen angel, then why cannot this star also be one?

3. At Work in the Early Church:

The Bible unlocks the door for us in Acts 8 to identify this star. This chapter speaks of a man who mingled with the converts of Philip at Samaria when Peter was sent here to lay hands upon the baptized believers so they might receive the Holy Ghost. This man Simon, observing that the Holy Ghost was given by the laying on of Peter's hands, was filled with envy and jealousy. He no doubt saw Peter as a superior magician and thus a threat to him. He offered Peter money so he too might be able to perform this fascinating and mysterious miracle.

Peter rebuked him and said, "I perceive that thou art in the gall of bitterness, and in the bond of iniquity." Menge translates, *Ich sehe dass du in Galle der Bitterkeit, und in Bande der Ungerechtigkeit geraten bist.* Translated, this reads, "I see that you have fallen into the bondage of unrighteousness, Gall and bitterness." It is clear from this statement that Simon was in bondage, and bondage is from Satan.

Fausset's *Bible Encyclopedia and Dictionary* states:

> Simon Magus the Samaritan practiced magic, 'bewitching the people of Samaria, giving out that he himself was some great one,' so that all said, 'This is the power of God which is called great.' His followers reported of him saying, 'I am the word of God, the paraclete, omnipotent,' in fact, the incarnation of the word, the Logos. By being baptized by Philip, he would be initiated into communion with some powerful spirit through whom he could do greater wonders than before.(1)

Volume 4 of *The Interpreter's Dictionary* (Abingdon) states:

> Simon was a professional magus like all Magi, a Shaman caste of the Medes, who later became Zoroastrian priests of Persia. In the Mediterranean world they were known as professional persons engaged in astrology, necromancy, incantations, exorcism, etc. He was known by the people of his day as the 'Great,' with the 'power of God.' It is said he committed suicide and had himself buried with the promise of rising on the third day.(2)

I am not suggesting that Simon Magus is this falling star. But I do suspect, because of his jealousy, that he fell into "this bondage of iniquity of gall and wormwood" from whence this poisonous practice originates. He was a disciple of that demon power of the air which administers this lethal draught. Everything that Simon was, he became because of his bondage and allegiance to this angel named Wormwood.

4. Looks Like A Star — But Burns Like A Lamp:

This star demon, through the power of Satan, has produced many impostors, beginning with Semerimis and her son, Tammuz, who set themselves up as Babylonian deities. These two spiritually poisoned not only the Babylonians, but much of the world. Nebuchadnezzar, Belshazzar, Darius, Baal, Ashtaroth, the many sun gods of Greece and Rome, many of the popes, gurus, and an unending list of other humans are among those who have accepted worship unto themselves. They have been poisoning the waters of religion throughout the centuries with their blasphemy.

The Trinity has always been the object of imitation and attack. God has been replaced by Allah, emperors, popes, and fuhrers. Today in Los Angeles alone, there are over 150 persons claiming to be Jesus. The most recent New Age movement makes contact with departed spirits who have become "spirit guides," obviously an attempt to replace the Holy Spirit.

This fallen star is an impostor "holy" spirit. He poisons the fountains of truth as did the serpent in the garden. He is not the true light or water of life. He looks like a star, but his light is only "as it were a lamp" and his water is the water of death. Just as eating of the fruit in the garden brought death, so shall drinking of the poisoned waters bring death during the tribulation.

5. A Great Star:

The prophets, when speaking of Jesus' coming into the world, said, "He shall be great." The disciple of this star, according to Acts 8:9-11, "gave out that himself was some GREAT one," which is exactly what John saw when he said, "And there fell a GREAT star from heaven." Every devil worshipping leader proclaims himself to be great.

6. Now Drink It:

Finally, John definitely states that "his name is Wormwood," which is what Peter named as Simon's bondage by using the words "gall and bitterness." While it is true that Peter does not use the word "wormwood," the inference certainly exists. In Lamentations 3:19, the words are used interchangeably in "remembering mine affliction, the wormwood and the gall."

The prayers of the martyrs under the altar in Revelation 6:9-11 infer that many of the tribulation judgments are based upon revenge. What score is God trying to settle with this poison angel?

In Revelation 16:4-7, the third angel pours out his vial upon the rivers and fountains of water. The results are more devastating than those of the third trumpet angel who poisons a third of the waters. One hundred percent of all drinking water is turned into blood here. What is significant are the words of the guardian angel over the waters,

> Thou art righteous, O Lord, which art, and wast, and shalt be, because thou hast judged thus. For they have shed the blood of saints and prophets, and thou hast given them blood to drink (Rev. 16:5).

Can we not deduce from the above revenge that in the case of the poison angel, God is finally leveling the balances of justice? Could it not be said that because of jealousy and envy against the Trinity, those who have poisoned the minds and hearts of children, youth and adults in schools, media, and even churches will be given poison to drink? Revelation 9:13-21 discloses that one-third of the population will die because of demon endoctrination administered by the sixth trumpet. There must be a correlation here with the poisoning of one-third of the waters.

7. Famine For Water:

Is it contradictory that the poison angel would destroy those who faithfully embraced and defended the doctrines of Satan? Not when you look at the character of Satan. The devil has, and still is, doing this very thing today. People build churches and write books in his honor while engaging in channeling, spiritualism, astrology, fortune-telling, transcendental meditational exercises, and a host of other satanic methodologies. And when they are completely possessed and obsessed, they commit suicide at Satan's command.

A famine for water seems almost unthinkable. I was a little lad when my father was forced to haul water for home use and livestock in the middle thirties. But there was never a time during the depression of the dirty thirties in Saskatchewan that water was not available somewhere. Water will become scarce not only because of one third of it being poisoned, but we must not forget about the effect of the three-and-a-half-year drought that Elijah pronounces upon the world at the outset of the tribulation.

IV. THE FOURTH TRUMPET - THE CONSTELLATION ANGEL (Revelation 8:12-13)

And the fourth angel sounded, and the third part of the sun was smitten, and the third part of the moon, and the third part of the stars; so as the third part of them was darkened, and the day shone not for a third part of it, and the night likewise. And I beheld, and heard an angel flying through the midst of heaven, saying with a loud voice, Woe, woe, woe, to the inhabiters of the earth by reason of the other voices of the trumpet of the three angels which are yet to sound!

We can be reasonably sure that the first two trumpet judgments are instigated by man. The forests and grasslands being burnt up appears to be environmental warfare. The naval holocaust on the Mediterranean Sea almost certainly describes the results of a nuclear blast. Both of these attacks are away from populated areas, and cities are not affected. It would be expected that in the use of nuclear weapons, a limited restraint would be exercised by man at the outset.

The third trumpet judgment comes "from heaven." Here the principalities and powers of the air are involved as the poison angel lethalizes the clear waters which God created on the third day.

In the fourth trumpet judgment, the luminaries (which God hung in space on the fourth day of creation) are attacked. As we will shortly discover, the fifth and sixth trumpet judgements are attacks from the underworld through the release of fiendish demons into the world. The seventh trumpet, which multiplies into seven vials, is reserved for God and His wrath.

1. Satan In Perspective:

You will recall in our study of the seven tribulation participants, more specifically the pregnant woman whose child Satan tries to devour, that the archangel, Michael, defends the woman (Israel). The woman flees into the wilderness to hide for three and a half years. We are not told how long Satan and Michael fight; the record simply states that Satan "prevailed not."

Immediately following Satan's defeat, he will be cast out of Heaven. The sounding of the fifth trumpet, which is also the first woe, almost certainly marks the time at which Satan will be ejected because of the "woe" associated with it (Rev. 8:13, 12:12).

2. His Last Stand:

Satan knows at this point that his days are numbered wherein he has access to the throne of God. Any devastation against the luminaries which may be on his agenda would have to be carried out soon.

3. God Lengthens the Leash:

Shortly after this time, Satan will be allowed free course on earth. God will give the tribulation inhabitants what they have always wanted. The world is determined to serve Satan and now God will allow him to reach farther than ordinarily allowed.

Satan will be permitted to touch the sacred sources which provide light for the entire universe. He knows that his son, the antichrist, is soon going to run into terrible turbulence and his crash is imminent. Satan is aware that the only way he can help his son, when he tumbles, is to pull the blinds down one third of the way on the luminaries. He knows that "men love darkness rather than light" because of their evil deeds.

4. Not the First Time:

This is not the first time God has done something like this. In the Book of Job, Satan accuses God of building a hedge around Job so that he cannot be harmed. Satan then challenges God that this is the reason why Job is serving Him. God replies, "...All that he hath is in thine power..." (Job 1:12). Here we discover how far God will actually allow Satan to go at certain times.

The balance of the chapter tells how God gave success to robbers in plundering Job's oxen and asses and to murderers who killed the servants. Satan was allowed to use "the fire of God" to burn up the sheep and then the Chaldeans robbed Job of his camels and killed the servants in charge. Finally the unthinkable happens; God allowed Satan to use the "wind" to crush the house in which his sons and daughters were eating and drinking and they were all killed.

If God allowed Satan to use "the fire of God" and the "wind" to persecute a friend of God, could not God allow Satan to respond to the blast of the fourth trumpet by interfering with the sun, moon, and stars to persecute his enemies?

5. A Turn Later:

God knew what He was doing in Job's time, for the world has an everlasting memorial in Job. True children of God do not serve Him for ulterior reasons, but because of their great trust that what He is doing "will work out for the good to them that love him" (Rom. 8:28).

We have preachers today who say it is not God's will that any of His children should be poor or sick. I refer to the positive confession, health and wealth gang. The reason they say this is because such a doctrine, when embraced by gullible people, will work out for the good of those who proclaim it — through the many offerings they receive. I believe in divine healing, and I believe "God will supply all our needs according to his riches in glory." But I do not believe in proclaiming divine healing and divine supply for His children for my own ulterior purposes.

In the case of Israel (whose remnant Satan persecutes during the tribulation), God wants to teach the tribulation inhabitants the same lesson He taught the friends of Job. It will not matter how many miracles the false prophet performs or how treacherous the antichrist becomes or how much spit fills the faces of abused Jews. The Jews will be so soundly converted and convinced that Jesus is the Messiah, no disaster will be fierce enough for them to renounce Him.

There are only three more trumpets, also known as woes. After God has raptured Israel to himself, He will show us how dark it can get when He pulls the curtains and how undrinkable the waters can get when He pollutes them. God will show how hot the sun can become when He rolls the curtains up again, how barren the Euphrates River can get when He dries it up and how deep and how far the blood will flow when He smites humanity with His sword!

6. Life Is In The Light:

We know that "life is in the blood." However, John 1:4 declares that "in him was life; and the life was the light of men." John is speaking here of the spiritual life, but the analogy has credence in regards to natural light as well.

Without the light of the sun, moon, and stars, this planet would become an unending wasteland and desert. One third of the sun's energy denied would be sufficient to kill every growing plant, with the possible exception of those that thrive in the shade. The suns rays are also necessary to penetrate the waters to sustain food for every living thing in the sea. The loss of one third of the sun's strength during the day, the loss of one third of the moon's rays by night, and the shortening of each day and lengthening of each night by four hours, would surely result in frost at every sunrise, even in July and August.

This fourth trumpet judgment will only intensify the famine and starvation. I have heard it said many times that there is a very delicate balance in the placement of sun, moon, and stars as relating to the axis upon which the planet rotates. A little nearer to the sun and everything would burn up. A little farther from the sun and everything would freeze.

7. Woe, Woe, Woe; Three More To Go:

The word "woe" is not good news. Our Lord put these words here not only to inform us of the severity of the last three woe trumpets, but, more specifically, that we would know that the falling star at the outset of chapter nine is Satan.

The words of Revelation 12:12, "...Woe to the inhabiters of the earth and of the sea! For the devil is come down unto you, having great wrath, because he knoweth he hath but a short time," disclose that Satan will create great "woe" for the inhabiters of the earth in the "short time" remaining. The fact that Revelation 8:13 closes with the words, "Woe to the inhabiters of the earth," forces us to conclude that it addresses the same judgment. This confirms the belief that the falling star of Revelation 9:1 is indeed Satan and that the first two woe trumpets are instigated by him.

V. THE FIFTH TRUMPET - THE PAIN ANGEL
(Revelation 9:1-12)

The "short time" referred to in Revelation 12:12 is a period of 586 days, the time Satan is confined to earth after being cast out of heaven. This time frame includes the five months of Revelation 9:5, the 391 days of Revelation 9:15, and the forty-five days required to pour out the vials of God's wrath.

> And the fifth angel sounded, and I saw a star fall from heaven unto the earth: and to him was given the key of the bottomless pit. And he opened the bottomless pit; and there arose a smoke out of the pit, as the smoke of a great furnace; and the sun and the air were darkened by reason of the smoke of the pit. And there came out of the smoke locusts upon the earth: and unto them was given power, as the scorpions of the earth have power. And it was commanded them that they should not hurt the grass of the earth, neither any green thing, neither any tree; but only those men which have not the seal of God in their foreheads. And to them it was given that they should not kill them, but that they should be tormented five months, and their torment was as the torment of a scorpion, when he striketh a man. And in those days shall men seek death, and shall not find it, and shall desire to die, and death shall flee from them. And the shapes of the locusts were like unto horses, prepared unto battle, and on their heads were as it were crowns like gold, and their faces were as the faces of men. And they had hair as the hair of women, and their teeth were as the teeth of lions. And they had breastplates, as it were breastplates of iron; and the sound of their wings was as the sound of chariots of many horses running to battle. And they had tails like unto scorpions, and there were stings in their tails: and their power was to hurt men five months. And they had a king over them, which is the angel of the bottomless pit, whose name in the Hebrew tongue is Abaddon, but in the Greek tongue hath his name Apollyon. One woe is past; and, behold, there come two more hereafter.

The next two woe trumpets initiate an entirely new and horrific era of tribulation judgments as Satan mobilizes the world of evil departed spirits and demons. The bottomless pit and Hell are opened and the wicked men and demons contained in them will be released to inflict severe suffering upon the tribulation inhabitants.

1. Are You Who We Think You Are:

This woe trumpet judgment begins with John seeing a star falling to earth. The star is Satan whose ejection is described in Revelation 12:12. We know that one third of the angels (here called "stars") followed him in his rebellion against God. If his fallen angels are called "stars," then we would expect that he himself must also be a "fallen star."

In referring to this star, "he" carries a key and is capable of unlocking the bottomless pit. He is a personage. I cannot agree that the being carrying a key in Revelation 20:1 is the same as the falling "star" of Revelation 9. In Revelation 20:1, nothing is said of the key that this personage carries as being "given" to him, implying that he owns it. The "star" personage of Revelation 9:1 carries a key that was "given him."

"Woe to the inhabiters of the earth, for the devil is come down unto you having great wrath." The devil will be very angry and agitated because he and his son, the antichrist, have only 586 days left to turn things in their favor. The Jews will not bend, for their allegiance to Christ has been established. Having killed so many Jews will begin to concern these two, for if world opinion turns against them because of their crimes, the antichrist could be called to stand judgment in a world court.

In this state of mind, Satan will become very unpredictable, fully capable of doing the unthinkable. The worst possible scenario will become a reality.

2. The Bottomless Pit Unlocked:

Who else but Satan would be interested in the bottomless pit? This is where the angels who sinned and followed him in the heavenly rebellion long ago are now imprisoned. Second Peter 2:4 and Jude 6 state that these demon angels are kept here waiting for their judgment day. Satan needs all the help he can get, so he calls upon his reserves from the universal demon prison for assistance.

We cannot imagine what sort of crime this is. These are the worst criminals known to God or Man. Every one of them is a proud, arrogant, conceited, contemptuous, insolent, and haughty insurrectionist against holiness. They have conspired against the highest Authority,and along with their coup leader Lucifer, were de-throned.. Angry over their long imprisonment, they will be eager to be freed so they may avenge themselves. God, however, places a restraining order upon them to prohibit them from killing anyone during their five month vicious rendezvous.

God is giving man what he thought he always wanted, fellowship with the devil and his demons. Such unholy alliances are getting to be quite commonplace in these days. If it is not the Holy Spirit who is guiding, it can only be an unholy spirit.

I am very concerned about the people today, many of them prominent, who are becoming involved in the New Age movement. I am sure they are not aware of what is happening when they allow themselves to find strength from "within" themselves. I am convinced from testimonies I have heard that something unnatural and sensational does indeed take place. However, because this experience is not found through prayer in the name of Jesus Christ, only one other option remains.

3. Man, Woman, Horse, Lion, Locust, or Scorpion:

The strange creatures described in Revelation 9:3-11 portend terrible possibilities. This is not an existing creature that we now know. God has given it this outrageous appearance so that we might realize that each phase of its construction has special meaning.

We first note that this creature comes from the tightly secured prison called the "bottomless pit." This is not the Hell that wicked and unprepared souls are consigned to, like the rich man of Luke 16:19-31. This place is where fallen angels, now called demons, are consiged to "chains of everlasting darkness" (2 Pet. 2:4; Jude 6). These are the same demons who entreated the Lord not to send them back to the abyss, but to allow them to enter the herd of swine (Luke 8:26-36). They are fierce man-haters. Their greatest delight is in tormenting men, as exemplified by the man of Gadara who was possessed with legions of them.

To open the door to their prison house and allow them to roam this earth, stinging men everywhere for five months, will create a scene of suffering which cannot be imagined.

Second, this creature's anatomy is a composite of six known beings. The locust, bird, horse, man/woman (mankind), lion, and scorpion. These six beings represent six different species of living beings created by God who have been victims of the curse of sin. The locust represents the kingdom of insects, the horse represents domesticated animals, the man and woman represent the kingdom of man, the lion represents wild beasts, the scorpion represents the reptile kingdom, and the wings of this creature represent the bird kingdom.

The message of this six-part creature is that the curse of sin has enslaved every living thing and kept them in bondage. These are now depicted as a composite demonic being over which Satan has control, and Satan orders it to bring suffering upon the inhabitants of the earth.

4. The Reign of Pain:

The principal word of chapter nine is "hurt." We have in the excruciating sting of this creature the accumulated pains of a woman in the pangs of childbirth and a man eating his bread "by the sweat of his brow." We have the pain of a horse under the slavery of cruel taskmasters, the pain a lion inflicts upon the creatures he consumes for his livelihood, and the starvation and desolation a locust creates by his voracious appetite. The creature also depicts the excruciating pains of the strike of a scorpion and the hardships birds endure. As a composite, this creature symbolizes the pain demon, borne of the curse of sin — the very substance of the bottomless pit.

5. No Sedative:

The sting of a scorpion can be fatal, but the sting of this demon creature will be worse. Any sedative strong enough to alleviate this pain would surely cause brain damage, cardiac arrest, a stroke, or insanity. Death will be the only relief, but dying will not be an option during these five months (Rev. 9:6).

These demons administer the sting of sin which prohibits the relief of death. This is the tribulation. The ultimate tragedy is that men, women, and young people can all avoid the tribulation if they will only accept the grace of God and the sacrifice of His Son — but many will not. This is not God's fault or desire, for "God is not willing that any should perish, but that all should come to repentance."

6. Tribulation Mosquitos:

The proliferation of this infernal creature will be of such magnitude that their number will form a dark cloud so dense that the sun will be darkened. We have all seen large swarms of mosquitoes forming a cloud, but these are not mosquitoes. They are spirit creatures, with a form that can be seen, which possess intelligence because they recognize the 144,000. They cannot be captured, handled, or killed. There is no pesticide which can eradicate them. The only known antidote for demon domination is the blood of Jesus Christ.

John saw them as little horses the size of a scorpion which would probably be the size of a gopher or squirrel. Joel 2:9 seems to describe the same thing that John was seeing, creatures that climb walls and enter houses through windows. They will fill the earth. There will probably not be a tribulation earth dweller who will not be bitten at least once during those five months with the exception, of course, of the 144.000 (Rev. 9:4).

7. King Abaddon or Appolyon:

Permit me to speak a word here to seancers, mediums, clairvoyants, psychics, spiritualists, astrologers, mystics, channelers, and the like. Check out the origin of your spirit guides. I have heard New Age people say the name of their guide is Abaddon (Rev. 9:11) which actually means "destroyer." One day you may discover that you have become one of his slaves. You say your spirit guide is guiding you in this present world. You say right, but you are wrong when you think it is upon a good path. Satan's paths all have "dead" ends.

VI. THE SIXTH TRUMPET - THE RIVER ANGEL
(Revelation 9:13-21)

And the sixth angel sounded, and I heard a voice from the four horns of the golden altar which is before God, saying to the sixth angel which had the trumpet. Loose the four angels which are bound in the great river Euphrates. And the four angels were loosed, which were prepared for an hour, and a day, and a month, and a year, for to slay the third part of men. And the number of the army of the horsemen were two hundred thousand thousand, and I heard the number of them. And thus I saw the horses in the vision, and them that sat on them, having breastplates of fire, and of jacinth, and brimstone: and the heads of the horses were as the heads of lions; and out of their mouths issued fire and smoke and brimstone. By these three was the third part of the men killed, by the fire, and by the smoke, and by the brimstone, which issued out of their mouths. For their power is in their mouth, and in their tails: for their tails were like unto serpents, and had heads and with them they do hurt. And the rest of the men which were not killed by these plagues yet repented not of the works of their hands, that they should not worship devils, and idols of gold, and silver, and brass, and stone, and of wood which neither can see, nor hear, nor walk. Neither repented they of their murders, nor of their sorceries, nor of their fornication, nor of their thefts.

1. Tribulation Intensity Ratified:

As the tribulation progresses, it increases in intensity. In comparing the fifth angel trumpet woe with the sixth, the duration of the plague is extended from five months, approximately 150 days, to 391 days. The composition of the demon creature has increased from a scorpion-sized horse to an average-sized horse. The fifth trumpet creatures were not permitted to kill men, while the sixth trumpet creatures kill one third of those remaining upon the earth. Their faces imply a more barbaric character in having exchanged the face of a man to that of a lion. Their breastplates have changed from iron to fire, jacinth, and brimstone. Their stings have changed from that of a scorpion to a serpent, signifying a more destructive disposition.

2. This Is Not The Army of the People's Republic of China:

I cannot agree with those who see the Chinese army in this 200,000,000 creature cavalry. The "kings of the east" are involved only in the battle of Armageddon. This is, in fact, not a battle; it is a "plague" (Rev. 9:20). Furthermore, this is not a cavalry of horses. Horses do not have lion's heads or mouths spewing fire, smoke, and brimstone. Neither do they have tails with snake heads at the end of them. This is the second woe and is again satanic in nature. This demon creature originates from Hell, which man has limited information about.

Some scholars see a 200,000,000-fighter-bomber attack in these semi-metallic, smoke-spewing creatures. If John was seeing bombers or fighter planes, he would surely have described them as eagles, storks, or big birds of some kind making noise like thunder. There is no country in the world that can boast an air force of 200,000,000 fighter planes. John is describing exactly what he saw.

3. Angel Five and Six are Half-Brothers:

The fifth and sixth angels' father, origin, and mission are very closely related. Angels one and two are also half-brothers because their judgments are the instigations of man. Angels three and four are half-brothers because their judgments are the instigations of Satan's power of the air. The instigators of the judgments of angels five and six are

Satan's demons from the underworld, depicted in horrendous figurative language portraying the portent of their mission.

4. The Master Key: "Neither repented they of their murders, nor of their sorceries, nor of their fornication, nor of their theft" (Rev. 9:21).

This is the last judgment before the sounding of the momentous seventh trumpet. God is sending this judgment upon the world to bring repentance to as many as possible. It is God's intent to warn men how futile and destructive service to the antichrist and the rewards of Satan really are. God is trying to intervene and divert the fearful consequences of the worship of devils and idols of gold, silver, brass, stone, and wood as stated in verse twenty. To show men what the end reward of such a religion is, He looses four demon angels who are in charge of promoting the four paramount sins which will be rampant at the close of the tribulation — murder, sorcery, fornication, and theft.

As a minister of the gospel of Jesus Christ for thirty-two years, let me send out this solemn warning. It has been my experience that people engaged in any one of the above sins are vulnerable for exploitation by the evil one. These sins produce a fertile spiritual field in which Satan will plant a multitude of other vices which can eventually lead to demon possession. People coming to this moral and spiritual state of affairs have great difficulty in freeing themselves from their bondage. Our Lord said, when freeing one His disciples had been unable to help, "This kind can come forth by nothing, but by prayer and fasting" (Mark 9:29).

5. Four Horns, Four Rivers, Four Angels, Four Weapons, Four Sins:

This woe trumpet judgment is best explained in the reverse order:

- The reason for this judgment (FOUR SINS)
- The manner in which this judgment is delivered (FOUR WEAPONS)
- The origin of these sins (FOUR ANGELS)

- The domicile of these angels (FOUR RIVERS)
- The call for justice (FOUR HORNS)

The creature we see in this woe is also not a real animal. No beast is able to spit fire, smoke, and brimstone out of its mouth. The two witnesses of chapter eleven are able to spew fire from their mouths only because they are God's witnesses. These creatures are demons and their four weapons, fire, smoke, brimstone, and the sting in their tails, have to be symbolic. Nowhere else in Scripture have demons ever been depicted as having this kind of ability.

It needs also to be noted that these demons have a will of their own. They have a rider, but he is just a pawn of the destiny determined by his ill-fated demon steed. These demons are on their own, without a leader, and out of control. There seems to be no organization to their ranks and no limitations to their sphere of death.

The fire, smoke, and brimstone are named as the three fatal weapons. The sting in the tail is said to hurt men, which is not to say that the sting cannot kill. It simply means that the sting's destruction is not of the same proportion and magnitude as the fire, smoke, and brimstone. These four weapons are not only the instruments of this great slaughter, they are also the vehicles which first perpetrated the four sins of murder, sorcery, fornication, and theft (which is what this plague is all about).

The fire is symbolic of sexual lust which will be burning out of control during the tribulation. The sin of fornication is symbolized by the fire. The smoke represents Satan worship and incense offered up to demons. It also typifies the sorceries and devil worship rampant during the tribulation. The word sorcery comes from the word *pharmacopoeia* meaning drugs, impure sensuality, and occult practices, which all accompany the drug culture.

The brimstone symbolizes a smashing down, as in the case of Sodom and Gomorah where brimstone falling from heaven pounded a valley into the plains which today cradle the Dead Sea. It represents violence, destruction, and thievery. The serpent-like tail represents Satan, the serpent of Eden who brought death into the world. It represents the sin of murder.

If these 200,000,000 demons could actually spew literal fire, smoke, and brimstone out of their mouths, the results would be far more devastating than here recorded. If each demon were to kill only five people per day, they would more than destroy the entire population of the earth in a week. What kind of havoc would they contrive in 391 days? The power of this plague comes out "of the mouth" (Rev. 9:19), indicating it is an indoctrinational scheme of the devil having to do with persuasion and discipling. It is a deliberate attempt to stifle the evangelization ministry of Moses, Elijah, and the 144,000.

These demons are sent by Satan to demoralize the populace by encouraging fornication through the doctrine of sensuality and the stirring up of lust. This is typified by fire proceeding from their mouths. The 144,000 promote purity by the preaching of their mouths. The report regarding their pure lives is that "they are virgins" and "in their mouth was found no guile" (Rev. 14:4-5).

These demons further teach men how to be thieves as typified by the brimstone doctrine of violence and destruction proceeding from their mouth. They also promote Satan worship as typified by incense smoke doctrines spewing from their mouths. Finally, many people are hurt with the sting of death through the serpent-tail which follows at the end of the beast. Death is always the end result of Satan's doctrines.

The key to understanding this trumpet woe is to be found in the fact that it is the mouth that does the damage. Ironically, it is also with the mouth that confession is made unto salvation. In this case, it is with the mouth that indoctrination unto damnation is proclaimed. These demons are teachers sent from Hell.

The four angels which are bound "at" the Euphrates (as translated in the original Greek) are four right-hand accomplices of Satan. As Jesus had an inner circle while here on earth, Satan also had higher ranking angels which formed part of his coup when he rebelled against God. Names like Belial (2 Cor. 6:15), Beelzebub (Matt. 12:24), and Legion (Mark 5:9) give evidence that rankings do exist in the world of demons. The fact that these four angels are "bound" indicates that they are evil angels and are from among those who were ejected with Satan at his fall.

According to Menge's translation of 2 Peter 2:4, two hells are named: *Tiefsten abgrund*, which means "bottomless pit," and *Ketten der finsternis*, which means "chains of darkness." The Greek uses the plural "pits," which renders the Menge idea of two places as correct. Revelation 20:1 and 15 name two different hells. The infernal creatures of the fifth seal were released from the bottomless pit, which means that these four angels must be the keepers of the hell where darkness is the chain of bondage. The command to "release" these four angels substantiates the idea of this second hell or the chains of bondage from which they are set free.

It should not be surprising to find that Hell should be "at," or somewhere in the vicinity of, the Euphrates river. This is the cradle of humanity, the location of the Garden of Eden where Adam and Eve fell into sin. Here the first murder was committed. The great apostasies of Noah's day took place here. The tower of Babel and Babylon were built here where Nimrod's wife, Semerimus, institut-ed the mother/child worship of Tammuz. Here is where the three Hebrew children were cast into the fiery furnace and Daniel was cast into the lion's den for refusing to worship the king of Babylon. This is where Daniel wrote his prophecy and first saw the little book which contains the seven seals. Here the Hebrew nation was held captive for seventy years. God called Abraham from this area. If the world had its beginnings here, it would naturally be the place where Hell would be located.

It is interesting to note the statement of Genesis 2:10, "A river went out of Eden to water the garden; and from thence it was parted, and became into four heads." Essentially, the very river that watered Eden and provided so much blessing and well being for Adam and Eve flowed out and divided into four rivers. One of these is the Eu-phrates from which the four main sources of all iniquity (murder, sor-cery, fornication, theft) flow into all the world to water Satan's fields of sin. These fields have produced a great harvest of tares which shall return to this hell at the Euphrates to be burned. It is from this hell that Satan, through his demons, will poison the minds and hearts of the deluded tribulation inhabitants of this 391 day period.

This is the hell where the spirits of evil men, those who will in-carnate themselves into 200,000,000 horse-like infernal creatures, spewing their iniquitous doctrines of murder, sorcery, fornication, and theft into the tribulation world, are kept. These 200,000,000 de-mon spirits are the souls of the most wicked men who have lived and died throughout the centuries. These specialists in murder, sor-cery, fornication, and theft will be sent out as Satan's tribulation mis-sionaries.

Even as the 144,000 are organized into twelve groups of 12,000, these demonic beings could well be organized into four groups. Fifty million of them will spit out the doctrines on the burning fires of immorality and fornication. Fifty million will belch out the satanic smoke of sorcery and the religion of the drug culture. Fifty million will be specialists in the art of the destructive smashing and brimstone theft doctrines. Fifty million will specialize in the serpent-tail sting of murder.

For God's people, it all started in a garden at the Euphrates and will end in a garden near Abraham's promise, the New Jerusalem. For Satan's people it all started at Babylon and will end with the destruction of Babylon (built on the Euphrates) with their souls being consigned to the lake of fire.

This thirteen-month, thirteen-hour, period of demon domination will see the world sink into an unprecedented moral morass. Ministers of the gospel get weary, downhearted, and discouraged as they see their converts slipping back into the sins from which they were delivered. Their hearts break when they see childish, peevish Christians souring the fellowship with their hot and cold testimonies.

But think of the trials of Moses and Elijah, both of whom will be killed during the reign of these four angels commanding such spiritual devastation. Think of the 144,000 servants of God savagely outnumbered, trying to stem the tidal wave onslaught of 200,000,000 devilish demons, demons spiting hot fornication lust, blowing satanic occult smoke-storms, snorting brimstone, smashing and stealing doctrines, and swinging serpent-headed murderous tails among a tribulation society.

6. False Teaching is a Plague: "The rest of the men which were not killed by these plagues yet repented not of the worship of devils" (Rev. 9:20).

The worship of devils is responsible for the very plagues which killed a third of the populace. It may further be assumed that because they did not repent of this evil, the sights of judgment are still set upon them.

Rhetoric, eloquence, and oratory have always been powerful tools in every aspect of society. Whether you are a minister, politician, lawyer, teacher, or salesman, the degree of your success will depend upon your ability to communicate. Jim Jones proved that he could make people believe whatever he wanted them to believe. Hit-

ler convinced Germans that he had the answers to the world's di-
lemmas. This period represents nearly one-third of the entire tribulation, time enough to twist minds and warp characters to cause
enough crime so as to kill a third of the world's people.

The chief tribulation religion will be Satanic ritualistic worship requiring thousands of lives as human sacrifices. The devil will deceive people into thinking that when enough humans have been
sacrificed upon his altars, relief will come. The sorcerers and the drug
culture participants will die by the thousands, either through the sacrifice of humans to Satan, through overdosing, or through fierce battles between competitive drug lords.

Policemen will be unable to control break-ins because of looting
and stealing to support drug addictions. Citizens will take the law
into their own hands, and thousands will be shot on the spot of the
robbery. Murder will be the popular sport of the day.

7. Where is God?:

At this point, God will simply drop the reins and let the demon
horses run wild. Second Thessalonians 2:11-12 makes an almost unbelievable statement:

> And for this cause God shall send them strong delusion, that
> they should believe a lie: that they all might be damned who
> believed not the truth, but had pleasure in unrighteousness.

There will come a time when God will permit Satan to have his
way with man. Man will be too blind to see that he is killing himself with his own lust and desire. Repentance will be a thing of the
past. When the "voice from the four horns of the golden altar" commands the sixth angel to loose the four demon angels who release
200,000,000 demon spirits into the world, God will no longer be saying, "Choose ye this day whom ye will serve." The choice will have
already been made and God will allow sin to run its course.

Revelation 10 reveals another vision interjected between the seals,
trumpets, and vials. In order to establish a scriptural chronological
continuity after chapter nine, keep in mind that the sixth trumpet is
called the "the second woe." The chronological order may be resumed by turning to Revelation 11:14 where the consummation of

the the second woe is confirmed and the announcement is made that the third and last woe is about to begin. The third woe begins with the sounding of the seventh trumpet (Rev. 11:15). Before we consider this seventh trumpet, there are some very important events in Revelation 10 to consider.

And I saw another mighty angel come down from heaven, clothed with a cloud: and a rainbow was upon his head, and his face was as it were the sun, and his feet as pillars of fire: and he had in his hand a little book open: and he set his right foot upon the sea, and his left foot on the earth, and cried with a loud voice, as when a lion roareth: and when he had cried, seven thunders uttered their voices. And when the seven thunders had uttered their voices, I was about the write: and I heard a voice from heaven saying unto me, Seal up those things which the seven thunders uttered, and write them not. And the angel which I saw stand upon the sea and upon the earth lifted up his hand to heav-

en, and sware by him that liveth for ever and ever, who created heaven, and the things that therein are, and the earth,
and the things that therein are, and the sea, and the things
which are therein, that there should be time no longer: but
in the days of the voice of the seventh angel, when he shall
begin to sound, the mystery of God should be finished, as
he hath declared to his servants the prophets. And the voice
which I heard from heaven spake unto me again, and said,
Go and take the little book which is open in the hand of the
angel which standeth upon the sea and upon the earth. And
I went unto the angel, and said unto him, Give me the little
book. And he said unto me, Take it, and eat it up; and it
shall make thy belly bitter, but it shall be in thy mouth sweet
as honey. And I took the little book out of the angel's hand,
and ate it up; and it was in my mouth sweet as honey: and
as soon as I had eaten it, my belly was bitter. And he said
unto me, Thou must prophesy again before many peoples,
and nations, and tongues, and kings (Rev. 10).

When comparing this vision with the vision of Revelation 1:12-
16, there is little doubt that the mighty angel is Christ himself. The
lion which John hears roaring after the book is opened is the same
lion of Revelation 5:5 who "was found worthy to open the book."
Christ is the lion because He took the book from the Father's hand
and opened its seals. Who else then but Christ would still be in custody of the book and displaying it as being "open," which is to say
that whatever the seals represent will be consummated with the
sounding of the seventh trumpet. The book seen open, or blank if
you will, indicates that it is ready to be rewritten.

After the lion roars, John hears thunder rolling through the heavens seven times. The seven thunders were an audible message to
John. He was told in Revelation 1:11 to write everything he hears
and sees, and he was about ready to record the messages of the sev-
en thunders when the Lord told him to "write them not," to "seal
up the messages of the seven thunders." These messages were not
to be included in this Book of Revelation. They were to be sealed by
John, as the messages of the sealed book were sealed by Daniel.

John was told to eat the book, which means it was to become a
part of him. It was sweet to his mouth because it contained a new

plan of God for another age. In the seven thunders is contained another revelation, similar to the Book of Revelation, which will probably be written for the inhabitants of the 1,000 year reign of Christ. At that time, the revelation will contain seven thunders instead of seven seals.

The book was bitter to his belly because the next assignment for John was hard for him to digest as he discovers that he was appointed to be the seer for this second prophetical message as well. John will be responsible to see that its message is delivered to the next seer, just a Daniel was responsible for delivering it to John (Rev. 10:11).

There are three very important verses in this tenth chapter, verses five, six, and seven. In verses five and six, the angel (Christ) who made the oath in Daniel 12:7 reappears and makes a second oath that "time should be no longer." The seventh verse states that "the mystery of God (regarding Israel's salvation) should be finished as he hath spoken unto his servants the prophets."

Paul, one of the prophets who spoke of this mystery, said; "Don't be ignorant about the mystery of Israel's salvation, for they will be saved when the fullness of the Gentiles has come in" (Rom. 11:25-27, paraphrased by author).

The fact that something is finished is substantiated by several facts. The book (containing the tribulation judgments which bring about the conversion of Israel) is seen "open" in the angel's hand. The prayer of revenge offered by the souls under the altar has now been answered and the time "for the killing of the rest of the brethren and fellow servants has been fulfilled" (Rev. 6:11). The scattering of the power of the holy people (meaning Moses, Elijah, and Israel) is also finished (Dan. 12:7). The time for the sounding of the seventh and last trumpet has come.

VII. THE SEVENTH TRUMPET - THE KINGDOM ANGEL
(Revelation 10)

1. Fulfillment of the Mysterious Mystery:

> But in the days of the voice of the seventh angel, when he shall begin to sound, the mystery of God should be finished, as he hath declared to his servants the prophets (Rev. 10:7).

Regarding the days of the seventh angel "when he begins to sound," the Greek translation is, "whenever he is about to trumpet." Philips translation is, "There shall be no further delay in the days which shall soon be announced by the trumpet-blast of the seventh angel, the mysterious purposes of God shall be completed, as he assured his servants the prophets."

We need to be aware that while only a few seconds of time elapse, like the "twinkling of an eye," from the time the angel takes up the trumpet and prepares to sound it to the time he actually sounds it. This is a very significant interval in terms of the many prophetical turnovers transpiring at this split second.

When the last trumpet sounds, Christ takes over the reins of world leadership (Rev. 11:15). When this happens, many changes are made. There are many things which are "finished" as the angel lifts the seventh trumpet. The reign of the antichrist and the false prophet expire, and Satan's "short time" in which to persecute Israel is finished. Israel's hiding and the conversion of Israel are finished. The martyrdom of Israel for its faith in Jesus, the testimony of Moses and Elijah, and the scattering of the "holy people" are all finished.

The term "is finished" is not the same as the term "it is done." From the "is finished" when the angel lifts the last trumpet to the "it is done" in Revelation 16:17, there are forty-five days during which time the seven vials are poured out.

When the seventh angel lifts his trumpet, many things are "fulfilled". However, when he sounds the trumpet, many things take place and begin to happen. The dead in Christ are raised, Israel is raptured away before the pouring out of the vials of Gods wrath, the sun and moon are darkened, and the powers of the heavens are shaken. The great and terrible day of the Lord begins.

We are now at the 1,290-day point Daniel referenced (Dan. 12:11). He also spoke of an additional forty-five days, totalling 1,335 days, of which he said anyone surviving to this point could consider himself blessed (Dan. 12:11-12).

2. Now Let the Trumpet Sound:

> And the seventh angel sounded; and there were great voices
> in heaven, saying, The kingdoms of this world, are become

the kingdoms of our Lord, and of his Christ, and he shall reign for ever and ever. And the four and twenty elders, which sat before God on their seats fell upon their faces and worshipped God saying, We give thee thanks, O Lord God Almighty, which art, and wast, and art to come; because thou hast taken to thee thy great power, and hast reigned. And the nations were angry, and thy wrath is come, and the time of the dead, that they should be judged, and that thou shouldest give reward unto thy servants the prophets, and to the saints, and them that fear thy name, small and great; and shouldest destroy them which destroy the earth. And the temple of God was opened in heaven, and there was seen in his temple the ark of his testament: and there were lightnings, and voices, and thunderings, and an earthquake, and great hail (Rev. 11:15-19).

The foregoing Scripture annunciates that something momentous has taken place. We might well expect this, for this trumpet bears the number seven. Heaven's command center responds to this trumpet with great voices saying, "The kingdoms of this world are become the kingdoms of our Lord, and of his Christ, and he shall reign for ever and ever." The twenty-four elders fall on their faces in worship saying, "Thanks, O Lord God Almighty, which art, and wast, and art to come; because thou hast taken to thee thy great power."

The saints of all ages, small and great, are depicted as standing before the throne receiving their rewards. Terrible words are heard, "Thy wrath is come, that thou shouldest destroy them that destroy the earth." The tones of the seventh trumpet are both glorious and terrible, a song of major victory chords with a minor key funeral dirge heard in the background. The exuberance accompanying these pronouncements assertively indicates that a new commander, Jesus Christ, has taken control, and the antichrist and false prophet have been dethroned.

3. The New Commander:

Revelation 11:7-11 records the short-lived victory over the powers of Moses and Elijah. The people will have applauded the power of the beast when he successfully liquidated the prophets of God, presuming that the plagues the prophets brought upon them have ended. The antichrist will feel very good about himself because of having broken the "power" of the holy people. He will probably be postulating that this is the feat that will turn things in his favor, not realizing that this despicable act will invoke the irrevocable wrath of God.

After three and a half days, the unburied prophets will rise to their feet in the streets of Jerusalem. A "great voice" will be heard from heaven saying, "Come up hither." A cloud will appear, and Moses and Elijah will disappear into it. This cloud represents all the dead in Christ who shall rise at "the last trump," along with believing Jews who "are alive and remain" after the tribulation. Together, they and the prophets are raptured away before the vials of wrath are poured out. Jesus ascended into heaven in a similar way. His cloud was composed of the sleeping Old Testament saints our Savior preached deliverance to when He descended into Hell during the three days His body lay dead in the sepulcher.

Within that same hour, an earthquake will seize the city of Jerusalem and shake it like an angry dog until a tenth of the city crumbles and 7,000 are dead. A fear never felt before will blanket the holy city. This is how God will deliver His final sermon at the close of the tribulation. If ears will not hear the words of the 144,000 and eyes cannot believe the miracles of Moses and Elijah, then perhaps 7,000 bodies buried under one tenth of the city's infrastructure will get their attention. And indeed it does, for the entire remaining populace "gives God the glory."

How quickly God can bring man to his knees — from rejoicing, making merry, and sending gifts around the world over the death of Moses and Elijah to "great fear" with quivering voices "giving God the glory." This is a moment of truth. Who is the God of Israel? Is it the antichrist (the leader of the European Economic Community) who lied his way into power and then, by flattery and miracles, deceived the Jews and many others into signing a fraudulent peace treaty? Or, is it the God who can raise prophets from the dead, shake cities to ruins, and make cursing men bow their knees in prayer?

The announcement that "the kingdoms of this world are become the kingdoms of our Lord, and of his Christ" means that the phony messiah is now on the run and the Messiah of God will corner him before too long.

4. The Sons of Abraham Rejoice:

> And I saw another sign in heaven, great and marvelous, seven angels having the seven last plagues; for in them is filled up the wrath of God. And I saw as it were a sea of glass mingled with fire: and them that had gotten the victory over the beast, and over his image, and over his mark, and over the number of his name, stand on the sea of glass, having the harps of God. And they sing the song of Moses the servant of God, and the song of the Lamb, saying, Great and marvelous are thy works, Lord God Almighty; just and true are thy ways, thou King of saints (Rev. 15:1-3).

The sea of glass upon which the victorious multitude stands represents the raptured Church and those who ascended with Christ at His ascension. Some may question this idea because a multitude standing upon a multitude seems out of character. In reality this does not present a problem.

In Revelation 17:15, the whore is depicted as sitting upon waters which represent many people. If she (the world church) can be depicted as "sitting upon" many people, why cannot this multitude be depicted as "standing upon" many people? This multitude consists of the tribulation converts of Moses and Elijah. This we know from the song they have been taught, for they sing "the song of Moses." Special mention is made of their four-fold victory, which means they are a distinct company coming out of an exclusive era, "...They had gotten the victory over the beast, and over his image, and over his mark, and over the number of his name..." (Rev. 15:2).

THE RAPTURE OF ISRAEL OR THE "TRUMP RAPTURE"

MY BASIC PREMISE

The fact that a controversy exists between reputable Bible scholars as to whether the church does or does not go through the tribulation is in itself conclusive evidence that a rapture exists before and after the tribulation.

It is time to reconcile our pre-, mid-, and post-tribulation theories. It is clear to me that pre-tribulationists err in thinking that 1 Thessalonians 4:16-17 is talking about the rapture of the Church before the tribulation, when indeed it is talking about the rapture of Israel after the tribulation (as verified in Matt. 24:29-31). Likewise, the last "trump" of 1 Corinthians 15:52 is indeed the same as the seventh and last trumpet of Revelation 10:7 and 11:15. Furthermore, the resurrections of Revelation 11:18; 1 Thessalonians 4:16, and 1 Corinthians 15:51-52 are one and the same event, the first resurrection (Rev. 20:5).

Mid-tribulationists have erred in thinking that the "come up hither" of Revelation 11:12 and the "finished mystery of God," as seen in Revelation 10:7, refers to the Church and thereby marks the middle of the tribulation. Rather, it is the end as evidenced by Christ taking control in preparation for His millennial kingdom. They must realize that the Bible speaks only of a three-and-a-half-year tribulation and nowhere teaches a seven-year tribulation. They must also agree that the pouring out of God's wrath as recorded in Revelation 16 could not possibly cover a three-and-a-half-year period of time

Post-tribulationists have seriously erred in thinking the pregnant woman is the Church instead of Israel. It is Israel — not the Church — which is raptured at the call of the "last trump" (Matt. 24:29-31), which means Israel — not the Church — will go through the tribulation

My personal theory is not important. I hope my position never becomes a theory, for such are not compatible with the Bible. The Bible contains only truth. When four theories exist, however, it is obvious that at least three of them are wrong, and you have a right to question the remaining one you have chosen to defend.

I see God dealing with Israel in the same manner as He has with the Church. The Church has already gone through its tribulation beginning with the persecutions by Rome and all of the sufferings of the Age of Grace, and it will be spared, raptured away, before the tribulation begins. The Jews, for the most part, have not shared in the proclamation of the gospel of Jesus Christ through the missionary mandate given to us by the Lord. They will get their turn at this mission during the tribulation. When their task is done, and their suffering fulfilled, they will be spared, or raptured away, before the wrath of God is poured out upon a persecuting world. This issue is dealt with extensively (see chapter four) under "The Rapture of the Church."

A new and fresh understanding of the Book of Revelation is being presented to you here. It is up to you, the reader, to judge its credibility. For centuries now, the Church has been teaching certain theories regarding the coming of Christ. By doing this, we have created divisions, and sometimes ill will has entered the fellowship of believers because of disagreement. As a result, Christians have forsaken and ignored the study of the Book of Revelation because the mere mention of a new theory certainly does not generate too much excitement. How can we inject a new interest and enthusiastic return to the study of the only book of the Bible which was authored by our Lord himself? The following are a few suggestions:

Attitude

The Gentile bride of Christ, or more specifically the Christian Church, will need to change its indifferent attitude toward the Jew and the Old Testament. He who assumes an indifferent attitude towards the Jew and the Old testament is not a Bible scholar. When the born again believers stop presuming that they are the beginning and ending of all of God's plans and purposes for mankind throughout eternity, we will all be well on our way to understanding the second coming of our Lord and Savior Jesus Christ.

When the Christian will finally concede that the Bible is indeed referring to the Jew when words or phrases such as "the elect," "tribes," "chosen," "holy people," "saints," "they that keep the commandments and faith of Jesus," "they who sing the song of Moses and the Lamb," and other similar expressions are used, then the Book of Revelation will start making sense.

Serious Personal Pursuit for Truth

Lethargy and laziness are the enemies of spiritual growth and biblical comprehension. It is easy to go to a book store and buy a book that addresses the issues surrounding the second coming of Christ and that is not wrong. However, just simply to accept everything in such books without serious research on your own will not open your understanding to all that God has for you.

I challenge you to take your Bible and check out my research. I would want to be the first one to discover that I may be disseminating a falsehood. After thirty-two years of study, I am amazed at how the Bible has its own way of vindicating itself. You can be sure you are on the wrong path when it is necessary to bend Scriptures at certain places to "make them support" questionable ideas. Never allow this to become a practice in your pursuit for truth.

Restrain Your Prejudice

Be willing to put your preconceived notions on hold for a while. Does the Bible, or does it not, speak of two raptures? It cannot be denied that what Jesus is saying in Matthew 24:29-31 and Mark 13:24-27 is not the same as what He is saying in Matthew 24:36-44 and Luke 17:34-36. Neither is Paul's topic in 1 Thessalonians 4:13-17 the same as that of 1 Thessalonians 5:1-9. Paul and Jesus are not contradicting themselves. The problem is not with them, rather with our failure to recognize two raptures, at two different times, for two different classes.

In Matthew 24:36-44, Jesus is describing the times in which we now live,

> But as the days of Noe (Noah) were, so shall also the coming of the Son of man be. For as in the days that were before the flood they were eating and drinking, marrying and giving in marriage....

Then very abruptly, a rapture takes place. Jesus describes it as,

> Then shall two be in the field; the one shall be taken, and the other left. Two women shall be grinding at the mill; the one shall be taken, and the other left.

The climate is friendly and peaceful, as suggested by being in the field, grinding at the mill and sleeping in bed. The event occurs as unexpectedly "as a thief in the night" and "at such a time as ye think not." Paul describes this rapture in 1 Thessalonians 5:1-9 in a very similar manner. This is the rapture of the Church and could quite appropriately be called "the pre-tribulation thief rapture."

In Matthew 24:15-28 Jesus describes a tribulation that will erupt in Judea because of an image called "an abomination" which will be erected in the temple in Jerusalem. He continues in verses 29-31 by saying, "Immediately after this tribulation shall the sun and moon be darkened, and the powers of heaven shaken." Jesus is saying that when the tribulation in Judea is over, another tribulation (that great and terrible day of the Lord) will follow. However, before this second tribulation erupts, verse 30 declares that "then shall appear the sign of the Son of man in heaven." We note that the purpose of this coming is not to establish His kingdom as some have taught for centuries, rather to gather His "elect" (the Jews) from the four corners of the world before the second tribulation breaks out.

This "gathering" is obviously a rapture for Israel which could appropriately be called "the post-tribulation trump rapture." This same rapture is described by Paul in 1 Thessalonians 4:15 in a very similar manner. This is not a peace-time rapture, for here Paul speaks of those who are "alive and remain" (those who survive the Judean tribulation) who shall be caught up to meet the Lord in the air. It is not a secret rapture, rather a trumpet sounds and an archangel shouts to awaken the dead and to gather Israel.

Many Bible scholars have said for centuries that the "thief rapture" is for the purpose of removing the Church before Israel's tribulation begins, and they were correct. However, they were incorrect in linking the Church "thief rapture" of Matthew 24:36-44 with the "trumpet rapture" of Israel as described in 1 Thessalonians 4:13-17. What has been overlooked is that a "trumpet rapture" for Israel takes place after the first three-and-a-half-year tribulation in Judea.

The failure to recognize a rapture for Israel, and the mistaking of the rapture of Israel as being the rapture of the Church, is in itself the crux of all misunderstandings which have spawned several theories as to whether the Church goes through part, all, or none of the tribulation. The rapture of the Jews who accept Christ during their tribulation (heretofore overlooked) will take place at the sounding of the "last trumpet" just prior to the forty-five days when the vials of God's wrath are poured out.

Honesty Can Do No Harm

Acknowledging that the Bible does indeed teach a rapture for Israel strengthens the cardinal teachings surrounding the events of Christ's return. A new path, free of conflicting eschatological obstacles, is cleared by yielding biblical right of way for such a rapture. This new insight not only identifies the problems which existed in the pre-, mid-, and post-tribulation theories, but also solves the old conflict surrounding the "the last trump" and "the first resurrection." The righteous dead cannot be harmed by the tribulation and thus are not raised at the rapture of the Church, rather at the Jewish rapture when all the dead in Christ are raised. Thus, there is only one resurrection of the righteous, which is precisely what the Bible as been saying all along (Rev. 20:5).

The honest Bible scholar will see that obstacles which once hindered the understanding of the Book of Revelation have disappeared, creating a new, understandable, and irrefutable approach to eschatology. When Jesus gave us the Book of Revelation, He intended for us to understand it. We owe it to the Church, and to the world, to halt the skeptical attitude which complains about the many views which now exist, resulting in a deliberate ignoring of the Book of Revelation.

Understanding Paul's Answer

The Thessalonians somehow got the impression, either through Paul or someone else, that Jesus had already returned or that His return would take place within the very near future. The question they wanted Paul to answer was, "If Jesus has already returned, or will return within a few days or weeks, what will happen to our loved ones who have died recently? Will they be left behind as we go to meet the Lord in the air?" Most Bible scholars completely miss the question Paul was asked and see only that part of his reply which speaks of a rapture. They assume that because he is writing a letter to a "church," the rapture here spoken of refers to the rapture of "the" Church. This is not the case.

Paul is using the "Jewish rapture event" as a time-reference point in answering the question regarding the dead. His answer is, "They will rise from the dead when they hear the sound of the trumpet, and together with those who are "alive and remain" (survive the tribulation) shall be caught up to meet the Lord in the air" (1 Thess. 4:16-17, paraphrased by the author). The believers surviving the tribulation will be mostly Jews, which means the rapture alluded to here is for Jewish believers. Paul was very much aware of the fact that at the time the dead would be raised the Church would already have been raptured away.

If Paul would have been asked how the Church would be raptured away, he would have answered it with the words, "For yourselves know perfectly that the day of the Lord so cometh as a thief in the night" (1 Thess. 5:2). This passage further declares that the "thief" Church rapture will take place before the tribulation "when they say peace and safety" (1 Thess. 5:3). Still speaking about the Church, Paul assures them "God hath not appointed us to wrath..." (I Thess. 5:9).

Paul, in attempting to answer the question regarding the dead of 55 A.D., was very much aware that there would be no Gentile Church on earth when the dead would rise. So he answered this question from the perspective of what he saw, which was a Jewish remnant who were "alive and remain" after the martyrdom of the Jews who refused to bow to the antichrist.

Information regarding the question as to the whereabouts of the raptured Church is found in Matthew 24:28, Luke 17:37, and Revelation 5:9-14. We are instructed that the "eagles are to be found wherever the body is." Eagles, who find great enjoyment in "the air," represent the Church. The body, of course, is that of our Lord, upon whom we feed as typified in the Eucharist.

We should not expect to find a great deal of information regarding the Church in the Book of Revelation. This revelation is, in its greater context, specifically written regarding the end of the world which has to do with God's dealings with the Jews.

In trying to pinpoint the time when the dead would be raised, Paul made reference to a "great falling away first," after which the Holy Spirit would be removed to allow "the man of sin" to be revealed (2 Thess. 2:3). This "great falling away" does not refer to the miserable spiritual state of affairs of the last days. It is true that Paul and Jesus speak of false teachers and false christs (Matt. 24:24; 1 Tim. 4:1-2). Jesus and Paul also speak of "iniquity which shall abound" and "perilous times" (Matt. 24:12; 2 Tim. 3:1-4). We know these conditions will exist antecedent to Christ's return. But the "great falling away" that Paul was seeing was much greater than any of these apostasies.

In trying to explain to the Thessalonians the exact time when the dead would be raised, it was necessary for Paul to begin with his day, delineating the signs along the pathway of Church history which marked out a trail to the resurrection of the righteous. What Paul saw happening first, long before the dead would be raised, was a "great falling away." The Church in Thessalonica, the seven other churches listed in Revelation 2 and 3, and many others would fall from the faith. Paul saw Christianity becoming all but obsolete in that part of the world which he evangelized (now Turkey, Greece, and Rome). I believe the "great falling away" which came "first" is what is known in Church history as the "dark ages." The second great event that Paul uses as a time-reference point, a sure sign that the resurrection of the dead was near, was the "man of sin" sitting in the Jewish temple and declaring himself to be God (2 Thess. 2:3-4).

At this point, Paul speaks of "our gathering together unto him," which means the time for the Jewish rapture and first resurrection is very near (2 Thess. 2:1-2). Jesus declares that this gathering of the "elect" (Jews) will take place after the tribulation. This is the "trump" rapture and resurrection. Because the Gentile Church will already have been raptured, the only "church" left to be raptured are the "elect." Paul is telling his Thessalonian brethren that the dead in Christ would be raised "first," and, together with those who are "alive and remain" (survive the tribulation), would meet "the Lord in the air."

What Difference Does it Make?

I feel that a correct understanding of the order of events is crucial to the salvation of many people. The world has always had its procrastinators. The notion that the Church must go through the tribulation has created an "I'll wait and see" attitude with the rationale that there is sufficient time to repent during the tribulation. Those who are unfortunate enough to insist upon this attitude will thus be caught like Jesus said, "unawares," or as Paul expressed it, "asleep,"

315

while the Church is being secretly raptured away like a "thief in the night."

5. The Judgment Seat Of Christ:

During the forty-five days when the wrath of God will be poured out upon a Jew-killing, God-hating and Church-persecuting society, the saints will be standing in line at the judgment seat of Christ, eagerly awaiting their rewards (Rev. 11:18). Paul clearly teaches that such a judgment will take place,

> For we must all appear before the judgment seat of Christ, that every one may receive the things done in his body, according to that he hath done, whether it be good or bad (2 Cor. 5:10).

I am not sure whether this will be a sad or happy time. Here the genuine Christians will surface. Those who loved the accolades and praises of men already have their rewards. Those who quietly worked behind the scenes doing what seemed to be the meaningless tasks in the name of Christ will "shine as the stars forever and ever." In 1 Corinthians 3, Paul classifies the works of Christians in categories of hay, wood, stubble, gold, silver, and precious stones. He warns that these will be tried by fire. If our works are typified as belonging to the dead flammable variety, they will be lost, but we will be saved "so as by fire." If our works are typified by materials which can only become more refined by fire, we shall receive a rich reward. You cannot fool God. You will only have waiting for you in eternity what you sent on ahead during time.

There is not a Christian who at some time has not shrunk back and felt a chill of uncertainty while contemplating this happening. Satan has told you many times, "You will never make it to this judgment, because you sin every day and sinners cannot appear here." Satan is a liar, of course, but here is the truth of the matter:

> If we walk in the light, as he is in the light, we have fellowship one with another, and the blood of Jesus Christ his Son cleanseth us from all sin (I John 1:7).

316

Walking in the light means fellowship with God. Those in fellowship with God enjoy the continuous cleansing process provided by the blood of Jesus Christ. His presence in our lives keeps us clean and always prepared to meet Him.

Sin will not be judged at this judgment. Sin was judged at the cross, and those trusting Christ for salvation are forgiven, cleansed, and pardoned. Their sins are removed from them as far as the "east is from the west" (Ps. 103:12). Those who have not trusted Christ for salvation must appear at the Great White Throne Judgment where unforgiven sin will be dealt with (Rev. 20:11-15).

Someone who has never heard about being born again may be reading this book. You may feel this new birth is not within your grasp. You are not a member of any church, you do not feel worthy of holy communion, and you do not have access to a priest to whom you may confess your sins. I assure you that none of these are necessary! The dying thief never heard of the new birth, in fact he even prayed the wrong prayer. He should have prayed, "Lord be merciful to me a sinner, and forgive me for Christ's sake." Instead, he prayed a selfish prayer, "Lord, remember me when thou comest into thy kingdom." The Lord overlooked everything the dying thief did wrong and did not understand and replied, "Verily I say unto thee, this day shalt thou be with me in Paradise."

This forgiven sinner bypassed confessing his sin to a priest or minister. He did not partake of holy communion. He did not write a letter or make a phone call to a television evangelist. He did not go to an altar when they were singing, "Just as I Am," and he did not sign a decision card or take a new believers' class. He did not join a church or put money into the offering plate. In fact, he was not even baptized. But this forgiven sinner went to Heaven.

Be sure of this one thing — that dying robber's experience is God's way of telling us that all that is necessary to salvation is this:

> If thou shalt confess with thy mouth the Lord Jesus, and shalt believe in thine heart that God hath raised him from the dead, thou shalt be saved. For with the heart man believeth unto righteousness, and with the mouth confession is made unto salvation (Rom. 10:9-10).

6. The Wrath to Come:

> And the nations were angry, and thy wrath is come, and the time of the dead, that they should be judged, and that thou shouldest give reward unto thy servants the prophets, and to the saints, and them that fear thy name, small and great; and shouldest destroy them which destroy the earth (Rev. 11:18).

The words "shouldest destroy them which destroy the earth" is a signal of the terrors to come. This is what the seven vials will be all about. The destruction of the wicked is still future at this point, but the sleeping saints and raptured Church are seen at home with the Lord (Rev. 15:1-4).

7. Where Do We Go From Here:

Revelation 12 and 13 are not part of the consecutive chronological order. As stated earlier, they are interjected visions (between the seals, trumpets, and vials) of the tribulation participants whose interrelationships create the tribulation. It is not difficult to find our way back to a consecutive chronological order if we constantly remind ourselves that nothing can happen on earth during the tribulation unless it is ratified by the heavenly tribunal established in Revelation 4. We must always follow the path of this command center.

Revelation 11 closes with the temple seen as "open in heaven," displaying the "ark of his testimony." You will recall earlier that I stated whenever God moves to a new method of symbolizing judgment (e.g. from seals to trumpets or trumpets to vials), a response is heard from the heavenly command center. This will be in the form of voices, thunder, lightning, or an earthquake proceeding from the throne. We know that such a change is now about to take place, because chapter eleven concludes with the execution of the seventh trumpet and closes with such a demonstration.

To resume a chronological consecutive study, we need to search for some clue which has to do with the "open door" and the "ark of the testimony," as this is what was in view at the end of the seventh trumpet (Rev. 11:19). Our consecutive chronological order is reestablished in Revelation 15:5, where these again come into view.

CHAPTER SEVEN

FORTY-NINE PRONOUNCEMENTS
CONCERNING THE SEVEN VIALS
(Revelation 16)

The seven vials containing the wrath of God are poured out upon those men who accepted the mark of the beast. This takes place during the last forty-five days of human history here on earth. Daniel delineates these days in the following manner: "From the time the daily sacrifice is taken away (until the end) there shall be 1,290 days." The first thirty of these 1,290 days follow immediately after the image of the beast is set up in the temple. They are designated by the antichrist for the administration of the mark of the beast and to cause all people to bow and worship his image. The daily sacrifice and prayers to God are also forbidden during these days as foreshadowed in Daniel 6:7. The refusal by the Jews to accept the mark or to worship the beast during these thirty days ushers in the 1,260 days of "Jacob's trouble," known as the great tribulation. When these two time periods totalling 1,290 days have expired, then will follow the last forty-five days of human history on earth. Concerning these days, Daniel says, "Blessed is he who survives to the 1,335 days" (Dan. 12:12).

I. THE FIRST VIAL - THE BLAIN ANGEL
(Revelation 16:1-2)

And I heard a great voice out of the temple saying to the seven angels, Go your ways, and pour out the vials of the wrath of God upon the earth. And the first went, and poured out his vial upon the earth; and there fell a noisome and grievous sore (blain) upon the men which had the mark of the beast, and upon them which worshipped his image (Rev. 16:1-2).

1. A Great Voice:

The voices heard at the execution of the first four seals are those of the four living ones (beasts). At the sounding of the seventh trumpet, voices are heard in Heaven, but we are not told who or what they are. Prior to the pouring out of this first vial, a great voice is heard in Heaven. There is only one great voice and He is called the Word. There can be no mistake as to the identity of this "great voice." It is the "great voice" of a trumpet which John heard in Revelation 1:10. It is the voice of Christ who is now in command (Rev. 11:15). He is about to make the first move in bringing about the great and terrible day of the Lord.

This is the voice who created every letter and word in every language, for He is "The Word which was made flesh and dwelt among us." This is the voice with complete control over death that called, "Lazarus, arise!" This is the voice which the dead shall hear at the first resurrection. This voice gave the command, "Peace be still," to the storm. This voice commanded demons to depart and they sought refuge in bodies of frightened hogs. This voice asked, "Whom seek ye?" and soldiers fell over backwards. This voice taught us to pray, "Thy kingdom come, Thy will be done, on earth as it is in heaven, for thine is the kingdom, the power and the glory, forever and ever." The time has come when He shall "make his enemies his footstool."

2. The Seven Angels:

John was electrified at the sight of these seven angels. He describes the scene as a "wonder, great and marvelous." The appearance of these angels was similar to the single person he saw in chapter one and must therefore bear some relevance to Him. The golden girdle about the seven angels' breasts (Rev. 15:6) symbolizes the judiciary authority as that worn by Christ in Revelation 1:13. These seven angels represent the seven-fold power of Christ as represented by the seven horns of Revelation 5:6. These are special powerful cherubim or seraphim, judiciaries of an executive class. Their white splendor represents purity, perfect judgment, holiness, and righteousness.

Not only does the appearance of these angels transfix John, but he marvels over the seven golden vials they are given.

3. The Wrath of God:

Our knowledge of the character of God—His thoughts, objectives, and design for man—is best expressed by Jesus' coming in the flesh. The character of God is personified by His love, mercy, and grace. The greatest expressions of His love are exemplified by His incarnation and birth at Bethlehem, His death upon the cross at Golgotha, His power over death from the tomb, His ascension into Heaven from the Mount of Olives, and His promise to return. All of these bear witness to the fact that God gave the best Heaven had in order to save men from the worst Satan would perpetrate. It was John, the disciple of love, who wrote, "For God so loved the world, that he gave his only begotten Son, that whosoever believeth in him should not perish, but have everlasting life" (John 3:16). It is, therefore, no wonder that John marveled when he saw these judicial angels holding vials filled with the wrath of God.

The seven vials contain a venom called the "wine of the fierceness of the wrath of God, poured out without mixture" upon a sin-thirsty world. It is a poison resulting in eternal death. The cleansing blood of Christ dare not be spilled where the wrath of God has been poured. All overtures towards repentance are too late. Once the world "falls into the hands of an angry God," weeping and praying will be a "vanity of vanities." God has His own way of exacting justice and retribution and when His wrath overflows, there will be found no place for man to hide.

4. Go Your Ways:

This command of Christ is spoken simultaneously to all seven of His special envoys. There is no "and after this" between the vials being poured out. These seven angels depart all at once, as a unit. This means that the effects of all of the seven vial plagues will be felt concurrently during these forty-five days. There will be no moratorium, reprieve, or healing time from one plague to another. This means that the sores of the fifth vial (Rev. 16:11) will be the same unhealed sores of the first vial (Rev. 16:2). It means that while men were suffering the scorching of the fourth vial, they were also suffering from the plagues of the first three vials as expressed in Revelation 16:9.

These forty-five days will witness a world of grief, sorrow, and sobbing from the rising of the sun to the rising of the sun. It will be a time of agony, distress, and affliction. It will be a time of despair and hopelessness, cursing and blasphemy, bitterness and hostility. According to verse fourteen, it will affect the entire world.

5. Blains and Blotch:

That there may be a collation between this first vial and chemical warfare cannot be dismissed. While the sores seem to be similar to those in Exodus 9:9 when Egypt was smitten with plagues, they are not limited to a small geographic area like Egypt — they are universal. This plague must surely be the fulfillment of Deuteronomy 28:27 and 35.

God will use His own power, the wrath of Satan, demons, and Man himself to punish this sinful world. There can be no doubt that when the kings of earth become possessed with the spirits of devils (Rev. 16:14), there is nothing within their destructive capabilities that they will not deploy. This includes environmental, biological, chemical, nuclear, and conventional warfare.

It would appear that the sores of the first vial are caused by poisonous mustard gas or some other chemical or biological warfare that produces these kinds of effects. Philips translates the words "noisome grievous sores" as "loathsome malignant ulcers." The Living Bible translates the same words as "horrible malignant sores." In either case, they are cancerous, fitting the description given in Deuteronomy 28:27 of sores "which cannot be healed."

It is no secret that radioactive weaponry and other chemicals used in warfare are the causes of much of the cancers we have in the world today. There are still thousands of people suffering in Japan today with cancers as a result of the bombing of their cities at the end of World War II.

6. Only Those Men with the Mark of the Beast:

The mark of the beast will initially be given as a signet of survival. Man will not be able to buy or sell unless he produces it. As is always the case with Satan, his promise is completely opposite to his product. He promised Adam and Eve that they would not die and that they would become wise gods knowing good and evil. Satan made fools, instead of intellectual gods, out of them, and death came not only to Adam and Eve, but to the entire human race. When God came in the evening to commune with Adam and Eve, they were hiding because they were naked. It appears that God is reminding men that what happened when He came to the garden will happen again when He comes back to earth, when He says, "I am coming soon, take care of your garments lest you be found naked" (Rev. 16:15, paraphrased by the author).

During this last forty-five days, the mark 666 will be anything but a mark of survival. In Revelation 9:4, it was this mark which the fallen angel-demons sought for in identifying those whom they were allowed to sting. Here it is the men with the mark who are plagued with sores (Rev. 16:2). In Revelation 14:9-11, a special angel is seen flying through heaven warning the world that:

> ...If any man worship the beast and his image, and receive his mark in his forehead, or in his hand, the same shall drink of the wine of the wrath of God, which is poured out without mixture into the cup of his indignation; and he shall be tormented with fire and brimstone in the presence of the holy angels, and in the presence of the Lamb: and the smoke of their torment ascendeth up for ever and ever; and they have no rest day or night, who worship the beast and his image, and whosoever receiveth the mark of his name.

According to this Scripture, the mark of the beast does not represent survival — it represents identification, betrayal, and doom. The mark of the beast will be a curse and an identification for suffering and torture to its wearer. It will have no purchasing power during these forty-five days, because there will be little left to purchase.

7. An Irrevocable Decision:

Revelation 15:7-8 reveals that once the vials are placed into the custody of the seven angels, the temple throne tribunal chambers will fill with smoke and no one can enter into it (meaning — no decisions can be altered) until after the plagues are executed upon this world.

Man can go too far in his blasphemy against God. There is a point of no return. Matthew 12:31-32 warns that there is a state to which Man can come, through the hardness of his heart, where he grieves the Holy Spirit to the point where forgiveness is beyond his reach. Jesus instructed Nicodemus that without the work of the Holy Spirit eternal life is impossible. Hebrews 6:4-8 and 10:26-31 teach that there comes a time when persistent, wilful sinning eventually invokes the wrath of God upon man and mercy is forever squandered.

John warns that there is a sin unto death (I John 5:16). These tattooed tribulation disciples of the antichrist will probably have committed all of these sins and there will be absolutely no hope for them.

II. THE SECOND VIAL - THE SEA ANGEL (Revelation 16:3)

And the second angel poured out his vial upon the sea; and it became as the blood of a dead man: and every living soul died in the sea.

1. Cause or Effect:

It is difficult to determine whether the vial of this second angel was intended to ruin the waters which in turn would kill all aquatic life, or whether its intent was to slaughter all aquatic life and the blood from such a slaughter would redden the waters. I suppose the cause is not significant. The effect remains the same and the waters are turned into blood like that of a dead man. All life in the water dies.

2. Sea or Ocean:

We are not told here whether this is the Mediterranean Sea or whether the sea represents all of the oceans of the world. The Living Bible translates it, "The second angel poured out his flask upon the oceans." I believe this interpretation is probably correct. The Mediterranean sea has already been smitten by the second trumpet angel of Revelation 8:8-9. This is not to say that it cannot be attacked again. Only a third of the waters were turned to blood and a third of all creatures died during the first attack.

If the Mediterranean Sea is meant, eventually the contents of the vial would reach all of the oceans of the world, as they are connected by the Mediterranean through the Strait of Gibraltar and the Suez Canal. The contents of the vial of this second angel are very toxic as depicted by the extent of the marine carnage. These are the vials of God's wrath, and one would have to suppose that what is happening here is probably a direct act from God.

3. The Blood of a Dead Man:

In order to understand the horrific immensity of this tragic judgment, let us consider the descriptions by several translators. The Living Bible says it will be like the "watery blood of a dead man." The Amplified Bible translates, "It turned into blood like that of a corpse (thick, corrupt, ill-smelling and disgusting)." Philips translates, "Fluid like the blood of a corpse." *Die Gutte Nachricht* translates, *Wasser zu Blut wie von einem Ermordeten,* meaning "water like the blood of on e who was murdered." Menge translates, *Leichenblut,* meaning "corpse blood."

4. Implications for Ocean Navigation:

It is impossible to imagine just how far-reaching the implications and consequences of this judgment might be. Blood thickens when it cools, as expressed by The Amplified Bible. What will this mean for ocean liners, ships, and all sea-going craft? One might reason that it makes little difference when there are only forty-five days remaining. The people who will be living during the tribulation, for the most part at least, will not know this. While the darkness over the "kingdom of the beast" may conceal the fact that their waters are blood, they will nevertheless be aware that something terrible has happened because of the terrible stench filling the air.

5. Implications for Acquatic Life:

It seems incomprehensible that every fish, whale, shark, and every form of ocean life should be gone. At this point, the famine and drought of the three and a half years of tribulation will have so depleted food supplies, that the ocean would seem to be the only most likely source of food remaining.

What a terrible scene this plague will create. Every beach in the world will be littered with rotting carcasses of sea animals. Polar bears, penguins, otters, whales, sharks, sea lions, walruses, porpoises, dolphins, gulls, and myriads of other creatures will die.

6. Implication for Air Pollution:

These last forty-five days will stink, and closing the windows will not help. Those in the tribulation will fall asleep and awaken with a terrible stench. They will eat and drink with it, many living with perpetual nausea. If time were extended beyond forty-five days, a pestilence would fill the world with an epidemic of diseases killing every living creature on earth.

7. Carbon Dioxide:

We were taught many years ago that carbon dioxide is a toxic gas, the product of respiration and emissions from the burning of millions of tons of fuel each day. It is the ocean that absorbs carbon dioxide and converts it into useful bicarbonates. If the oceans are turned to blood, will they still be capable of converting carbon dioxide into bicarbonates? Or, will people breath raw carbon dioxide and cough their way into a Christless eternity?

III. THE THIRD VIAL - THE RIVER ANGEL
(Revelation 16:4-7)

And the third angel poured out his vial upon the rivers and fountains of water; and they became blood. And I heard the angel of the waters say, Thou art righteous, O Lord, which art, and wast, and shalt be, because thou hast judged thus. For they have shed the blood of saints and prophets, and thou hast given them blood to drink; for they are worthy.

1. A Star Versus An Angel:

The initial impression is that there must be a correlation between the falling "lamp" star of Revelation 8:10 and this angel. In addition to them both being the third in their class of judgments, the results of the two are also somewhat similar. The third vial angel's judgment is more severe in that it is 100 percent effective, while the third trumpet angel claims only one third.

They are, in fact, opposite in their original source. The star angel of Revelation 8:10-11 is the angel whose name is "Wormwood." Satan has placed this evil angel in charge of promoting all sorts of devil religions and false teachings like those practiced by Simon the sorcerer. The waters which this angel gave people to drink was wormwood or absinthe, a lethal substance. The angel of Revelation 16:4 is Christ's servant and the waters which he gives people to drink is blood, and no one is said to have died from these waters. The effects of this judgment are brought upon them for another reason.

2. They Have Shed the Blood of Prophets:

The tribulation dwellers will be a wicked generation, but we must not blame them for every judgment that is executed during this forty-five day period. Prophets lived a long time ago and this judgment is directed upon the system which is guilty of killing them.

The harlot called Babylon killed the prophets of the Old Testament and the apostles and saints of the New Testament. In Revelation 14:8, an angel flying through Heaven makes the announcement that God has destroyed her because she "made all nations drink of the wine of her fornication." Revelation 16:6-7 must be speaking of the the world church, because Revelation 19:1-3 unquestionably speaks of her judgment. The words used to describe her judgment, "True and righteous are thy judgments," are the identical words used in Revelation 16:6-7 in describing the judgment of that which killed the saints and prophets.

While the actual drinking sources are turned to blood by this third angel, it appears that a second purpose for this judgment is intended. The harlot is depicted holding a golden cup which she administered to her adherents. The contents of the cup are called the "wine of her fornication." The Eucharistal wine represents the blood of Christ. Because the harlot exploited the blood of Christ while giving drink to her adherents from the filthy rivers and streams of her false teaching, God forces her to drink the draught she imposed upon her trusting followers. She is also reminded not only of her part in the shedding of the blood of Christ, but her guilt in the killing of His servants.

3. A Double Judgment:

There is a danger in overemphasizing the judgment of the great whore, thereby distracting from the judgment which comes upon all who agreed, supported, and defended the world church. I cannot help but feel that God turns the rivers and fountains to actual blood so that every time hands are washed, sores are bathed, and water is drunk, man would be reminded that Christ shed His blood. This is a chillling reminder that If His blood would have been appropriated during the convenient season of grace, it would have saved them from every misery of the inconvenient season of wrath.

That a double judgment is here intended is to be seen from the double response. The angel of the waters agrees to the judgment of blood upon the waters by saying, "Thou art righteous, O Lord...because thou hast judged thus." Whereupon the voice of a second angel is heard from the altar (which has to do with holy sacraments) saying, "Even so, Lord God Almighty, true and righteous are thy judgments." The fact that those who are forced to drink the blood water have something to do with the altar and holy things reaffirms our suspicions that the finger is pointing at the world church.

4. For They Are Worthy:

These words certainly belong to a different dispensation than that of grace in which we now live. The Bible seldom depicts the sinner as being worthy of the suffering he must endure because of his sin. God has no delight in the death of the wicked. He has always loved the sinner and felt sorry for him.

Grace, mercy, forgiveness, cleansing, justification, regeneration, sanctification, and love are the benefits of salvation which will be withheld during this forty-five day dispensation. Every man must pay for his own transgression. There will be no ram caught in the thicket, no serpent lifted up in the wilderness, no cross, no tomb, no resurrection. There will be no one present to show the way to those who are worthy to drink the blood water.

5. The Angel of the Waters Says Yes:

God has guardian angels watching over all of His creation. If this were not so, Satan would have dispatched robbers to confiscate our possessions, released a tornado to kill our families, and transmitted sores to afflict our bodies just as he did when God allowed him to touch Job. The angel who has guarded the drinking water since the fall of man does not restrain the third angel which destroys the rivers and fountains.

It appears as though God just pulls the landing gear out from under His creation. Because the curse of sin has so disfigured it, God has decreed that it is beyond restoration. The only thing to do is to let it self-destruct and then start all over again by creating a "new heaven and new earth, wherein dwelleth righteousness."

6. The Angel of the Altar Says Yes:

Our Lord asked the question one day, "When I come again, shall I find faith?" The answer is no. The faith that is in the world is to be found in the Church which will be raptured before the tribulation. The faith which will be in the world during the tribulation will be in Israel who will be raptured away after the tribulation. During the remaining forty-five days, there will be absolutely no faith in God in the world. This sixteenth chapter speaks only of blasphemers "who repented not to give God the glory." The word that best describes the world church is "harlot," and God saw no hope of repentance in her. He sends out the call, "Come out of her, my people, that ye be not partakers of her sin, and that ye receive not of her plagues" (Rev. 18:4).

The angel who has guarded the holy things of God upon the altar agrees to the judgment. There is no objection raised to the third angel poisoning the fountains of what was to be truth and destroying the harlot and making her drink what she has always been giving her patrons to drink, dead blood, "even the wine of her fornication."

7.   God Unscathed:

Affirmation of the justice and righteousness of God in executing these catastrophes is heard twice. The sentences, "Thou art righteous, O Lord, which art, and wast, and shalt be, because thou hast judged thus" and "Even so, Lord God Almighty, true and righteous are thy judgments," confirm the fact that the justice of God has been retained through all of these horrors (Rev. 16:5-7).

Every overture of grace was extended to man. Every provision for salvation, pardon, and restoration of the life lost in Eden was made by His Son upon the Cross. Every spiritual armour for battling Satan was provided when the Holy Spirit was sent to guide us into all truth. Churches, Bible colleges, hospitals, homes for children and invalids and the aged were all built in the name of Christ. The Church, through relief agencies, shipped food and clothing all over the world whenever a crisis presented itself. Missionaries went everywhere proclaiming the good news of the gospel of Jesus Christ. Young men and women committed their lives to full-time service in all kinds of Christian ministries. Radio and television networks broadcast the gospel into every corner of the world.

God owes man nothing more. The judicial verdicts agreed upon are based upon the multiplied ways in which God has reached out to Man in love, providing opportunities for repentance that he might have been saved. The heavenly tribunal was once a part of this great enterprise to spread the gospel on earth. Their witness is against Man.

IV.   THE FOURTH VIAL - THE SUN ANGEL
(Revelation 16:8-9)

And the fourth angel poured out his vial upon the sun; and power was given unto him to scorch men with fire. And men were scorched with great heat, and blasphemed the name of God, which hath power over these plagues: and they repented not to give him glory.

1. We Live By the Sun:

The sun has fascinated humans from time immemorial. Men still worship the sun today, feeling that somehow it has the power to make them happy, give life, and provide the seasons of the year. They see in it a godlike force, capable of destroying Man and his world. Worshipping it may keep them in its appeasing graces and good favor.

The sun was created by God on the fourth day of creation (Gen. 1:14-19). It is the fourth angel who pours his vial upon the sun, interfering with the relationshp existing between the location of the earth and sun. The results of the slightest change in this relationship would have catastrophic consequences. Not only would man and beast either freeze or roast, but all other forms of life dependent upon the sun for survival would disappear.

I cannot tell you what this angel will do to the sun in order for it to scorch men with heat. I do know that the disciples of the beast acknowledged in their blaspheming of God that He had "power over these plagues." He does indeed control the sun. What will happen here is not the fulfillment of the prophecies of our scientists. The world will not come to end some day because the sun will burn itself out as the wise ones of today try to make us believe. The world will come to an end because of sin.

In this plague, God will use the sun, the greatest blessing of the universe, to punish the worshippers of the beast. The sun provides rain through the evaporation of the earth's surface water, and, when the sun gets too hot, it will burn up the evaporation which forms clouds of rain. The lack of rain will dry up the forests and all vegetation which provide oxygen, food, and shelter for wild life. The worshippers of the beast will have so provoked God that the very things He created, saying "they were good," will become instruments of terror and objects of blasphemy.

I am not surprised that God will smite the sun and turn the oceans, rivers, and fountains of water into blood to deny the beast, worshippers the blessings these wonders of creation provide. What surprises me is that He hasn't taken them away from us today, with so many denying that He ever created them. God has been patient for a long time when we consider how Man struggles so to deny Him the honor and praise He deserves for these glorious acts of creation. It amazes me that judgment has been so long in coming. I can only conclude that God has a lot more love, mercy, grace, and patience than I ever thought.

The Book of Revelation records many instances where God is praised precisely as the Creator — expressions such as: "The first and the last," "the beginning of the creation of God," "worship him that made heaven and earth, and the sea, and the fountains of waters," and several others affirming God as the Creator. This should be a warning to Man that withholding honor is not looked upon lightly by the Creator.

2. Not Within the Power of Man:

What is happening here seems to be beyond the ability of Man. This is probably the fulfillment of Malachi 4:1 where we read: "For, behold, the day cometh, that shall burn as an oven...." The prophet does have an encouraging word for us in verse two which states, "But unto you that fear my name, shall the Sun of righteousness arise with healing in his wings...." Fearing His name results in healing by the Sun of righteousness. Blaspheming His name results in suffering from the sun of wrath.

Scientists fear that the depletion of the ozone layer will one day culminate in a sudden complete breakdown of the entire ozone function. This could very well have effects similar to those described in this vial. I rather doubt that this is the case here, for the breaking down of the ozone layer in no way affects the sun. The sun never increases or decreases in its power. John sees this angel pouring his vial "upon the sun" which would mean that the effect this vial has upon the sun is the primary cause of this plague and not the secondary cause as in the case of the loss of the ozone function.

3. Cursing, Habit, or Hatred:

Cursing is the work of the Devil. He deceives men into believing that every misfortune is God's fault, and, therefore, He becomes the object of their profanity and blasphemy. Profanity is a grave sin, and God included it as one of the ten commandments. "Thou shalt not take the name of the Lord thy God in vain; for the Lord will not hold him guiltless that taketh his name in vain" (Exod. 20:7).

For the breaking of any of the other nine commandments, there appears to be some advantage or profit to be realized by man. For the breaking of this third commandment, no such advantage is to be gained by the transgressor. Engaging in such useless and non-profitable exercise reveals how complete the deception by Satan can be. Its only reward is the deep displeasure of God and a perpetual guilt.

The men of this forty-five-day era will know God controls the scorching heat of the sun, but instead of asking Him for relief, they will blaspheme Him. They will be completely possessed of the devil, morally and spiritually out of control. The throttle of destruction is pulled out all the way with no braking apparatus in place.

4. Does Suffering Come From God?:

There are many atheists in the world today because they were the victims of suffering. Suffering is not the work of God. The garden of Eden exemplifies the comfort and serenity God planned for Man. God is nowhere depicted in Scripture as one taking delight in the suffering of mankind. God intended Man to have a paradise devoid of insects, thistles, hailstorms, drought, or blight, filled with perfect happiness. Sickness, pain, misery, distress, and depression were absent from the garden. The elements which constitute unhappiness are hatched from a single egg called sin. The serpent introduced this evil egg of sin in the garden of God which has since hatched all of the woes of Man. Man, for centuries now, has been cursing the wrong personage for all of his woes. I cannot give you all of the answers to why God allows suffering, but I can give you the source of suffering:

> And the Lord God said unto the serpent, Because thou hast done this, thou art cursed above all cattle, and above every beast of the field; upon thy belly shalt thou go, and dust shalt thou eat all the days of thy life. And I will put enmity between thee and the woman, and between thy seed and her seed; it shall bruise thy head, and thou shalt bruise his heel. Unto the woman he said, I will greatly multiply thy sorrow and thy conception; in sorrow thou shalt bring forth children; and thy desire shall be to thy husband, and he shall rule over thee. And unto Adam he said, Because thou hast hearkened unto the voice of thy wife, and hast eaten of the tree, of which I commanded thee saying, Thou shalt not eat of it: cursed is the ground for thy sake; in sorrow shalt thou

eat of it all the days of thy life. Thorns also and thistles shall it bring forth to thee; and thou shalt eat the herb of the field; in the sweat of thy face shalt thou eat bread, till thou return unto the ground; for out of it wast thou taken: for dust thou art, and unto dust shalt thou return (Gen. 3:14-19).

The above Scripture tells the saddest story I know. All of the aspirations of man, all of his hopes and dreams for well being, were squandered by one act of disobedience against God. Instead of enjoying all the blessing of Eden and the presence of God forever, life ends with a lament, "From dust thou art, to dust thou shalt return."

I am glad that this is not the end of this story. Jesus died our death and was delivered to our dust; by taking our penalty, He is able to restore the life that was lost. He is eagerly waiting for us to accept our reinstatement with our heavenly Father. We need to be careful in our conclusions as to the source of all suffering. We must not alienate ourselves from the one who can deliver us from it.

5. The Gravity of this Plague Upon Man:

This scourge cannot be explained with words. Imagine being covered with the malignant, festering, grievous sores of the first vial. In this painful, uncomfortable state, man must try to function in a world that reeks and stinks with dead and decaying sea and ocean life, the results of the second vial. The air Man must breathe is basically carbon dioxide because the blood in the oceans prevents their ability to transform carbon dioxide into bicarbonates. Think of having to drink the blood water of the third vial. Add to all of these torments the scorching sun of the fourth vial and the forty-five day darkness of the fifth vial. What words in our vocabulary could actually describe this calamity?

These are not single plagues with time lapses between them. All of these plagues become one plague wrapped in a thick darkness. The heat will be so intense, man's entire body will feel scalded. His sores will be so inflamed, itching, and painful that insanity will be but a heartbeat away. Infection and fever will drive men into delirium, with only blood water to wash the sores and to drink to reduce their fever.

6. The Gravity of this Plague Upon Nature:

There will be no rain for the entire three and a half years of tribulation and these forty-five days begin with an already nearly-devastated world. Can a tree planted beside a river survive forty-five days of scorching heat even if its roots are literally sitting in water? Will animals attempt to drink the blood water? Will there be a spear of grass left anywhere for them to eat? The answer probably is no.

7. Though He Slay Me, Yet Will I Not Repent:

Grace is gone and the Holy Spirit removed, making it impossible for Man to repent. Paul said that

> ...God shall send them strong delusion, that they should believe a lie: that they all might be damned who believed not the truth but had pleasure in unrighteousness (2 Thess. 2:11-12).

Pharaoh's heart was hardened to the point where nine plagues were necessary in order for him to submit to God and release the Israelites. During these final forty-five days, God forbears in punishing the world with but six plagues (the number of Man) and then follows with Armageddon. There is no opportuity or provision for repentance available to man during this era. Instead of a spirit of repentance, God sends him "strong delusion."

V. THE FIFTH VIAL - THE DARKNESS ANGEL
(Revelation 16:10-11)

> And the fifth angel poured out his vial upon the seat of the beast; and his kingdom was full of darkness; and they gnawed their tongues for pain, and blasphemed the God of heaven because of their pains and sores, and repented not of their deeds.

1. The Seat of the Beast:

It would appear that the word "seat" would refer to the headquarters or residence of the antichrist. We are not told where this may be. Since the Common Market Treaty was created in Rome in 1957, it has always been my sense that it will be Rome. A second possibility is that it could be the new city of Babylon which is to be rebuilt in the last days.

2. His Kingdom:

This refers to the geographical land mass encompassing the antichrist's domain. The "kingdom of the beast" will include the European Economic Community which is generally construed to represent most of the boundaries of the Old Roman Empire. The beast of Revelation 13 has seven heads and ten horns with crowns upon each horn. These represent seventeen countries. The beast is called the eighth head, which totals eighteen. This will probably be the membership of the European Economic Community at its inception. However, if the ten crowns upon each horn are to symbolize a country, then an additional ten would have to be added, totaling twenty-eight. Daniel further speaks of the antichrist making a "covenant with many" (Dan. 9:27), including Israel. These will probably be associate members of the European Economic Community. The actual scenario as to the total membership during the last forty-five days would be difficult, at this point, to ascertain.

It is not essential that we be informed regarding borders and membership at this time. But there are a few very important indicators of which we should be aware. These include the building of a temple in Jerusalem, the signing of the seven-year contract between Israel and the European Economic Community or the United Nations, and the development of a cashless monetary system where a concealed number "in the right hand or the forehead" authorizes the wearer to "buy or sell." Note that the mark is not "on" the hand or forehead, but "in" the right hand or forehead. I believe this means it is either a mark decipherable only by infra-red rays or it will be a minute computer chip surgically inserted beneath the skin.

The ability of the antichrist to overcome the insurmountable obstacle of putting together a peace plan that both Jews and Arabs can agree to will catch the attention of the entire world. The Bible speaks of a time of peace prior to the tribulation (I Thess. 5:3), referring to the resolution of the ageless animosity and impasse between Jews and Arabs. Each race claims to be the sons of Abraham and the benefactors and heirs to Palestine. This conflict has existed between these half-brother nations for centuries. More astounding than the miracle of bringing about a peace in the Middle East is the suddenness in which this peace evaporates and explodes into an irrevocable hatred.

3. The Darkness:

The ninth plague of darkness recorded in Exodus 10:21-23 covered only the land of Egypt in the days of Moses and Pharaoh. The plague of this fifth vial has its geographic limitations, too. It will cover a vast area of the world's land mass known as "the kingdom of the beast," affecting that part of the world which is in control of most of the world's trade. The effects of this darkness will be felt around the world.

Abject darkness, like that expressed here, must be a most terrifying experience, something only the totally blind could understand. Darkness is not pleasant even to an infant baby who awakens at night and cries because of fear, even though he has not yet learned that there is anything to be feared in this world. Jesus' coming into the world was to dispel darkness. "The people which sat in darkness saw a great light; and to them which sat in the region and shadow of death light is sprung up" (Matt. 4:16).

John (in speaking of Christ's coming) said, "In Him was life, and the life was the light of men." This fearful darkness is to be a reminder to the disciples of the antichrist that they did not want the light. They hated Jesus, the Light. They have now been granted what they've always wanted.

4. Sounds of Pain: "And they gnawed their tongues for pain."

The miseries portrayed here are very similar to those expressed in biblical descriptions of Hell. Hell is depicted as a place where "their worm dieth not and their fire is not quenched," a place of "weeping and wailing and gnashing of teeth," a place of "thirst, remorse, outer darkness and suffering." The gnawing of the tongue is a normal

339

human reaction to duress, pain, and great trauma. This is but the first lament of Satan's funeral dirge for all of those who insisted on blaspheming the God of heaven.

5. No Prayers:

The Bible contains the accounts of many long nights of spiritual battles, like the night when Judas betrayed the Lord and the night when Peter denied His Lord. Surely one of the most touching is the night when our Lord prayed in Gethsemane, "Not my will, but thine be done." Another memorable night of travail passed when Jacob wrestled with an angel until daybreak when his hip moved out of joint.

Night time seems to be conducive for spiritual battles. Distractions are limited, the wheels of industry for the most part have ground to a halt, and, as in the case of the jailer of Philippi, midnight seems to be the right time to cry out, "What must I do to be saved?"

There will be an iniquity at work during these forty-five days that will prevent the thickest darkness known to Man from inducing good refections about God into the heart of Man. There will be no sense of guilt, wrong doing, or fear of God. There will be no respect for holy things, troubled conscience, or fear of judgment or Hell. There will be no response to the memory of a praying mother or father or a desire to be with loved ones gone to heaven.

The death of deaths is to die to the call of the Holy Spirit, the agent of God's grace. Accepting the mark of the beast is a spiritual suicide so final that no resurrection unto contrition, remorse, or tears is possible. What kind of a world might one expect where every tongue is cursing God and not a single knee bows to pray?

6. The Deeds of Stony Hearts:

Galatians 5:22-23 tells us that "the fruit of the Spirit is love, joy, peace, longsuffering, gentleness, goodness, faith, meekness (and) temperance...." These are the fruit of the Spirit; however, the Holy Spirit will have left the world by this time. The fruit of the works of the flesh will be in full operation.

Now the works of the flesh are manifest, which are these; adultery, fornication, uncleanness, lasciviousness, idolatry, witchcraft, hatred, variance, emulations, wrath, strife, seditions, heresies, envyings, murders, drunkenness, revellings and such like... (Gal. 5:19-21).

The four cardinal sins of the tribulation are named in Revelation 9:21: murder, sorcery, fornication, and theft. These are not simply the "works of the flesh" as stated in Galatians 5:19-21; during the tribulation these will be the fruit of the worship of devils.

Sinners have been restrained by the Holy Spirit during the Age of Grace. When this restraint has been removed and the Devil becomes the sole dictator for the sinner, men will become more and more like him. Paul calls this class "fierce, despisers of that which is good" (2 Tim. 3:3). That is all one may come to expect when Man departs "from the faith, giving heed to seducing spirits, and doctrines of devils" (1 Tim. 4:2).

7. Every Man A Demon, and Every Soul A Legion:

God has angels in charge of every aspect of His interests in the world. Jesus taught that angels watch over the children (Matt. 18:10). Christ himself had an angel who ministered to Him in the garden of Gethsemane. Daniel told King Darius that it was an angel who shut the lions' mouths so they could not hurt him. We are told in Psalm 91 that God sends angels to take charge over us that we should not dash our foot against a stone. In Revelation 16:5, the guardian angel of the waters speaks. In Revelation 16:7, the angel of the altar speaks.

Satan has his ministering demon servants who promote his iniquity in this world. His activities will be especially intensified during the tribulation. The demons of alcohol, drug addiction, divorce, robbery, murder, Satan worship, blasphemy, lying, immorality, and every conceivable iniquity and transgression, will attempt to enter every man on earth. The man of Gadara said to Jesus, "My name is Legion, for we are many" (Mark 5:9). He is not only telling us that he was filled with many demons, but by using the pronoun "we," he identifies himself also as a demon.

341

In Luke 11:24-26, Jesus underscores the danger of demon possession. He warns how a demon once cast out of a man will not rest as he tries to regain his former position in that heart. Having succeeded in gaining a fresh foothold, he will bring in seven others (demons) more wicked than himself in an attempt to fortify his position more securely within this soul.

These last forty-five days on earth will not only be characterized by desolation in the environment, there will also be a desolation of human characters which will be depraved, marred, and scarred by demon possession. Man's thoughts will only be evil continuously. He will be so depraved and deceived by Satan that his only pleasure will be in destruction and death. There will be no Image of God to be found in Man in these days.

VI. THE SIXTH VIAL - THE EUPHRATES ANGEL
(Revelation 16:12-16)

And the sixth angel poured out his vial upon the great river Euphrates; and the water thereof was dried up, that the way of the kings of the east might be prepared. And I saw three unclean spirits like frogs come out of the mouth of the dragon, and out of the mouth of the beast, and out of the mouth of the false prophet. For they are the spirits of devils, working miracles, which go forth unto the kings of the earth and of the whole world, to gather them to the battle of that great day of God Almighty. Behold, I come as a thief. Blessed is he that watcheth, and keepeth his garments, lest he walk naked and they see his shame. And he gathered them together in a place called in the Hebrew tongue Armageddon.

1. Now That Day Is Very Near:

Much has been written, discussed, and (more recently) filmed about the battle of Armageddon. Eschatological hairs are being split over various terms which address the second coming of Christ. It is necessary for those who believe the Church will go through the tribulation (post-tribulationists) to make every inference to Christ's return represent both the rapture of the Church and the battle of Armageddon.

It is not fair to misconstrue the Scriptures to the extent that "the day of the Lord" (1 Thess. 5:2; 2 Pet. 3:10), "the wrath of the Lamb" (Rev. 6:16-17), and "that great terrible day of God" (Joel 2:11; Matt. 24:29; Rev. 11:18; 14:19-20; 16:1, 14;) all speak of Armageddon and the rapture happening simultaneously. Such deliberate misrepresentation of Scripture is a high price to pay in order to prove the rapture of the Church will take place after the tribulation.

If the Bible says "the day of the Lord" shall come (secretly) as a thief in the night, then how can the day of the Lord also be described as coming "with great glory, with angels, the shout of an archangel and the trump of God" (Matt. 24:30; I Thess. 4:16)? The day of the Lord which comes as a "thief in the night" can only mean the rapture of the Church and cannot be the same day as when stars are falling, the sun is black, and the moon is blood. Neither can it be the same day as when the Euphrates is dried up and the kings of the east meet at Armageddon. These do not describe the manner in which a thief comes.

Joel 2:28-31 speaks of Israel's conversion and the day of the Lamb's wrath. The prophet clearly relates God's words, "I will show wonders," or, as other translators state, "symbols" or "wonder signs." These are only "signs" and are not in themselves a judgment. No life is lost because of the sun turning black or the moon turning to blood. These signs come "before the great and terrible day of the Lord (Armageddon)" spoken of in Joel 2:10-11.

The wrath of the Lamb is a day of fear and prayer (Rev. 6:16). This is surely the fulfillment of Joel 2:28-29 which speaks of the conversion of Israel concurrent with these signs. There are no praying men in the days of God's wrath. It is said of them that "they repented not" and "they blasphemed the God of heaven" (Rev. 16:11). I cannot see the "thief" day, the "wrath of the Lamb" day, and the "wrath of God" day as possibly being the same days.

I will admit that the day of the Lamb's wrath has similar happenings as the day of God's wrath. That is to be expected. Nevertheless, there are some differences. The moon turns to blood only on the day of the Lamb's wrath, which comes "before" the day of God's wrath. There is nothing said of the moon turning to blood on the day of God's wrath. The words used are that "the sun and moon shall be dark." (Compare Joel 2:10-11 and Matt. 24:29 with Joel 2:31 and Rev. 6:12).

The answer as to how many days "before" the wrath of God will the wrath of the Lamb take place is found in Malachi 4:5-6. Here the prophet declares,

> See, I will send Elijah the prophet before that great and dreadful day of the Lord comes. He shall turn the hearts of the fathers to their children, and the hearts of the children to their fathers; or else I will come and strike the land with a curse (NIV).

The reason for Elijah's coming is to turn the hearts of Israel to the Lord which is what Revelation 6:9-17 is all about. According to Revelation 11:3, Elijah comes 1,260 days before Armageddon. If the "before" in Elijah's coming means three and a half years "before" Armageddon, does not the "before" as it relates to the day of the wrath of the Lamb also take place three and a half years "before" Armageddon (that great and terrible day of the Lord)?

2. . The Great River Euphrates:

The drying up of the Euphrates River is a most astounding phenomenon. The Euphrates is the largest and longest river in Western Asia, 1,800 miles long, from 30 to 1,200 yards wide, and from 10 to 30 feet deep. Its head waters originate from the Armenian mountains, winding down through Iraq and Kuwait until it finally empties into the Persian Gulf. The prophets, through the wisdom of God, knew that the last great battle of civilization would be fought in this area, which is also becoming very obvious to the world today.

It is astonishing that a vial of the wrath of God poured into this river would cause it to evaporate. This miracle will be so great that no room will be given for any kind of human intervention. This is the outright power of God at work. After the passing of three and a half millenniums, the Jews are still talking about the parting of the waters of the Red Sea and Jordan river. If God had such power over the waters then, why question it now?

Is God trying to tell the world to remember the Red Sea and Pharaoh's army? I think so. If there is any advice to be given to the armies of the world at this point, it would be to leave the Jews alone. Those who go down to Armageddon will not return! No army will ever capture Jerusalem, because a mighty warrior on a white steed will be standing guard on the outskirts of the holy city. This warrior's name is the Word, and He has a sword in His mouth. One word "breathed in wrath" over the armies of the world will kill millions of soldiers in a second.

3. The Kings of the East:

To the Eastern world, the Eurphrates has always been a logistical geographical divider. It was the boundary of Solomon's empire. In several places in the Scripture, it is referred to as the northeast limits of the territory promised to Abraham (Gen. 15:18, Deut. 11:24, Josh. 1:4). The Euphrates created a natural barrier of protection against invading armies. Even in modern times, the movement of large armies with tanks, trucks, and artillery becomes a challenge when trying to cross the Euphrates. Bridges are of little help in war time, for they are the first targets of destruction.

When God decides that it is time for the kings of the East to come up against Jerusalem, He will clear the path by drying up a vast stretch of the Euphrates River. It is quite possible that all of the Euphrates will be dried up, opening an obstacle-free frontier from the Black Sea to the Persian Gulf. News will hit the media headlines of every country in the world. The kings of the East, who are the kings of the Orient and Asia, will think this is the work of their gods and will hastily make their advance upon Israel. They will be certain their mission will succeed because the gods are on their side. They do not know that they have been deluded.

4. A Frog Trinity of Devil Spirits:

When God makes up His mind to make a fool out of a king, He often uses that king's own gods of wood and stone to do it. Here the trinity of evil, the dragon, the false prophet, and the beast, speak the word which mobilizes a military stampede towards Jerusalem. John sees three frog-like creatures, the spirits of devils, proceeding out of their mouths. They make their way to the kings not only of the East, but "all the world," inciting them to battle at Armageddon. When the spirit of the devil enters a man who is in a position of power, let all the earth tremble. David's prophecy in Psalm 2 warns:

> What fools the nations are to rage against the Lord! How strange that men should try to outwit God! For a summit conference of nations has been called to plot against the Lord and his Messiah, Christ the King. Come, let us break his chains, they say, and free ourselves from all this slavery to God. But God in heaven merely laughs. He is amused by all their puny plans. And then in fierce fury he rebukes them and fills them with fear. For the Lord declares, This is the King of my choice, and I have enthroned him in Jerusalem, my holy city. His chosen one replies, I will reveal the everlasting purposes of God, for the Lord has said to me, You are my Son. This is your Coronation Day! Today I am giving you your glory. Only ask, and I will give you all the nations of the world. Rule them with an iron rod; smash them like clay pots! O kings and rulers of the earth, listen while there is time. Serve the Lord with reverent fear; rejoice with trembling. Fall down before his Son and kiss his feet before his anger is roused and you perish. I am warning you — his wrath will soon begin. But oh, the joys of those who put their trust in him! (Ps. 2, The Living Bible)

5. Working Miracles As They Go:

Moses and Elijah, the tribulation miracle workers, will have been killed by the beast at this point. There is no one on God's side to counteract the miracles of the wicked frog-trinity. It is hard to tell just what these miracles will be, but we do know that the kings of the world are so impressed and convinced by them that Israel will easily be defeated.

6. No One Can Be More Deceived Than He Who Deceives Himself:

No one seems to recognize the fact that the drying of the Euphrates is an act of God. They do not see the omnipotent trap in this free passage. Probably the devil, the beast and the false prophet will claim responsibility for this miracle by telling the world the fire they called down from heaven dried it up. The kings of the East may claim their gods did it in order that Israel should finally be wiped from the map of the world and every Jew exterminated. In any case, they lead themselves like sheep to the slaughter. They seem not to realize that the battle is not against Israel at all; it is the battle of that great day of God Almighty!

What a mismatch this battle will be. It will be over before it really has a chance to start. God always makes a quick end of His battles with Man. Ask the Philistines who trusted in Goliath. Ask the Canaanites, Hittites, Perizzites, Jebusites, and Amalekites who trusted in their size and brute strength. Ask the general who was in charge of the Egyptian army which drowned in the Red Sea.

God makes a mockery of Man when Man insists upon battling with Him. He used a little shepherd boy with a sling shot to kill a giant. He used a woman called Jael to drive a nail into the head of Sisera, captain of the host of Jabin. He told Samson to take the jaw bone of an ass and kill 1,000 Philistines. It is exactly like King David said in Psalms 2, "The Lord in heaven shall laugh them into derision."

7. Armageddon, No Laughing Matter:

Regardless of what you call it, the Valley of Megiddo, the Plain of Esdraelon, the Valley of Jehoshaphat, or the Valley of Armageddon, it will be the scene of the destruction of the antichrist and blasphemers of tribulation times.

Armageddon is a chilling word. It represents defeat, wrath, blood, death, and sorrow. There has never been a battle like it, nor shall there ever be another one like it. It is the end of the world! Armageddon is a very bloody valley. Barak defeated Canaan, Gideon defeated Midian, Saul committed suicide, and Israel was defeated by the Philistines in the Valley of Armageddon. Here the beloved Josiah was killed in battle against Pharaoh Necho of Egypt. It will be in this valley that Christ will defeat all nations who come up against Jerusalem (Zechariah 14).

Armageddon. How can it be described? Songs, books, poems, and plays have been written about it. The theater has tried depicting it upon the silver screen. Artists have tried portraying it upon canvas. But the best actors, the best writers, the finest singers, and the world's most talented artists could never come close to depicting the tragedy of Armageddon!

In Revelation 16:18-21, John heard "voices," a disarray of humans crying in confusion, pain, and dying. He heard and saw crashing thunder and blinding lightning. Then came a tremendous earthquake, like none the earth has ever experienced, that divided the great city into three parts, and the cities of the nations fell to the ground. John saw the islands flee away, and the mountains could no longer be found! A hail storm with huge hail stones battered what was left.

The great winepress of the wrath of God will press out a harvest of the blood of all who belong to the "vine of the earth," the antichrist. As grapes are cast into the winepress, so shall sinners be cast into the wine press of God's wrath and crushed and squeezed until every drop of blood is compressed from them.

VII. THE SEVENTH VIAL - THE HAIL ANGEL
(Revelation 16:17-21)

And the seventh angel poured out his vial into the air; and there came a great voice out of the temple of heaven, from the throne, saying, It is done. And there were voices, and thunders, and lightnings; and there was a great earthquake, such as was not since men were upon the earth, so mighty an earthquake, and so great. And the great city was divided into three parts, and the cities of the nations fell: and great Babylon came in remembrance before God, to give unto her the cup of the wine of the fierceness of his wrath. And every island fled away, and the mountains were not found. And there fell upon men a great hail out of heaven, every stone about the weight of a talent: and men blasphemed God because of the plague of the hail; for the plague thereof was exceeding great.

1. The Great Vial:

This seventh vial, poured out by the seventh angel, concludes the judgments of God upon the world. The outpouring of the seventh vial culminates in the final victory of Christ over the blaspheming inhabitants of the world — the beast, the false prophet, and Satan. It results in Christ finally being betrothed to the wife-bride, Israel, and the great celebration called the marriage supper of the Lamb. Christ is finally crowned as King as He assumes authority over the world for the next millennium.

2. The Great Voice:

This single voice is heard in several other places in the Book of Revelation. This is the voice of the Alpha and Omega, the Word. It is this voice which cries as when a lion roars (Rev. 10:3). The voice which finally cries, "It is done," is the same voice which cried from the cross, "It is finished." He was the one who initiated the plan of salvation and He alone has the right to announce when it has been completed.

The words, "It is done," are the best words the world will hear. They announce to mankind that God is almost ready to love the world again. They say His wrath is almost over and His judgments are almost done. These words mean that Satan's grip upon the world for the past six millenniums is broken. The curse of sin which has brought suffering and heartache to the world for 6,000 years is done.

This is the voice which will usher in the "peace on earth, good will to men" as the angels proclaimed on the night of His birth. The words, "It is done," are the fulfillment of Isaiah 2:4, "...And they shall beat their swords into plowshares, and their spears into pruning-hooks: nation shall not lift up sword against nation, neither shall they learn war any more."

3. The Great Earthquake:

It would appear that this earthquake is a double judgment. The seventh angel pours his vial into the "air." In all likelihood, this means that in addition to the shaking by the earthquake (the work of God), there will probably be a great shaking taking place through nuclear warfare. The destruction of cities, the thunder, lightning, and hail are all elements accompanying nuclear explosions. It cannot be overemphasized that nuclear warfare is very much the language of the Book of Revelation. The very fact that man has built nuclear weapons reveals that he is capable of using them. When the frog-demons are through with their mission of devil indoctrination and mind warping, there will be little decency found even in the best of the "kings of the earth." Man will be so depraved that throwing nuclear bombs, missiles, and poison gas at Israel from the "air" is not impossible.

This earthquake was predicted by Paul (Heb. 12:26-29) and in Haggai 2:6, Joel 3:6, and Zechariah 14:4-5. This quake will be greater than all of the other earthquakes named in the Book of Revelation, including the ones in chapters six and eleven. There is no Richter scale that could possibly measure its intensity. The skyscrapers of the world will come tumbling down like a child's block houses, and, when it is over, the cities of the world will be nothing more than slight elevations. Everything will be leveled and reduced to rubble. The work of Man's hands for centuries will, in one moment, become chaos and ruin under the mighty hand of God.

4. The Great City:

The "great city" is Jerusalem, because of its association with the crucifixion. Jerusalem will not be destroyed like all of the other cities. It will however, be divided into three parts. I am sure there is a reason why God will divide Jerusalem. I confess I do not know the answer at the present time.

5. The Great Babylon:

That the ancient city of Babylon will be rebuilt is not beyond the realm of the possible. Scholars of prophecy used to be laughed at when such a suggestion was made. Today, we are hearing rumors of Saddam Hussein's ambition to do just that. God has a perfect memory. He has not forgotten about the golden vessels which Babylon confiscated from the temple in Jerusalem and used for drunken sexual orgies and drinking to the honor of the gods of Babylon in the time of Belshazzar. He has not forgotten the seventy-year captivity and imprisonment of the Jews. He has not forgotten the fiery furnace, the lion's den, and the thirty-day edict when prayers to Jehovah were forbidden.

He has not forgotten that the mother/child worship was introduced into the world from Babylon. He has not forgotten that the cults which have proliferated throughout the world originated from the magicians, soothsayers, Ziggurats, and all kinds of devil worship from Babylon. She has intoxicated and poisoned many of the fountains of truth. God remembers her in this final hour and mixes a fatal draught of His deep displeasure and wrath, and she is made to drink it before going under.

6. The Great Hail:

It will not be necessary to call insurance adjusters to assess this damage, for the world will be a total write-off. Nothing like this has ever been seen before. Hailstones about the weight of a talent (150 pounds or about 60 kilograms) will batter the earth. There is no man or beast that could possibly survive such a pounding.

This will be the worst thrashing that civilization has ever received. Houses built with conventional materials like plywood will have blocks of ice in their basements. Commercial buildings with corrugated steel roofs would be hard pressed to withstand this onslaught. Every moving vehicle will be flattened. It would be hard to imagine that anything could withstand this plague.

If my imagination has an answer as to what the wine press of God's wrath spoken of in Revelation 14 might mean, this pounding to a pulp may answer to it. Hailstones of this size have already fallen into the ocean from clouds formed after the testing of atomic bombs. Could this hail be the results of a massive atomic bomb attack?

The end of chapter sixteen is not the end of the "It is done" as announced in verse seventeen. The "it is done" announced here simply means that the seventh trumpet is done sounding. There is much more yet to be done. There are several great considerations yet to be presented.

7. The Great Victory:

I have previously said several times that when the consecutive chronological order of this book is broken, you need to look for instructions from the command center, the heavenly tribunal, which makes all of the decisions before judgments can proceed. Expressions like "heaven opened" or "voices, thunder, lightning, or an earthquake" are an indication that the chronological order is about to be resumed. When you skip over the interjected seventeenth and eighteenth chapters, you will find the continuity is again established in Revelation 19:11 with the words, "I saw heaven opened."

The continuity was broken in Revelation 16:15 with the words, "Behold I come as a thief." Some scholars seem puzzled about this out-of-context Scripture. This is merely an announcement that Jesus is coming quickly to confront the kings of the world at Armageddon and is not misplaced at all. John could not write both the account of the pouring of the seventh vial and the appearance of Christ on a white horse at the same time. He chooses to record the happenings of the seventh vial first.

When we go back to Revelation 16:15 and connect it with Revelation 19:11-21, the Scriptures now flow as Christ on the white horse confronts the enemies of Israel:

> Behold I come as a thief...And I saw heaven opened, and behold a white horse; and he that sat upon him was called Faithful and True, and in righteousness he doth judge and make war (Rev. 16:15; 19:11).

What follows reveals that this seventh pronouncement, the seventh vial poured out by the seventh angel, contains seven announcements of the seven victories of Christ.

THE SEVEN VICTORIES OF JESUS CHRIST

Christ's Victory Over Kings
(Revelation 19:11-19; 14:19-20)

As a young lad, I used to spend a lot of time pondering lines of the Bible which appeared in capital letters. I was sure they were very special and contained an extremely important message. Bible writers were very selective in granting this kind of literary honor.

Revelation 19:16 contains a sentence which to me seemed to stand out as the greatest of them all: "KING OF KINGS, AND LORD OF LORDS." I was not sure of the meaning of many of the capitalized lines, but even as a child, I was sure about the meaning of this sentence. Somehow I knew that the baby Jesus laid in the manger would grow up to be this King of kings, and Lord of lords. Nothing has changed since then. I still know of a certainty that the King of kings and Lord of lords is Jesus.

The world desperately needs this King of kings, the King of peace. Peace promulgated by selfish, sinful, unregenerate men has little hope for success. Peace enforced, imposed, and guaranteed by superior destructive powers is not true peace. Scientific and technological advantage in weaponry will only forge more sophisticated war machines and, sooner or later, our enemies will possess any destructive force we possess. We are in a ruinous military rat race, and the rats have as a good a chance of winning as anyone else.

It is not a better military defense or offense that will assure peace. Only when every man becomes "a new creature in Christ" and the "King of kings and Lord of lords" is enthroned in every heart can Man safely beat his swords into plow shares and his spears into pruning hooks. Our peace tables have been many shapes and made from many materials, but our politicians have not been able to hammer out a peace plan on any of them. Regardless of the geographical location, the weather, or the verbalized intent, peace meetings have brought no real peace.

A volatile peace will come soon. The leader of the E.E.C., with the aid of the United Nations, will soon sit down with Jews and Arabs and sign a seven-year peace treaty. When that happens, buckle your biblical seat belts for the world will be taken for the roughest political ride it has ever known. Regarding this declaration of peace, the Bible states, "When they shall say, Peace and safety; then sudden destruction cometh upon them, as travail upon a woman with child; and they shall not escape" (1 Thess. 5:3). All of Man's attempts at peace will end in a great slaughter in the Valley of Armageddon.

"It's Always Darkest Before the Dawn" is the title of a song we have been singing for a long time now. Armageddon will be the sunset of war, hate, and unrest. After this dark night in human history, the message of the angels, "Glory to God in the highest, and peace on earth good will toward men," will dawn upon the world. The Savior who was born in Bethlehem will establish His kingdom of true peace, which will endure for 1,000 years.

> And I saw heaven opened, and behold a white horse; and he that sat upon him was called Faithful and True, and in

righteousness he doth judge and make war. His eyes were as a flame of fire, and on his head were many crowns; and he had a name written, that no man knew, but he himself. And he was clothed with a vesture dipped in blood: and his name is called the Word of God. And the armies which were in heaven followed him upon white horses, clothed in fine linen, white and clean. And out of his mouth goeth a sharp sword, that with it he should smite the nations: and he shall rule them with a rod of iron: and he treadeth the winepress of the fierceness of the wrath of Almighty God. And he hath on his vesture and on his thigh a name written, KING OF KINGS, AND LORD OF LORDS. And I saw an angel standing in the sun; and he cried with a loud voice, saying to all the fowls that fly in the midst of heaven, come and gather yourselves together unto the supper of the great God; that ye may eat the flesh of kings, and the flesh of captains, and the flesh of mighty men, and the flesh of horses, and of them that sit on them, and the flesh of all men, both free and bond, both small and great. And I saw the beast, and the kings of the earth, and their armies, gathered together to make war against him that sat on the horse, and against his army (Rev. 19:11-19).

This passage is a continuation of Revelation 16:15. These are the same kings and this is the same beast out of whose mouth a frog-like creature emerged that went forth unto the "kings of earth" as in Revelation 16:13-14. Chapter sixteen records the happenings moments after the seventh vial was poured out. The initial catastrophes of this vial did not settle the score or finalize what God has ordained must be accomplished, for the last verse of chapter sixteen records that men were still blaspheming God. What happens in Revelation 19:11-20 and Revelation 14:14-20 is the final last tragic stand these men make against Christ. It will be a very gruesome, one-sided affair.

Christ, the rider upon the white horse, is seen going forth wearing many crowns. There has never been a king who has displayed his crowns before the battle was fought and won. Our Lord is not being presumptuous here. God has always been the Sovereign King of the universe and has never lost a battle. When He goes out to fight against Man, the consequences are predictable. The coronation comes before this conquest, because victory is assumed. His crown has been earned long ago upon the cross and is now bestowed.

Jesus, through His overcoming life and obedience "even unto death," is here being "highly exalted, and given a name which is above every name." That name here displayed upon His forehead cannot be divulged to mortals. He alone is granted the right to its revelation. At His birth they called Him Jesus, at His coronation He receives a new name. I wonder what it will be.

He is also wearing different garments. In Revelation 1, His countenance supersedes the brightness of the sun. Here His garments are described as a "vesture dipped in blood." Isaiah describes what John saw in the following manner:

> Wherefore art thou red in thine apparel, and thy garments like him that treadeth in the winefat? I have trodden the winepress alone; and of the people there was none with me: for I will tread them in mine anger, and trample them in my fury, and their blood shall be sprinkled upon my garments, and I will stain all my raiment. For the day of vengeance is in mine heart, and the year of my redeemed is come. (Isa. 63:2-4).

He will have a name on His thigh, "King of kings and Lord of lords," and Jacob (the elder of Israel) will recognize Him immediately. When he sees Him, I believe Jacob will say, *This is the angel I fought with all night at the brook Jabbok, and at sunrise He touched my thigh and I could scarcely walk. He said, You shall not be called Jacob anymore, but Israel.* I finished the days of my life on earth limping from place to place, and, from that day on, my children would not eat the meat from the hollow of the thigh where the sinew shrank which caused me to halt (Gen. 32:24-32, author's paraphrase).

Out of my thigh was born the name Israel. And now the angel who fought with me has a new name, too. I asked Him His name at Jabbok, but He only replied, 'Why do you need to know my name?' I was quite certain back there that I had seen God face-to-face. But now I know of a certainty that the angel was "THE KING OF KINGS AND THE LORD OF LORDS." He is our Messiah, for He identifies with us by wearing His name on the thigh, the place He touched me and said, 'You will be called Israel.' I saw Him again when I was dying and I said to my son, Judah.

355

The scepter shall not depart from Judah, nor a lawgiver from between his feet, until Shiloh come; and unto him shall the gathering of the people be. Binding his foal unto the vine, and his ass's colt unto the choice vine; he washed his garments in wine, and his clothes in the blood of grapes (Gen. 49:10-11).

The time has come for Jacob to see the salvation of the Jews. God's people will finally see the King of kings destroy Israel's ancient enemies.

...Babylon is fallen, is fallen, that great city, because she hath made all nations drink of the wine of the wrath of her fornication...And I looked, and behold, a white cloud and upon the cloud one sat like unto the Son of man, having on his head a golden crown, and in his hand a sharp sickle...And another angel...cried with a loud cry to him that had the sharp sickle, saying, Thrust in thy sickle, and gather the clusters of the vine of the earth; for her grapes are fully ripe. And the angel thrust in his sickle into the earth, and gathered the vine of the earth, and cast it into the great winepress of the wrath of God. And the winepress was trodden without the city, and blood came out of the winepress, even unto the horse bridles, by the space of a thousand and six hundred furlongs (Rev. 14:8, 14, 18-20).

I do not know why Revelation 14:14-20 is the conclusion to Revelation chapter nineteen, but I am convinced that it is because of the connection made for us by Joel. The prophet describes the battle in the Valley of Armageddon as the battle in the Valley of Jehoshaphat. Jehoshaphat and Armageddon are the same valleys. Revelation 19:15 abbreviates the description of this battle by simply stating that "he treadeth the winepress of the fierceness of God Almighty." God does not have two winepresses of His wrath, so this one must be the same as that of Revelation 14. Joel describes this same battle in the following manner:

Announce this far and wide: Get ready for war! Conscript your best soldiers; collect all your armies. Melt your plowshares into swords and beat your pruning hooks into spears. Let the weak be strong. Gather together and come, all nations everywhere. And now, O Lord, bring down your warriors! Collect the nations; bring them to the Valley of Jehoshaphat, for there I will sit to pronounce judgment on them all. Now let the sickle do its work; the harvest is ripe and waiting. Tread the winepress, for it is full to overflowing with the wickedness of these men. Multitudes, multitudes waiting in the valley for the verdict of their doom! For the Day of the Lord is near, in the Valley of Judgment (Joel 3:9-14, The Living Bible)

The above Scriptures confirm that Revelation 14:14-20 follows Revelation 19:11-21 and that Revelation 19:11-21 follows Revelation 16. The scenes described in these passages are a continuation of what is to happen to the kings of the earth. The following scriptural rearrangement clarifies the sequence of the story of Armageddon when recorded in this order:

And he gathered them (the kings of the earth) together into a place called in the Hebrew tongue Armageddon (Rev. 16:16)

...and behold a white horse; and he that sat upon him was called Faithful and True, and in righteousness he doth judge and make war (Rev. 19:11)

...And out of his mouth goeth a sharp sword, that with it he should smite the nations: and he shall rule them with a rod of iron: and he treadeth the winepress of the fierceness and wrath of Almighty God (Rev. 19:15)

...And I saw the beast, and the kings of the earth, and their armies, gathered together to make war against him that sat on the (white) horse, and against his army (Rev. 19:19)

...And the winepress was trodden without the city, and blood came out of the winepress, even unto the horse bridles, by the space of a thousand and six hundred furlongs (Rev. 14:20).

I am not completely comfortable about rearranging Scriptures in this manner, however, an objective consideration of what I have done will clarify the Scriptural sequence of the story of Armageddon. No violence has been done exegetically.

When the sun rises the morning after the sickle angel has harvested the grapes of wrath and sin and the winepress has been "trodden outside the city," it will illuminate a sight that both Heaven and earth shall never forget. The single sword of His mouth will have spoken the Word of wrath and before the eyes of the horrified survivors will be a crimson lake of blood as deep as to the horse's bridles. It will flood the Valley of Armageddon, stretching north and south for 160 miles. Floating upon that lake will be a hideous carnage of carcasses and bodies. Silhouetted against the eastern sky will be a black cloud of all kinds of ravenous birds responding to the call of an angel standing in the sun:

> And I saw an angel standing in the sun; and he cried with a loud voice, saying to all the fowls that fly in the midst of heaven, Come and gather yourselves together unto the supper of the great God; that ye may eat the flesh of kings, and the flesh of captains, and the flesh of mighty men, and the flesh of horses, and of them that sit on them, and the flesh of all men, both free and bond, both small and great (Rev. 19:17-18).

I know of no darker chapter in the history of mankind.

> I see the last dark bloody sunset
> I see the dread avenger's form.
> I see Armageddon's onslaught
> But I shall be above the storm.

> There comes a moaning and a sighing
> There comes the death clods heavy fall
> A thousand agonies of dying
> But I shall be above them all.

The descriptive words of the Book of Revelation are terribly similar to many of today's headlines in our daily newspapers. Daily, Jews are returning to Israel by the thousands. Jesus said that when we would see this, "The end is even at the doors" (Matt. 24:33). As you see these things beginning to take shape (which have been written in this document), if you have not made the choice to serve Him, acknowledge the God of Heaven and His Son, Jesus Christ, while there is still time.

The conquest of Christ at Armageddon is not being prepared by some kind of secret military build up in the heavens "behind" man's back. There are no tanks, trucks, planes, bombs, or bullets up there. God can, if He wishes, cause great walls to fall through the foolishness of marching as He did at Jericho. If you cannot believe in a God like that, you will not believe anything written in this book either.

The armies which follow Jesus Christ on white horses are not angels. They are the Gentile Church, which was raptured before the tribulation, and the Jewish Church, which was raptured after the tribulation. They are also the dead in Christ who were raised at the Jewish rapture along with the saints who ascended with Him at His ascension 2,000 years ago. They are following Him like they have all of their lives on earth. They have not come to fight, for their battles with the world are over now. They are wearing white clothes, not red ones like He is wearing. They have simply come to watch and hear Him speak with the same sword-Word of His mouth that has always made things happen.

I have always loved horses, and I expect to be riding one of those white horses along with millions of others on that day. We will follow our Lord on His white horse as He goes out to confront the antichrist and the kings of the earth. I wonder if the Lord will call to my mind on that day that I wrote about all of this in a book entitled *Europe After Democracy* while I was still back on earth.

Christ's Victory Over the Babylonians
(Revelation 14:8; 16:7, 19; 19:1-3)

...And great Babylon came in remembrance before God, to give unto her the cup of the wine of the fierceness of his wrath (Rev. 16:19)...And there followed another angel, saying, Babylon is fallen, is fallen, that great city, because she made all nations drink of the wine of the wrath of her fornication (Rev. 14:8)..."And after these things I heard a great voice of much people in heaven saying, Alleluia; Salvation, and glory, and honor, and power, unto the Lord our God. For true and righteous are his judgments, for he hath judged the great whore, which did corrupt the earth with her fornication, and hath avenged the blood of his servants at her hand. And again, they said, Alleluia. And her smoke rose up for ever and ever (Rev. 19:1-3).

Sin had its beginning in Babylon and it will end in the destruction of Babylon.

Christ's Victory Over the Beast
(Revelation 19:20)

And the beast was taken, and with him the false prophet that wrought miracles with him, with which he deceived them that had received the mark of the beast, and them that worshipped his image. These both were cast alive into a lake of fire burning with brimstone (Rev. 19:20).

When the leader of the E.E.C. makes his appearance, the world will be convinced he is the man for this age and hour. He and the false prophet will so perfectly imitate all the miracles and political expectations prophesied regarding the true Messiah of Israel that many Jews (the very elect) will be deceived by him. The question of Revelation 13:4 will be asked, "...Who is like unto the beast? Who is able to make war with him?"

But, after only three and a half years in power, he will break his agreement with Israel and become their persecutor instead of Messiah. In spite of his miserable treatment of Israel, he will succeed in swinging world opinion in his favor and against Israel. He will deceive the people, but he will not deceive God.

One might conclude that a man with a reputation of being a "beast" that no one could "make war with" would wage quite a sensational brawl against anyone attempting to stop him. What a mockery the Bible makes of his resistance to being captured—one little line in Revelation 19:20, "And the beast was taken, and cast alive into the lake of fire."

It is my hope that all records of history will be destroyed during the forty-five days of God's wrath against Man. The history of Mankind is too bloody and shameful to be worth remembering and recording. But if history will be retained and recorded, the antichrist will go down in its annuls as the most repulsive, arrogant, and wretched human being that has ever been born.

I am convinced that the antichrist is already born in this day. It is my firm conviction that he could very well take over domination of the European Economic Community in this decade. According to the survey of May, 1990, and the many people interviewed in Western Europe at that time, the people of Europe want to be autonomous. They would like to continue on as viable countries with their own governments.

The Bible does not predict this kind of an arrangement. Europe will become one large kingdom under one leader. Europe is the geographical land mass which once constituted the Roman Empire. As such, it is the hub and reference point for understanding prophecy with regard to the antichrist.

Christ's Victory Over the False Prophet
(Revelation 19:20)

There are many questions about the false prophet that are unanswered. Will he really not know that the antichrist, with whom he makes this unholy alliance, is a very murderous, proud, and selfish man? Or will the false prophet, in spite of his suspicions, proceed in cooperating with the antichrist because his own lust for power is stronger than his desire for integrity?

Perhaps the false prophet will have ambitions and ulterior motives of his own and think that somewhere down the road, through the whirl of events, he might replace the antichrist. Is he just another victim of deception and exploitation like many other leaders of the world?

It is impossible to answer these questions at this time. We do know, according to the account regarding him in Revelation 13:11-18, that the false prophet will deliberately deceive the people. He will demand that his constituents worship the beast. He will use his miracle-working power to deceive the populace into thinking that the antichrist is a messiah of some kind. He will demand that an image of the beast be built and placed in the temple to be worshipped. It will be the false prophet who will be responsible for issuing the order that a compulsory mark be assigned to every citizen with a death sentence for those who refuse. All of these things are in violation of the peace treaty that will be signed with the Jews.

His will be a most severe judgment, for he will be "cast alive into a lake of fire burning with brimstone." The Hell and Purgatory he pretended to be delivering men from, through his deceitful holy facade, is the one he will himself now be consigned to forever. His dragon mouth indoctrinated many souls unto damnation. Prophets in Israel were highly respected, and the Messiah was the hope of Israel. The antichrist and false prophet will claim these holy titles and sacred honors in exploiting the peoples of the world for the service of Satan. Christ alone is the author of the salvation of the soul and the rightful Messiah of God for Israel and all the world.

Christ will capture and subdue both of Satan's impostors. Neither of them shall ever have the privilege to choose eternal life or gain an entrance into the New Jerusalem. The evidence against them will fill the world, and they will be damned to eternal fire without a trial. Even if this wicked pair would surrender to Christ, it would be impossible to forgive the antichrist for literally destroying the world and Mankind. It would be equally impossible to forgive the false prophet for deceiving multitudes, through the harlot world church, into believing the dictator of the European Economic Community is the Messiah of Israel.

Christ's Victory Over Satan
(Revelation 20:1-3)

And I saw an angel come down from heaven, having the key of the bottomless pit and a great chain in his hand. And he laid hold on the dragon, that old serpent, which is the Devil, and Satan, and bound him a thousand years, and cast him into the bottomless pit, and shut him up, and set a seal upon him, that he should deceive the nations no more, till the thousand years should be fulfilled: and after that he must be loosed a little season.

This is the moment that saints have been dreaming about for centuries. This is the fulfillment of Genesis 3:15 where the promise to bruise the head of Satan was made. The capture of Satan is a disabling strike against sin. The binding of Satan paralyzes the ongoing program of the propagation of iniquity. When the origin of sin is removed, all functioning of sin must cease. This means the curse will also be be lifted. Consequently, brute creatures will lose their thirst for each others' blood and their hunger for each others' flesh. Sickness and death, which has come as a result of sin, will have lost their power. Thistles and thorns will become obsolete. What started in a beautiful garden just eastward from Eden will end in a world garden called "a new heaven and a new earth wherein dwelleth righteousness." The chaining of Satan will clear the way for a real New World Order.

If ever there was a maximum security prison, it is the bottomless pit. The angel who holds the key can only be Christ himself, for He declares, "I have the keys of hell and of death" (Rev. 1:18). In Revelation 3:7, Christ infers that because He holds the keys, no man openeth and no man shutteth. It is Christ who lays hold of the dragon and binds him for a thousand years, casting him into the bottomless pit. It is Christ who locks the pit and sets a seal upon him. Only kings can order the enforcement of seals and this king is Christ. This imprisonment will be implemented by Christ himself, and Satan will not be allowed to exit until Christ orders it.

The world will be at rest, for the millennial sabbath of rest will have begun. God's completed six days (6,000 years) will have finally brought an end to all suffering with the capture of Satan. Our children will no longer be tempted and trapped into iniquity. Homes will not be broken through the devices and sinister schemes of Satan. God will wipe all tears from sad eyes and "crying and pain will be no more." Man will finally agree that the source of all suffering was Satan. His capture will cause the "Sun of righteousness to rise, with healing in his wings." Oh, what glory that will be!

Christ's Marriage Celebration
(Revelation 19:5-9)

And a voice came out of the throne, saying, Praise our God, all ye his servants, and ye that fear him, both small and great. And I heard as it were the voice of a great multitude, and as the voice of many waters, and as the voice of mighty thunderings, saying, Alleluia: for the Lord God omnipotent reigneth. Let us be glad and rejoice, and give honour to him: for the marriage of the Lamb is come, and his wife hath made herself ready. And to her was granted that she should be arrayed in fine linen, clean and white: for the fine linen is the righteousness of saints. And he saith unto me, Write, Blessed are they which are called unto the marriage supper of the Lamb. And he saith unto me, these are the true sayings of God.

Prior to Christ's victory celebration known as "the marriage supper of the Lamb," a praise event will take place in Heaven. Heaven will erupt with thunderous verbal applause four times. In the first instance (vs. 1), John hears "a great voice of much people in heaven, saying, Alleluia; Salvation, and glory, and honour, and power, unto the Lord our God." The spotlight will be focused upon Christ and His victory over the great whore who brought so much sorrow to the true Church of Christ throughout the ages, as well as misery to the Jew during the tribulation.

The second wave of praise is recorded in verse four. Here the twenty-four elders and four living ones fall before the throne crying, "Amen; Alleluia." Heaven will be electrified a third time when a single voice, mysterious in origin, cries from the midst of the flood of white light engulfing the throne, "Praise our God, all ye his servants, and ye that fear him, both small and great." Then a fourth adulation bursts forth as the voice of a great multitude, in magnificent praise, filling the heavenly temple and saying, "Alleluia: for the Lord God Omnipotent reigneth." John appears to be stunned by all of this, and he fumbles for a sentence to try to explain this heavenly acclaim and plaudit. In his first attempt in describing this jubilation, he says it was as "the voice of a great multitude." Realizing his readers would not capture the magnitude of this exaltation, he adds the words that it was "as the voice of many waters." Even this statement falls short, so he further adds it was "as the voice of mighty thunderings."

What John heard that day was much greater and grander than all of these. His dissatisfaction with his portrayal of this scene is disclosed in the words "as it were." That is to say the explosion was only similar to a great multitude or the cascading of many waters and the crash of a thousand thunders. Only Heaven knows how to adequately praise our God and His Christ. What John was hearing has not yet happened. I intend to be in that great company of the redeemed when it does happen. Only then will we appreciate the difficulty John was having in trying to articulate the immensity of this praise happening.

Not only are we incapable of capturing the dynamics of this celebration, we also fall short of fully understanding and appreciating the vast expanses of redemption's benefits. Only when we finally stand in His presence and see the glories of the next world, with the perfection of all who inhabit it, will we realize what God intended for us to become. To be free from all that Satan and sin have perpetuated and to enjoy all that Christ has prepared now remains our blessed contemplation.

This will be a wedding banquet. The bride is called His "wife (which) hath made herself ready" (Rev. 19:7). The only time a bride can be called the groom's "wife" is in the case when a man remarries a woman he has divorced. This is precisely what is happening here. Contrary to popular opinion (which insists that the bride here is the Church), this bride is not the Church. The Church is nowhere called the wife of Christ in the Scriptures. Jesus is the "bridegroom" who came as a "thief" at midnight to meet the ten virgins. Only five of them were prepared. The prepared virgins are the Church. The unprepared virgins represent Israel.

The Church is not to "become" the bride of Christ, she already is His bride. Our marriage to Christ takes place at conversion. Our relationship to Christ after conversion is compared by Paul in Ephesians 5 as that of a husband and wife. The bride, which we are now a part of, goes into the marriage celebration at the rapture. "And they that were ready went in with him to the marriage" (Matt. 25:10). The first five virgins that were "ready," as seen in Matthew 25, went into the marriage. The other five went to buy oil, which is to say they were going to get ready. However, the door was shut while they were gone. We cannot forget that they were virgins like the first five. We must conclude that eventually they also obtained oil and became qualified to enter the marriage celebration, just as the first five did.

What became of them in the meantime? The unprepared virgins at the rapture of the Church are righteous Jews, those Jews who today wait and pray at the wailing wall for their Messiah. Why should praying Jews be regarded as unprepared? The answer is to be found in the parable of Matthew 25. The oil, which represents faith in Jesus

Christ, was missing. This rendered their virginity, prayer, and waiting as foolish, for their Messiah has already come.

As previously stated in our study of the pregnant woman in Revelation 12, Israel will be given similar opportunities to those given the Church. A second fountain will be opened and they will experience a second birth of Christ, a second pentecost, a second ascension, a second Moses and Elijah (John the Baptist), and a second rapture. Revelation 19 tells of the second marriage celebration. The bride is Israel, who was not ready for the first marriage celebration at the rapture of the Church, but who has now (through the trials of the great tribulation) "made herself ready." It is not surprising that the bride is called a wife. The Scriptures frequently call Israel the wife of Jehovah or call Jehovah her husband (Jer. 3:1-18; Ezek. 16:1-63; Hosea 2 and 3).

The statement, "And to her was granted that she should be arrayed in fine linen, clean and white: for the fine linen is the righteousness of the saints" (Rev. 19:8), is very significant. Fine linen, white and clean, is appropriately worn only by a virgin on her wedding day. However, because Israel will have repented and her sins will be washed away by the blood of the Lamb, a special provision is made for her. As the divorced wife of Jehovah, she is "granted" or allowed (because of this supernatural cleansing) to be adorned with the garments of a virgin bride.

What a glorious celebration will ensue when all of the blood-washed saints of God (the Gentile Church and the wife bride, Israel) shall join in this thunderous jubilation unto the Lamb.

But Israel must go through the most insane suffering this world has ever known in order to "make herself ready." To every Jew reading this message, I urge you to accept Jesus Christ as your Messiah now. Then you will enter the marriage celebration before the tribulation (at the rapture of the Gentile Church) and be saved much suffering and, in all probability, a terrible death.

Christ is King
(Revelation 19:11-16)

And I saw heaven opened, and behold a white horse; and he that sat upon him was called Faithful and True...and on his head were many crowns; and he had a name written, that no man knew, but he himself...and his name is called

366

The Word of God...and he shall rule with a rod of iron...And he hath on his vesture and on his thigh a name written, KING OF KINGS AND LORD OF LORDS.

And I saw in the night visions, and, behold, one like the Son of man came with the clouds of heaven, and came to the Ancient of days, and they brought him near before him. And there was given him dominion, and glory, and a kingdom, that all people, nations, and languages, should serve him: his dominion is an everlasting dominion, which shall not pass away, and his kingdom that which shall not be destroyed (Dan. 7:13-14).

And the angel said unto her, Fear not, Mary: for thou hast found favor with God. And, behold, thou shalt conceive in thy womb, and bring forth a son, and shalt call his name JESUS. He shall be great, and shall be called the Son of the Highest: and the Lord God shall give unto him the throne of his father David (Luke 1:30-32).

When the Son of man shall come in his glory, and all the holy angels with him, then shall he sit upon the throne of his glory: and before him shall be gathered all nations: and he shall separate them one from another, as a shepherd divideth his sheep from the goats: and he shall set the sheep on his right hand, but the goats on the left. Then shall the King say unto them on his right hand, Come, ye blessed of my Father, inherit the kingdom prepared for you from the foundation of the world (Matt. 25:31-34).

The subject of Christ's millennial kingdom is very extensive. The Bible is literally filled with references which point to the messiahship and kingship of Christ. I cannot do this subject justice in this volume, but permit me to reiterate once more. The struggle between nations in these last days has nothing to do with territory, oil, strategic advantages, or any other issue. These are only symptoms. All of the unrest in the Middle East has nothing to do with disagreements existing today.

The underlying, hidden problem is the ancient struggle between the forces of good and evil. From the beginning, Satan has vied for the mastery of the world. His ambitions are stronger today than ever before. He is using men in power, nations, and certain conditions as levers which he pulls to his own advantage.

By the same token, God is preparing to reinstate the garden of Eden environment. God loves this world and He wants everyone to live in peace and happiness. He gave his own Son that He might destroy the works of the devil and deliver us from our sins. We are now standing at the very threshold of the fulfillment of the ultimate plan of God. From the Scriptures quoted above, it is clear that Christ, the Son of God, will one day be King.

Once again, let me warn all nations turning against Israel. You will never annihilate or drive Israel into the sea. There is a force much greater than SCUD missiles, fighter planes, warships, and chemical and biological bombs. When you bomb Israel, you are bombing the chosen people of God. He has prophesied that all nations will be brought before the omnipotent tribunal and judged proportionately to their treatment of Christ's "brethren," the Jews (Matt. 25:31-46). Yes, Israel will get badly roughed up, and it will appear to her enemies that they can already hear death's rattle in her breast. But if this world only realized what awaits them at God's appointed hour, they would throw themselves prostrate before His mercy.

In closing, let me point out that the marriage supper of the Lamb with Israel, the wife as the bride, is not the end of the story. In fact, it is but the beginning of blessings for the holy people, the Jews. Revelation 21:9-27 reveals that John is taken to a high mountain where he was shown the bride, the Lamb's wife. Verse twenty-four declares that the kings of the earth will be in subjection to her.

There is hope after Armageddon. Hear the word of the Lord:

> And I saw thrones, and they sat upon them, and judgment was given unto them: and I saw the souls of them that were beheaded for the witness of Jesus, and for the word of God, and which had not worshipped the beast, neither his im-

age, neither had received his mark upon their forehead, or in their hands; and they lived and reigned with Christ a thousand years (Rev. 20:4).

In closing, let me extend God's overtures of grace, mercy, and love to those who neither care about nor believe in Jesus Christ. If you continue on this pathway, you are sure to suffer your greatest loss — the salvation of your eternal soul. Your soul will endure the miseries of Hell and you will miss the thousand-year reign of peace on earth, after which you must stand before the Great White Throne Judgement. You will hear the verdict of an everlasting existence in the lake of fire.

HEAR THE WORD OF THE LORD:

But the rest of the dead, (wicked) lived not again until the thousand years were finished (Rev. 20:5)...And I saw a great white throne, and him that sat on it, from whose face the earth and the heaven fled away; and there was found no place for them. And I saw the dead, small and great, stand before God; and the books were opened: and another book was opened, which is the book of life: and the dead were judged out of those things which were written in the books, according to their works. And the sea gave up the dead which were in it; and death and hell delivered up the dead which were in them: and they were judged every man according to their works. And death and hell were cast into the lake of fire. This is the second death. And whosoever was not found written in the book of life was cast into the lake of fire. (Rev. 20:11-15).

I have written this book with the hope that many will accept Jesus Christ as a personal Savior and be prepared when He comes "as a thief in the night" to remove His Church before the dark storm clouds of the tribulation hide His smile and favor from us.

SALVATION PRAYER

"O God, have mercy upon me. I have sinned against you, your Son and the Holy Spirit. I apologize for the wrong I have done. Forgive me and wash me clean through the blood of your Son. I believe and trust in you. I will serve and love you. I want to be ready when you come to take your Church unto yourself at the rapture. Thank you for saving me. AMEN!"

NOTES

CHAPTER TWO

1. Paul Brainerd Smith, *Church Aflame*, (Toronto: The People's Press, 1949), p. 5.
2. J. W. Van Deventer, "We shall shine as the stars,"in *Rodeheavers Gospel Solos and Duets*, No. 3 (Winona Lake, Indiana: Rodheaver Hall Mack, 1938), p. 163.
3. James Mongomery, "There is a death," in *From Death to Life Through Christ* (Grand Rapids:Zondervan, 1966), p. 10.
4. Alexander Hislop, *The Two Babylons*, (New York: Loiseaux, 1916), p. 70.
5. Clarence Larkin, *The Book of Revelation* (Philadelphia: Edwin W. Moyer, 1919), p. 22.
6. Arthur I. Brown, *Into The Clouds* (Fundamental Truth), p. 153.
7. Henry H. Halley, *Halley's Pocket Bible Handbook* (Chicago, 1948), p. 683.
8. Ibid., p. 684.
9. H. A. Seiss, *The Apocalypse* (Grand Rapids: Zondervan, Date of Publication unavailable), p. 88.
10. Gustav Just, *The Life of Luther* (St. Louis: Concordia, 1903), p. 22.
11. Henry H. Halley, *Halley's Pocket Bible Handbook* (Chicago, 1948), p. 696.
12. Ibid., p. 696.
13. Ibid., p. 696.
14. Mary A. Kidder and Frank M. Davis, "Is My Name Written There," in *Great Hymns of the Faith*, John W. Peterson, ed. (Grand Rapids: Singspiration, 1968), p. 260.
15. Ibid., p. 260.

CHAPTER THREE

1.   *Cassell's German-English Dictionary.* Karl Breul, ed. (London, Toronto, Melbourne, and Sydney: Cassell, 1909), p. 723.

CHAPTER FOUR

1.   *Encyclopedia Britannica,* s.v. Geopolitics.
2.   *Encyclopedia Britannica,* s.v. Geopolitics.
3.   Alexander Hislop, *The Two Babylons* (New York: Loiseaux, 1916), pp. 19-20.
4.   *Our Wonderful World Encyclopedia,* 1957 ed., s.v. Trade Routes.

CHAPTER SIX

1.   *Bible Encyclopedia and Dictionary.* A. R. Fausset, ed. (Grand Rapids: Zondervan, Date of Publication unavailable), p. 654.
2.   *The Interpreter's Dictionary of the Bible,* Volume 4, George Arthur Buttrick *et al.,* eds. (New York and Nashville: Abingdon, 1962), p. 360.

Other Exciting Titles From Bridge Publishing:

The 90's: Decade of the Apocalypse
Steve Terrell

As of December 31, 1992, the member nations of the European Common Market have dissolved all existing trade barriers between each other. They seek to establish their own trans-national currency system. They will elect their own president. *If you think this is all coincidence, read this startling book.*

ISBN 0-88270-707-8• Trade/188 pp.
$ 6.95

Heaven
Judson Cornwall

So much is written about hell, and so little about heaven! To address this disparity, we offer this typically excellent work by Dr. Cornwall. With his trademark command, simplicity, and thoroughness, see how he addresses questions like: What is heaven like? Where is it? Is it a place at all? Guaranteedto make you Homesick!

ISBN 0-88270-659-4• Trade /139 pp.
$ 6.95

Life in the Millennium
Mona Johnian

The Church has looked to it with joyful anticipation since the moment the Lord ascended into Glory, but what does the millennium *mean*, and what will it be like? Learn from one of the most sought-after teachers in the northeast as she simply and clearly illuminates the glory that is in store for the people of God!

ISBN 0-88270-705-1• Trade/195 pp.
$ 7.95